HOW TO FIND A BOOK

how

to

find

a

secondhand

or

antiquarian

book

by

drif

field

---

published by drif field guides, London 1992

ISBN NO 0-9510005-4-3

Published by drif field guides
41 North Road, London N7 9DP
Tel: 071 607 1757

Dedication

This book is dedicated to the American lady who came in to The Charing Cross Road bookshop, where I was putting on a guest appearance and asked if she could be directed to the department that specialised in early Elizabethan embroidery.

Whilst the official staff smiled to themselves I informed her that there was but one shop in Britain (Morton in Marsh) which had books on needlework, but that it was very unlikely to have anything on a subject so specific. However I told her that there was a lady in Todmorden who specialised in books on embroidery and if anybody had such books, she would have them.

She asked where Todmorden was, as if it was an extension of Tottenham Court Road. I explained that it was in Lancashire about 300 miles away. The lady turned away from me with a look of contempt and asked the gentleman behind the counter where she could get hold of somebody who *really* knew about secondhand books.

You and me both Madam, you and me both.

THIS BOOK WOULD NOT HAVE BEEN POSSIBLE WITHOUT THE ASSISTANCE OF THE FOLLOWING PEOPLE:

carol watkinson	paperwork
david mann	stickywork
jess abbo	inkwork
mark holmes	legwork

The following is written for the benefit of readers; It is unlikely to be of any use to Collectors or Dealers. Many Collectors and Dealers are indeed looking for books but what they are really looking for is cheap books. No consideration of prices is made in this article. It is solely concerned with finding a book when it is really wanted. No account has been taken of the prices charged by respective dealers in the index that follows. The only consideration is, is there a better than half chance that they will have the book and if they do not have the book will they be able to help you find it.

HOW TO FIND AN OLD BOOK

The best way to find a book is not to look for it; it is one of the very few guaranteed promises of life that the moment you start looking for a thing it will disappear. Objects that by their very presence seemed to have no other purpose than to annoy, take extreme delight in being unavailable when you really want them. Books seem to possess this anti talent more than most ordinary objects. They have a degree of malevolence hard to credit in something so allegedly inanimate. They have the ability to make dumb insolence look like Positive Thinking. It does not actually help not to look for them but it does not give the little cretons the chance to sneer when you cannot find them.

RING RING: This is Iain Sinclair, listen drif, I've got you a part in a film I've written. At last I shall be able to tell the truth about secondhand bookdealers, but we need a few jokes, come dressed as normal. SAY NOTHING I don't want you embarrassing me in front of my new literary friends. Oh and I want you to find a book: THE CARDINAL & THE CORPSE.
drif: But Iain, the only language I can speak is OUT! Alright, alright, consider it found.
RAYMOND CARVER: What about money?
drif: Listen BOMBHEAD, it's not the wages but what we can loot.

When I was asked to look for a copy of Gone With The Wind, I had almost spent all the money on a new Prince of Wales check suit before I got down to the trivial business of actually coming up with the book. It is not a book I would stock, because it is too common; I found that the shops in the Charing Cross Road did not stock it either because they thought it was too common, but all of them assured me that I would have no trouble finding it - elsewhere. I then attempted to go to all the shops on the Northern Line in ascending order from Wimbledon to Edgware, the higher I went the more my temper and irritation rose. Eventually I rang my tailor and told him I would be unable to make the next day's fitting because I had to go out and find a poxy book. He asked me what book it was and I told him. "I have a very nice hardback copy of that Sir, I can bring it in if you like!" he said.

Gone With The Wind is the greatest selling novel of all time, because of this I had assumed that I would have no trouble picking up a copy. Because I am a secondhand bookdealer it did not occur to me to look anywhere other than a secondhand bookshop. I did not think to look in a new bookshop nor did I even consider the notion of buying a paperback copy.

The first thing to do when you are looking for a book is to establish the correct title, the correct author, the correct date and place of publication and if possible the size of the book. The reason for this is that memory plays strange tricks and the title that you recall is not necessarily the correct one.

My own favourite request for a book is: The Seven Pillars of Willesden; it is a book that deserves to be written but somehow I cannot see T. E. Lawrence writing it.

The easiest way to check the author and title is through a publication known as Books In Print which is stocked by most new bookshops - usually on microfiche - or in bookform by many secondhand bookshops. Most Public Libraries also possess a copy. More books are in print than you might imagine and despite the renowned incompetence of publishers it is invariably easier trying to obtain a new book than it is getting hold of an old one. Unless you are a collector or a dealer the chances of your requiring a genuinely out of print book are slim. Do not dismiss the notion that a book will be out of print simply because it seems to be old; the Oxford University Press had a Greek translation of the Bible in print for 300 years.

If you cannot find the book you want in Books In Print you should try the British Library Catalogue which can usually be obtained at major public libraries. The Catalogue is alphabetical by author, but there is some cross indexing, and it gives you more details than Books In Print. It is especially good for listing other works by the author which can be very helpful if you have made a mistake. If it is not in the British Library catalogue you have a problem. My own solution to this problem is to declare anything that is not in as not being a book. Thus neither I, nor the British Library authorities define directories, shop trade catalogues or privately printed material as being books.

Having established the correct title and author & date you can set about considering the best way to look for the book. There is currently an advert on television which shows a gentleman called J R Hartley looking for a fishing title which he manages to obtain after five or six calls on the telephone. Gentle reader, this advert is a lie. It is a fraud of which Robert Maxwell would have been proud. Doctor Goebbels would have named it his advert of the year. The Reverend Moon would give away all his followers to be able to tell such stories. The chances of your finding a secondhand book by using the local yellow pages are the same as Maxwell, Goebbels and Moon getting together to form an equal partnership. BT encourages you to use the phone because they know you are almost bound to fail; If you could find the book on the first attempt they would lose money. The more calls you make, the more those crooks profit.

I do not own a television set (I did have one once, but I sold it to a collector; it was so old the pictures were in sepia). Despite this cultural poverty that advert has entered my consciousness. I cannot now stand in a secondhand bookshop without some more thick resonant asking me if I am looking for the book on fly fishing.

If you are looking for a general book then the best thing you can do is go to a general secondhand bookshop; If you are looking for a specialist book then the best thing you can do is go to a specialist. In neither case are the bunch of fraudsters who call themselves a telephone company going to be of any assistance to you.

You are more likely to find a secondhand book by accident than by design. Nonetheless, you should try in places where secondhand books are available and ask everybody, even the most unlikely people. The only trouble is that you often find they are looking for the same book.

Ringing a general secondhand bookshop is aa complete and utter waste of time. You try finding a specialist through the glory that is now directory enquiries. First you have to know his name, his full address and what he specialises in, then if you give them 47.5pence BT will tell you his or her telephone number.

CALL ME ISHMAEL

When BT introduced the 47.5p charge - what a wonderfully conceived figure - I thought it was just a try-on and that they knew they would be forced to reduce the amount down to the figure they really wanted to charge. What a fool I was, because I have seen sheep fighting back against the dog in North Wales, because I have herd Nuns taking the name of the Lord in vain (when they had me as a pupil), I did not believe that they would be able to get away with this monstrous piece of crookery. But nothing happened, not a word of dissent was spoken not a murmur raised. This charge is not so much inertia selling as inertia mucking. What are you going to do with a telephone number other than ring it. They are making a profit twice. When you go in a restaurant do you pay to see the menu? When you go to a railway station do you pay to get information about the train? It is because they removed all the telephone directories from coin boxes that you have to keep ringing them up to find out the number.

Not only do this junior bunch of Mafiosa now charge when you ring directory enquiries, the service - for want of a

RING RING: Listen Truthpaste, I don't mind being portrayed in your film as the only greying skinhead in the NF, but I was wondering if you would be prepared to pay for a small item of apparel to help soften the image? What do you mean you asked for a book called THE CARDINAL & THE CORPSE, I distinctly remember it being somebody attractive...
RAYMOND CARVER: How did you get involved with somebody who wrote a book called BROWN CLOUDS? He's also a misogynist.
drif: A what?
RC: A person who thinks sex is what the Scots carry coal in.

better word - is worse. You have to know the full name, you have to know the full address; if you know these things it seems unlikely to me that you will not know the number. You cannot now ring them up and say you want the telephone number of the bookshop in Carlisle, any bookshop, because all the records are now on computer, and you cannot be told the piece of information next to the one you want. Even if they fail to get you the number you want they charge 47.5p

How can it possibly cost 47.5p to find out a single number. (Stand by for a letter from the PR department of BT saying that you can have two enquiries for your 47.5p). What do they think people do with these numbers? I have yet to hear of anybody collecting telephone numbers in the same way as they collect train numbers. When I was younger I did collect telephone directories; if only I had hung on to them I would have been worth millions today.

You could try ringing your local secondhand bookshop for a general book, but my advice is don't bother; I personally feel that the next piece of advice is worth more than the 47.5p those bunch of phonies would charge you for giving out the number.

There is an unofficial competition in secondhand bookshops to see who can get rid of telephone enquirers the fastest. The outright winner is Mr. Derrick Nightingale of Norbiton, who is able to answer the telephone, politely fend off the enquirer and restart his conversation with a genuine customer in under six seconds. There are some bookshops that can do it faster but they do not do it with as much skill or

PERSISTENCE IS EVERYTHING, whether you are writing a book or looking for one, it took Iain Sinclair ten years as my chauffeur before he had enough material to write the opening of WHITECHAPPEL SCARLETT TRACINGS. It took Mr Lambrianou fifteen years to find a decent ghost writer, and it took DEREK RAYMOND twenty five years to become an overnight success.

flair. Some shops even go as far as to pretend they have left the desk to go in search of the book - these are the ones where the owners aspire to being actors - unless it is an exceptional book there is no way that the owner of a bookshop can remember all the stock he may or may not have. Good shops sell the books fast; bad shops have no idea what they are holding.

I realise it will come as a dreadful shock for at least 96% of the population but if you want to find a general secondhand bookshop, phoning, writing or sending your maiden aunt will just not work.

The reason sending somebody else does not work is that most people who are looking for books have more knowledge of the book than they might imagine. It is they who can remember the shape, without being able to realise it, it is they who can remember the exact shade of green, without being able to describe it. I was very impressed by the confidence of a lady who went into a Brighton secondhand bookshop and asked for a book she could not remember the name of, but which she was sure the owner of the shop would recognise immediately for as she said it was the green book. If you go yourself you will be able to decide what substitutes are acceptable, if you send a substitute you may not get a substitute book.

It was not until I started looking for books for people that I discovered that most people imagine that most bookshops have similar stocks. Most of my enquirers seemed to imagine that I had only to look through my own stock to find a particular

RING RING: LISTEN TRUTHPASTE, I don't mind slumming it in low rent barbers. I don't mind wearing cheaper clothes than PRINCESS DI. I will even wear her clothes if you like but if that spear carrier for the Krays puts his arm round my shoulder once more I will start wondering if his sexuality is as patent as his shoes and his lies.

book. Bookshops only compete on price position and politeness. One of the reasons that bookshops are so rude is that they do not have to bother about what the customer thinks. One of the reasons they are in such obscure places is that they have even more obscure books. The paradox is that most secondhand bookshops have incredibly low prices relative to other items but this is because other people do not go in to them. It is an even more strange paradox that if books were even more expensive then the bookshop owners would make more effort to see if they have them on the shelves. Most bookshops make 80% of their profit from regular customers; there is thus no incentive to give away a book for £3 to someone who is never likely to come in again.

It is an almost impossible task, and one of my few ambitions, to find out how many books there are in the world. People unfamiliar with books often behave as if it was possible to store all the books ever published in one place, if only the bookdealers were a little better organised. The British Library has six million books on catalogue and many more that it does not know it has. The Library of Congress has nine million on file but only about half of that number in stock because Congressmen have not bothered to return them. The Lenin library has 12 million in stock; about nine million of these are believed to be works of Lenin. I don't think there is a bookstore in Britain that has more than half a million and most of those are either duplicates, triplicates or whatever the word for 36 copies is - a Scallep?

It is the belief that you are going to find a book which is paramount. You should ignore remarks that the book is extremely common, nor should you take any notice of remarks that it is extremely rare. There are only two types of books:THE ONES YOU HAVE GOT AND THE ONES YOU HAVE NOT GOT. Everything else is bookdealers flannel.

When you do eventually succumb to going into a secondhand bookshop you could then indeed ask the owner or his staff for a particular book but it is not something I would recommend for in most cases you will be told either that they have sold the book yesterday, or that they have never heard of the book or most unpleasant of all you will witness the "Suck Job".

Suck Jobs consist of the sudden inhalation of breath between the teeth as if the perpetrator was trying to say FFFFFFF backwards. It is usually accompanied by an unsightly grimace and the screwing up of the eyes. The intensity of this reaction is in inverse proportion to the actual difficulty of finding the book; it is more a demonstration of the owner's lack of enthusiasm to help you do so.

Many Askersafterbooks appear to be of the confirmed opinion that it is the job of the bookshop manager to go in diligent search of the title when asked by the Askersafterbooks. I have talked to many bookshop managers regarding this and it is their opinion - by almost ninety per cent - that it is their job to point the Askersafters in the right direction. Quite how this confirmed difference of opinion arose I am unsure but it is indeed a common sight.

For most Askersafterbooks Suck Jobs are more welcome than what they see as dumb insolence. The Askersafters cannot believe it when they are told by the bookshop owner that they have never heard of the book. To save time and effort most bookdealers simply lie and pretend they do know the book but say that they do not have a copy

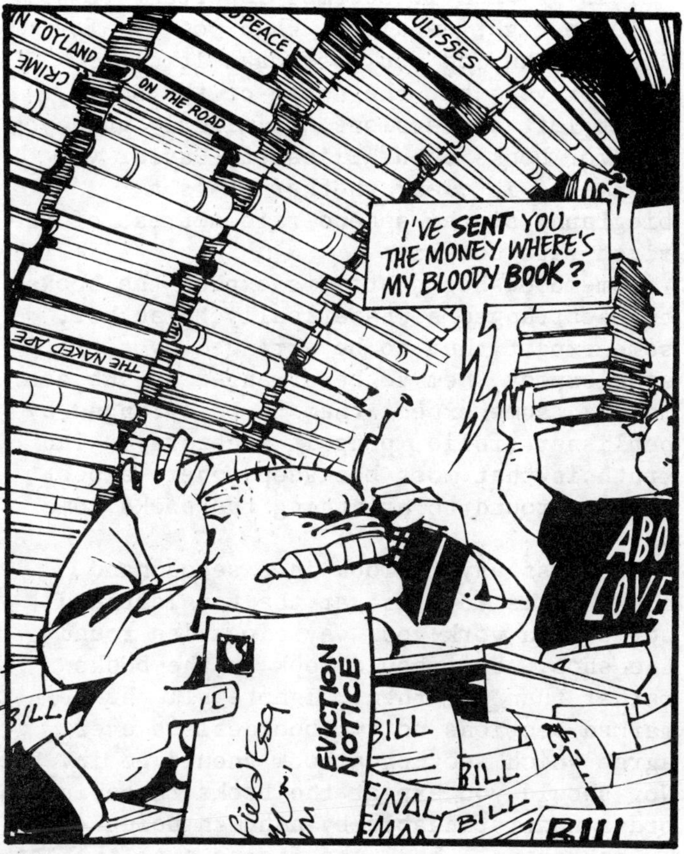

RING RING: Listen Truthpaste, if that barrel of rotten olives casts aspersions on my sexuality again I shall be pitting him.
TRUTHPASTE: I thought he would be your ideal cellmate.
drif: With him, I wouldn't share a brain cell let alone the K**Y JELLY.
TRUTHPASTE: Well lets have it straight, are you homosexual or not?
drif: ARE YOU BUYING OR SELLING?

at the moment.

This is when it becomes important to have all the right details. When you ask for Room At The Top you must make it clear whether you want the novel or the book about loft conversions. Similarly when you ask for books about Elizabeth Taylor you must make it clear whether it is a biography of the second rate actress of the first rate novelist.

Some bookshop customers expect the books to be arranged alphabetically by author, some expect them to be arranged by title, some expect them to be arranged by subject matter, some expect them to be arranged by publisher (folio, penguin etcetera). The truth is that most bookshop owners expect to get around to arranging the books some day.

The best way to look in a secondhand bookshop is to start at the top lefthand corner and work your way clockwise round the shop. You should look at the books rather than _for_ them. Ignore all the marked sections no two bookdealers ever agree which section a book should go in. Nor should you expect the books to be in an order understandable by a human being.

The reason I have the footnote at the top of this article regarding it being for Readers rather than book collectors is that the next piece of information seems so stupid that it makes me look like a complete moron for giving it. The way to look at bookshelves is from left to right. That may sound ridiculous to most people who go in for the first time have no idea that this is what you do. They seem to imagine that you follow the management's

Quite often a book will be in the last place you would expect to find it, above all never give up and keep looking everywhere.

finger and the books will be directly there. That finger is but a vague notion; it is an indication where the book might be if they had it. It is a means of ridding the bookshop owner of having to explain to the customer the little possibility there is going to be of their finding a copy of the O'Brien family (limited to fifty copies). I have indeed heard a gentleman asking for this book or to be more precise, he asked to see all the copies of the History of the O/Brien Family that the shop had available.

Most bookshops know when College terms begin for it is then that they see students, usually for the first and the last time. They enter waving multi page lists filled with obscure bibliographic details of books without which the compilers of these lists are convinced it is not possible to be educated. These lists are indeed a vital part of the students education. They teach the sensible ones never to have any faith in the compilers of the list. To send one person off in search of the books on these waste pieces of paper is a mistake to send off fifty is somewhere between megalomania and moronicness.

These lists usually contain exact dates, publishers and editions and page numbers as if only those copies would supply the education the student needs. The truth is that one text book on economics is much the same as another, as are books on English Grammar and on English Law.

If you are a student and you have been issued with one of these required reading lists you will be doing more to increase your education by going back to the person who issued the list and asking him or her specifically where you are to obtain the books. It is not enough for them to say that you can get them in secondhand bookshops: Tell them you want exact details of which bookshop. If this does not work you may hire my services at less than BT charges for each single piece of information to roundly berate these morons.

If what I have suggested sounds far too tedious, far too labourious, far too difficult and far too time consuming, then I would humbly suggest that you contact the people who call themselves Bookfinders; they will do none of these things. They advertise in Yellow Pages and some distribute leaflets through the secondhand bookshops. The largest acts as an in-house service for the booksellers, Waterstones. They should more accurately be called Booksearchers, for as far as I can work out they succeed on only 20% of occasions.

I contacted ten of them under an assumed name and asked for a real book that I was looking for. A few weeks later adverts started appearing in the Bookdealer magazine which is issued weekly to the trade in Britain (it contains about 10,000 of these adverts). Of the ten I contacted only seven actually seemed to list the book I was looking for. When I rerang the others they seemed to have forgotten my request, but two did manage to get the adverts a few weeks later. Of those that did advertise a significant number got the author's name wrong. This is why you, as the Askerafter a book, must attempt to get it right. It is just about possible to degarble once, but doing it twice is a trifle more difficult.

About a fortnight after the adverts appeared I began to get some quotes from the bookfinding service. The strange thing was that I had sent quotes to each of them - under another name and from another address - quoting the book I was looking for, a copy of which I already possessed, but did genuinely want another. Even more strange was the fact that most of the Booksearching services seemed to be quoting back the copy I quoted to them. Not one seemed to come up with anybody else's book. It is true that the book I was looking for was a non-mainstream collector's book. Slightly more interesting to me was the modest level that they charged as a commission. Waterstones & Twiggers both seemed to charge twice the price that I had been quoting.

The third booksearch service wrote and told me as the quoter of the book, that I was asking far too much for it, without even telling me as the searcher how much they had had it quoted to them at.

Many secondhand bookdealers do subscribe to this notion that there is a fixed market price at which books should be sold. This is slightly ridiculous. It is surely up to the buyer to decide what price he or she will pay. The price of books in bookshops or in catalogues or at bookfairs, is the price that collectors will pay, and the range of books at these venues is surprisingly small. Paradoxically, it is becasue so many books are so cheap that they are difficult to find. If you want a First Edition of the Gutenberg Bible, all

Whatever happens keep calm, do not lose your temper, do not make snide remarks that J. R Hartley never had this trouble. No matter how many people you have asked remember that the next one could be the person with a copy.Be polite; it may be the person behind you who has the book you want.

it requires is money. You could have one today. But if you want a thing known as a paragraph bible you will have to go in search of one, and I assure you it will be a long chapter.

You could try advertising yourself, but alas the primary medium of communication for bookdealers in Britain, The Bookdealer Magazine, does not allow private people to use itst hallowed columns. The next alternative The Book & Magazine Collector is so slow that it is not sure what year it is, but if you are looking for the type of book which is popular among bookcollectors then this would well be a possibility. Far more likely is to advertise in the appropriate magazines, thus if you are looking for a nautical book, try a nautical magazine, if an aircraft one then the aircraft magazines.

The only other possibility is me, but I feel I should warn you that I charge more than you could ever believe. This is partially due to my ambition to become the world's most expensive bookdealer and partially to offset the fact that I can only obtain books by mixing with other bookdealers, most of whom I loathe. I will only do the things I have listed above; I may do it with a little more determination but my main qualification is that I don't give up. I guarantee to find you any book in the world and if I don't I have got some wonderful explanations.

The bookdealers listed in this index are the first five that I would ring if I were looking for a book on a particular subject. Most of them are very helpful on the phone - for bookdealers - and you will find that

RING RING: drif, drif, where are all my copies of the CARDINAL & THE CORPSE? I only worked with you talentless freaks so that I could advertise that book in my catalogue which comes out the same day as the film. You promised to make me rich if I gave you a walk on part in that film. If you don't come through the only thing I shall ever be putting you in is the ... drif, drif, are you there? I have never heard you keep quiet for so long.

MRS PATEL: Ah Cardinal Sinclair I presume. I have extremely patiently been waiting for your call, that lovely Mr Drif has told me that you owe his company which I now own, several millions of pounds in copyright fees for putting him in your novels, and that you will be giving me even more for a very rare book, would you like one thousand copies or two?

this can be just as useful as getting the actual book, speaking to somebody who has seen the book does reassure you that it is indeed available.

The reason I have listed only five on each subject is not just laziness on my part, but related to my belief that if you cannot find a trace of the book in the first five, then you are going to have serious difficulties. There are certainly more than five people who specialise in illustrated books for example, but in my experience the only people who want illustrated books per se are all book cellectors. This list is compiled mainly for the benefit of readers.

RAYMOND CARVER WRITES: There is one thing that natterjack toad has deliberately omitted to tell and that is that if he does find the book of your dreams he will not only inflict more financial damage than Reg & Ronnie ever dreamt of, but that the book itself will become somewhat of a disappointment, for after all what can you do with a book other than read it. All the pleasure in book collecting is in hunting the book, in going round secondhand bookshops....

drif: Send off now. For drif's guide. Now, to Secondhand Bookshops. Now (alright Ray you get the copywriting job back). I never knew that was what ordinary people did with books. Pity about yours, but don't worry I have been asked to find a writer who is dead & keen.. sorry that should be dead keen and with drive. the interview is this afternoon so go and get the motor car and we will take a saunter down to palatial Parkhurst to meet our new client. There is no need to rush, he will not be going anywhere for eight years or so. I honestly think Reg Kray will have to go a long way to find somebody better than you to ghostwrite his poems.

A C A D E M I C

HOWES Hastings 0424 423 437

BLACKWELL'S Oxford 0865 792 792

DILLON'S London 071 636 1577

DEIGHTON BELL Cambridge 0223 353 939

See Student Texts.

A C U P U N C T U R E

BRIAN MILLS Newcastle 091 261 5380

A D V E R T I S I N G

See ART & DESIGN

A E R O N A U T I C S

See AVIATION

A F R I C A N A

TAIKOO York 0904 641 213

ORIENTAL & AFRICAN BOOKS Chester 0743 352 575

JANET BOX North Wales 0407 740 374

VICTOR BURKE South Brent 0364 43502

YESTERDAY'S BOOKS Bournemouth 0202 302 023

A G R I C U L T U R E

PHENOTYPE BOOKS Cumbria 0768 630 49

AGRICOLA BOOKS Headcorn 0622 890 331

A L D I N, C E C I L

MAYNARD & BRADLEY Leicester 0533 532 712

HALSON Cheshire 051 420 3276

See also BOOKDEALERS

A N A R C H I S M

HAMMERSMITH BOOKS London 081 876 7254

PORCUPINE BOOKS London 071 837 4473

A N G L I N G

JOHN & JUDITH HEAD Salisbury 0722 327 767

HEREWARD BOOKS Ely 0353 740 821

PHILIP M. HOPPER Essex 081 598 9999

WIGLEY BOOKS Pershore 0386 554 125

See HUNTING SHOOTING & FISHING

A N T A R T I C

WALCOT West Midlands 021 382 6381

A N T I Q U A R I A N

MAGGS BROS. London 071 493 7160

QUARITCH London 071 734 2983

SIMON FINCH London 071 499 0974

JAMES BURMESTER Bath 0272 327 265

CODEX RARE BOOKS Cumbria 0697 741 156

A N T I Q U E S & C O L L E C T I N G

POTTERTON BOOKS North Yorkshire 0845 401 218

JOHN IVES London 081 892 6265

ARS ARTIS Oxford 0865 770 714

COTHAM HILL Bristol 0272 732 344

HENEAGE London 071 930 9223

A R A B I A

TAIKOO BOOKS York 0904 641 213

JOPPA BOOKS Surrey 0932 868 269

REMINGTON London 071 836 9771

ULYSSES London 071 637 5862

A R C H A E O L O G Y

A.P. & B. BAKER Wigton 098 843 348

UDO POLCZYNSKI Surrey 081 689 6274

CASTLE BOOKSHOP Holt 0829 270 382

CASTLE HILL BOOKS Kington 0544 231 161

MUSEUM BOOKSHOP London 071 580 4086

A R C H E R Y

IAIN PUGH Worcestershire 0386 552 681

A R C H I T E C T U R E

SOTHERAN'S London 071 439 6151

THOMPSON'S BOOKSHOP Cirencester 0285 655 239

INCH'S York 0904 627 082

R.H.P. HASKELL Poole 0202 744 310

MONMOUTH HOUSE BOOKS Gwent 060 085 236

A R D I Z Z O N E

NIAL DEVITT Leamington Spa 0926 315533

BOOKS & THINGS London 071 370 5593

A R M Y

see MILITARY HISTORY

A R T R E F E R E N C E

ANNE CREED London 071 836 7757

THOMAS HENEAGE London 071 930 9223

ARS ARTIS Oxford 0865 770 714

MAINSFORD Bath 0225 445 107

See also DESIGN

A R T I L L E R Y

see ANTARTIC

A S T R O L O G Y

See OCCULT

A S T R O N O M Y

ARUNDEL BOOKSHOP West Sussex 0803 882 680

A T H L E T I C S

DENIS AMOS Cheshunt 0992 30486

ATHLETICA Worthing 0903 200 434

A U S T R A L I A

FLINDERS London 071 388 6080

PETER MOORE Cambridge 0223 411 177

A U T O G R A P H S

MAGGS BROS. London 071 493 7160

JOHN WILSON Oxford 0865 880 883

SKLAROFF I.O.W. 0983 754 960

See MANUSCRIPTS

A V I A T I O N

FRANK SMITH Newcastle 091 265 6333

THE AVIATION BOOKSHOP London 071 272 3630

COX East Anglia 0473 254 776

A V O N

see WEST COUNTRY

B A E D E C K E R S & M U R R A Y S

THE TRAVELLERS BOOKSHOP London 071 836 9132

DR. R.H. HIGHLEY Sheffield 0742 366 306

B A L L G A M E S

DENIS W. AMOS London 0992 30486

B A N K I N G

ALISTAIR GIBB Fife 0592 269 045

B A W D E N

BALLANTYNE & DATE London 071 242 4249

B E A R D S L E Y, A U B R E Y

PAUL SHERMAN London 081 556 2366

B E A T N I K

BEATNIK BOOKS Dingwall 0349 830 724

B E E S

B & K BOOKS Haye on Wye 0497 820 386

BEE BOOKS OLD & NEW Bridgwater 0823 698 781

B E L L R I N G I N G

J.M. FARRINGDON Swansea 0792 405 267

B E L L O C

AIDAN MACKAY Bedford 0234 57760

B E R K S H I R E

ETON ANTIQUE BOOKSHOP Eton 0753 855 534

RICHARD WAY Henley 0491 576 663

INVICTA BOOKSHOP Newbury 0635 31176

B I B L E S

HUMBER BOOKS 0482 802 239

ASPIN Hay on Wye 0497 820 437

B I B L I O G R A P H Y

MAGGS BROS. London 071 493 7160

HOWES BOOKSHOP Hastings 0424 423 437

DAWSON'S Folkestone 0303 850101x131

GEORGE'S Bristol 0272 276 602

DEIGHTON BELL Cambridge 0223 353 939

B I G G A M E H U N T I N G

VANDELEUR London 081 878 6837

BOBBY MARTIN Northern Ireland 08494 73778

COCH-Y-BONDDU BOOKS Machymleth 0654 702 837

see also HUNTING,SHOOTING,FISHING

B I N D I N G S

MAGGS BROS. London 071 493 7160

HARRINGTON'S London 071 352 5689

BAYNTUN Bath 0225 466 000

See FURNITURE

B L A C K S T U D I E S

SPURRIER Canterbury 0277 462 764

HAMMERSMITH BOOKS London 081 876 7254

B L A C K, A & C

ANDERSON, J C & N Guildford 0483 893 418

OLD CATHAY FINE BOOKS Hertfordshire 0707 271 006

B L Y T O N, E N I D

JULIA SESSERMAN Kent 081 658 6123

B O A R D G A M E S

See CHESS & DRAIGHTS.

B O E R W A R

BOER WAR BOOKS York 0904 654 698

B O O K S E A R C H E R S

WATERSTONES London 071 434 1195

TWIGGERS Bristol 0272 682 155

STERLING BOOKS Weston Super Mare 0934 625 056

BRUCE CASTLE BOOKS London 081 808 3222

A. & R. BOOKSEARCH Cornwall 0503 220 246

B O R N E O

EASTGATE BOOKS Beverley,Hull 0482 868 579

B O W L S

CHEQUER BOOKS Abingdon 0235 528 172

B O X I N G

P F & J R McINNES Bournemouth 0202 394 609

DAVID BENNET Sheffield 0226 767 497

R A HARTLEY London 081 904 6413

B O Y' S S T O R I E S

NORMAN SHAW London 081 771 9857

ROBERT KIRKPATRICK London 081 968 9033

B R I T I S H T O P O G R A P H Y

See INDIVIDUAL AREAS - such as East Anglia, Scotland, W

B R O A D C A S T I N G

L.V. KELLY Devon 0884 256 170

B U C H A N

BALLANTYNE BOOKS London 081 340 1953

B U C K I N G H A M S H I R E

SQUARE EDGE Aylesbury 0296 89480

B U S I N E S S

See ECONOMICS, but best to try new

B U T T E R F L I E S

DAVID DUNBAR London 081 455 9612

C A M B R I D G E S H I R E

See EAST ANGLIA

C A N A L S

M & M BALDWIN Geobury Mortimer 0299 270 110

C A R I C A T U R E

LOUIS BONDY London 071 405 2733

C A R P E T S

ABINGTON BOOKS Abington 0223 891 645

See ANTIQUES or ART

C A R R O L L, L E W I S

See CHILDRENS

C A R S
See MOTORING

C A R T O O N S
FACET BOOKS Nottinghamshire 0636 814 735

C A T A L O G U E S
NEWCASTLE BOOKSHOP Newcastle 091 261 5380

C A T S
M.C. ASTON Coventry 0203 711 711
BOOKLINE Down Parick 039 687 712

C A V I N G
CAVERS BOOKSHELF Wales 0239 831 371

C E N T R A L E U R O P E
ANTHONY HALL London 081 898 2638
HAMMERSMITH BOOKS London 081 876 7254
DE VISSER Cambridge 0223 425 746

C E R A M I C S
REFERENCE WORKS Dorset 1929 424 423
ANTIQUARIAN BOOK CENTRE Hanley 0782 261 352

C H A U C E R
See LITERATURE

C H E M I S T R Y
See SCIENCE & TECHNOLOGY

C H E S H I R E
IAIN CAMPBELL Cheshire 0829 41499
EARLS EYE Chester 0244 319 688
MACCLESFIELD RARE BOOKS Cheshire 0625 610 861

C H E S S & D R A U G H T S

BARRIE ELLEN Southend 0702 338 763

K. WHYLD Lincolnshire 0472 851 374

S.V. DICKENSON London 071 629 3644

C H E S T E R T O N

AIDAN MACKAY Bedford 0234 57760

C H I L D R E N' S

GREEN MEADOW Nottinghamshire 0949 81723

J.J. RIGDEN Canterbury 0227 769 911

E & C FOX Maidstone 0622 754 774

M & D REEVE Oxford 0865 61709

DAVID MILES Canterbury 0227 464 773

C H R I S T I E, A G A T H A

ELGO BOOKS London 071 482 4431

C H U R C H I L L

MARK WEBER London 071 225 2506

ALAN TAYLOR-SMITH Kent 0959 561 561

C I N E M A

A.E. COX Southampton 0703 447 989

IMPRINT Stroud 0453 759 731

C I R C U S

PLEASURES OF PAST TIMES London 071 836 1142

IMAGES Staffs 0543 264 093

C L A R I C E, H A R R Y

BOOKS & THINGS London 071 370 5593

C L A S S I C S

THE CLASSICS BOOKSHOP Oxford 0865 726 466

C L E V E L A N D

See NORTH EAST

C L O C K S

HADFIELD Leicestershire 0509 503 014

RITA SHENTON London 081 894 6888

ROGERS TURNER London 081 853 5271

C O I N S & M E D A L S

SPINK & SON London 071 930 7888

SEABY London 071 495 2590

C O L E R I D G E

COLERIDGE BOOKS Somerset 0278 733 338

C O M P U T E R T E X T B O O K S

SKOOB London 071 404 3063

See SCIENCE & TECHNOLOGY

C O M P U T E R S

GRAHAM WEINER London 081 883 8424

C O N A N D O Y L E

RUPERT BOOKS Cambridge 0954 781 861

S. HAMILTON Berwickshire 0361 82922

CONAN DOYLE BOOKS Leatherhead 0372 453 147

See Crime Fiction.

C O O K E R Y

COOKS BOOKS Rottingdean 0273 302 707

T. JACKSON Yorkshire 0943 601 947

BLACK CAT BOOKS Berwick 0289 382 953

JANET CLARKE Bath 0225 723 186

C O R N W A L L

NEW STREET BOOKS Penzance

PENZANCE RARE BOOKS Penzance 0736 62140

BROWSERS Falmouth 0326 313 464

BOOKENDS Fowey 0726 833 361

AMBRA BOOKS Bristol 0272 741 962

C O S T U M E

JUDITH MANSFIELD Lancashire 0706 816 487

JOHN IVES London 081 892 6265

BLACK CAT BOOKS Berwick 0289 382 953

A LA MODE London 081 886 2436

C R I C K E T

J.W. MacKENZIE Epson 081 393 7700

ORCHARD BOOKS Gloucestershire 0594 516 030

APPLEBY'S Keswick 07687 74054

C R I M E

See DETECTIVE FICTION or TRUE CRIME

C R I M E F I C T I O N

A1 CRIME FICTION Sherbourne 0935 814 989

BLACK BIRD BOOKS London 071 221 0269

ERGO BOOKS London 071 482 4431

R. ANDREWS Cheltenham 0242 820 904

C U M B R I A

HOLLET Sedbergh 0539 620 298

MICHAEL MOON Whitehaven 0946 62936

EWEN KERR Kendal 0539 720 659

C Y C L I N G

ANGEL BOOKS North Walsham 0692 404 054

D A N C E

DANCE BOOKS London 071 836 2314

D A R T M O O R

DARTMOOR BOOKSHOP Ashburton 0364 53356

D A R W I N

M.E. KORN London 081 883 5251

D E L A M E R E

KEITH SMITH Leabury 0531 5336

D E R B Y S H I R E

ALAN HILL Bakewell 0629 814 841

D E T E C T I V E   F I C T I O N

A1 CRIME FICTION Sherborne 0935 814 989

BLACKBIRD BOOKS London 081 455 3069

ERGO London 071 482 4431

MURDER ONE London 071 734 3483

D E V O N

HONITON OLD BOOKSHOP Honiton 0404 47180

AMBRA BOOKS Bristol 0272 741 962

EXETER RARE BOOKS Exeter 0382 438 021

LINDY'S Newton Abbot 0626 62221

D I C K E N S

JARNDYCE London 071 631 4220

VALENTINE'S London 081 254 4225

SOTHERAN'S London 071 439 6151

BOZ BOOKS Hay on Wye 0497 821 277

D I C T I O N A R I E S

KAREN THOMSON London 081 741 1327

JOSEPH BIDDULPH Ponty Pridd 0443 492 243

D I R E C T O R I E S

RAY SPARKES Staffordshire 0543 472 274

D I V I N G

See UNDERWATER

D O G S

DOGGIE HUBBARD'S Aberystyth 0970 85224

G. YORK Devon 0404 41727

HALSON BOOKS Cheshire 051 420 3276

STEVE RIBBONS Manchester 0484 684 043

D O L L S & D O L L H O U S E S

MULBERRY BUSH Sussex 0273 493 781

THE STAFFS BOOKSHOP Lichfield 0543 264 093

See also CHILDRENS BOOKS

D O R S E T

ANTIQUE MAP & BOOK SHOP Dorchester 0305 848 633

D U L A C

JOSEPHS London 071 493 8353

MAGGS London 071 499 7160

MARCHPANE London 071 836 8661

D U R H A M

See NORTH EAST ENGLAND

D Y L A N, T H O M A S

DYLAN'S BOOKS Swansea 0792 55255

CORRAN BOOKS Laugharne 0994 427 444

E A S T A N G L I A

FERROW Great Yarmouth 0493 843 800

CROWE Norwich 0603 624 800

COX Ipswich 0473 254 776

HEREWARD BOOKS Ely 0353 740 821

SUFFOLK RARE BOOKS Sudbury 0787 72075

E A S T E R N   E U R O P E

ANTHONY HALL London 081 898 2638

HAMMERSMITH BOOKS London 081 876 7254

E C O N O M I C   H I S T O R Y

BAT BOOKS London 081 514 5243

E G Y P T O L O G Y

ULYSSES London 071 637 5862

BOOKS B.C. London 081 864 0580

E N G I N E E R I N G

MOSTLY BOOKS Barrow in Furniss 0229 836 808

JULIA ELTON London 081 747 0967

RUSSEL JONES Berkshire 0628 824 237

E N T O M O L O G Y

L. CHRISTIE London 081 672 4024

E P H E M E R A

IAIN CAMPBELL Chester 0829 41499

THE OLD NEWSPAPER & EPHEMERA SHOP London 071 235 7788

KEN'S Newport Pagnell 0908 610003

E Q U E S T R I A N

R.E. & G.B. WAY Newmarket 0638 507 217

ALLEN & CO. London 071 834 5606

E R O T I C A

BATH OLD BOOKS Bath 0225 422 244

DELECTUS BOOKS London 081 963 0979

G & L TYSON Bath 0225 420 845

E S O T E R I C

See OCCULT

E S S E X

See EAST ANGLIA

F A I R Y T A L E S

See Children's Books.

F A L C O N R Y

R & H SMITH Hampshire 0264 773 938

ADRIAN WALKER Dunstable 0582 605 824

F A N T A S Y

See S/F

F A R M I N G

RUSSEL JONES Berkshire 0628 824 237

See also AGRICULTURE

F E M I N I S M

E. CRAWFORD London 071 278 9479

See WOMEN WRITERS

F E N C I N G

LYDIAN BOOKSTORE Buckinghamshire 0491 571 218

F I R E A R M S

PROSPECT BOOKS Gwynned 0492 640 111

F I S H I N G

JOHN & JUDITH HEAD Salisbury 0722 327 767

HEREWARD BOOKS Cambridgeshire 0353 740 821

WIGLEY BOOKS Pershore 0386 544 125

PHILIP HOPREL Essex 081 598 9999

See HUNTING, SHOOTING & FISHING

F O O T B A L L

JOHN W. WHITTAKER Durham 091 384 3202

BOOKMARK London 081 905 6993

See BALL GAMES

F O R E I G N T R A V E L & T O P O G R A P H Y

TAIKOO York 0904 641 213

ULYSSES London 071 637 5862

See TRAVEL & TOPOG

F O R R E S T E R, C. S.

MARTYN KEENE King's Lynn 0485 520 201

F R A N C I S, D I C K

NIGEL BIRD Tregaron 097 423 281

F R E N C H

ASPIN Hay on Wye 0497 820 437

G A R D E N I N G

LLOYD'S London 081 940 2512

MIKE PARK London 081 641 7796

IVELET BOOKS Redhill 0737 768 282

SUMMERFIELD BOOKS Cumbria 07683 41577

G E N E O L O G Y

JOHN TOWNSEND Berkshire 0734 785 463

G E O L O G Y

BALDWIN'S BOOKS Witham 0376 83502

BOW WINDOWS Lewes 0273 480 780

HONITON BOOKSHOP Honiton 0404 47180

G E R M A N

ROGERS TURNER London 081 853 5271

SPECULUM MENTIS Bath 0225 426 243

G H O S T   S T O R I E S

ENIGMA BOOKS Honiton 0404 891 266

JOHN EGGLING Todmorden 0706 816 487

G I L E S

FACET BOOKS Nottingham 0636 814 735

G I L L,   E R I C

SHERLOCKS Suffolk 0449 740 397

G I R L' S   B O O K S

GIRLS GONE BY Lancashire 0257 271 347

TRISHA MARSHALL London 071 286 0828

E.B. DYER & D.F. BRUCE Amersham 0494 433 895

G L A M O U R   &   P I N U P

NOSTALGIA York 0904 624 901

YESTERDAY'S PAPER Lincolnshire 0507 609 017

G L O U C E S T E R S H I R E

VALENTINES BOOKSHOP Nailsworth 0453 832 483

THOMPSONS Cirencester 0285 655 239

G O L F

FURNISS Scotland 0387 75624

GRANT Worcestershire 0905 778 155

SARAH BADDIEL London 071 408 1239

QUARTO St Andrews 0334 74616

G R A M O P H O N E S   &   R E C O R D S

THE HISTORIC RECORD Sheffield 0742 460 275

G R E E K

NICOLAS BOOKS London 081 445 9835

HELLENIC BOOK SERVICE London 071 267 9499

ZENO London 071 836 2522

G R E E N E, G R A H A M
GLOUCESTER ROAD BOOKSHOP London 071 370 3503

G U I D E S
See SCOUTS & GUIDES

G U N S
PROSPECT BOOKS & PRINTS Wales 0492 640 111

G Y P S I E S
BORDER BOOKS Lancashire 0706 814721

H A G G A R D, R I D E R
R.T. ALLEN Whitley Bay 091 252 4516

H A M P S H I R E
GILBERTS Winchester 0962 53932
PETERSFIELD BOOKSHOP Petersfield 0730 63438
TRAYEN'S Guildford 0483 572 424

H A R D Y, T H O M A S
ANTIQUE MAPS & BOOKSHOP Puddlestown 0305 848 633
SWAN GALLERIES Sherborne 0935 814 465
BOOKS AFLOAT Weymouth 0305 797 774

H E A T H R O B I N S O N / C & W
BOOKS & THINGS London 071 370 5593

H E R E F O R D / W O R C S
HEREFORD BOOKSHOP Hereford 0432 357 617
KEITH SMITH Ledbury 0531 5336
THE MALVERN BOOKSHOP Malvern 0684 575 915

H E R T F O R D S H I R E
BOOK CABIN Harpenden 0582 768 581
THORPES St Albans 0727 65576

H I S T O R Y

ABBEY BOOKS St. Albans 0727 867 904

HOWES Hastings 0424 423 437

WINGHALE BOOKS Lincolnshire 0652 678 752

See MEDIEVAL

H I S T O R Y - M E D I E V A L

BENNETT & KERR Abington 0235 832 587

MARK CHRISTODOLOU York 0904 641 389

H O M O S E X U A L I T Y

GAY'S THE WORD London 071 278 7654

H O R S E S

R.E. & G.B. WAY Newmarket 0638 507 217

ALLEN London 071 828 8855

See EQUESTRIAN

H U M B E R S I D E

See YORKSHIRE

H U N T I N G, S H O O T I N G & F I S H I N G

HEREWARD BOOKS Ely 0353 740 821

FURNISS Scotland 0387 75624

I L L U S T R A T E D

IMAGES Lichfield 0543 264 093

DRUMMOND London 071 836 1142

SHERLOCKS Suffolk 0449 740 397

JOSEPHS London 071 493 8353

BALLANTYNE & DATE London 071 436 4829

I L L U S T R A T E D - 2 0 T H C E N T U R Y

BOOKWORKS Letchworth 0462 673 189

I L L U S T R A T E D - 1 9 T H C E N T U R Y

IAN HODGKIN Glos 0453 764270

I N D I A

BOOKS ABOUT INDIA Wetherby 0937 586 453

BOOKS OF ASIA London 071 630 5331

I N D U S T R I A L   H I S T O R Y

BOOK HOUSE Kirkby Stephen 05396 23 634

BALLANTYNE & DATE London 071 242 4249

I R I S H

NAUGHTON BOOKSELLERS Don Laoghaire 0103531 2804392

EMERALD ISLE BOOKS Belfast 0232 370 798

CATHACH BOOKS Dublin 0103531 718 676

DE BURCA Dublin 0103531 2882159

DAVIDSON 0238 562 502

I S L E   O F   W I G H T

HERITAGE BOOKS Ryde 0983 62933

VENTNOR BOOKSHOP Ventnor 0983 853 706

SKLAROFF Totland 0983 754 960

J A Z Z

SCORPIO BOOKS East Anglia 098 684 245

BEATNIK BOOKS Dingwallia 0349 830 724

J E W E L L E R Y

NIBRIS BOOKS London 081 946 7207

See COSTUME & NEEDLEWORK

J O H N S O N,   S A M U E L

THE STAFFS BOOKSHOP Lichfield 0543 264093

CLARKE HALL London 071 353 4116

J O Y C E,   J A M E S

ULYSSES London 071 637 5862

see also IRISH BOOKDEALERS

J U D A I C A

JOHN TROTTER London 081 203 6350

MANOR BOOKS London 081 349 9484

K E N T

CHRISTINE SWIFT Kent 0233 713 730

MARRINS Folkestone 0303 53016

DAVID MILES Canterbury 0227 464 773

K I N G, J E S S I E M

MARCHPANE London 071 836 8661

K I P L I N G

BOOKSHOP FAVERSHAM Kent 0795 532 873

L A K E D I S T R I C T

EWEN KERR Cumbria 0539 720659

L A N C A S H I R E

BOB DOBSON Blackpool 0253 886 103

GREAT GRANDFATHERS Leyland 0772 422 268

HOLLET Sedbergh 0539 620 298

ROCHDALE BOOK CO Rochdale 0706 31136

L A N C A S T E R, O S B E R T

BOOK BAZAAR London 071 352 6810

L A T I N A M E R I C A

BURTON GARBETT London 081 540 2367

L A W

WILDY & SON London 071 242 5778

L E F T L I T E R A T U R E

PATERSON Cambridge 0223 321 658

L E F T I E P O L I T I C S

PORCUPINES London 071 837 4473

SPURRIER Canterbury 0227 462 764

L E I C E S T E R S H I R E

MAYNARD & BRADLEY Leicester 0533 532 712

L E T T E R S, M A N U S C R I P T S, D O C U M E N T S

HENRY BRISTOW Verwood 0202 826 979

MAGGS London 071 493 7160

L I N C O L N S H I R E

HARLEQUIN Lincoln 0522 543 217

STANILAND Stamford 0780 55800

BRIDGE BOOKSHOP Deeping St James 0778 343 175

P J CASSIDY Holbeach 0406 26322

L I T E R A T U R E - 1 9 T H C E N T U R Y

JANDYCE London 071 631 4220

VALENTINE'S London 071 254 4225

M A G A Z I N E S

TILLEY'S Sheffield 0742 752 442

KEN'S Newport Pagnell 0908 610003

M A G I C / M U S I C H A L L

ANNE FITZSIMMONS Carlisle 0228 513 815

PLEASURES OF PAST TIMES London 071 836 1142

M A N U S C R I P T S

JOHN WILSON Oxford 0865 880883

RICHARD FORD London 081 993 1235

M A N U S C R I P T S - A N T I Q U A R I A N

SAM FOGG London 071 495 2333

MAGGS London 071 493 7160

M A R I T I M E

ANTHONY J. SIMMONDS London 081 853 1727

McLAREN Clydeside 0436 76453

GREEN'S London 081 997 6454

BOOKS AFLOAT Weymouth 0305 779 774

FISHER NAUTICAL Hassocks 0273 890 273

M A T H E M A T I C S

F.E. WHITEHEAD London 081 699 3225

M E D I C I N E

ROBERT CONNELLY London 071 430 1394

F.E. WHITEHEART London 081 699 3225

MICHAEL PHELPS London 081 785 6766

M E R S E Y S I D E

BROADHURSTS Southport 0704 532 064

KERNAGHAN Southport 0704 546 329

M I C R O S C O P E S

TURRET HOUSE Norfolk 0953 603 462

ROGERS TURNER London 081 853 5271

SAVONA BOOKS Humberside 0964 535 195

M I D D L E   E A S T

JOHN TROTTER London 081 445 4293

TAIKOO York 0904 641 213

FINE BOOKS ORIENTAL London 071 636 6068

M I L I T A R Y   H I S T O R Y

P.G. DE LOTZ London 071 794 5709

CHELIFER BOOKS Wigton 0228 711388

THE COLLECTOR Halifax 0422 363 895

GEORGE HARRIS Worcestershire 0299 402 413

DEREK HAYLES Maidenhead 0628 39535

M I N I A T U R E   B O O K S

LOUIS BONDY London 071 405 2733

COOPER HAY Glasgow 041 226 3074

MICHAEL GARBETT Bristol 0454 617 376

M O D E R N   F I R S T S

ULYSSES London 071 637 5862

BERTRAM ROTA London 071 836 0723

BELL BOOK & RADMELL London 071 240 2161

HALVEDENE Liverpool 051 708 0780

M O D E R N   B R I T I S H   I L L U S T R A T E R S

BALLANTYNE & DATE London 071 436 4829

BOOKWORKS Herts 0462 673 189

SKELLOCKS Suffolk 0449 740 379

M O T O R I N G

LES WILSON Manchester 0942 893 632

CHRIS WINDER North Yorkshire 0423 521 187

EOIN YOUNG Surrey 04865 3311

BALLANTYNE & DATE London 071 242 4249

CHATERS London 081 568 9750

M O U N T A I N E E R I N G

JARVIS BOOKS Matlock 0629 55322

JOHN O'REILLY Derby 0332 365 650

ANGLESEY BOOKS Holyhead 0407 760 988

M U R R A Y' S

See BAEDECKER'S

M U S I C

MAY & MAY Shaftsbury 0747 830034

KENNEDY & FARLEY East Sussex 089 285 3141

LISA COX Exeter 0392 55776

TRAVIS & EMERY London J071 240 2129

ARCHIVE BOOKS London 071 402 8212

M U S I C A L   I N S T R U M E N T S

F. TROTMAN Dorset 0308 862 293

N A P O L E O N I C A

PROSPECT HOUSE Belfast 0232 245 787

N A T U R A L   H I S T O R Y

WHELDON & WESLEY Hitchin 0438 820 370

DARTMOOR BOOKSHOP Dartmoor 0364 53356

HOLBOURNE BOOKS Worcester 0905 27824

BOOKS FOR NATURALISTS Devon 0598 3538

N E E D L E W O R K

JUDITH MANSFIELD Lancashire 0706 816 487

BLACK CAT BOOKS Berwick 0289 382 953

See also Costume.

N E W   Z E A L A N D

SQUARE EDGE Aylesbury 0296 89480

N O R F O L K

See EAST ANGLIA

N O R T H   O F   E N G L A N D   T O P O G R A P H Y

HOLLET'S Sedburgh 05396 20298

N O R T H   E A S T   O F   E N G L A N D

STEEDMAN Newcastle 091 232 6561

JOHN TURSON Durham 0388 747 600

N O R T H A M P T O N S H I R E

OLD HALL BOOKSHOP Brackley 0280 704 146

WOOTAN BILLINGHAM Northampton 0604 34531

PARK BOOKSHOP Wellingborough 0933 222 552

N O T T I N G H A M

G BLORE Nottingham 0602 626 059

MAYNARD & BRADLEY Nottingham 0602 484 824

N U M I S M A T I C S

SPINK London 071 930 7888

O C C U L T

UROBOROUS Glasgow 041 332 4924

ATLANTIS London 071 405 2120

WATKINS London 071 836 2182

ALPHA BOOKS London 081 348 2831

OCCULTIQUE Northampton 0604 27727

O P E R A

GEORGE BURKE Newburgh 0337 40231

O R I E N T A L

AD ORIENTAM St. Leonards 0424 427186

FINE BOOKS ORIENTAL London 071 636 6068

HAN-SHAN-TANG London 071 731 2447

TAIKOO York 0904 641 213

O R I E N T A L A R T

RICHARD LYON West Sussex 0273 832 255

O R N I T H O L O G Y

WHELDON & WESLEY Hitchin 0438 820 370

F.N. CRACK Lancashire 05242 61244

O X F O R D U N I V E R S I T Y P R E S S

WOODSTOCK BOOKSHOP Oxfordshire 0993 811005

O X F O R D S H I R E

TOBY ENGLISH Wallingford 0491 36389

RICHARD WAY BOOKS Henley 0491 576 663

WATERFORDS Oxford 0865 721 809

SANDERS Oxford 0865 242 590

P A P E R B A C K S

VORTEX London 071 254 6516

RICHARD WILLIAMS South Humberside 0724 840 645

P E A K E, M E R V Y N

SKLAROFF IOW 0983 754 960

HOWDEN BOOKS Yorks 0482 845 567

P E N G U I N

RICHARD WILLIAMS South Humberside 0724 840 645

BLACK CAT BOOKS Leicestershire 0533 512 756

P E R F O R M I N G A R T S

PLEASURES OF PAST TIMES London 071 836 1142

ANNE FYTZSIMMONS Cumbria 0228 513 815

P E R F U M E R Y

BUTTERBURR & SAGE Reading 0734 314 484

P H I L O S O P H Y

THOEMMES Bristol 0272 291 377

JOHN PRICE London 071 837 8008

MAIR WILKES Fife 0382 542 260

P H O N O L O G Y

CHEVERTON BOOKS Wareham 092 95 54808

P H O T O G R A P H Y

BALLANTYNE & DATE London 071 242 4249

BOOKS & THINGS London 071 370 5593

J.F. HOLLEYMAN Hove 0273 410 915

INCH'S York 0904 629770

P O E T R Y

THE POETRY BOOKSHOP Hay on Wye 0497 820 305

BERTRAM ROTA London 071 836 0723

ALEX ALEC-SMITH Humberside 0482 869 453

ULYSSES London 071 637 5862

P O E T R Y - 1 9 T H C E N T U R Y

DEREK WISE Brighton 0273 400 559

P O E T R Y - 2 0 T H C E N T U R Y

PETER RILEY Cambridge 0223 327 455

P O E T R Y - W W 1

PALLADOUR BOOKS Shaftesbury 0747 539 42

P O L A R E X P L O R A T I O N

P.J. WALCOT West Midlands 021 382 6381

P O L I T I C S

HAMMERSMITH BOOKS London 081 876 7254

NICK SPURRIER Canterbury 0227 462 764

DILLONS London 071 636 1577

P O P M U S I C

BEATNIK BOOKS Dingwall 0349 830 724

C.T. BENFORD Hampshire 0705 753 325

P S Y C H I A T R Y / P S Y C H O L O G Y

MAIR WILKES Fife 0382 542 352

SOCIAL SCIENCES BOOKSHOP Middlesex 081 902 3659

P U B L I C S C H O O L S

THE RUTLAND BOOKSHOP Uppingham 0572 823 450

P U P P E T R Y

DA SILVA BOOKS Marsham 0263 733 882

R A C K H A M

MAGGS London

DRUMMONDS London

MARCHPANE London

R A C K H A M, A R T H U R

MAGGS London 071 493 7160

DRUMMOND London 071 836 1142

MARCHPANE London 071 836 8661

R A I L W A Y S

EDWARDS East Anglia 0787 247 771

PATTERSON & LIDDLE Bristol 0272 731 205

HENRY WILSON Chester 0829 40693

ROBERT HUMM Stamford 0780 66266

N J BRIDGER Berkshire 0635 200 507

R A V I L L I O U S

BALLANTYNE & DATE London 071 242 4249

R E L I G I O N

CHARLES HIGHAM SPCK London 071 387 5282

LINDY'S Newton Abbott 0392 436 021

LAURIE GAGE Southend 0702 715 133

PENDLEBURY'S London 081 809 4922

R E P T I L E S

STEPHEN SIMPSON East Sussex 0273 727 328

J.G. BOOKS London 081 764 4669

R O W I N G

RICHARD WAY Henley 0491 576 663

VANDELEUR London 081 393 7752

R O Y A L T Y

PICCADILLY RARE BOOKS Kent 0892 750 201

C. PAUL KNIGHT Essex 0702 335 408

R U P E R T S

HALL London 081 898 2638

R U S S I A N   B O O K S

ANTHONY NEVILLE Rye 0797 224 552

S C H O O L   H I S T O R I E S

THE RUTLAND BOOKSHOP Uppingham 0572 823 450

DELPH BOOKS Manchester 061 764 4488

S C I E N C E   F I C T I O N

TOBY ENGLISH Oxon 0491 36389

FANTASY CENTRE London 071 607 9433

JOHN EGGELING Lancashire 0706 816 487

FERRET FANTASY London 081 767 0029

HOWDÉN BOOKSHOP Yorkshire 0430 432 071

S C I E N C E   &   T E C H N O L O G Y

E.A. WHITEHART London 081 699 3225

GRAHAM WEINER London 081 883 8424

ANTHONY PARKINSON South Port 0704 547 016

M.A. STROH London 071 359 7666

S C I E N T I F I C   I N S T R U M E N T S

ROGERS TURNER London 081 853 5271

S C O T T I S H

DONALD MacCORMICK Edinburgh 031 447 2889

MAIR WILKES Dundee 0382 542 260

ABERDEEN RARE BOOKS Aberdeen 035 887 275

COOPER HAY Glasgow 041 226 3074

S C O U T S & G U I D E S

JOHN HOGGARTH Whitby 0947 873 38

S H A K E S P E A R E

VAUGHAN Stratford on Avon 0789 205 312

S H E E T M U S I C

ARCHIVE London 071 402 8212

HOLLEYMAN & TREACHER Brighton 0273 28007

WORDS & LYRICS London

See also MUSIC

S H O P T R A D E C A T A L O G U E S

KEN'S Newport Pagnell 0908 610003

NEWCASTLE BOOKSHOP Newcastle 091 261 5380

CAROL HOGBEN London 081 789 0311

S H R O P S H I R E

QUARRY BOOKS Shrewsbury 0243 361404

20TH CENTURY BOOKS Ludlow 0548 4441

S M O K I N G

JOHN IVES London 081 892 6265

S O M E R S E T

See WEST OF ENGLAND

S P O R T

DAVID ELLIS London 081 520 4032

S T A I N E D G L A S S

M & J VENABLES Bristol 0272 507 362

S U F F O L K

CLAUDE COX Ipswich 0473 254 776

T E N N I S

THE TENNIS BOOKSHOP Hampshire 0425 480 518

T H E A T R E

DECORUM London 071 278 1838

COX Southampton 0703 447 989

T H E A T R E - T E C H N I C A L B O O K S

BOOK BAZAAR London 071 352 6810

T H E O L O G Y

see RELIGION

T R A N S P O R T

BALLANTYNE & DATE London 071 242 4249

FALCONWOOD London 081 303 8291

T R U E C R I M E

CAMILLE WOLFF London 071 221 0269

CLIFFORD ELMER Cheadle 061 485 7064

ONYX BOOKS Bristol 0934 822 781

T U R K E Y

OXUS BOOKS London 081 870 3854

T Y P O G R A P H Y

CLAUDE COX Ipswich 0473 254 776

U N D E R W A T E R / D I V I N G

WYE & SEVERN BOOKS Gloucestershire 0452 760 368

DIVER & WATERSPORTSMAN'S LIBRARY Paignton 0803 551840

BARAK Sussex 044 236 229

W E I G H T L I F T I N G

D. WEBSTER Strathclyde 0294 72257

W E L S H

DYLAN'S Swansea 0792 655 255

CAPITAL BOOKSHOP Cardiff 0222 388 423

YSTWYTH BOOKS Aberystwyth 0970 617 511

TOM LLOYD ROBERTS Mold 0352 720 276

CARMARTHEN BOOKS Carmarthen 0267 235 676

W E S T O F E N G L A N D

AMBRA BOOKS Bristol 0272 741 962

EASTWOOD Bridgewater 0278 683 894

HONITON RARE BOOKS Honiton 0404 47180

EXETER RARE BOOKS Exeter 0392 436 021

ROTHWELL & DUNWORTH Taunton 0823 282 476

W I L L I A M S O N, H E N R Y

CLEARWATER BOOKS Winborne 0202 893 263

W I N E & S P I R I T S

A.J. SHEPERDSON North Humberside 0262 603 472

JOHN THORNE Essex 081 592 0259

JOHN ROBERTS London 081 876 1534

W O D E H O U S E, P. G.

NIGEL WILLIAMS London 081 693 0464

W O M E N W R I T E R S

LYDIAN BOOKSTORE Buckinghamshire 0491 571 218

W O R C E S T E R S H I R E

See HEREFORD & WORCS

Y O R K S H I R E

AXE Yorkshire 065 384 486

SPELMANS York 0904 624 414

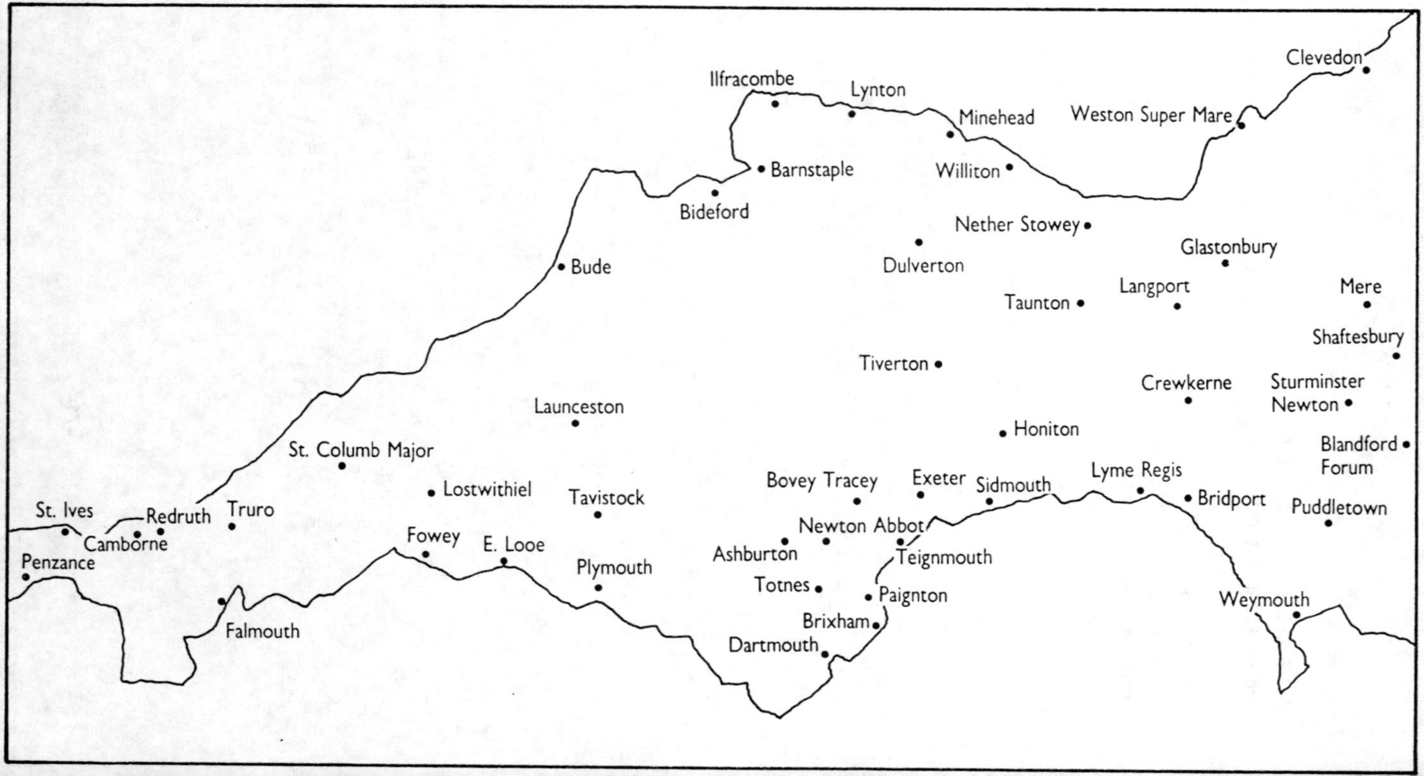
Clevedon
Ilfracombe
Lynton
Minehead
Weston Super Mare
Barnstaple
Williton
Bideford
Nether Stowey
Glastonbury
Bude
Dulverton
Langport
Mere
Taunton
Shaftesbury
Tiverton
Crewkerne
Sturminster
Newton
Launceston
Honiton
Blandford
Forum
St. Columb Major
Bovey Tracey
Exeter
Sidmouth
Lyme Regis
Lostwithiel
Tavistock
Bridport
Puddletown
St. Ives
Redruth
Truro
Newton Abbot
Camborne
Fowey
E. Looe
Ashburton
Teignmouth
Penzance
Plymouth
Totnes
Paignton
Weymouth
Brixham
Falmouth
Dartmouth

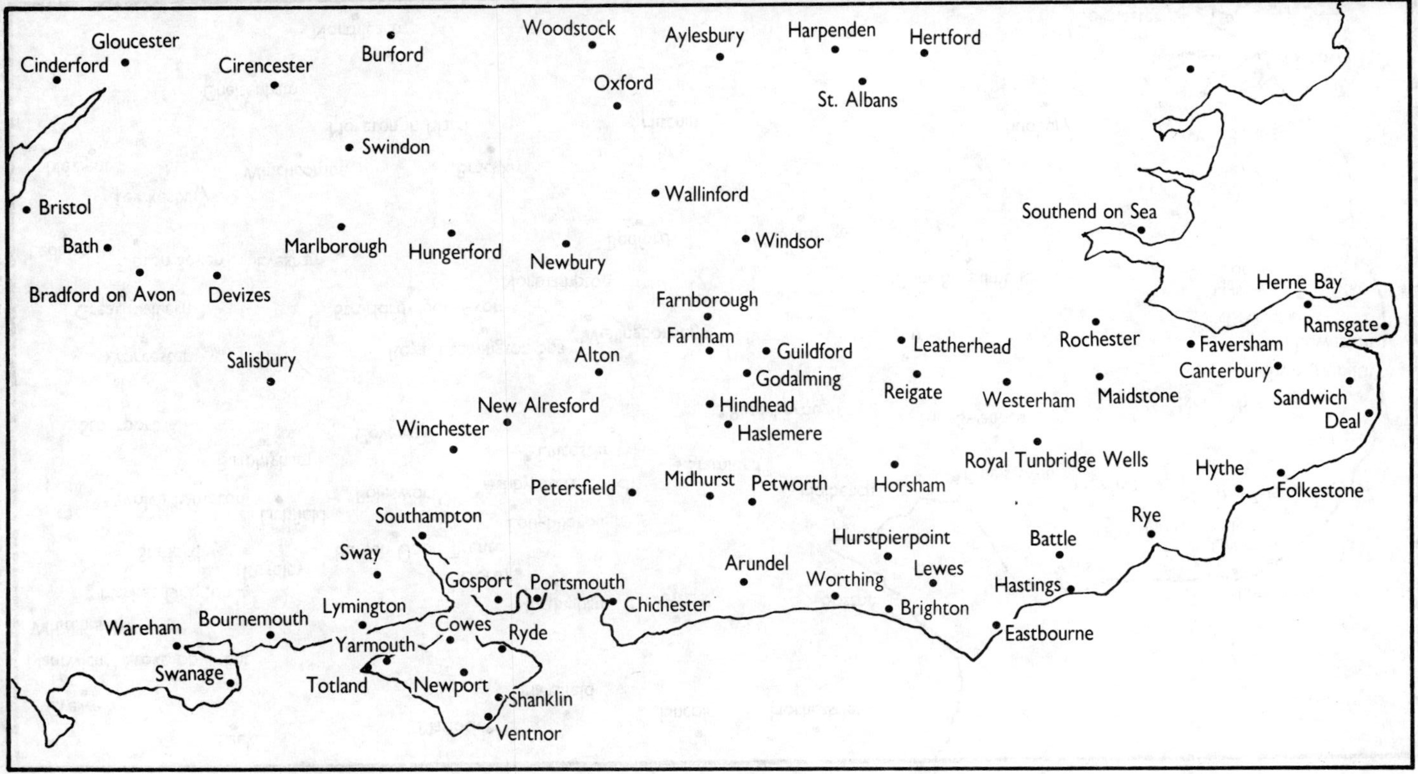
Gloucester
Cinderford
Cirencester
Burford
Woodstock
Aylesbury
Harpenden
Hertford
Oxford
St. Albans
Swindon
Wallinford
Southend on Sea
Bristol
Bath
Marlborough
Hungerford
Newbury
Windsor
Bradford on Avon
Devizes
Farnborough
Herne Bay
Ramsgate
Farnham
Leatherhead
Rochester
Faversham
Salisbury
Alton
Guildford
Godalming
Reigate
Westerham
Maidstone
Canterbury
Sandwich
Deal
New Alresford
Hindhead
Winchester
Haslemere
Royal Tunbridge Wells
Hythe
Folkestone
Midhurst
Petworth
Horsham
Petersfield
Southampton
Rye
Hurstpierpoint
Battle
Sway
Arundel
Lewes
Gosport
Portsmouth
Worthing
Hastings
Chichester
Brighton
Lymington
Cowes
Eastbourne
Wareham
Bournemouth
Ryde
Yarmouth
Swanage
Totland
Newport
Shanklin
Ventnor

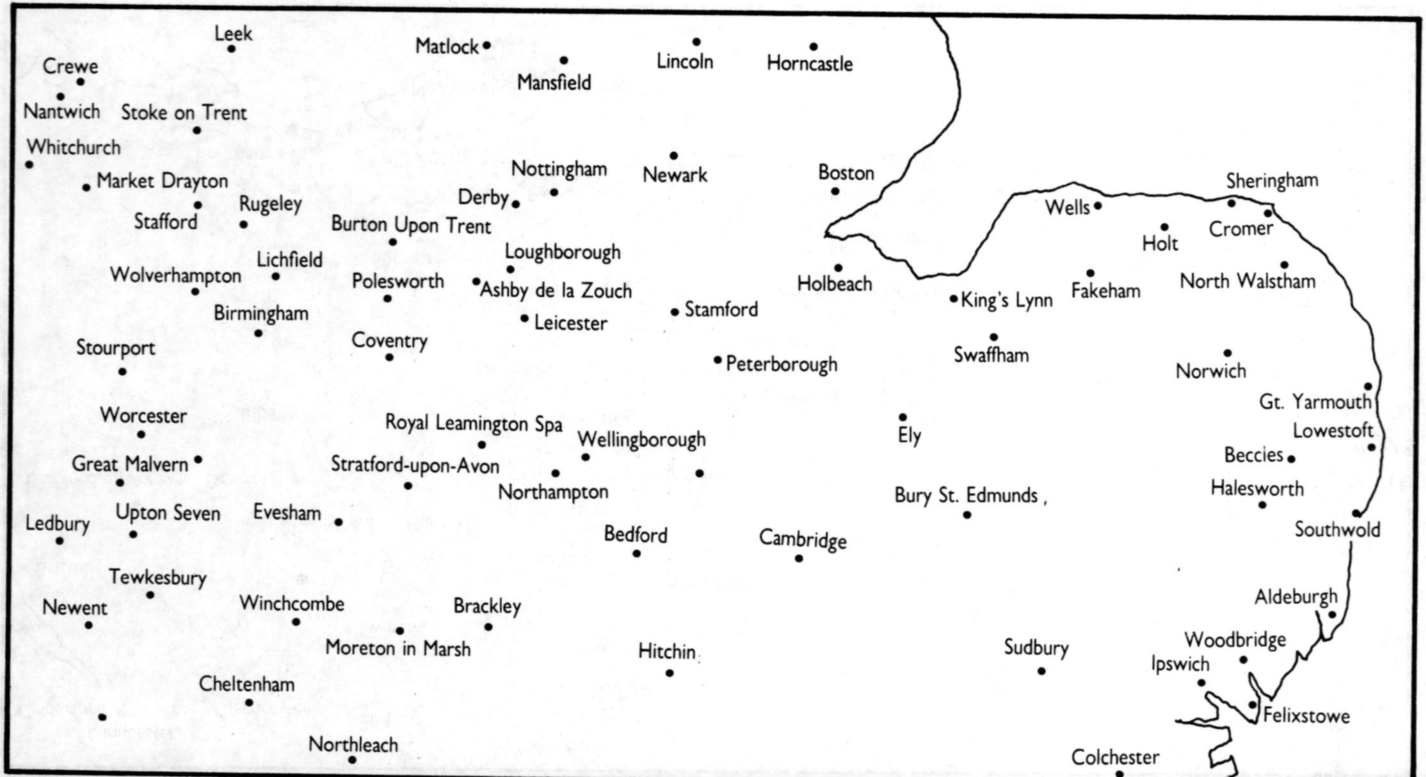
Leek
Matlock
Lincoln
Horncastle
Crewe
Mansfield
Nantwich
Stoke on Trent
Whitchurch
Nottingham
Newark
Boston
Sheringham
Market Drayton
Derby
Rugeley
Wells
Stafford
Burton Upon Trent
Cromer
Holt
Loughborough
Lichfield
Wolverhampton
Polesworth
Ashby de la Zouch
Holbeach
North Walstham
King's Lynn
Fakeham
Stamford
Birmingham
Leicester
Coventry
Stourport
Swaffham
Peterborough
Norwich
Gt. Yarmouth
Worcester
Royal Leamington Spa
Ely
Lowestoft
Wellingborough
Beccies
Great Malvern
Stratford-upon-Avon
Halesworth
Northampton
Bury St. Edmunds
Southwold
Upton Seven
Evesham
Ledbury
Bedford
Cambridge
Tewkesbury
Aldeburgh
Newent
Winchcombe
Brackley
Woodbridge
Moreton in Marsh
Hitchin
Sudbury
Ipswich
Cheltenham
Felixstowe
Northleach
Colchester

Wales

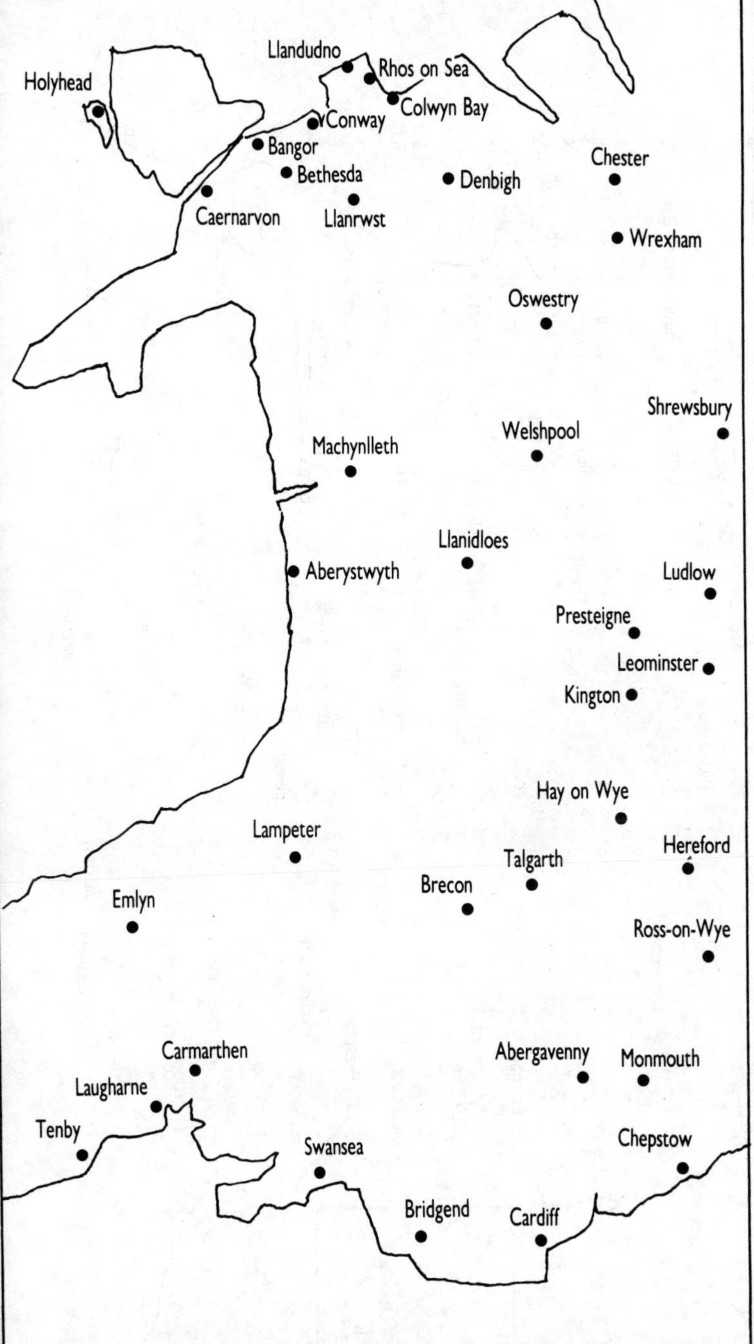
Holyhead
Llandudno
Rhos on Sea
Colwyn Bay
Conway
Bangor
Bethesda
Caernarvon
Llanrwst
Denbigh
Chester
Wrexham
Oswestry
Shrewsbury
Welshpool
Machynlleth
Llanidloes
Aberystwyth
Ludlow
Presteigne
Leominster
Kington
Hay on Wye
Lampeter
Hereford
Talgarth
Brecon
Emlyn
Ross-on-Wye
Carmarthen
Abergavenny
Monmouth
Laugharne
Tenby
Swansea
Chepstow
Bridgend
Cardiff

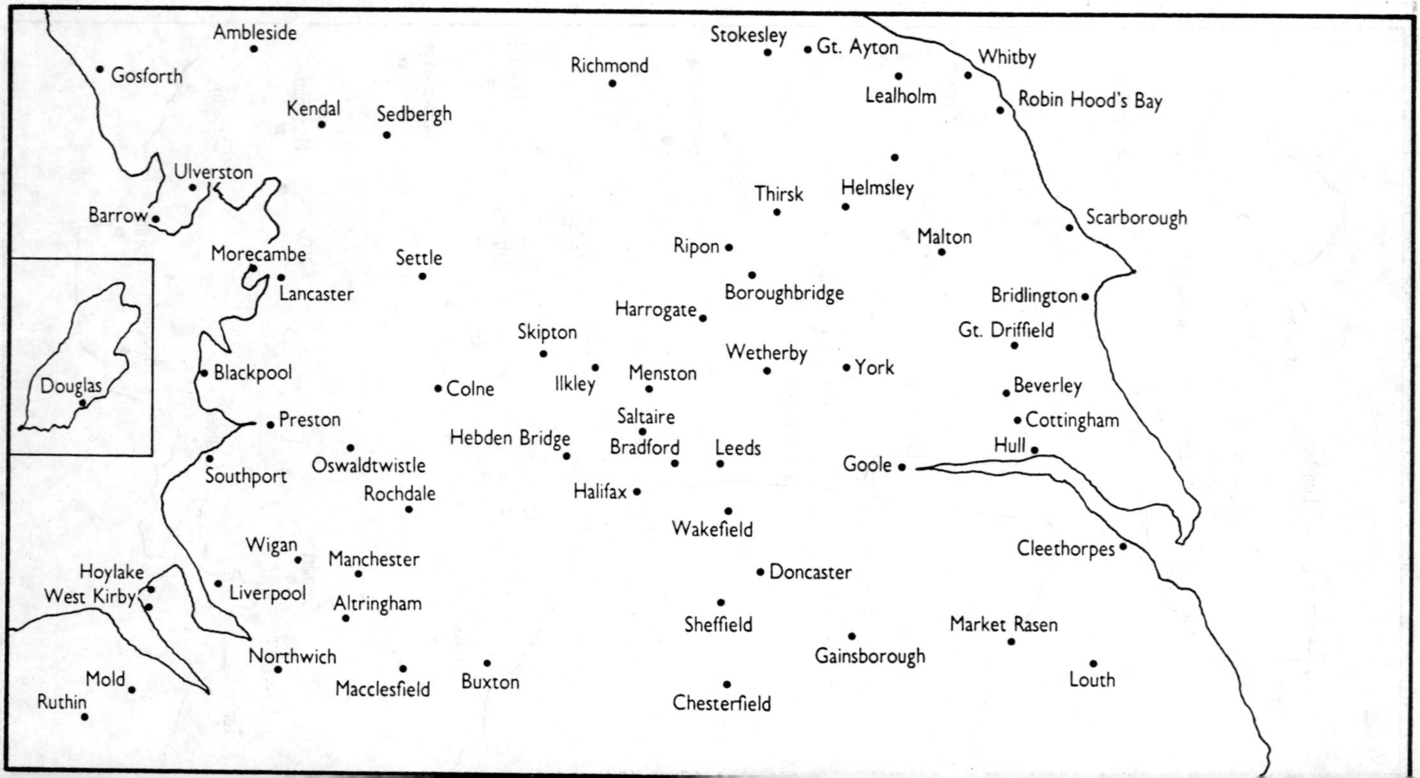
Ambleside
Gosforth
Kendal
Sedbergh
Richmond
Stokesley
Gt. Ayton
Whitby
Lealholm
Robin Hood's Bay
Ulverston
Barrow
Thirsk
Helmsley
Scarborough
Malton
Ripon
Morecambe
Settle
Lancaster
Boroughbridge
Bridlington
Harrogate
Skipton
Gt. Driffield
Wetherby
York
Menston
Ilkley
Blackpool
Colne
Douglas
Beverley
Saltaire
Preston
Cottingham
Hebden Bridge
Bradford
Leeds
Hull
Goole
Oswaldtwistle
Southport
Halifax
Rochdale
Wakefield
Cleethorpes
Wigan
Manchester
Hoylake
Doncaster
West Kirby
Liverpool
Altringham
Sheffield
Market Rasen
Gainsborough
Northwich
Mold
Macclesfield
Buxton
Louth
Ruthin
Chesterfield

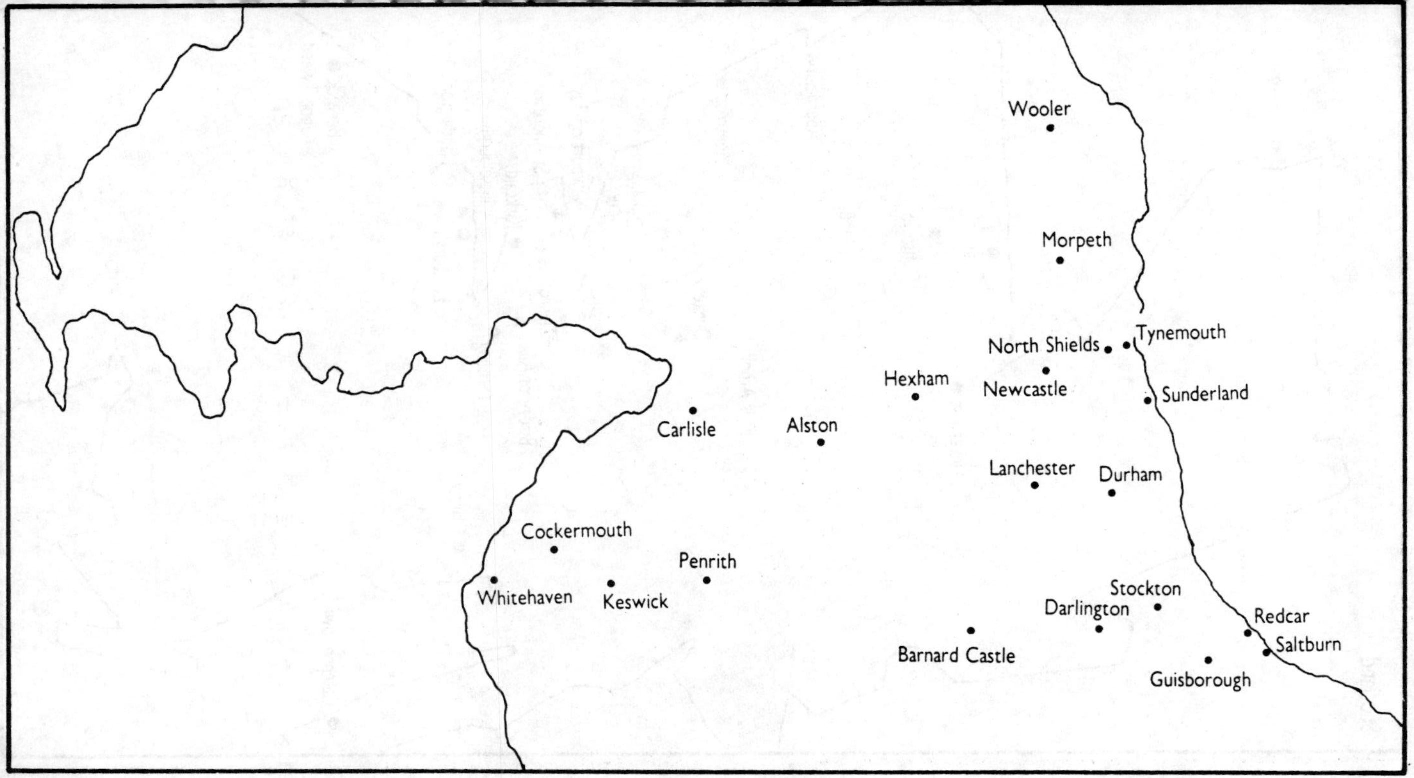
Wooler
Morpeth
North Shields
Tynemouth
Hexham
Newcastle
Sunderland
Carlisle
Alston
Lanchester
Durham
Cockermouth
Penrith
Whitehaven
Keswick
Stockton
Darlington
Redcar
Saltburn
Barnard Castle
Guisborough

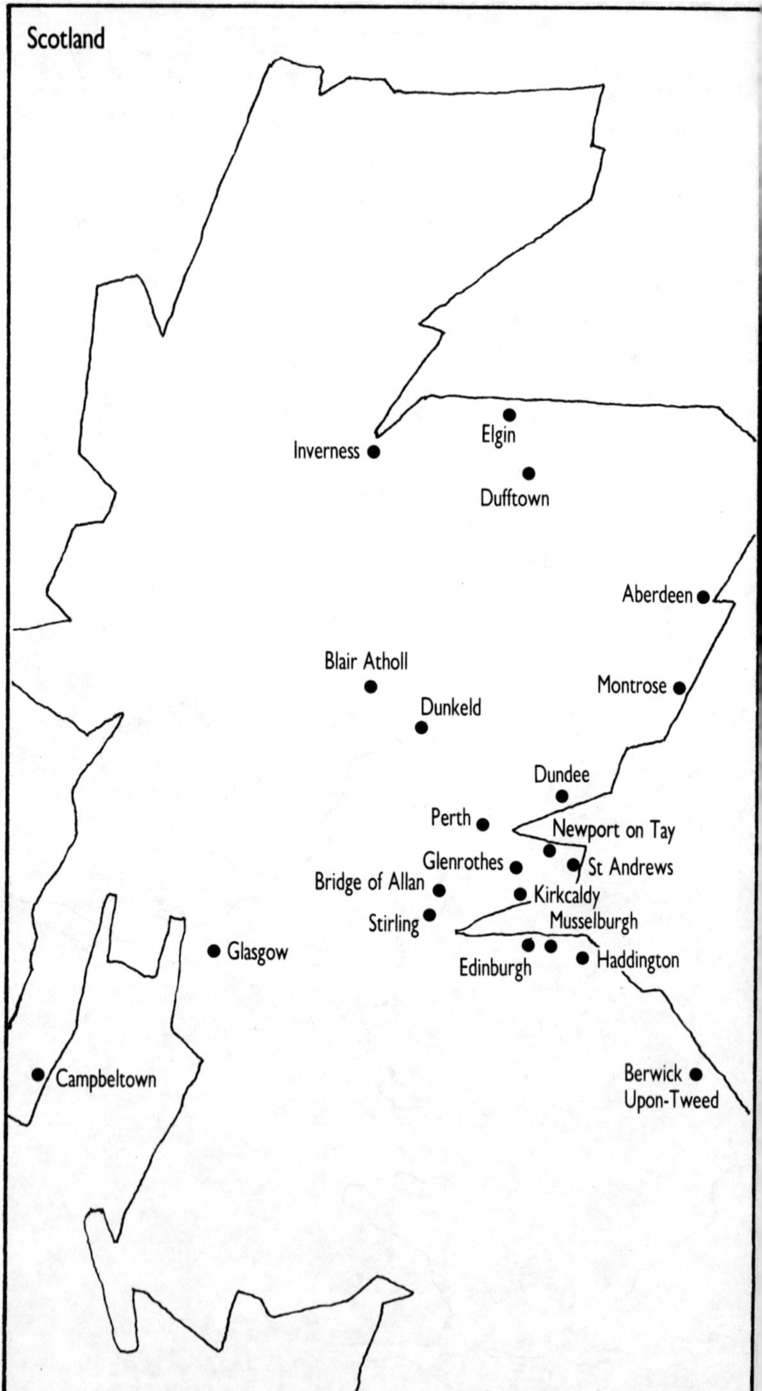
Scotland
Elgin
Inverness
Dufftown
Aberdeen
Blair Atholl
Montrose
Dunkeld
Dundee
Perth
Newport on Tay
Glenrothes
St Andrews
Bridge of Allan
Kirkcaldy
Stirling
Musselburgh
Glasgow
Edinburgh
Haddington
Campbeltown
Berwick
Upon-Tweed

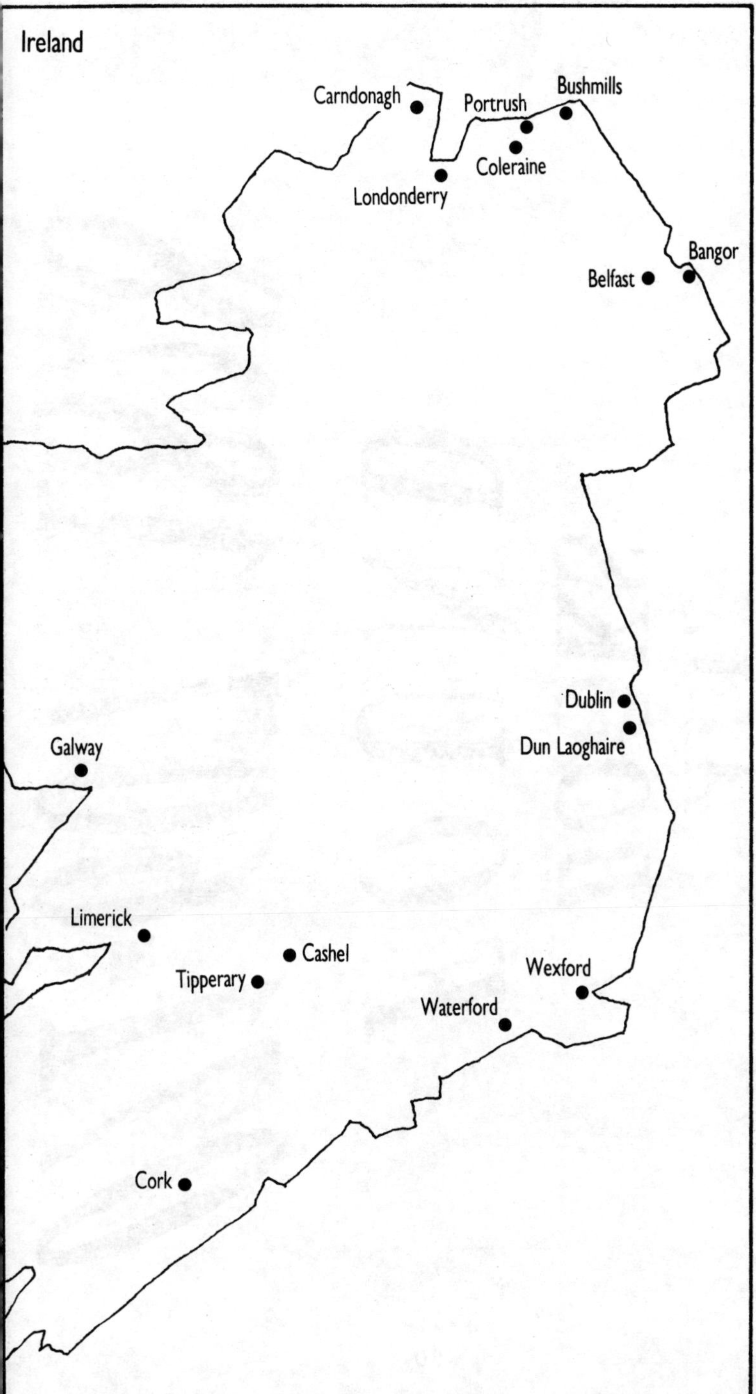
Ireland
Carndonagh
Portrush
Bushmills
Coleraine
Londonderry
Bangor
Belfast
Dublin
Dun Laoghaire
Galway
Limerick
Cashel
Tipperary
Wexford
Waterford
Cork

For Mylan.
with lots of love from
June xx
Christmas 1992.

drif's guide 1992-93

drif's guide to and for the better secondhand bookshops of the british isles 1992-93

by

drif

field

---

published by drif field guides, London 1992

published by drif field guides,
London 1992

41 North Road, London N7 9DP
Tel: 071 607 1757

ISBN No: 0-9510005-4-3

THIS BOOK IS DEDICATED TO

PEOPLE WITH FORGETTING DIFFICULTIES

ACKNOWLEDGEMENTS

I wish to acknowledge the immense assistance of the Arts Council, the Antiquarian Booksellers Association, The Provincial Bookfairs Association, the Bookdealer magazine, The Book & Magazine Collector Monthly, the secondhand bookshop owners of Britain and Bookfairies everywhere. If it were not for their encouragement and financial help this book would not have been possible.

CONTENTS

This book would not have been possible without the help of the following people:

ABBREVIATIONS

AB	ABOVE
ACAD	ACADEMIC, STUDENTS, SCHOLARLY
AMT	AMOUNT
ANTQRN	ANTIQUARIAN
ARS	ART RELATED SUBJECTS
ASTRL	ASTROLOGY
AV	AVERAGE
AWYW	ASKS WHAT YOU WANT*
BGNS	BARGAINS
BIB	BIBLIOGRAPHY
BKS	BOOKS
BKSP	BOOKSHOP*
BKRM	BOOKROOM
BKST	BOOKSTALL
B&MC	BOOK & MAGAZINE COLLECTOR
BL	BELOW
BR	BRITISH RAIL
BSMT	BASEMENT
BSN	BIBLIOGRAPHICALLY SUBNORMAL
BTA	BETTER THAN AVERAGE
BTR	BEST TO RING
C's	COLLECTOR(s)
CAL	CALIBRE
CLOT	CANDIDATE FOR LIBRARIAN ON THE TITANIC
CLSD	CLOSED
CND	CONDITION
D's	DEALER(s)
DIFF	DIFFICULT
DIS	DISCUSSIONS
EC	EARLY CLOSING
EMPHON	EMPHASIS ON
ESPEC	ESPECIALLY

ETF	EASY TO FIND
ETGOW	EASY TO GET ON WITH
FARTS	FOLLOWS AROUND RECOMMENDING THE STOCK
GOB	GRAND OLD BORE
GIOPOC	GROSS INCOMPETENCE ON PART OF THE COMPILER
HSF	HUNTING SHOOTING & FISHING
ILL	ILLUSTRATED
IMPOSS	IMPOSSIBLE
INBies	IMPORTANT NECKWEAR BRIGADE
INT	INTERESTING
IR	IRISH RAIL
KEEN ON	KEEN ON STOCKING IF THEY COULD GET IT
KUTI	KEEPING UP THE IMAGE
L	LUNCH
LG	LARGE
LIT	LITERATURE
LT	LONDON TRANSPORT
LTHRWR	LEATHERWARE*
MED	MEDIUM
MOD 1STS	MODERN FIRST EDITIONS
NAST	NOT A SHORT TREK
NAT HIST	NATURAL HISTORY
NEB	NOT ENOUGH BOOKS
NETGOW	NOT EASY TO GET ON WITH
NFDA	NO FURTHER DETAILS AVAILABLE
NO NO.	NO NUMBER SHOWN IN STREET
NRLY	NEARLY
NSOC	NOT STRONG ON CONDITION
NV	NOT VISITED
OPP	OPPOSITE
OOS	OUT OF STATION

OOSH	OUT OF SHOP
OWOWS	OVERSUPPLIED WITH ONE WAY STREETS
P	PARKING
PBKS	PAPERBACKS
POCS	PROLIFERATION OF CHARITY SHOPS - (see Footnote pp 74 - 85)
POSS	POSSIBLE
R's	READER(s)
REL	RELIABLE
RES STK	RESERVE STOCK
SR	SCOTRAIL
S/F	SCIENCE FICTION/FANTASY
S/H	SECONDHAND
SIOL	SHOP IS ON LEFT
SIOR	SHOP IS ON RIGHT
STN	STATION
STK	STOCK
SPEC	SPECIALIST
T	TRADE
TOPOG	TOPOGRAPHY
TWC	TRADE WITH CARD
UNINT	UNINTERESTING
UNR	UNRELIABLE
V	VERY
VETGOW	VERY EASY TO GET ON WITH
WAD	WORTH A DETOUR
WAP	WORTH A PILGRIMAGE
WEBCOC	WAS EXPECTING A BETTER CLASS OF CUSTOMER
WYLAH	WATCHES YOU LIKE A HAWK

* (see Terminology)

TERMINOLOGY

ANORAKSIA NERVOSA SPECIAL
A shop so cold that you have to bring your own heating, the strange thing is that most of the owners of these shops have a warmth of personality that nearly makes up for it: The classic example is Mr Rolph of Lowestoft.

ASKS WHAT YOU WANT
What I want in a secondhand bookshop is to be left alone. Most people do not even have the courage to go into secondhand bookshops and asking those of us who do manage to summon it up is intimdating, which is possibly the main purpose, but it only acts as a further deterrent the next time we might think of going in one. Unfortunately most secondhand bookshop owners only ever see the people who do come in, they never get a chance to meet the 96% of the population who don't. If people want help then they will ask for it; if the dealers are trying to ensure that the potential customers are going to treat the books properly - which indeed most don't - then what they should do is have a separate section where you do have to ask, establish your credentials and show your ability to handle the books properly before you are allowed in.

When I was looking for books with photographs of naked midgets and the AWYWers interrogated me I told them the truth, most just burst out laughing and assumed that I had made it up, but I did have a customer. He had already gone round asking for the same item and had become so embarrassed that he had been driven to using my egregiously overpriced service to find the books for him. I never ask people what they want the books for: It is my job to find them, not pass judgement.

The only person who has come up with a reasonable compromise is the owner of the main shop in Westerham who says 'If I can be of assistance, please ask' and then he retreats to behind the desk. I think what I shall say to AWYWers from now on is: 'If I think you can be of assistance I will ask'.

A SAMUEL BECKETT SPECIAL
A secondhand bookshop where it is not always possible to tell what is going on, the windows often have just two or three drearily strange books in them, it is not always clear how to open the door and when you go in there is a strange sense of wonderment, especially about when the last person did, and what happened to him or her.

A BOOK & MAGAZINE COLLECTOR SPECIAL
A bookshop where the owners have not got a clue and spend their lives consulting a magazine of the same name in the offices of which they also publish the Record Collector Magazine and on the wall there is a notice; 'RECORDS ARE THE ROUND ONES, BOOKS ARE THE RECTANGULAR ONES'.

A BOOKDEALER SPECIAL
Any shop which has at some time or other advertised in The Bookdealer, an alleged Trade Magazine which comes out weakly. It is not considered relevant that these shops often do not have any secondhand books in them, what IS important is that they speak kindly of the editor after whom a prize has been named. The Barry Shaw prize for never sullying a secondhand bookshop. The classic example is Allen's in London which claims to deal in secondhand books on horses. There are no secondhand books in it, but because it is advertised on the front page of the Bookdealer it is considered to be a secondhand bookshop and is regularly classified as such in other directories, which encourages Mr Shaw's surrealist belief that you can tell how well the secondhand booktrade is doing by the number of new bookshops which advertise in his journal. A Bookdealer Special therefore is an alleged secondhand bookshop with no secondhand books. Mr Shaw is an alleged editor of a secondhand book journal without a secondhand brain.

BIBLIOGRAPHICALLY SUBNORMAL
A secondhand bookshop where they have taken to inscribing unheard of bibliographic details such as 'first thus' because it was published by a book club, much favoured by bookfairies.

BOOKFAIRIES
Bookfairies are beings who strip secondhand bookshops of the most obvious fruit which they then attempt to sell to other locusts who swarm at bookfairs. The good news is that they invariably fail, the bad news is that it does not stop them breeding. Bookfairs are like the froth on a glass of beer. It is the most obvious feature and the first part most people take any notice of, but it contains very little real liquidity and is only sustained by the action underneath - that is in secondhand bookshops. And like locusts it is not so much the actual creatures as the number of them which is detrimental.

BOOKSHOP
For the purposes of this guide, the term Bookshop refers only to secondhand bookshops, New book shops are described thus..

DOGS
Books which are so unsaleable most bookshop owners can hear them barking a mile off. Not all dogs are cheap and even the most expensive establishment can have more than its fair share.

A DRIF SPECIAL
A shop so low key that most dealers cringe at the thought of going in it which is precisely why I like it so much. The books are even lower rent than I am, but I am quite often in better condition than them...just.

A SINCERE APOLOGY

A HELEN HANFF SPECIAL
A Bookshop which looks great from the outside, preferably three thousand miles away. The owner is usually very good at talking and writing but the books are terrible. The good news is that these shops soon go out of business: The bad news is that it does not stop people writing about them and reinforcing the Hollywood image of what secondhand bookselling is like. The unforgettable book - whose name no American can ever remember - is constantly being quoted in the press as reflecting the way bookdealing is. Miss Hanff is one of those people who would not go to the toilet without ringing the newspapers first. The end result is the same: a dark smear on a clean sheet.

I sincerely wish to apologise for the above remarks, I should of course have spelt her name **Helene**.

LEATHERWEAR SPECIALISTS
Shops which sell books solely as furniture which is not bad in itself, but I strongly object to their calling themselves Antiquarian Bookdealers, see also Libricides.

LIBRICIDE SPECIAL
A Libricide tears the colour plates out of books and sells them separately. These establishments often call themselves specialists in Natural History or Travel because they are too ashamed to admit to what they actually do, to which I have no objection, after all when the plates were in the books they were merely in the chorus but the print dealers make them into stars. What I do object to is the fact that they call themselves bookdealers.

LITERACE (to rhyme with Liberace)
An establishment where the books are extremely showy, very flash and unnecessarily expensive. More effort is put into the display than into the content.

NATURAL ROUTES
From now on I shall be working on the basis that my readers are attempting to get into as many secondhand bookshops in a day as is humanly possible. I shall thus only be listing those shops which are open four or more days a week and are sensibly positioned or on the way to other bookshops. It

is not the distance from another bookshop or a major conurbation which makes it difficult to get to but whether you can go to other bookshops in the same area. As a dealer I need to try and get to ten secondhand bookshops in a day. I know from personal experience that only seven will actually be open, and that I will more than likely only buy books in three of them. For a bookshop to position itself in a town or village which has no sensible transport connections either by road or rail is madness beyond belief and typical of the mentality of secondhand bookshop owners. From now on other than to distill the vitriol I shall be ignoring such malevolent dumps, which are attempting to use up my time to fuel their failure to think about where potential customers are coming from. I am not against secondhand bookshops being in obscure places, but I am against bookshops being in places where I have to detour from sensible shops to visit their premises. Thus I am still eager to visit the shop in Iona which has always defeated me, but I regard the bookshop in Clare in Suffolk as being one of the worst positioned in Britain. You cannot go to Clare without skipping two other places. The nearest railway is ten miles and it is a branch line. To go to Clare from London takes an entire day of determination. There are not enough people in Clare to support a secondhand bookshop and so the shop is dependent on visitors.

NOUVELLE CUISINE
A bookshop usually influenced by the bookfairies which has a minimalist stock and books you have to have a degree in semiotics to understand the importance of. THE CLASSIC EXAMPLE is Ballantyne & Date in London.

PARKING
I am perhaps the worst person in the world to be giving advice on parking, my abhorrence of motor cars is only exceeded by my indifference to the fate of their owners. In my experience of chauffeurs they divide into those who would park outside of Downing Street during a bomb scare in Whitehall, to those who will happily spend their lives searching out the great parking spaces of the world. My advice is aimed at those people who are in between.

ROAST BEEF
A bookshop which is attempting to sell the same books as were popular fifty years ago. It may seem strange but the truth is that the styles of bookshops change considerably over a short period of time. It is not so much the books themselves that make a Roast Beef shop, but the way the shop price and value them.

INTRODUCTION

HOW TO USE THIS GUIDE

This guide book is compiled with me in mind: If enough people buy it I shall be able to retire and achieve my life's ambition of becoming a layabout: If not enough of you buy then I shall have to continue at a task of even lower status, that of being a secondhand bookdealer. As far as I can work out I shall still be the only person to whom the whole of the guide book will be of any use. Several people complained that the last edition was unusable by anyone other than me: This was completely incorrect: I could not use it either.

If somebody else were to compile this guide book then I would like them to tell me about all the newly opened secondhand bookshops, about all the bookshops that have closed down and all the shops where there have been major changes.

Several people do tell me about newly opened shops, but their definition of what constitutes a secondhand bookshop and mine seem to differ somewhat. For me a secondhand bookshop is somewhere where you can walk in and walk out again: Thus I do not count places where you have to telephone or places where you have to ring a bell to gain entry.

The only places I count as being secondhand bookshops are those with secondhand books. My definition of a secondhand book is that it must previously have been owned by a punter. I do not count shops that buy books solely from reviewers or from publishers as being secondhand bookshops. I am not exactly certain what they are but secondhand bookshops they are not.

This guide begins with what I consider to be the worst secondhand bookshop in the British Isles and makes its way to what I consider to be the best. It starts in Northern Ireland, continues through Eire then moves to Scotland, Wales and England. The bookshops are listed in what I consider to be natural routes. These routes are the way I think it easiest to visit all the shops in an area. If I do not consider it worthwhile visiting a shop either because it is too far off the beaten track, has absurd opening hours, or would be likely to be unprofitable, then it is not included in the guide: It should however be included in the directory. All the bookshops in the guide have been visited by me in 1992, many of the shops in the directory have likewise been visited but I do not consider them worth going to.

The names of the secondhand bookshops in this guide are the names which appear on the fascia. Those bookshops which are called with that inspiration and creativity for which secondhand bookshops are renowned, Bookshop, are given what I in my conformity and lack of imagination believe is a more appropriate name, this is denoted with an asterisk by the name. Those shops which have no name at all are similarly treated. No separate account is taken of those shops which are convalescent homes for bookfairies, which reminds me, those pricks - and I have yet to meet a woman who does this - who call their shops by long and absurd names have been castrated.

The address is that which I say it is. Bookshops and other shops have taken to not displaying a number and I often have to guess. I appreciate the bookshops' attempts to keep me happy, but I have a vague feeling that most people do not have as much time as I have to go hunting up and down streets. The element of chance also seems to increase with the deterioration of street names. Some are so unobvious or absent that not even the locals are aware of what they are called. Because of the chainstore massacre it is not always easy to tell which High Street you are in and many is the time that I have had to stop and try to think where I am, and where I should be. For this reason I define London as being anywhere within the M25 motorway and I define the other cities of Britain by the available one day travel card boundaries. Thus I define Selly Oak as being in Birmingham, and North Shields as being in Newcastle. This may seem a somewhat cavalier approach for a roundhead such as myself, but it is encouraged by bookshops' refusal to divulge details of their official address. If the secondhand bookshops of Britain would place a small postcard in the window with the name, the full address, post code, area code and telephone number, together with their opening hours, it would be much appreciated by me. I realise that this would involve vast amounts of effort on their part but that is exactly my intention. They would then be able to understand when I get it wrong after doing it 750 times!

THE OPENING HOURS OF BOOKSHOPS

For those of you who have not had the great fortune to be born British, I should explain that the opening hours of secondhand bookshops posted - if they are - should be seen more as an act of intention, an ideal, a new years' resolution, not a firm and binding commitment.

Thus if a bookshop says it will open Monday to Saturday, no sensible person would expect it to open such incredible hours. The odd monomaniac may go round complaining about it, but nobody serious would expect a secondhand bookshop to open Monday to Saturday just because they had said so in the window, or in a trade directory or in the phone book. After all Britain is renowned for its liberal traditions.

What the notice means is that if the owner does not have better things to do, such as recovering from the bookfair hangover, returning from a buying trip in Zamboanga or attending the funerals of dear aunts in Brighton (I have a vague suspicion that there are more aunts in the book business than there are in the novels of P. G. Wodehouse) and if they have nothing better to do they will consider opening up.

It tends to be the younger more literary element, the ones with the university education and no confidence who put up notices apologising for their absence. The more experienced self taught bookdealers know that making excuses is the thin end of the wedge. Next people will start asking for them to open on time.

In the same way as nobody civilised turns up at a party at the stated hours on the invitation so it is similarly considered bad manners to turn up at the times posted in directories. For those of you who do not understand why this is, I shall explain; it gives the game away, you have been buying guide books and thus did not know but had to learn what the correct form was.

RC: "How did you find that out? Nobody has ever invited you to a party in your whole life, and anyway I thought it was my job to go to parties on your behalf."

Thus, if a secondhand bookshop says it is going to open at 9am, nobody is expected to turn up at 9am and you are clearly the pushy type if you turn up at 9.30am.

This trait (no sensible secondhand bookdealer would see it as a deficiency) is Universal, from Charing Cross Road to Inverness.

One of the things that irritates me most about the owners of secondhand bookshops is their seeming belief that somehow I have just turned up there by accident; that I had nothing better to do than amble into their shop and spend pots of money; that I was just admiring the idyllic rural village and happened to spot their delightful premises.

All I ever do is hunt down books. For me getting into secondhand bookshops is more of a military campaign. I have to plan it with extreme care, but above all I have to put enormous financial resources into doing it. It is my life and I don't mind wasting it, but I do get a trifle upset at the way bookshop owners behave as if somehow I had just turned up completely by accident. The accident was my parents' fault, not mine. I go into bookshops because I mean to be there.

There is nothing I enjoy more than going off hunting for secondhand books, for me there is never a time when I do not feel some sort of optimism about what I am going to find in a particular bookshop. Personally I consider all the remarks I make a load of rubbish, because you never know where you are going to find a particular book that you are looking for. That said, I do believe that you are more likely to find good books in good bookshops, but I also feel it is always worth trying any others: I do not know how, but I also feel that most secondhand bookshops are likely to improve and I am always willing to give them another chance.

I awoke one morning at 5am, skipped having a bath (I don't mind this, but a lot of other people complain), cycled to Paddington Station and got the 6am train to Cardiff and began my favourite breakfast - The Independent, The Guardian and The Times. The train arrived at Cardiff and I changed to another train to Newport where I was very sad to have to miss the remainder shop which has secondhand books. The train got to Swansea at 10.30 and I was even sadder to have to miss going to the 4 bookshops there, but I had seen them the previous week. I arrived in Carmarthen at 11.45 and was just in time to catch the bus to Laugharne. I was a bit upset to be leaving as there is not only a good bookshop in Carmarthen, there is a wholefood shop with a lovely cafe attached. This cafe serves soup of which I have had dreams. If I ever have to queue for a soup kitchen, this is the soup kitchen I shall queue at. Instead, I got the bus to Laugharne, I enquired of the bus driver when the next bus was due out and he said the service was hourly. The bus service in Wales has improved out of all recognition. I got to Laugharne some 8 hours after I had set off only to discover that the shop was closed. I consulted my trusty guide book which did indeed say that the shop was unreliable about its opening hours, but not that it went for lunch. I consulted the trinket shop next door where they said that they had not seen the shop open at all that day or on previous days.

There was no sign on the door giving any information whatsoever, someone had tried putting a brick through the window, but unfortunately I could not find another. I went off and hunted a phone box and did what I am really loathe to do which is ring up and ask if they will open the shop, but there was no reply not even from the home number. Admittedly this was a sunny Spring Tuesday and a seasoned bookshop hunter had no right to expect a bookshop to be open on such a day. After all the Sunday Telegraph was not calling to write an article about the shop being the longest in Britain - maybe I misread that article and what it said was the bookshop with the longest wait in Britain, but as I stood there thinking of the hours that I had spent trying to get into this and other bookshops, and dreaming of the soup I was missing, I cursed that shop with a venom that even I am loathe to print.

What the halfwits who open these shops in the middle of nowhere imagine they are doing is almost beyond comprehension. Of course, they are not going to have any local custom, nobody lives in these places. If you want to open a shop in the middle of nowhere just because it has literary connections, you should also consider whether it has transport connections. This type bookshop cannot survive other than by attracting collectors and dealers.

Well I have had enough, from now on it is no more Mr Nice Guy, instead I shall be Ogre the top. I don't need these literary arse lickers to waste my life for me, I have been doing it quite successfully for years and I have other things to spend my money on, other than helping British Frail to even bigger losses. Just because this pair of idiots wanted to breathe the same air that Dylan Thomas puked up, in the belief that it brings them closer to literature, I have to spend my life gallivanting round, missing bowls of soup. If a veggie cafe in Carmarthen can open hours that I do not have to calculate with a computer, why can't bookshops? Why should I have to put up with it? If you cannot open a secondhand bookshop four days a week then you should not open it at all and in future I shall not be going to those places which are simply refuges for people too ashamed to admit that they are unemployable.

RC: "Needless to say there was no soup left when he got back to Carmarthen. He'll be there next year don't worry."

It is unreasonable for secondhand

bookshops to expect everybody else to make the effort to find out their hours, they are behaving like modern novelists who expect everybody to make the effort to read their books. The job of a secondhand bookshop is to sell books. You cannot sell books if you are closed. It is the same with modern novelists, they do not sell books because they have closed minds. Putting up long and unrememberable notices on the door is about as useful as appearing on the Late Show: It looks wonderful and makes you appear very erudite, but it does not sell books. However I am not against all notices in bookshop windows, my own favourite was in the secondhand bookshop in Cowes. It said: "BACK IN FIVE MONTHS" and on the appointed day the owner did indeed return to post another notice "CLOSED FOR HOLIDAYS". A few weeks later there appeared in the trade press yet another: "THRIVING BOOKSHOP FOR SALE". So far there have been no further developments but I hope something happens in the next year or so as the suspense is killing me.

"BACK IN FIVE MINUTES"

"BACK IN FIVE MINUTES" does for the well read what "Are you or have you ever been ...." does for the slightly red: It makes them change colour, but it does it with much more economy and with much greater terror. The person who first dreamt up this notice deserves to be up there with Stalin, Pol Pot and Goebbels; their reign has ended but the legacy of the anonymous Torquemada lives on.

Those five minutes of which they are talking are not the five minutes in which you could hard boil an egg, but rather they are the five minutes that your father assured you it would take to do your homework if you did it properly; the five minutes that your mother promised you it would take to keep your room tidy if you did it every day; the five minutes that London Transport claim for the regularity of its bus service; the five minutes that photocopier salesmen will take to reorganise your life; the five minutes that insurance salesmen need to explain all the benefits of mortgage endowment policies; the five minutes Jehovah's Witnesses need to explain what the Bible really meant; the five minutes a day that Charles Atlas needed to look the way he did and which nobody else would want to, not even for five minutes.

In truth I look forward to that notice, I have read more books in that five minutes than I managed in the entire time of my alleged education. I have met more interesting people in that five minutes than at any other time of my life. I look upon that five minutes as a time when I can genuinely do nothing without having to defend myself.

If the lady of my dreams' husband were to return unexpectedly and shout through the bolted and barricaded door (I believe in practising safe sex) that I should come out immediately and face the consequences like a man, I would plead for five minutes in which to adjust my dress, and further I would ask for the five minutes that bookdealers are going to be back in for my last session of adulterated pleasure.

And if he were to depart in a towering rage at my daliance and return with a shotgun threatening suicide unless I behaved like a gentleman I should seek to spend five minutes of my time encouraging him to carry on.

And when I was accused of aiding and abetting suicide (I could not begin to explain to you the complications of the British Legal System even if I were to have ten minutes of the five minutes that bookdealers are going to be back in) I do not doubt that I would be found guilty in less than the five minutes that bookdealers are going to be back in.

When the judge asked if I had anything to say in mitigation I would ask if I could speak for the bookshop owner's five minutes. I sincerely doubt if any British judge could live that long. And were the establishment to bring in some fresh young blood, as they call anybody under the age of seventy, then I would ask for a last five minutes with my beloved: The five minutes that booksellers are going to be back in!

If the executioner were to offer me five minutes for a quick smoke before I ascended the gallows then I would choose the five minutes that booksellers are going to be back in despite the proven scientific chance of my getting lung cancer before I was hanged.

If after a life of complete rejection, total contempt and spirited spurning, God with that mercy for which s/he is so renowned in the Christian world was to offer me five minutes in which to repent and tender a plea of mitigation at the Last Judgement then I would undoubtedly choose the five minutes that secondhand booksellers are going to be back in, for despite my willingness to change sides as necessity dictates, I would have an unshakeable faith that no God, no matter how all seeing or all knowing, would believe the length of time that I had total faith in that notice. No God would ever suspect that I could have been so stupid, so trusting, so gullible, not even God's main PR agent on earth, the Christian Church which is not exactly famed for its honesty would have had the audacity to perpetrate such an out and out lie.

RC: "For Christ' sake nobody say anything about lunch or we will be here all bloody day."

As to lunch hours, I can only say in the short amount of space allotted to me, that I am against them.

The one piece of good news is that more and more secondhand bookshops are opening late in the evening, especially in London.

THE SIZE OF SECONDHAND BOOKSHOPS

I only acknowledge three sizes of bookshops, small, medium and large. In my experience the size of a secondhand bookshop is in inverse proportion to its quality. It is not always true that small bookshops are good but it is invariably the case that large bookshops are bad and the larger they are the worse they are. The only stock I measure is that which can be seen by the general members of the public. I am always interested in finding out about reserve stocks, and how to get at them, but the reserve stock has no relation to my definition of size.

All descriptions of stock type are on average. It is possible for very bad shops to get very good books, once or twice but the question really is what can you expect on average.

Similarly for the prices.

I divide secondhand bookshops into four main types: Readers, Collectors and Dealers, and the subsiduary Specialist shop which usually has no books for Readers. These are usually abbreviated to R,C,D and Spec. I only judge stock on what can be seen, I am not concerned with what the owners of the shop say. If I cannot see the books, or if I fail to recognise that they are experts in Modern First Editions or Art, then it is not my fault. I do not classify a shop as having a speciality unless I consider it is worth travelling to see that speciality. Where shops have a significant number of books on a subject, but not quite enough to make it worth travelling to, I define them as being "keen on". I judge stock on average. It is my belief that you can tell what type of stock a bookshop has from just one visit. It is not necessary that I should actually obtain a bargain before I define a shop as being one where bargains are available, which brings us onto the even more delicate subject of price.

Nothing upsets secondhand bookdealers more than describing them as being expensive, but the truth is that all secondhand books are unbelievably cheap in comparison to any other similar item. In comparison to antiques they are about one tenth the price. In comparison to going to the cinema a paperback is about half the price. For the price of a theatre ticket you could buy the complete works of Bernard Shaw. It cost me less to buy a beautiful book about the work of Otto Dix than it did to go to the exhibition. Nothing is as cheap as books. That is why I like them so much; I am the ultimate cheapskate, and when I make statements about one dealer being expensive, it is relative to other dealers in similar subjects.

Discounts should always be discounted. If you cannot afford a book at the price it is marked then making the discount the line between buying it and not is a mistake. Most bookshops give ten per cent to "recognised dealers". I have no ambition to be recognised and do not ask for a discount if the bookshop owner gives me one then it is up to them. In my experience Discounts and Discussions are only really useful if you want to annoy a particular dealer.

I feel slightly unqualified to discuss the subjects of discounts and trade discussions, because the bookshops where I go regularly have now started saying my lines before I do. I have however discovered a new way to intimidate bookshop owners, and that is to find a book in the window which looks reasonably expensive but whose price you cannot see, and when you march in the shop just say I will have that book in the window naming the item, and when they attempt to show it to you just put it at the bottom of your pile without at any time looking at the price. It really unnerves them. It is almost worth paying the price, whatever it is, just to see how much it upsets bookdealers.

WARNING!

Under the Prevention of Death by Boredom Act I am legally obliged to warn you that the following article is unlikely to be of any interest, unless you have a substantial fascination for the economics of Railway Planning, and for those of you who do I should warn you that the article deviates (if that is the right word) into the subject of public toilets.

It is not just my desperate desire to see all my pensees in print, but my latest belief that it is up to those of us who are regular users of a service to do something about it. Such critiques may seem slightly out of place in what alleges to be a guide book, but I honestly feel that unless something is done about the near terminal state of British Frail that I for one will be doing no more travelling.

I am eager to feel that if there is another Mr. Maxwell lying out there, I shall be the one to discover him, and possibly join forces. I do not wish to end up like the rest of the British Press which stood idly by whilst he looted £900 million for himself. I realise they had much more important things to do such as ensuring that no newspaper had a page that did not have at least one reference to the Royal Family, or lack graphic details of other peoples' sex lives. And I am hoping that I shall not be alive long enough to see these two staples merged into one. Of course they could not have left out these earth shattering events to waste time on one of their own, and any way, as they now keep telling us (at least it makes a change from the Royal Family and sex) they were prevented by the hideous libel laws of Great Britain. It is my unhumble opinion that if they could not take on Mr Maxwell then they should have been fighting the libel laws, it was their job to clean out their own stables and if they did not have the tools to do it then they should have sought out those tools. It may well have been true that it would have been a long tedious and possibly fruitless campaign, but at least they could have stood up and said 'We told you so.' I already know that nothing I say will make British Frail change one iota, but at least I went down waving a flag.

RANTING AND RAILING

There is no better way to start the day than with a slow breakfast on a fast train dreaming dreams and anticipating adventures.

Despite every effort by the management of British Frail travelling by train is still the most efficient and civilised way to visit the majority of the secondhand bookshops of Britain.

British Frail is ashamed to be in the mass transport business. It secretly dreams of becoming an airline, this is why its stations now look like airports. This is why it has airline style announcements. This is why it has a bird as the symbol of inter-city, but the most conclusive proof that it lives with its head in the air is that the price of its tickets is sky high!

It costs more to get to Tenby than it does to Tenerife. When the clerk told me the price of a first class return to Newcastle I had to tell him I only wanted to go there, not buy the place. British Frail used to run an advert saying that for the price of a first class ticket you could see the landscape of Constable; for the price of a first class ticket you could BUY the landscape of Constable. It is true that there are cheaper tickets, but no sane person let alone somebody who is mad enough to travel on British Frail can understand all the permutations. Indeed most of the staff do not. If you do not like the price at one window it often pays to go to another.

For British Frail to charge the prices it does is worse than lunacy it is criminal negligence whilst 80% of its trains are travelling 80% empty 80% of the time. This may come as a surprise to the commuters and holiday makers but to those of us who travel regularly it seems like a gross under-estimate.

In this time of alleged recession when tour companies have cut their prices, when airlines have cut their fares, when even property companies have cut their charges the only thing British Frail has cut is the service it gives.

The one thing all of us inherited no matter how poor we may have been born is the finest railway network in the world. British Frail is doing its utmost to disband it. If only half the energy it applies to this task was actually applied to running a mass transport system then we would be better off.

They are bankrupt; they are bankrupt financially, they are bankrupt spiritually and they are bankrupt of ideas. Closing down a line or reducing a service is not an idea. They should not be allowed to squander the only inheritance most of us have.

On a train it is possible to get to 80% of the cities of England and get home again the same day. In a motorcar you can get everywhere, eventually, and you can make it back the same day if you are willing to risk life and limb, but if you don't kill yourself that day, you will certainly feel dead the next.

Paradoxically it is the very emptiness of

trains that makes them so pleasant. On a train you can plan what you are going to do, stand by for ritual guffaws, eat (if I had to choose blindfold whether I was going to eat in the average British cafe or on a train I would choose the train every time), you can read the papers, you can stare out of the window, and you can go to the toilet. Not even in a chauffeur driven limousine can you do most of these things. Why is it then that the trains are so empty that British Frail loses more money than even Mr Maxwell dreamt of. Why is it in this allegedly ecologically oriented age that British Frail has so little sympathy from its customers?

It is because of what British Frail imagines is management, that is why. If the management of British Frail knew about the prostitutes at Kings Cross they would more than likely open up a boutique selling chastity belts.

Not even as a secondhand bookdealer can I buy enough books to read to withstand the waits that I have endured on obscure British Frail stations and I have often been reduced to studying British Frail's advertising. Currently there is one pen wash poster which consists of portraits of what I take to be British Frail's ideal passengers. It is usually after being driven out of a buffet by the great British Yobbo, holding one of the interminable rounds of the vomiting championships, that I am driven to studying this poster in detail. It has that chocolate box cover air about it. There is a city gent in a bowler hat and an old school tie, possibly looking for his chauffeur. There is a man whose previous occupation would appear to be as a model on the cover of romantic novels, there is a young career girl in a business suit wearing one of those scarves round her neck that you only ever see on women who appear on television a lot. Even the tennis player is wearing a neckerchief. All of them even down to the boy scout are well groomed and have teeth aglow ready to face the challenges of life. Indeed in a rare example of wit the token old age pensioner looks exactly like Mrs Thatcher. The only thing that all the people in this advert have in common is that they are wearing important neckwear. There is even what I take to be an American tourist wearing a bootlace tie, why do I never get on trains like this? I was once booed by all the other passengers when I got on a train at Crewe wearing a jacket and tie. The booers with whom I had to endure a journey to Edinburgh were all uniformly dressed in teeshirts, leather jackets, jeans and trainers. There was not one tie amongst them, not even to hold up their jeans. The off the buttock look was de riguer. It is exactly this latter group, the booers, whom British Frail should be trying to attract, the people without cars, the feckless, the indigent, the rail nutters - it is they who fill the pubs, the football grounds and the betting shops. It is they who spend the entire journey from London to Edinburgh reading the Sun newspaper and keeping Mr. Murdoch extremely happy. It is they who have made videos such a profitable enterprise.

British Frail cannot stand the sight of these people and nor can anybody else, but that is not the point. British Frail is supposed to be running a mass transport system, just because the masses look like they would have been transported in the nineteenth century, British Frail should not be able to give up or allowed to have fantasies about whom it would really like to have as a passenger. Nobody likes to look these horrors in the eye, the customers that British Frail dreams of are the ones you see at eye level on the newsagents shelf - the Country Lifers, the Homes and Gardeners, the Readers Digesters. British Frail is determined not to look up to those whom are most likely to make a profitable railway - the pornographic gross individuals who lie legs a kimbo, their dress permanently in a state of disarray. All British Frail does is avert its eyes but even then it cannot bring itself to admit that the next to bottom shelf in the newsagents rack is the one with whom it can also sleep. The Special Interest Groups.

I used to be a member of a special interest group until British Frail forced me to become a member of the Important Neckwear Brigade.

RC: "Stand by for a long and even more boring article about British Frail and Uncle drif's bicycle."

You can always tell when a British journalist has just lost his licence for being drunk: They write an article about the gross inefficiency and dreadful unreliability of British Frail trains. What those besotted with the idea of punctuality for the first time in their lives do NOT realise is that those of us who travel regularly are in favour of late trains. It was that Italian moron drunk with his own power who first promulgated the notion of trains running on time, and he used to arrive everywhere in a motorcade.

If those who speak so volubly would just shut their big mouths and use their little brains for one moment they would realise that British Frail is also in favour of running trains on time. It is they who have to provide spare staff when trains run late; it is they who have to provide extra trains when the scheduled ones do not arrive; it is they who have to provide an alternative service when no train at all appears. It is those of us who travel regularly who are in favour of late trains.

The last "Official" train for London used to leave Leeds at 7.35. In Leeds is a particularly good vegetarian restaurant.

RC: "Stroll on..."

This restaurant did not open until seven in the evening and it was thus impossible to eat in it comfortably and get back to London the same day, officially. However there was another train which left Leeds at 9.30 and arrived in York at 10.20 which did not seem a lot of use as the Edinburgh/London train was supposed to stop/pass through York at 10.15, but "supposed" is the operative word, it never did. There was never a night when that train arrived on time and it used to be possible to ring up British Frail and ask how late it was but not any more, because the Important Neckwear Brigade (INBies) have made British Frail obsessed by PR and it will not tell you how late the train actually is. It is an absurdity to be obsessed by minutes when you are travelling hundreds of miles. If you are driving to Formby from Bognor you do not ring up and say I will be there at 7.30, what you say is I hope to be there between 7 and 8 if nothing goes wrong. Many is the time I have been saved having to sleep on railway benches by late running trains, mind you given some of the new trains I prefer the railway benches. It is not the lateness or otherwise which is the crucial issue but the frequency.

The reason that you do not have to know the timetable on London Underground is that the trains are so frequent. It used to be possible to get back to London at any time of night, but not any more, these days British Frail only wants to run an eighteen hour service not a twenty four hour one.

All you had to do was get yourself to Crewe or York and you could get home but now things have been "improved" and it is no longer possible to do this. The reason that British Frail ran all night trains was primarily to deliver newspapers. These trains were often very slow, but they did get there in the end. Many is the happy nights sleep I had on the train that took eight hours to get from Sheffield to London. The only people who want to do it in three hours are the INBies. Then British Frail started reducing the number of trains that went at night, not a lot just one or two here and there but it was enough to make the newspapers think about getting alternative services, but it was still cheaper to deliver the newspaper by train. British Frail having got away with eliminating one service then wondered if it could do it again. I tell you that having British Frail's management in charge of scheduling trains is rather like having King Herod in charge of school outings. The number of trains was cut each year and very little reduction in profits was noted, but the newspapers did note a difference. When they missed a train it was three or four hours before the next one came along, and this made the delivery in rural areas more spasmodic. It was then that they seriously began to think about delivering newspapers by truck.

I told you this article was going to be long and boring, I would give up if I was you, there are not going to be any jokes and from here on in I shall be going into extremely technical matters.

British Frail was at this time becoming obsessed with Mussolini fantasies. The thing to have done was to delay the trains until the newspapers arrived at the stations. As a passenger at 2 in the morning you are not in the least bit bothered about what time the train arrives (as long as it does), but British Frail was about as flexible as prison bars, even that is too liberal as people have been known to get through prison bars, but nobody has ever got through to British Frail.

Having lost the newspaper contract, British Frail then started increasing the price to its other major customer: The Post Office, which despite having most of its sorting offices next to railway stations found that it could deliver its mail more cheaply by truck.

Slowly but surely British Frail reduced the night time passenger services because it claimed they were unprofitable. There was no admission that they were unprofitable because British Frail made them that way.

There used to be a train called the Nightrider (this is what happens when you employ PR men who have been to University and read Auden). It left Edinburgh at midnight and was due to arrive in London at 7am, but more crucially the one way ticket cost £20.00. That train was jam packed every night including Saturday/Sunday (British Frail no longer runs any service on Saturay/Sunday). It was an all night party. I don't know if the passengers were celebrating having got away from Scotland or tanking themselves up to fight the battle of life in London, but the amount of alcohol consumed on that train would have made the average British journalist blanch.

I once tried to get on that train at York, it was so packed I had to physically fight my way on. I was desperate to get to sleep but the only place I could find was in the toilet and I had to share that with two other people. When that train arrived at Kings Cross I doubt if most of the passengers knew what day it was let alone that the train was "officially" late.

I delivered a book and then went back to Kings Cross in order to return to York. It was the same train; (I would know that toilet anywhere) but it was almost empty. I could hardly recognise it. The only passengers were a few INBies busily telling their secretaries how inefficient the management of British Frail was because the buffet did not serve Perrier water. You do not need a university education to work out that British Frail must have made more money on the Nightrider than it did out of the INBies.

The Observer Newspaper is currently running a campaign to find out why people fall out of trains, only a British journalist could be so thick and/or hypocritical as not to understand why it happens: It is because they are drunk. In the last twenty years 500 people have fallen out of trains. In the same period 35,000 have died on Britain's roads. If British Frail was to employ somebody to push drunks out of moving trains it is unlikely to get to that total. There is no shortage of drunks on British Frail, they are not going to run out; I don't know what the Observer is so worried about. I can only conclude that most of its writers are so drunk that they are worried they might be forced to travel by train. One of my few ambitions is to find the way to get drunks to shut up. If pushing them out of speeding trains is the only method I would be keen to volunteer my assistance, with luck I might even be able to push out a few Observer journalists.

The average British yobbo is firmly convinced that the train will not run unless he has a dozen cans of lager in front of him. I often wonder if they think the trains are fueled by urine, which brings me onto one of the few things for which British Frail can truly be congratulated. In Britain you can tell what class a person is by their reaction to the next word: Toilets...

"SOME TIME A GREAT MOTION"

The working class just laugh if you try to treat the subject of toilets seriously. The middle class say nothing and wait for the subject to change (well I have bad news for the middle classes I shall be continuing on this subject for about another ten pages). The upper classes, all dream of rushing off and writing books about the decorative ones. These are not the toilets which I am interested in. The ones I am very interested in are the ones you pee and shit in. You come out of the average British Public Toilet feeling worse than when you went in. It is only that you have invested so much time and are desperate that you would go into most of them. The one place where they are truly convenient is on British Frail and I would like to take this opportunity to congratulate them on this splendid achievement. You may well laugh but I assure you I am not taking the piss, for those of us who travel regularly toilets are an important matter.

The middle classes who run the local councils in Britain have been closing down the toilets with gay abandon. I would be prepared to abandon my abhorrence of the word gay if homosexuals would campaign for more public toilets. The working classes have started peeing in the streets with a vengence. According to the middle classes who run the councils this does not happen: The truth is that they avert their eyes. If you are not going to provide somewhere for people to pee then you cannot complain when they do it in the street. Public toilets are a mark of civilisation even more so than bookshops. It is up to those of us who do not wish to see people peeing in the streets to provide somewhere where they can do it in private. British Frail is the only public utility which has taken its responsibility seriously. One of the groups that fail miserably in this respect are the owners of secondhand bookshops. It would be an extreme convenience if all the secondhand bookshops of Britain were to allow the public to use their toilets. It would also aid sales. Many is the time I have had to leave a bookshop because I could not concentrate because I wanted to go to the toilet. Only on trains is it possible to be sure to find a toilet. So few people go in secondhand bookshops that it would be no great imposition for them to open up their toilets, and if other people were to learn that bookshops often provide them then more people would come into the bookshop.

I am not against paying to get into public toilets nor would I be against paying to use a bookshop toilet. I know that there are indeed many uncivilised people who have disgusting habits but I feel that it is up to those of us who claim to be civilised to try and put up with them. We, after all, are supposed to know better.

In some ways it is surprising that British Frail is so good at providing toilets, perhaps because it is a mass interest they have not felt spurred to do anything, however in the case of minority interests they are determined to eliminate every deviation - as they see it.

I used to belong to what British Frail and the newsagents call a minority interest.

RC: "See I told you stand by for an even more boring diatribe than the one on toilets, he only put that in to try and prove me wrong."

It used to be possible some ten years ago to turn up at a railway station and go off to exotic places such as Chelmsford from where you could cycle to Maldon quite easily (Maldon does not have a train station any more). Or for the more energetic it was possible to put a bike on a train and go to Aberdeen and cycle to Perth - there is no direct route between these two places.

In those days cycles and trains went together so perfectly that it must have featured in the dreams of ecologists and keep-fitters, then things began to change, or as British Frail would say 'improve'.

The 125 train was introduced on the London/Edinburgh route. The guards van was about the size of British Frail's collective brain. It worked perfectly when there was just one or two cyclists but during the summer problems arose if more than half a dozen cyclists wanted to get on. To solve this problem British Frail introduced a compromise; it began to charge £3 if you took your bike on a train. In truth this did not make a lot of difference as most guards did not have the gall to collect the money for what is essentially baggage. There was another feature that was especially irritating and that was that you were supposed to pay the £3 every time you got on and off. If like me you get off ten times between London and Edinburgh in theory you were supposed to pay £30 for the bike.

British Frail then introduced sliding door trains on some of its local routes. The trains were designed by INBies for INBies; there was no guards van, but provision had been made for post sacks and if the guard felt so disposed you could store your bike there after he had unlocked the door. This needless to say slowed down the train and did not make cyclists over popular with the other passengers. British Frail then introduced limitations: 'you were not allowed to take cycles on these trains during the rush hour'. This was not too bad for those people who used the same train every day but for those of us who have not the privilege of living in Nottingham knowing the idiosyncrasies of the timetable there is somewhat difficult.

Some lateral thinking cyclists began buying two bikes and leaving one at either end of their journey. British Frail soon did its best to curtail this imaginative idea; they began enforcing the regulation that you could not chain your bike to a British Frail railing - you had to put it in a designated part of the station - usually platform 76 where it was left to the tender mercies of the British vandal. Given the amount of vandalism that goes on near railways I often wonder why British Frail does not sponsor a vandal team. They must be able to give the youngsters several good lessons.

Over the years it became less and less easy to use a bike on British Frail unless you carefully planned your journeys, but if like me you were a permanent traveller there is no sensible way you can plan your journeys. Professional travellers do not say they are going to get the 6am to Newcastle, they wait until they get to the station and then they see what trains are available; this is by far the most efficient method of travel, but British Frail's determination to only have the INBies as customers has ensured that those of us who do this can no longer take our bikes with us.

More and more British Frail brought in 'New and improved trains' all of which had sliding doors, if they did not have such they had some very strange names on the doors. The London/Bournemouth train guards van is entitled; 'Not for public use'. You are allowed to take a bike on but you have to know this first. British Frail's use of words is extremely interesting.

AWAY WITH WORDS

I once got to Bath station - without my bike but late - and was delighted to find that the train was still there. The reason it was late was that the guard was having a dispute with a passenger about his alleged invalid ticket. I was extremely interested in this debate because my ticket was only valid from Birmingham to London and I might have to do some explaining as to how I ended up in Bath (by taking the first available train). The ticket collector was becoming somewhat irate at the hold up and stormed off in search of a policeman who was on the train but was off duty and on his way home, after presumably a tiring day.

The policeman behaved with such diplomacy that I began to suspect he was in the wrong profession, but still the passenger would not surrender his ticket.

"I've shown that bastard my ticket three time if he can't read he shouldn't be on this train." The sentence was actually twice as long as this was interspersed with a word beginning with 'f' every other word.

"Don't worry about him sir, if you will show me your ticket we will all be able to get home this evening."

By this time the ticket collector had had enough of what he thought to be namby pamby shenanigans and had stormed off in search of what he considered to be a serious policeman. He returned with two, one of whom was a woman and she then took up the debate with the passenger. She was as determined as he was reluctant and when she made a very unfeminine grab for his ticket he took a swing at her, but she was prepared, and ducked, and the policeman who was originally dealing with the affair got hit full in the face. There must be a motto to this story somewhere but I have yet to find it. The passenger then locked himself in the toilet but unbeknownst to him the guard has a special key which can open the toilet in exactly these circumstances. I did indeed feel sorry for the policeman who had been so polite at the beginning for he too had to leave the train to ensure that the correct charges were brought. I feel sure that he was cursing that ticket collector almost as much as the passenger, but under his breath.

The train then started and the ticket collector made an announcement... "We are dreadfully sorry for the late departure of this train it was caused by ....." You could hear the thoughts rumbling in the ticket collector's brain. He knew he could not say in British Frail Speak what had actually caused the delay.

It was not until the train had left Chippenham that a full communique was disembargoed.

"We are sorry about the delay to this train, it was caused by a passenger having trouble getting off at Bath."

It was the INBies who conned British Frail into improving the look of its trains. British Frail surrounded by so much ugliness, not least from its passengers, was eager to hear the message. The evangelical claptrap of the designer decade could not have found a more crippled listener, ready to be converted at the slightest sign from on high, and oh how the newspapers cheered and got their chauffeurs to drop them off at the station when British Frail announced the new improved trains with the sliding door safety measures. All of it doomed to failure. What is the point of having deluxe trains and a bright new advertising campaign for the great British yobbo to vomit all over. Instead of wasting the money on fancy trains, British Frail should improve the frequency of its service. This does not look wonderful in bright PR shindigs but it encourages the passengers which British Frail seems unaware is the purpose of a mass transport system. It constantly complains that it has to compete unfairly against road traffic. I do not care whether this is true or not. We already have the world's best network all we have to do is put some trains on it. The road to profitability is cheap fares. If you ask a motorist the cost of a journey to Birmingham from London they will only tell you the cost of the petrol. Similarly if you ask the Great British Yobbo the cost of a train journey from London to Birmingham, they do not tell you of the vast amounts that they spend in the buffet.

Millions have been spent by British Frail bringing in the advanced passenger train, which now rots in Crewe. The sliding door trains on the local routes which suffer from what British Frail call 'teething troubles' - how the hell can British Frail have teething problems after being in the railway business for 150 years!

A railway is like a hotel. If you do not fill the seats on that day you are never going to fill them again. It costs just as much to run an empty train as it does a full one with the difference that you can make money out of a full one on the drinks, the food and the ancillary services such as shops on the station. Last year British Frail lost over £1,000 million. As usual British Frail is not willing to admit the truth. They claim they lost £145 million, they do not accept the £850 million subsidy from the government as being part of the loss. Indeed British Frail measures that money as ticket receipts. All you had to do was stand on any station at the beginning of the year and you could have predicted that British Frail was losing more than ever, and of course British Frail blames the recession. It also blames the recession because it cannot sell its properties at quite the inflated price that it previously managed.

The government's policy (policy is a mistake you can't rectify) is to sell off the railways. You can already hear the patter of tiny Rolls Royces round to the banks. Times are hard, and the Maxwells of this world have been reduced to car pools with the editors of British newspapers.

It does not take a lot of imagination to work out what will happen when the trains are privatised. Firstly they will begin charging for train information a la the telephone company; then they will reduce the number of lines because they are uneconomic a la bus companies; then they will increase the fares, "for long term investment" a la the water company; then they will sell off the properties. That there is a recession and British Frail cannot sell the properties now will only mean that the privateers will reduce the price. What happens in the long term is of no concern to them. It will not be so much Canary Wharf as an Albatross Armada.

In the immortal words of my ex chauffeur Lenin: What is to be done? I have absolutely no idea.

RC: "You mean we have been reading all this tripe and you have not one suggestion, I don't believe it.."

I do however have a few minor thoughts... It could not be any worse than the present situation if the railway lines of Britain were owned by a form of National Trust. Each line could be run separately by those people who use it regularly. That instead of charging for the length of journey you should simply be charged a fare for entry into the system as happens with letters where there is a flat fee whether you send the letter round the corner or to Inverness. Those of you who do not travel may feel that it is not a good idea that passengers be treated like parcels, but I assure you that we would prefer that to being treated as cattle or sheep. The collection and issuing of fares should be the responsibility of the guard on the train. This is the only system that cannot be defeated by ticket fraudsters, thus all the money is collected at the point of entry which means that the small provincial lines would not be considered a drain on the big inter city lines, the more points of entry the more passengers the railway system would have. It is a dreadful mistake for the railways to even allow potential passengers to have thoughts of motor cars, for once they have purchased a motor car they will never consider going by train.

One of the lines I use most regularly is the North London line which goes from Woolwich to Richmond via Hampstead. This line is almost a complete North London circular line. People who have not travelled on it are extremely wary of it because the trains are unreliable, the stations are dowdy, the information about it is meagre, and British Frail is ashamed of it. It looks too much like a railway. If the line was held in trust by those of us who wish to use it then methods of improvement could slowly but surely be introduced.

Firstly the number of trains could be increased, trains currently run, officially every twenty minutes, British Frail could not have introduced a more irritating schedule if it had tried. Twenty minutes is the exact length of time needed to drive passengers to distraction. It would be possible to withstand this length of time in the country but in London it is unreasonable to expect passengers to wait so long, it is not only unreasonable, they will not do it. And in London they don't. They either walk to the nearest tube or take a bus. The first improvement would be to make the trains every fifteen minutes, this could be done by using the old slam door trains that British Frail got rid of some ten years ago and which now act as practice boards for graffiti artists at Royal Oak depot. This would encourage the cyclists who abound on this line but who are currently treated as social pariahs because there is nowhere for them to put their bikes on the sliding door trains. The sliding door trains are known to British Frail as improvements, that is they are lighter and more susceptible to leaves on the line.

Twenty minutes might be an acceptable length of time if the trains ran regularly, but they don't. And when one train is cancelled it means a wait of forty minutes which is a sure fire method of driving passengers away. If the train ran every fifteen minutes it would come closer to providing a genuine twenty minute service.

The stations on the North London line have also been improved. They now look like the sets for B movies about prisons. They all have automatic ticket machines - an attempt by British Frail to reduce staff - the reduction in staff has encouraged a new breed of armed robber. They come to steal from the ticket machines which cost £100,000 each and which have an average of less than £100 in them and have necessitated the installation of closed circuit television cameras by British Frail. It is true that ticket collectors on trains would be susceptible to robbery, but there is no reason why ticket collectors should actually have to collect money. All they have to do is ensure that the passengers have valid jetons which could be purchased at newsagents in the same way as travel cards are now.

It is reassuring to passengers that there is a known official on the train. The guards who are currently employed are about as visible as the knickers on a nun. To ensure that the passengers have tickets British Frail has installed turnstiles which appear to be designed for anorexics and when people with prams or bikes try to get on the platform there is an almighty confrontation, there is even more of a confrontation when people who want to get out of British Frail's property meet those people who want to get in. The truth is that most people will put up with appalling conditions as long as they can get from A to B.

There is no information system so if you are standing at Highbury and Islington there is no way of knowing if a train has been cancelled other than by judging the number of passengers. British Frail has also done away with the clocks, possibly to ensure that passengers do not know how late the line is. This negative approach is somehow indicative of British Frail's will to actually run a railway. It does not believe that there are any more passengers out there despite the fact that more people travel on the railways each year. The strange fact is buried away on page 2397 of British Frail's annual report, the reason British Frail loses money on them is that they are all travelling on concession tickets. British Frail has a vested interest in the commuters.

It is they who currently make railway profits, or rather who ensure that the losses are not so catastrophic, but they are the worst possible customers. They only wish to travel at very specific times. It is rather like having a restaurant where people only wish to eat between seven and eight in the morning. It just does not make sense. Nothing should be done to encourage these stupid buggers to travel untold miles from their homes at peculiar hours and then repeat the journey at night because they wish to live in what they imagine is a rural idyll. Quite why the government has chosen to subsidise the commuters is not easy to understand. The INBies are the worst possible customers. To them it is a matter of life and death that they should arrive at 8.30 so that they can join the next jam.

The railway should be made so cheap that it is jammed at all times. It is a myth that people dislike jammed trains. In truth it is very much part of being a Londoner. It is a tragedy of Herculean proportions that British Frail does nothing to increase the number of passengers during the day. You can only fill a train once to allow trains to travel 80% empty is to demonstrate that you are 80% incapable of running a railroad service 80% of the time.

Inverness
Aberdeen
Dundee
Perth
Leuchars (St.Andrews)
Stirling
Glasgow
Edinburgh
Newcastle
Carlisle
Darlington
Whitehaven
Scarborough
Barrow
Lancaster
Harrogate
Blackpool
Preston
Halifax
Leeds
Liverpool
Huddersfield
Holyhead
Llandudno
Manchester
Colwyn Bay
Sheffield
Bangor
Conway
Chester
Lincoln
Llanrwst
Crewe
Nottingham
Wrexham
Stoke
Derby
Blaenau Ffestiniog
Stafford
Leicester
Kings Lynn
Macbynlleth
Wolverhampton
Shrewsbury
Peterborough
Norwich
Aberystwyn
Welshpool
Ludlow
Birmingham
Coventry
Knighton
Leominster
Northampton
Ipswich
Hereford
Cheltenham Spa
Cambridge
Carmarthen
Tenby
Abergavenny
Colchester
Oxford
Swansea
Gloucester
Southend
Cardiff
Newport
Faversham
Bristol
Bath
Chatham
Ramsgate
Canterbury
Deal
Salisbury
Castle Cary
Folkestone
Southampton
Crewkerne
Havant
Exeter
Bournemouth
Portsmouth
Newton Abbott
Weymouth
Plymouth
Paignton
Truro
Falmouth Town
Penzance

GET LOST

The directions I give are from Railway Stations. There have been many complaints about this choice of starting point, not least from BR who very much object to my being a passenger on their services. But I am at a total loss to understand where else I should begin. I am as unlikely to recognise a car park as I am a car, but this has not been the sole cause of disappointment with my magnum opus and in my experience the armchair critics are far more vociferous.

Mr Richard Boston in the Guardian took me to task for giving the next closest bookshop to the Upper Street Bookshop in London as being the Brixton Market Bookshop. As they say in Brixton but possibly not in the Guardian "as the crow flies". This is indeed untrue however I recommend that you should keep to particular tube lines in London. For those people not used to them it is difficult enough staying on the same line, and if a guide book is not written for people who have not been to a particular place, then who is it written for? In the case of Mr Richard Boston it is difficult to say, for he then goes on to give the directions to what he considers to be the next nearest shop, that of Boutle & King in Sadlers Wells and I quote "From Upper Street OOSH turn left" and I will quote no more.

If you were to follow this direction it would work perfectly, if you continued to Highbury and Islington Tube, got the BR train to Liverpool Street, from there got the train to Stansted and thence flew to Schipol, which has direct connections with Australia and brief stopovers in Singapore. From Australia you then get direct flights to Los Angeles and New York, and from there you fly to Heathrow. From there I would recommend that you take the tube to Kings Cross and then change to the Northern Line (you must be extremely careful at this point not to go wrong and take a south bound train to The Angel. Only on London Transport could The Angel be described as being south of Kings Cross). From The Angel you should come out of the station, turn right towards the crossroads, turn left at the Goswell Road, turn first right and first left into Arlington Way. The shop is on the left.

The above scenic route may well be the one that most British journalists would choose by preference, purely in a desire to add local colour, however I have my doubts about this: I do not feel that most journalists would take the tube from Heathrow after what would have to be described as a somewhat tiring journey. In my experience most British journalists feel that the only direction ever needed is to the local cab rank.

Previously I have assumed that this guide is going to be used only by the sweaty anoraked worms of book collectors and I have attempted to give what I consider to be reasonable directions.

I had also assumed that most motorists would carry atlases of Britain in their cars, I carry an atlas of Britain at all times and all I have is a briefcase, and I have been everywhere. What you have to remember is that the High Streets of Britain are now so bland that only Mr Major could be impressed. No sensible person would attempt to look for anything in London without having an A-Z of the streets which by no means marks you out as a tourist; in my experience most cab drivers have an A-Z in their cab. What does mark you out as a tourist is not carrying one. Asking people in the street is the worst possible thing you can do, especially in London. Most Londoners only know the way to work or the SS offices, the way home and the way to the West End. They regard everywhere else as being where unfortunates live.

RC: "You used that line in the last guide!"

drif "It is my line I can use it again can't I?"

RC: "There is no need to get shirty and you should not use 'can't I?' on the end of a sentence, it marks you out as being a Londoner."

Asking people in the street is frought with disaster, there are those who use pubs as landmarks, those who use traffic lights and those who use streets that were there 25 years ago, asking them where a secondhand bookshop is is doomed. Only 4% of the population ever goes in a bookshop of any kind. Secondhand bookshops tend to be in the cheaper parts of towns along with the health food store. The one guaranteed place to ask is in a charity shop. The old bats in those places only work there so that they can find out everybody else's business.

When it says OOS turn left, it means if you are standing at the door of the station you turn left, if it says into town it means you ignore all the side roads and wait until you get to the shopping area before you start worrying about directions. When it says third left it means the third major left not alleyways, not paths and not shopping precincts. I would be happy to give the names of streets but alas the councils of Britain are now eager that the names of streets should not be a burden on the budget. When it says not a short trek (NAST) it means a walk of more than twenty minutes from the railway station.

It is always best to look for a sign saying books, as the shops of Britain now feel that the needs of design preclude them from identifying themselves in any particular way especially numerically. I have one minor suggestion to make. If the designer beggars who now haunt most of the thoroughfares of Britain were to learn the streets within a given area such as the Charing Cross Road, Chelsea, Cheltenham or the Cotswolds, they could set themselves up as information services. All they would have to do is have a street atlas and a label on their lapels saying INFORMATION GIVEN beneath which, a tray, in the style of buskers. It is my belief that people would give them more than they get as beggars and they would be performing a useful service. In the Charing Cross Road the newspaper vendors would be delighted to see them, as would the secondhand bookshops which are bored rigid with having to explain where Foyles is. They could position themselves outside stations all around the capital and learn the required useful pieces of information such as when the last bus went by, and when the next one is - genuinely - they could learn where all the local landmarks that people would genuinely like to go to are. One piece of information that I am always keen to find out in English towns is the site of a large supermarket (they tend to be the only places in the Provinces which can supply my bizarre dietary needs). I realise that it might come under the definition of work, but it has to be far more profitable than lying in doorways asking for spare change. **RC: "You can tell it was a long time since he went near a beggar. When did you last see one with a lapel?"**

Until this halcyon time comes, in fact I think I shall have a go at doing this myself. I shall be changing the system under which I give directions. I shall assume that you are the type of person who comes out of secondhand bookshops backwards and I shall further assume that you are only intent on visiting the bookshops within one mile of your office. I shall further assume that you spend your life in the back of cabs studying local colour. I shall even further assume that you are intent on taking what can best be described as the scenic route, but most of all I shall assume that you do not have to worry about time and efficiency. This new and 'improved' set of directions will hereinafter be known as THE BOSTON ROUTE.

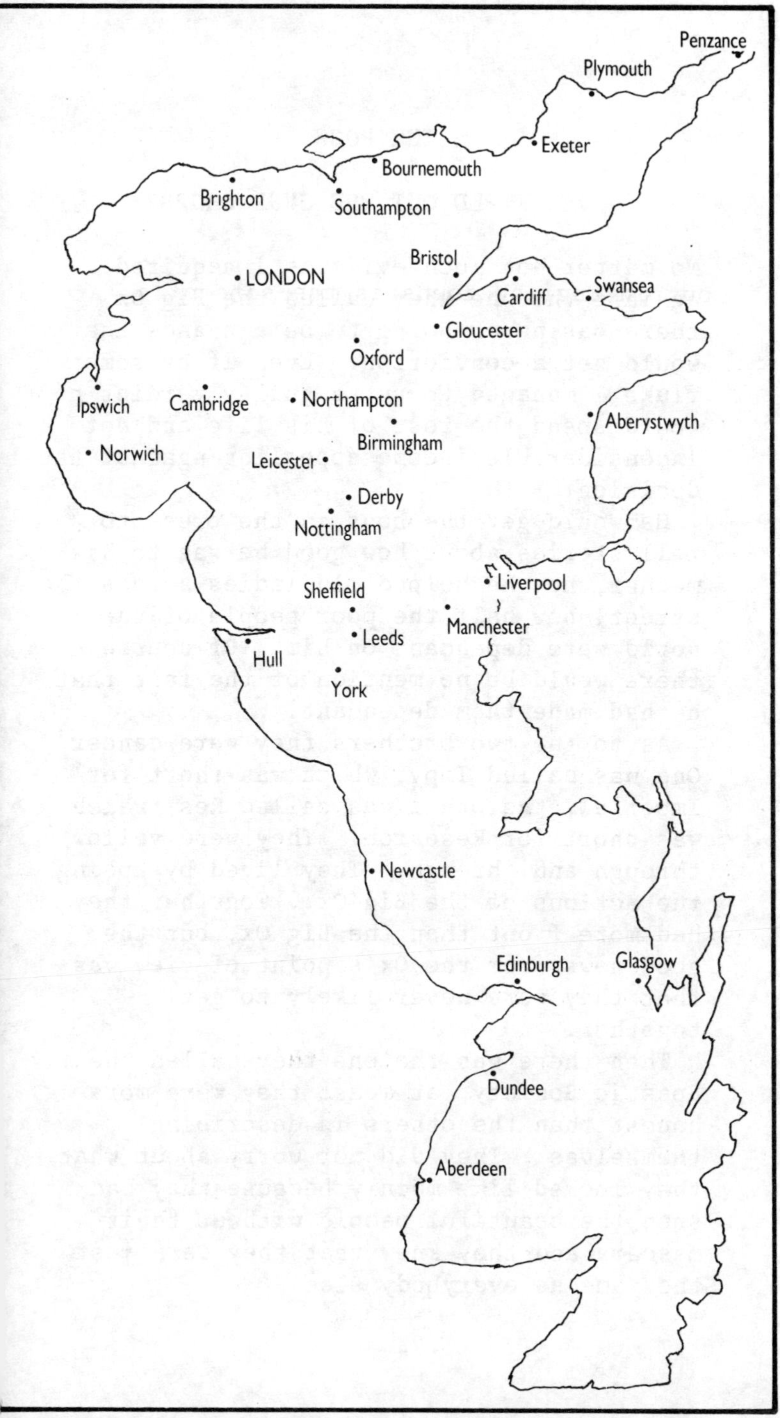
Penzance
Plymouth
Exeter
Bournemouth
Brighton
Southampton
Bristol
LONDON
Cardiff
Swansea
Gloucester
Oxford
Ipswich
Cambridge
Northampton
Aberystwyth
Birmingham
Norwich
Leicester
Derby
Nottingham
Liverpool
Sheffield
Manchester
Leeds
Hull
York
Newcastle
Edinburgh
Glasgow
Dundee
Aberdeen

THE POCS

WHO WIPED OUT THE JUNK SHOPS?

No matter how much evidence I acquired against the one they called the Big Ox, there was never going to be a chance that I would get a conviction. Even if by some fluke I managed to get a guilty verdict he would spend the rest of his life and not inconsiderable income appealing against the decision.

He would get the boys in the press to tell stories about how good he was to his mother, how he helped old ladies across the street, how half the poor people of the world were dependant on him. Of course there would be no mention of the fact that he had made them dependant.

As to the two brothers they were cancer. One was called Impy, which was short for Imperial, the other was called Res, which was short for Research. They were yellow through and through. They lived by apeing the actions of the Big Ox. Together they had more front than the Big Ox, but the good news from the Ox's point of view was that they were never likely to get together.

Then there was the one they called the Spastic Society, at least they were more honest than the others in describing themselves. They did not worry about what they looked like mainly because they had seen the beautiful people without their mascara and they knew that they were just the same as everybody else.

The female interest was provided by an old gal called Sue Ryder. You would have expected her to be the most elegant of the lot, but the truth was that she was the most down at heel, but it was all just a front. She had more sites than most of the others put together. She paid nothing for them because it looked like she did not have two ha'pennies to rub together and she only ever employed the oldest most worn out dames.

Then there was Doc Barnardo, nobody ever found out what he was a doctor of. It seemed to me that he just called himself that so that he could take an interest in little kids.

There were a whole host of other minor characters, with even more outlandish names, but they came and went like dandruff in adverts for shampoo.

I knew that nobody was ever likely to talk out against them. The omerta was absolute and they were more sanctimonious than nuns and tougher than the mafia. Sign language might help, especially hitting them with an enamel one.

Everybody knew it had to be them, only they had the muscle, only they had the opportunity and only they stood to benefit. All I had to do was prove it. Nobody was going to help me. Nobody had ever taken on this mob before, nobody had ever considered speaking against them. But I had one small advantage - I had been at the death of the last junk shop - it was not a pretty sight. And nobody, no matter how low, deserved to die that way, but in their arrogance the perpetrators had left one small piece of evidence: an ice pick. Where else in

Britain would you get an ice pick except in a charity shop?

My real problem was that I didn't have much time... I had just sold my appartment, in the nice part of Brixton, I had changed pounds into real money and I was due to start a real job in LA investigating some hoodlum who had wasted police equipment when six of them defended themselves. There was no way he was going to get away with wasting so much police effort; we had a video showing him doing it. I had sent all my possession to the States and my boss had given me this job as a tail end accomplishment. Everybody knew who did it: It was just getting the evidence.

I knew I wouldn't get very far but I had to show I was going through the motions, so I started with the biggest and boy what a motion that turned out to be, I did not rate an interview with the big man himself, but according to the bimbo I got fobbed off with, there was no such person. She certainly did not look like she got her clothes from Oxfam.

According to her Oxfam started up in Oxford during the war. I have never been to Oxford but the way she talked about it made it sound like a cross between Detroit and Harvard, mind you I have never been to Harvard either. She claimed that they were trying to raise money to help the poor: Aren't we all? I felt like asking if I could have my share now, but she was in such flow that I did not have the heart to stop her. According to her their purpose was to relieve world hunger: They had volunteers in every town who started up shops and people 'gave' them donations and

The man who asked for
charity in a charity shop.

they 'sold' the goods and gave the money to the poor, and people sent them money all the time, so that World Hunger could be relieved.

"Fifty years and there are still a lot of hungry people in the world," I said.

"That is because not enough people have given us money," she replied.

I decided to ask her straight:

"Did you have anything to do with the death of the junk shop?"

She just stood there looking at me and I did not get the feeling that she was trying to work out what size shoulders I had. Before I knew it I had been grabbed round the neck in a choke hold the LAPD would have paid money to keep secret. Even though I hadn't used them in a long time I now had proof that I had testicles. All the time she just kept smiling as if it was nothing to do with her, and indeed it wasn't. The only time she acknowledge my presence was to dismiss it.

"Thank you girls, if you could show this gentleman out I am sure he will not be casting any more aspersions".

She was right, her mob had moved far above ice picks a long time ago.

When I awoke the one consolation was that things could only get better, but that was before I discovered I had lost all my clothes, and then when I lifted my head it felt like I was hitting a girder, but the shock of that was nowhere near as bad as realising I had lost all my money. I could hear words but they were too much for me to take in ...

"Youhadbetterdrinkthisoryou'llfreezetodeathherelookI'llgetyouacoat..."

Eventually I translated it as he began to remove his own top layer. It looked like the skin of that great British delicacy, a weak old Steak and Kidney pie. I was sure I saw creatures run for cover under his other layer. It was not so much an overcoat as a disused incubator. As he put it round me I wondered what would start crawling all over my body.

"What happened to my clothes?" It sounded like an accusation even though I said nothing about the money.

"What were you doing before this?" He asked me.

"I was in the charity shop across the street."

"Say no more, I know all about these bleeding bitches, they pretend to go round giving to us poor people and all the time they are keeping all the best stuff for themselves. I know their game, they cream off everything so that they can get their 'advisers' from Sotheby's to have a look, and they've got more advisers than South Vietnam. All those toffee nosed old bats spraying air freshener every time you walk in the shop. If they had a bath they would not smell so bad, they always stink and have you noticed how they are always bitching: 'I made the tea last week, I don't mind doing my fair share but she's come in late three times in the last six months' .. they're just a bunch of old pratts whose idea of a good fantasy was getting a job at Harrods. You know why they open so late in the morning, its 'cos it takes them three hours to put their make up on so that they look vaguely human. They think of that make up as being some sort of nuclear protection suit against all the low lifers but you have noticed you only ever see middle class people in charity shops. You see all those notices they got, I reckon they have a competition to see who can come up with the best notice, and the winner - she's the one who gets to say 'this shop is now closed' at four in the afternoon. The reason they have to close so early is that their make up won't last much longer than six hours. My favourite notice is the one they have in Hoaxfam, NO FOOD AND DRINK. What are they doing, looking for new customers? I reckon they are fed up with flying all those hungry people to different parts of the world so that they can show them on television programmes, and now they are hoping to get more customers nearer home. You go to Wimbledon, they got 13 of those charity shops - they don't have any in poor areas - you go to the north they got none at all! I think they are practising to become a rugby team. The All Blacks would run a mile, if they had any sense. I don't know why those television people don't start one of them soap operas about them, they would not have to learn any lines. I can see it now:

'Oh Daphne, do you really think it is san Michelangelo?'

'Of course Penelope, everybody knows that trainers were invented in Italy.'

Those old pratts they know as much about antiques as I know about Pre Menstrual Tension. You don't want to start telling them about PMT they will stary trying to sell it as a kind of rope. Now that they have driven all the junk shops out of business they have started selling anything they can lay their hands on."

Maybe this was the informant I so desperately needed if I was going to crack thise case, but I had to check his credentials first. I did not like the sound of that remark about Vietnam. It made me wonder if he was what the Britishers call a liberal.

"Give me your name and address?"

"Buckingham Palace."

"What street is it in?"

"Why do I get all the nutters in this alley, you will have to ask the servants its not something I take any interest in, I only come here when they are tidying up."

I could not work the old guy out. He dressed in a tee-shirt that you could have held an archaeological dig on, it had a perfect record of every meal he had eaten for the last three months. He looked the way I often felt. He talked to me like I was a Radio Four audience. I wondered what had gone wrong, how had he ended up like this. Maybe there was something I could do for him, but what? If I gave him a five pounds he would only buy himself a bottle. If I gave him fifty pounds he might just be able to buy himself a meal and some new clothes - as long as he didn't shop at Oxfam - if I gave him five hundred pounds he might just be able to find a room somewhere and change his way of life, but what he really needed was some get up and go, and he needed someone to help him through the pitfalls of life and I knew I was not that person. But, I thought I had better make an effort, after all charity begins at home and this appeared to be his home... but now I did not have my $20,000!

"You surely cannot really enjoy this life you're leading?" I asked.

"You have too many adverbs in that sentence, but what do you mean?"

"Well, living like an old tramp."

"I'll have you know I was the winner of the Eric Korn Memorial Prize for best dressed bookdealer. I try to help you out when you're down on your luck and this is all the thanks I get. I get more kind words from those old bats in the charity shops."

"But in that case what are you doing here?"

"I'm carrying out research on behalf of the ABA to find out what happens to all the books charity shops get. Nobody really knows what happens, thousands of books get given to them every day, and not one good one ever comes out. The occult booksellers think it is some sort of Bermuda Triangle; the first edition dealers think they have a contract with that new shop Ulysses; the travel dealers have some half baked theory that they are sending them off to Africa to be read. The Childrens' bookdealers think they employ all those YTS kids to crayon in them but nobody knows for sure, and so I am carrying out a scientific survey. Do you know they have now started opening up bookshops? But you got as much chance of getting an interesting book out of one of those places as you have of getting a leg over."

"A leg over?"

"Its a technical term much used in book dealing. Those old bats get given books every night, after 4.30. I then go over there and tab the books and I try to follow what happens to them, but so far I have had no luck." He looked at me as if I was supposed to say something.

"If you really wanted to help me," he said, "you could get a job in a charity shop and then we would be able to find out what happened to all the books."

"But I am investigating the death of the junk shop."

"We all know those creeps did it, what you really mean is you would like to get the goods on them."

"The goods on them?" I wondered if this was another British double entendre, he surely could not mean ... not with the ladies in charity shops ... could he?

"The evidence. Now that the charity shops have driven out all the junk shops by sheer weight of numbers....."

I could see I was in for another session of Radio Four Speak. I tried to cut him off but it was no good, he was convinced I was so thick that unless he explained to me several times I would not understand. Maybe he thought I was Mr Major come among the people.

"Listen, I'll get a job in a charity shop if you will just get me some clothes so that I can get home."

"Well if that is all you want why didn't you just say so." And with that he walked across the road and dragged back a huge plastic bag that some kind soul had left outside the shop.

"I can't wear these! Some kind person has left these for poor people."

"Well what are you? You are naked, you haven't eaten in hours and you have no home to go to."

"I have got a home to go to, I just do not have the keys."

"Well maybe you would like to give me somewhere to stay for the night?"

"No .... a friend of mine is staying and she is of a very nervous disposition and all the bedrooms are taken."

"I can take a hint, but don't worry us bookdealers are used to living rough."

I pulled on the clothes in the bag, not only did they make me feel like a convict they made me look like one. I did get home but I had to pay £50 to a locksmith to break in to my very own home, in the nice part of Brixton.

That evening I was even more determined than ever to find out who had killed the junk shop, but I could not face having to go near them. I felt so guilty about stealing the clothes and I was sure one of them, or even the old man might come out and denounce me. I tried every other avenue of investigation, but nothing worked. I mulled over what had happened. I had gone to a charity shop, then I had lost $20,000, then I had woken up in that alley. There was no doubt about it, this case was getting the better of me. I resolved to solve it the next day.

My eyes ambled over the books in my library, one was even older than the guy in the alley. Maybe it was worth money. Maybe I could give it to him and he could sell it and set himself on the path to prosperity but that would leave me with only one book, Norman Vincent Peale on Positive Thinking, I decided to read it. The Alcoholics Anonymous tome was getting a bit boring.

There is no gainsaying the power of great literature. There and then I decided to return to the alley, the old man and the charity shops. I don't think I could have faced another page of Norman Vincent Peale.

The street looked vaguely familiar but somehow different, but then all those charity shops look the same. But as I studied the fascias I realised there was one I had not seen before. Inside it seemed to sell nothing but books, but unlike most secondhand bookshops I had seen - I used to go into them by accident until I discovered they were not places where you could place a bet - this one was neatly layed out, and the books were all well organised. A very pleasant looking gentleman in a suit stood behind a counter reading a book. I knew he could not be a REAL secondhand bookdealer, I had never seen one of them doing that, I asked him when this shop had opened.

"Today."

"And what is it in aid of?"

"The purpose is to help poor distressed secondhand booksellers many of whom have been going through a hard time recently sir."

"Oh I know one you might be able to help. He lives closeby, in fact when I last saw him he was in an alley round here somewhere but I can't seem to find it."

"The only alley sir is the site this bookshop is on. Our sponsor had a special attachment to it. He said it was where he made his greatest find - a book that was worth $20,000 - and with that money he set up this shop."

"Can you tell me where I can find an ice pick?"

THE GUIDE BOOK

NORTHERN IRELAND

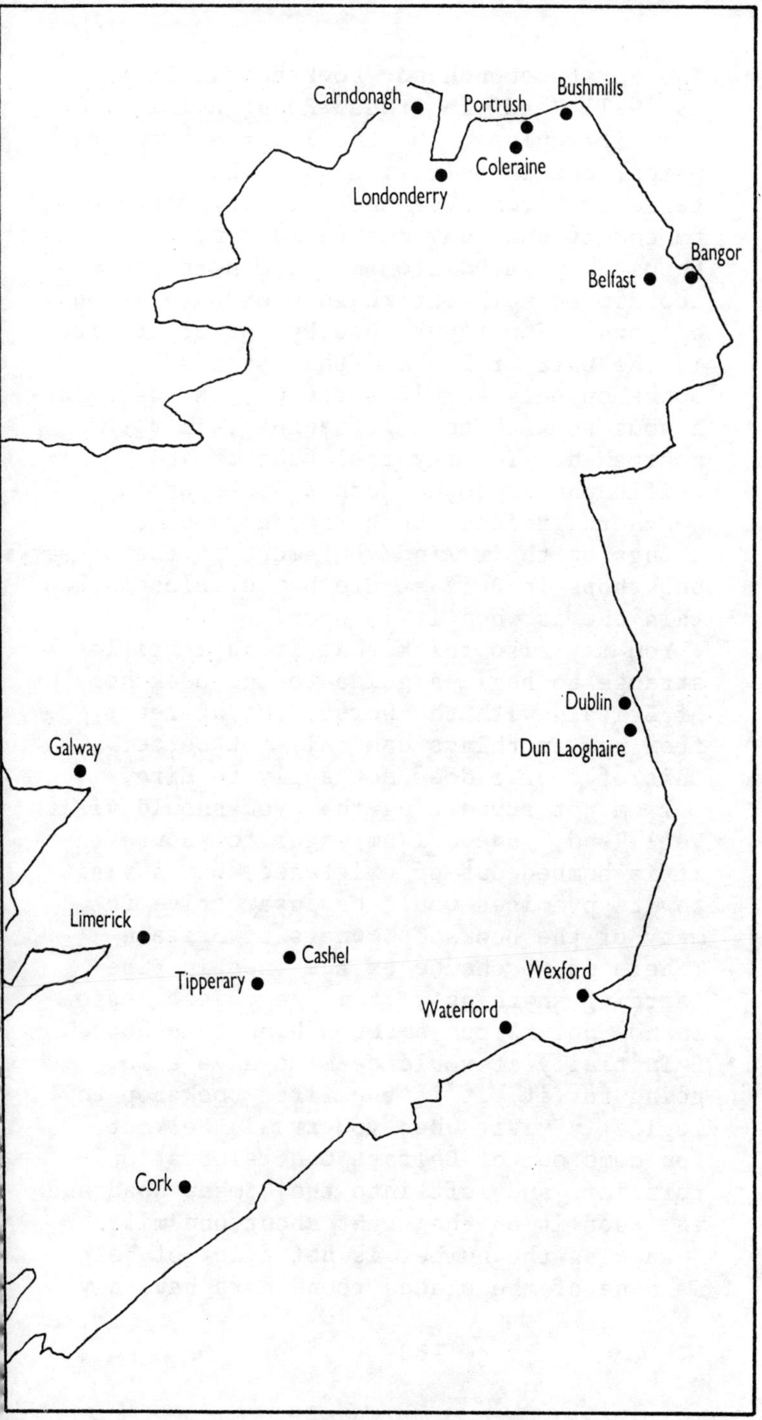
Carndonagh
Portrush
Bushmills
Coleraine
Londonderry
Bangor
Belfast
Dublin
Dun Laoghaire
Galway
Limerick
Cashel
Tipperary
Wexford
Waterford
Cork

The worst secondhand bookshop in Britain is 'Well Read' in Ormeau Road, Belfast. In Eire it would not be the least bit out of place, but in Belfast it is like a terrorist from over the border who has come to commit some day return mayhem, has become separated from his brethern and was too dim to work out where the south is on his own. For future use by terrorists it is the part of Ireland that stinks. This bookshop only survives because it swims in a soup so rich that it cannot fail to be nourished. You may feel that it is a trifle unfair to condemn a bookshop in Northern Ireland where they have other things on their mind, but most of the other bookshops in Belfast are better closed than this one is when it is open.

You may also think that it is a trifle strange to begin a guide to the bookshops of Britain with the worst, but at least from now on things can only get better. This of course does not apply to Eire.

I am not suggesting that you should visit Well Read, indeed I am eager to ensure that it is bombed out of existence, but a visit to its premises would be instructive to many of the bookshop owners of Britain (there is no chance of the ones in Eire learning anything), it is an object lesson in how not to run a secondhand bookshop.

Initially it would seem to have a lot going for it, it is the first bookshop to logically visit when you are in Belfast. You come out of Belfast Central Station, turn left and left into the Ormeau Road and the shop is on the right about one mile.

Knowing the number is not a lot of help as none of the places round here have any posted (having a number in Belfast is seen as a political act; it helps the troops). What you should do is look for a boarded up shack slightly set back from the road. The only thing I do like about this shop is the name, but that the name is so splendid only goes to irritate me even further. This name sits on a corpse just as a vulture sits waiting for its prey to die. A far better description would be Well Ignorant.

The hardboard that covers the window is an improvement; it hides the appalling vista inside. There is no sign saying what time the shop is open, I only discovered by a process of elimination - a task which took a considerable time, and by the time I did find out the shop was closed - it possibly was a good job that it was not open as I would have willingly eliminated on it.

The owner claims to be open from 1pm to 6pm six days a week. I would have no objection to these hours, if they were true, but speaking as a regular visitor to the charity bookshop round the corner in Rugby Avenue (last year, the year before that and the year before that) it is my considered opinion that he is lying.

Inside it looks like something the Saatchi's might buy or you could see exhibited at the Hayward Art Gallery. The exhibits do tend to change more regularly in Ormeau Road mainly because it is so damp that they rot faster. The one great consolation of modern art is that there is not going to be a lot of it in the future. It is physically decomposing faster than the prices are going up, but alas this does not bring much improvement. At the time I was there, several large slabs of concrete decorated the middle of the floor, in the revolutionary new upright position, I suppose if I live to be about 1000 I might just begin to understand this type of art but its early days yet. Strangely enough I did begin to get an inkling as the books are so dreary that it became more interesting studying the concrete, at least it was upright.

The books are not so much placed on the shelves but slung in like recalcitrant loonies. You are loathe to touch them because they are wet with unmentionable substances, like street ranters they constantly repeat themselves and yet there are very few of them. Their books are not placed in any regular order but seem to fight a guerrilla action, one volume is lurking in a corner, the other hides behind a concrete pillar, that is just the text, the covers have gone completely underground.

I spend my entire life looking for books that no other dealer wants but the strange thing is I do not find them in shops such as these. This type has no taste but even then it is the wrong type of no taste.

All this would have been completely forgettable were it not for the owner, for I did indeed find a book which my perverse tastes desired. It had no price. I don't mind being taken for a moron and indeed I have often found that it helps (sometimes if I don't like the price in a book I rub it out and then give the owner another chance), when they see how thick I am they never have the courage to charge the price originally marked. I presented the book for pricing and explained that it had none marked. He looked at me as if I had rubbed it out - I take strong exception to being falsely accused. He then informed me that the price was £10. I declined. He then asked how much I would pay. I don't mind being taken for an English mug, but I really expect that only to happen in Eire. I said that I would be willing to pay £5 at the most but that I would need to have it sent to me in London as it was so large and I did not wish to carry it.

The look of horror that came over him was almost as bad as the sight of the book. I explained to him that I was a visitor to Belfast and that I was going to be returning to Dublin that night and that I did not wish to carry the book with me owing to a little local difficulty there are no places to leave anything in Belfast. Nor does having a car help much as there always has to be two people. One has to sit in the car at all times or the police just blow it up. I informed him that I was willing to pay the postage and that there was no rush as I was going to Eire first.

"Sending books is far too much effort and anyway it will cost money."

"I will happily pay the postage."

"I have not got time!"

I could see that in some ways he was right, he more than likely had to organise the next exhibition of modern concrete in the middle of the floor. I left the book on the desk and walked out but I think what upset me most was his parting remark.

"If you knew anything about books you would buy that book."

In my defence all I can say is that there

are not many people in the world who would buy an odd volume of work on electrical engineering. I should also say that my temper was not improved by the sight of the Post Office directly opposite.

To cheer myself up I went to Prospect House in the Dublin Road; alas it was closed. But in their case there was a notice in the window saying when they would be back and a telephone number to ring if you wanted to get anything in the bookshop. Prospect House closed is better than most bookshops open, just looking in the window was a sheer joy. The books had been chosen with a discrimination that made the race relations act look like a work of Enid Blyton. There is more hope in that window than there was in any other bookshop in Ireland and much of Britain and this is the crucial element that secondhand bookshops should be in the business of cultivating.

Without hope there is nothing. It is not possible to go into a secondhand bookshop and buy books every time, but what is possible is to go into a bookshop and want to buy the type of books that they have. All the skill in bookdealing is in the choice of the books and finding them. In this shop I found a book on malingering, they had books that I thought it was worthwhile my working hard enough to get the money to buy. The books were chosen with an intelligence that I would like to have. By its very presence this bookshop proclaims the glory that is books. No new bookshop can ever be as civilised as this one, new bookshops can only ever stock what publishers produce and supply it with. But the number of secondhand books in the world is so great that a secondhand bookshop offers ample opportunity to make a valid statement; as those of us who attend art galleries say, the books themselves are not the important matter it is just as possible to do it with paperbacks as it is with fifteenth century illustrated books; it is not necessary that the bookshop owner should know about the subject with experience it is possible to tell whether a book is good or not just by looking at it. Good books always weigh more, not just the paper but the text. It has a certain solidity which an odd volume on Electrical Engineering lacks.

A few months after I had stood outside the window of Prospect House living in the longing to be in it, it was blown up. It was not blown up by intention, but by 'accident' as the terrorists say.

When I was in Northern Ireland five men were shot because they worked on a British Army base. The rate of unemployment in Northern Ireland is the highest in Britain. The terrorists claimed they were collaborators and the British press was happy to print this statement just as the British press is happy to print that a particular terrorist group claims responsibility. I would like to know what is 'responsible' about blowing up five men who were trying to earn a living. It is blame. Killing people is not a responsible act, and the British press is collaborating with the terrorists every time it prints such statements. They are giving those pathetics publicity for a half baked cause. Twenty years they have been at the last bout and they have not moved one inch further forward. If they have such great popular support as they keep claiming how come the situation is no different to that it was in 1972?

During the Gulf War (remember that?) a bomb went off in Downing Street, for a few brief hours it was not possible to know whether it was the lunatics in the Middle East or the local branch of Lost Causes International. This is exactly the situation we should try to encourage. Let them bomb as much as they please. I quite enjoy the sound of buildings going up myself, but the British press is the true collaborator for giving these pathetics so much publicity. Taking notice of bombers is like taking notice of screaming children, the more you give in the worse it gets.

By all means give them publicity every time they bomb somewhere, but why give them credit. I don't doubt that these psychopaths will bomb even more, but the good news is that they usually get the wrong target and in the end they would blow up themselves. All we have to do is be patient as most of the people in Northern Ireland.

When I was walking across the bridge into East Belfast there was a security check. Twelve soldiers are necessary for this to take place, but only one actually looks in the car, the rest are there for his protection. One of the soldiers said "Good afternoon Sir" as I passed. I don't know if they have been instructed to say this and it makes little difference but not once in Northern Ireland did I receive such a polite gesture so spontaneously given. There is a type of fanaticism that is extremely difficult for an ignorant Englishman to pin down. In England we see history as a form of punishment. In Northern Ireland they see it as a form of torture to be applied to the other side.

Another thing you see in Northern Ireland is adverts in the newspapers saying that such and such a company is no longer supplying goods or services to the British Troops in Northern Ireland. I would like it known that I am happy to supply books to the British Army in Northern Ireland, I am not only happy to do this I will reduce my prices to the level that British soldiers can afford. Furthermore, I would like it known that I shall be looking at the Well Read bookshop again in November, I think the fifth would be an appropriate date and I will be happy to announce that I am collaborating with the British Army, and if the terrorists attempt to bomb the living daylights out of me, I feel confident that with their usual accuracy I will take the Well Read Bookshop with me.

If I die, I will not feel that it has been in vain and if as I fully expect that they only eliminate the bookshop I shall look forward to calling it the Well Dead Bookshop.

RC: "It's not all going to be like this is it?"

drif: "What do you mean?"

RC: "Well that's eight pages and you have only got two bookshops in, I would mind all the political junk if you told them that you are the only greying skinhead in the National Front. Nobody wants to read this rubbish its Chinese torture, its the long slow drip. What they want is the quick

knee in the groin - I don't think there was one one liner in that was there?"

drif: "The Bookdealer magazine accused my last guide of being a joke!"

There are two bookshops to the south of Prospect House both of which are worth a look if you have the time, but more interesting is to go towards the City Centre and the Smithfield market area, the shops are fairly low key but they have fairly low prices as well. There is also an antique shop with books on the Antrim Road. The shop on the Woodstock Road in the East side of Belfast is a lot of effort for very little reward. There are two low key shops also in Bangor by the railway station, but far more rewardingly there is a truly interesting shop in Coleraine (The Coleraine Bookshop). If you are keen to go to Londonderry (as we prods call it) then it can be worth looking in at the shop in Rushmills and Port Stewart which is almost unique in Northern Ireland in being open on a Sunday.

The shop Bargain Books in Londonderry is a definite drif special, not least for the armed guards, but the shop on the other side of the bridge is well worth avoiding.

There is a shop in Cardonagh which is in Eire but is in the North of Ireland which I have not visited, it sounds interesting, possibly because I have not visited it.

E I R E

Bombing is too good for it! Certainly none of the bombers ever seem to try it there. Its not until you go to Eire that you can see what most of the people in Northern Ireland are against. The place is offensively poor whilst being even more offensively expensive. Now that Americans avoid it - they are all so thick that they are unable to tell the difference between Northern Ireland and Eire, which only goes to show their lack of familiarity with the country - the Irish have become more ravenous of anyone who looks like he might have more money than them.

The hotels are amazingly overpriced. In Britain I hold a contest to find the cheapest place to stay (£6.50 in Llandudno) but in Eire this is just a no hoper. I booked into a hotel that the official travel agency said cost £15 but wanted £20 the moment they heard I was English. This happens all over the country. The Bed & Breakfast places do not put up signs saying vacancies or even that they ARE a Bed & Breakfast. When you go to the door they make a decision about you and then try to work out how much they can charge you. Thus when you do find somewhere to stay you will quite often find other people paying a lot less than you.

CABBAGES, BACON AND POTATOES

The reason so many Irish people died during the famine has nothing to do with absentee landlords or British imperialism. Almost the sole cause is the appallingness of Irish restaurants. If anything things have got worse, the whole of Dublin now consists of Burger joints separated by fast food takeaways. Adolph Hitler would have given his right arm to find out how cardboard could be made palatable, and the Irish are still working on it. The French always sneer at the English but in truth they are only showing how ignorant they are, they have obviously not been to Ireland. It is a great place if you want to go on a diet. As a veggie who has survived in eel and pie shops in deepest Dalston, I live in the belief that it is possible to survive anywhere with a little imagination. I have become expert at indoor picnics, but Eire defeated me. There are no large supermarkets - which in England always have delicatessens attached - and thus it is almost impossible to create a meal of any kind for yourself. I did find one place in Dublin which claimed to be a delicatessen, I think they should have been arrested under the Trades Descriptions Act, for when I asked where I could find the olives they suggested Greece.

The first natural stop for books is Dublin; after that it is definitely best to go home. In Eire they now stock only two types of books. Irish and 'we don't have it'. This monomania has become worse over the last few years and it leads to some slightly strange results. If you are looking for a book about engineering and it is by Kelly then Dublin is the place to try, no matter that Kelly was born and bred in Chile.

If someone from Eire wants to buy a general book s/he goes to Belfast, where they are also keen on Irish literature but not to the exclusion of everything else simply to supply the demand, most of which comes from the dealers of Eire. When I was in Ireland I kept asking if the people in the north went in for northern books and the people in the south for southern books, but I kept being assured that there was no such dichotomy, this is true. The Irish dealers in Eire will buy anything they can get their hands on.

As to taxis, my advice is don't. I had been to Belfast for the day, and come back laden with books - this was the day the gentleman in Ormeau Road declined to send my parcel for me. I got into the cab at O'Connell Street Station and told the driver to take me to the north side of town giving him the address of the hotel. Because I was carrying so much he assumed that I had just arrived and did not know where this hotel was. When we arrived by what even a Cubist would have described as a circuitous route he told me that the fare was £11.50 (the Irish punt currently has parity with the pound). He switched off the meter the moment I began to dispute this fare, which I have a vague feeling is not allowed even in Eire. I then pointed out to him that the same fare had cost me £3.50 the previous evening. He then offered a deal whereupon I was only expected to pay seven fifty. I declined this generous offer and directed him to the police station so that we could sort the matter out. I was a bit surprised when he accepted my offer. We then drove to the police station whereupon he got out and rushed in. A few seconds later a policeman came out and said I would have to pay the fare. I offered to pay the fare, but I declined to pay the £11.50 and asked the policeman if that was the normal charge from O'Connell Street to the hotel. The policeman said that this was a civil matter and that it was nothing to do with him and went back into the station. I suggested to the driver that we go to his office and ask them how much it was. He declined this offer and countered with a suggestion that I should pay a fiver. I agreed provided he took me back to the hotel for as I explained to him I had to be up early in the morning as I wanted to catch the train to Westport.

"I will drive you there" he said, "we can negotiate the fee."

I was glad that one of the books I had bought in Belfast was an Irish atlas.

The best way to get round the whole of Ireland is to pay as you go. The Rover Tickets are all egregiously expensive. Unlike England, single tickets can be a lot cheaper than you would imagine on the railways. You are not supposed to break your journey, but everyone believes you when you tell them you are a dumb Englishman who does not know about such things.

James Joyce and I are in complete

agreement about our attitude to Dublin; we both try to leave at the earliest opportunity. Unfortunately it is the most central place if you wish to get to the other parts of Ireland. Thus it is easy to get to Belfast, Cork, Limerick, Galway and Londonderry. As a place to stay, I prefer Belfast but unfortunately you then have to move to Dublin if you want to visit the other parts of Eire.

In Eire there is a type of secondhand bookshop that you do not see in the rest of Britain. They are most like popular book centres, in so far as they operate a swap system, but the books are extremely low key, they are seldom ever the type of books that a collector would be interested in. I am very much in favour of bookshops for readers but the strange thing is that you do not actually see many readers in these shops. They seem to do very little business.

In Dublin, despite the disappointing absence of bombs there are security guards at the doors of most shops. This is not to stop things being brought in but a particular group of people; the free range urchins who seem to be such a virulent part of Dublin life. Anything that is not nailed to the floor they regard as being their own. You will even have difficulty finding a cardboard box in Dublin.

All this would lead the reasonable person to believe that the secondhand bookshops would be very keen to get your money, and they are, they just do not believe that they should do anything for it. What they want is for you to go in pick up a right load of old tat and give them the money.

There are a few shops in Dublin which gave better books such as Cathack Books and Cathair Books but they charge more than even an innocent American millionaire would be prepared to pay. All of the books that they have you could get in England at far less than they charge in Dublin. They do not seem to have any Irish books that English dealers do not have, just more of the same, and the moment they hear you are not interested in Irish Literature they lose all interest, which is good news until you discover they have nothing else. I don't know what has happened to all the other books, they used to have them a few years ago. Maybe the IRA has gone round silently assassinating them. Perhaps they give new recruits the task of eliminating all English books from the shelves. Maybe the kids think that green jackets are a type of cover.

There is one redeeming feature in Eire and the person who thought of this should be up there with James Joyce and Saint Patrick. As you enter a built up zone there is a sign painted into the road saying: SLOW. When you ignore this sign and speed on for another fifty yards there is another sign saying: SLOWER, which makes you smile for a few yards, but then you go on and there is another sign which says: EVEN SLOWER.

In central Dublin the best secondhand bookshop is The Winding Stair on Lower Ormond Quay. Not the least of its attractions is that it has a cafe attached and acts as an information exchange. I found out more about other secondhand bookshops in Eire sitting talking to the other deadbeats in this place than anywhere else in Ireland. This is the only bookshop I have ever seen where they have successfully managed to combine with a cafe, I would have been happier if it had been veggie, but I am afraid that cabbage and bacon is about as close as the Irish get.

Running a cafe or restaurant is performance art, and you have to do it well every day, running a bookshop is much more passive, and the people who are good at one are not necessarily good at the other, but there must be many passive customers just like me.

The shops on the north side of the Liffey Bridge are somewhat cabbage like, those on the south feel that they are the bacon, if you want hot potatoes you have to go to Blackrock and Dun Laoghaire.

The Naughton Bookshop in Dun Laoghaire is without doubt the best secondhand bookshop in Eire. It opens hours that Saint Patrick would describe as industrious, it is reliable, the books are interesting, in good condition and well chosen. The prices could not be described as low but in relation to the other bookshops in Eire they are distinctly value for money. There is a reserve stock which seems to produce much that is tempting. The person who works in this shop seems to know more about Irish Literature than most of the other bookshops in Ireland put together, and does not treat moronic enquiries from dumb Englishmen, as to why they had a book of Guinness Advertising in the local history section, with the disdain deserved (well I am a tee totaller, how was I supposed to know?)

They specialise in Irish books but not to the exclusion of all others, they seem to be much more outward looking than any other bookshop in Eire. I don't think us Imperialist oppressors can claim that it is because they are so relatively close to England as not many of the shops there are as high a calibre as this one. If I lived in the North of Wales, I think it would almost be worthwhile getting one of the cheap day trips to Dun Laoghaire just to go into this place, indeed if I have any recommendation it is that they should open one evening a week, and those of us who have an aversion to Irish hotels could do all the bookshops in Dublin in one day. For this bookshop is the dessert that it would be worth eating your greens for.

They may have Opera in Wexford but there is no sign of any left over libretti.

The bookshop in Waterford would be worth crossing to if it was not for its neighbour which lives up to the name of the word that it dwells in: Cork. I have been there two years running and never found it open. If I go a third time and it is closed I shall be taking a broken bottle to it and the cork will be even more useless.

When you get to Tipperary station you will find out why the song made the town famous, but there is a drif special there - its run by a German. I was summarily summoned to his summer shop in Cashel but did not make it. Instead, I was lured to Limerick which always makes me feel homesick for Marylebone High Street which only leaves Galway, and I left it.

If you mention Galway to most book people in Ireland, they mention Kenny's. If you go in the local tourist office and ask about any other bookshops they tell you that there is only Kenny's. It is like the Foyles of Galway, but much worse. It has almost as many books as it has arrogance, but the arrogance is not as new. What it does have which is secondhand is pomposity. It is so full of itself that if it were a balloon it would be able to cross the Atlantic in record time. And across the Atlantic is the direction it looks, however there are currently no Americans looking in its direction. The enquiry as to whether they can help you is more to establish the nasal nature of your accent. At one time they would have turned up their nose at anything less than mid Atlantic but now they will dig into any fodder even English turnips. A brief lecture on the glory of the Irish countryside, which round here is mainly bogs, a short dissertation on the glories of Irish literature, which this shop is bogged down in. If only a bookshop was like a restaurant you would at least be able to get rid of the waiters by telling them that you do not wish to order any more. Some of the books are mighty fine things, but who wants a third American edition of At Swim Two Birds, when you can buy a paperback? The one group of books that I was interested in were all hidden behind yet more buys of Irish literature. It is like going in an Italian restaurant where they only have spaghetti and nothing else. Some of us would like a little sauce. There is no seasoning of any other kind after a while it is like eating wallpaper paste.

The only serious secondhand bookshop in Galway is Byrne's in Dominick Street, it is not over large, but it is over interesting. There is a type of obesity which seems to effect secondhand bookshops, but ones this size are never likely to suffer from it. It is almost unique in Eire in that it has general books, that is ones that do not officially have an Irish connection. It is when you see this place that you realise the others are just shamming. There is also an antique shop with books at the far end of the street on the left, far more worthwhile than Kenny's.

S C O T L A N D

WALL TO WALL SCOTT versus THE BONNIE PRINTS

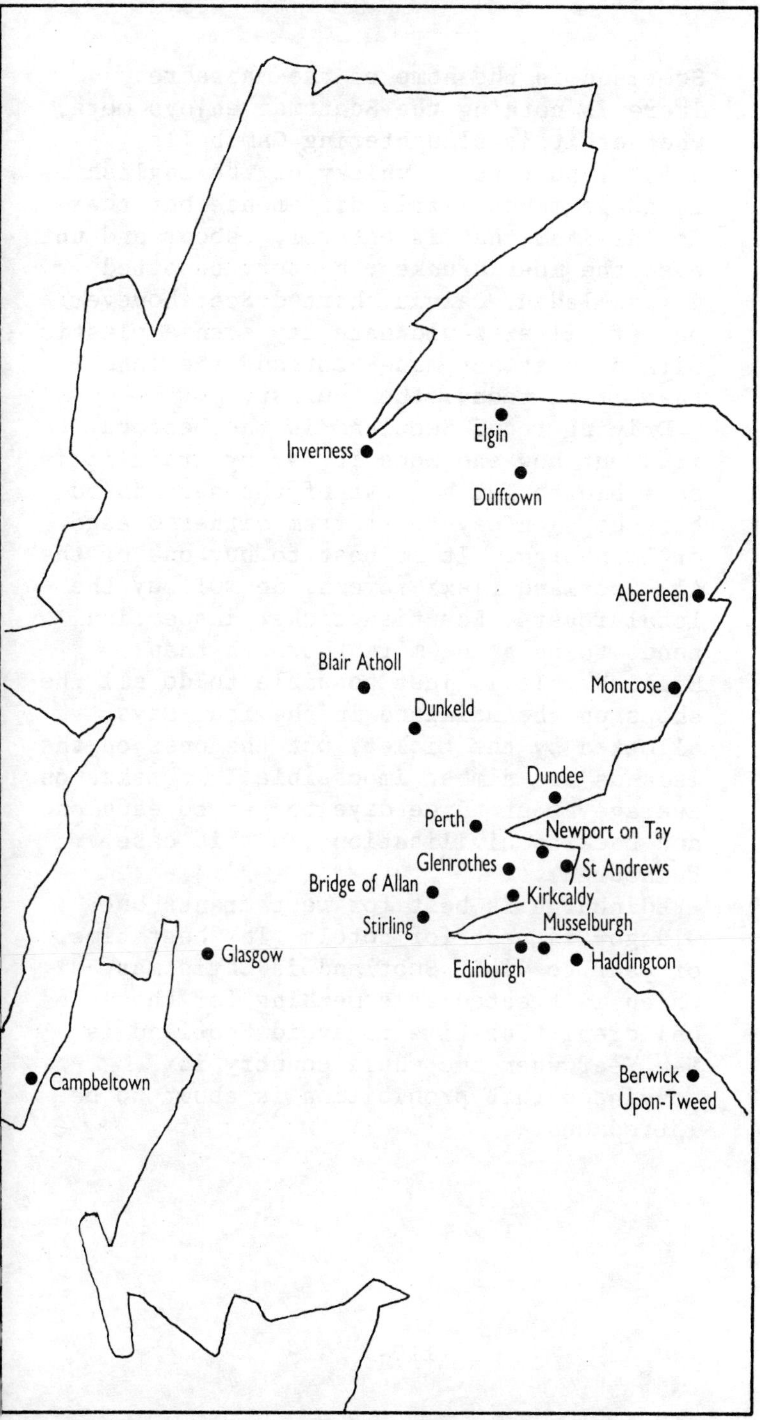
Elgin
Inverness
Dufftown
Aberdeen
Blair Atholl
Montrose
Dunkeld
Dundee
Perth
Newport on Tay
Glenrothes
St Andrews
Bridge of Allan
Kirkcaldy
Stirling
Musselburgh
Glasgow
Edinburgh
Haddington
Campbeltown
Berwick
Upon-Tweed

Scotland is the home of the massacre. There is nothing the Scotsman enjoys more, whether it is slaughtering Campbells, grouse, bottles of whisky or the English language makes little difference but there is one item that is entirely taboo, and not even the most drunken, history besotted, grouse laden, Calvin skirted Scot however out of kilter would dare lay even a plastic dirk on what has made Scotland the land that it is today: the tourist.

Driving round Scotland is the best way to find out how enormous it is, by train it is possible to get to most of the secondhand bookshops on day tours from either Glasgow or Edinburgh. It is best to buy one of the All Scotland flexi rovers, do NOT buy the local rovers, Scottish ticket inspection tends to be a lot more thorough than English. It is just possible to do all the shops on the mainland in the four days allotted by the ticket, but the ones on the islands are almost impossible. It takes on average about three days to get to each one and back to civilisation (in this case, Edinburgh).

Edinburgh is best for restaurants but Glasgow is best for hotels The best time of year to visit Scotland is Christmas which is treated as something for the children. The time to avoid Scotland is New Year when the whole country is convinced that prohibition is about to be introduced.

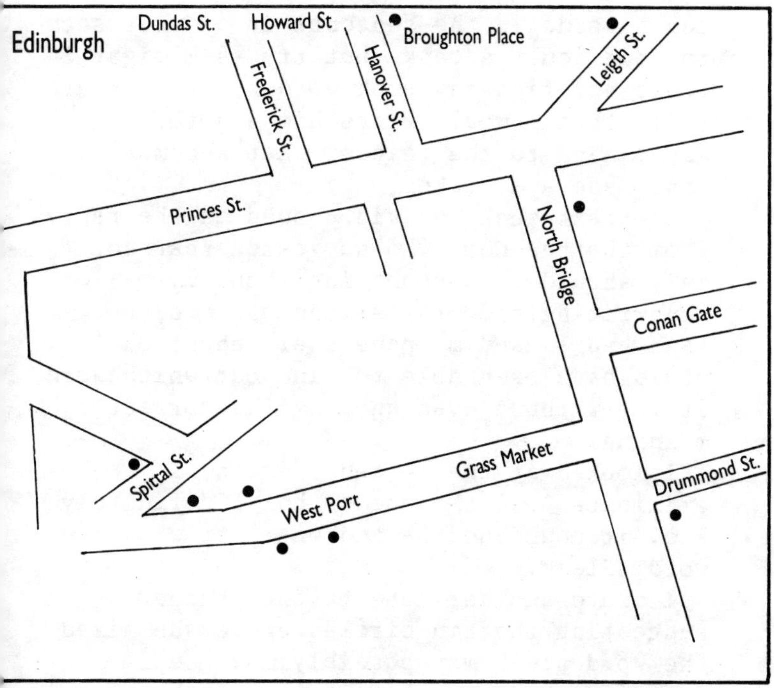

EDINBURGH

SLEEK CITY

I used to have a job as a baby sitter - well you didn't think I earned enough money as a bookdealer did you? One evening the brother of the child I was supposed to be looking after, a child who thought Just William was a wimp, asked me if I would help him with his homework there was one question which the teacher had set him again and again which was that he had to find a word in a sentence that meant self satisfied or smug. As there were only seven words in the sentence it did not seem too difficult a task, but try as I might I could not find any such word. I told that child that I would write him a note, explaining to the teacher that she must have made a mistake.

The next week the kid showed me the reply from the teacher, who suggested that not only should I do something about my handwriting and grammar and manners, but that had I used my powers of deduction I would have been able to find out which word it was without even knowing the correct meaning.

I looked at the sentence again, I eliminated all the words that I definitely knew it could not be and was left with one word: Sleek.

I wrote another note to the teacher suggesting that in circles where she mixed the word sleek may possibly mean self satisfied and smug but it is not the way we would use the word in deepest Brixton and I described the teacher, to the child, in words that elevated me to a position just slightly higher than that of Just William.

I wish to apologise to that teacher, for I have now found a place to which that word is highly applicable. Edinburgh is indeed a sleek city.

I still have not found out what they do in the mornings in Edinburgh, but it has been suggested to me that if the Betty Ford Clinic wished to open an European then Edinburgh would be a good place.

If you arrive on the overnight train, which is definitely the most romantic way, then the first shop to visit is Thin's, where the secondhand stock somewhat resembles the name, but no one could describe its opening hours as being anorexic. For this alone it deserves pride of place in the Edinburgh bookshops it is open at 9am and does not close until 10pm. It is a bit of a pity that other shops in Edinburgh seem to feel that 12noon till 6pm counts as full time. For those of us used to southern ways it is simply a long lunch.

Around the corner in Drummond Street GT is a semi remainder shop, but once again, it has the great advantage that it is open. The owner of the place does not exactly look like he is a member of the band of hope, mind you some of the books seem the worse for wear. The bookshops in Westport should suffer from Bulima: Several other Scots have expressed this opinion in more figurative terms than I am capable of describing, but if you are lacking the wherewithal I would humbly suggest that you try any of the eateries around here. One bookshop in particular (Grant & Shaw) deserves the Princess Di award for being both vomit making and attractive at the same time.

What is the point of having a bookshop that does not open? By having a shop which is only open when the owner feels like it you are using up the worlds stock of good will. Book collectors are addicts and if they do not get their fix on time they suffer withdrawal symptoms. By having a completely cavalier approach to opening times you are ensuring that as many collectors are deprived as possible, it is worse than not being there at all. The idea that customers are supposed to come back at a more convenient time is nonsense.

Why open a secondhand bookshop in one of the tourist streets of Edinburgh? I have attempted to get into Grant & Shaw several times and not once have the owners and I managed to be in the same place at the same time. It is somehow typical of the arrogance of the Edinbuggers that they are convinced that all the right people will come back.

Mr Peter Bell at least has the decency to put up notices saying when he will be there, but is far more reliable. The books tend to be somewhat academic, but at least the hours aren't.

Armchair Books is the first one to seriously visit in that it opens at ten thirty, and it genuinely resembles a proper bookshop. The books are not as high key as Bell or Grant & Shaw, but it is open, it is also much more pleasant to be in, and you get the distinct feeling that there are going to be some bargains, despite this last belief never having been proven right.

Old Grindles on the corner of Spittal Street has far more sensible opening hours 9 - 9 which is almost the perfect time for a bookshop to be open. The map you would have to draw of Edinburgh to get round the shops in a sensible order is so bizarre that not even I can be bothered to draw it.

The shops in Grassmarket and Conangate towards Holyrood House are so unexciting that it is better to go to the North side of Edinburgh not because they are open any earlier but at least they are interesting.

In Dundas Street the bookfairy Mr Pringle counts himself as a bookshop, but I'm not sure if I do. You have to go in for the use of the bell and he goes to lunch, the

Dundas Bookshop further down the street is far less problematical. The Broughton Bookshop has improved with the moving of the premises to Broughton Place.

By far the most interesting shop in Edinburgh is Second Edition in Howard Place. It too suffers from am tension, but you do feel that the wait is worthwhile, the books have been chosen with extreme care, the prices cannot be described as being on the low side.

There is an unvisited shop in Haddington, which has recently changed hands and there is a bike shop in Berwick which has books but not worth cycling all that way for. This should not be confused with Berwick upon Tweed which is on the border towards Newcastle where the shop is nearly into England, nearly interesting and nearly affordable. The Latto Bookshop in Musselburgh goes in for the Scottish Weekend, Wednesday to Saturday. There is also a rumour of a shop in Hawick, but I am not exactly certain of where that is. Far better than going south is to go north to Saint Andrews. On the way it is possible to visit Glenrothes which has a newly opened low key shop which is so cold it is almost a drif special, and Kirkcaldy where the books are about as far from mainstream as it is from the High Street.

LEUCHARS AIDE

If you travel by train to St Andrew's you have to alight at Leuchars and then get a bus or a taxi into the town which is five miles away, the taxis charge £15 for this trip, however if you go and stand at the bus stop they come along and offer their services at a reduced rate.

The four secondhand bookshops in St Andrew's are worth a visit as long as you can tolerate Americans on their four A's Teeth a glow, voice a pierce, enthusiasm a gush, platitude abound: If you need some solid culture it is best to go to Mair Wilkes in Newport on Tay just south of Dundee, which specialises in books on Psychiatry and Scottish History. It is not strictly a bookshop but they are so knowledgable and pleasant that it is well worth visiting and I always enjoy perusing the books on psychiatry.

When I was a kid my mother was always threatening to have me put away in a loony bin, I was very scared of this because I had no idea of what a looney bin was actually like. The only one I had ever seen was a prison like a gothic monstrosity which looked like it could offend more than good taste.

One day much to my horror she told me she had actually made an appointment, but other than running away from home, again, there was very little I could do to avoid it.

The day came, and my trepidation was increased when my mother made me have a bath. The journey was conducted in complete silence. The place was surrounded by a wall that defied scaling, and even more deeply unsettling was the extremely neat flowerbeds, something I have since learnt which is the hallmark of the authoritarians worldwide.

As we walked up to the buildings I could hear the screams of a lunatic, but even more unsettling was that nobody seemed to take any notice, people just stood around discussing flowers.

We were soon called in to see the doctor who asked me lots of strange questions which I could not even begin to answer. He then asked me if I would like to wait outside. I did so. After a few minutes I heard raised voices, and then the doctor came out and said,

"We are going to be keeping your mother in, you will have to go home on your own".

I have had a lot of time for psychiatry ever since.

Aberdeen now has five shops which makes it worth a detour not least for the fact that it is such a different city to anywhere else in Britain, the books are not too great, indeed the whole place could be described as a drif special, but it does contain hope.

Hope is the one quality that a secondhand bookshop cannot do without. It is more important than the actual books. What you need to visit a bookshop is the belief that there is a possibility that the bookshop may have what you are looking for. No secondhand bookshop is ever going to have all the books that everybody is looking for at a price they are willing to pay, but if it can persuade a potential customer that

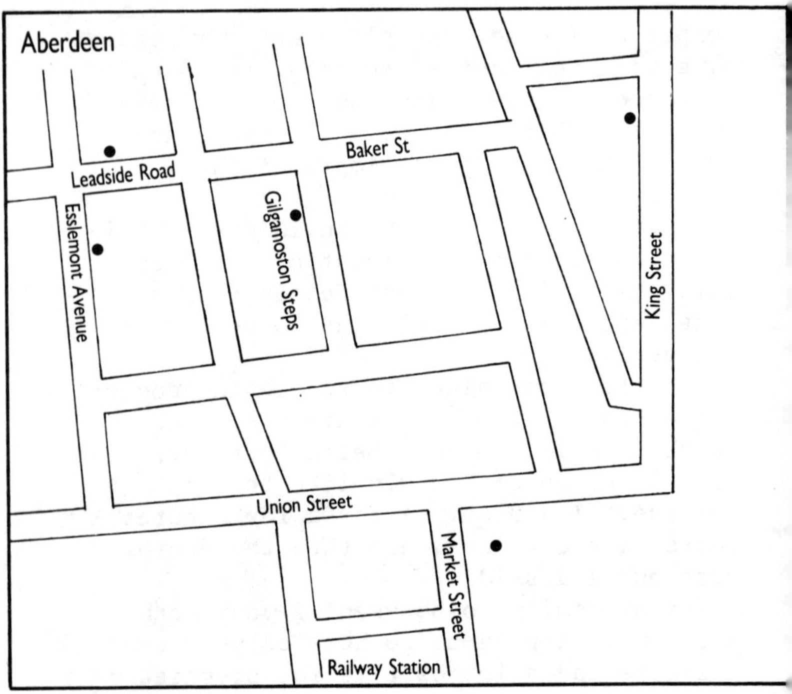

there is a possibility if s/he comes again that there might be a chance then the bookshop has succeeded. This is why it is that all unvisited bookshops are so tempting; you have not been disappointed by them yet. This is why it is an appalling abuse that places open as secondhand bookshops and do not have hours long enough that nobody other than the local burglar can get in.

Aberdeen is where you face a slight problem, the nearest bookshop is in Dufftown. Duff it ain't, but expensive it is. It is quite an interesting bookshop but they charge a lot more than the Charing Cross Road. Somehow there is a psychological feeling that bookshops in the middle of nowhere should charge a lot less than those in the centre of London. The books are not of a high enough calibre to make the trek worthwhile, nor is it easy to get to either by car or train. The shop in Elgin is now closed. If you are crossing to Inverness by car it is worthwhile going to this shop, but by train it is really a no hoper. If you are going to Inverness by train it is better to go via Perth.

The Inverness Bookshop overlooks the River Ness across which there is a footbridge. This bridge does not seem particularly impressive from the riverbank but as you step on to it it is like hearing a fairy story, a sense of wonder begins a spell. Outwardly it seems to be made of the same steel and wood as other bridges, but somehow ordinary materials have been made into something quite extraordinary and as you gain the middle of the bridge there is a wonderful bounce, echoes of the British Cavalry having to break step come to mind, but the planks on which this bridge are built thrive on bounce. They seem to be commuicating a message that they are proud to be where and what they are. This bridge is constructed with an economy that belies its strength. It is poetry cast in steel. It is an essay in what can be done with imagination. This is not a bridge along the lines of the Forth or the Humber or San Francisco but it is in many ways far superior to them. It is but a footbridge, and few people will make the trek to see it alone, but so rare is this simple but exquisite sight that it is an experience that will not be forgotten and yet it is much more, it is a work of art... It has majesty. It has not survived without the aid of much cash and effort but it is a worthwhile subsidy. There is another crossing of the river within sight which does the same job, but somehow it lacks everything that this bridge had. It is not the bridge itself that is so wonderful, for after all what is it other than a simple river crossing. What gives it life and denotes it as something special is that it has surpassed the mere materials from which it was made. In many ways it is similar to the Inverness Bookshop.

GLASGOW

QUELLE TIC & R'ANGERS

Glasgow looks like Gotham City with Leprosy. It smells like catfood diluted with vintage urine, it sounds like Billy Graham being sodomised. It has taste the same way as Barbara Cartland; in moderation. I like it.

The best shop for Dealers and serious Collectors is Cooper Hay which looks like the set for a Channel Four film about an Art Deco detective... the books are chosen with more taste than Le Corbusier could mange. It has prices that would make Mrs Thatcher feel proud. It has more interests than the Mafia.

The best bookshop for Collectors and Readers is the Caledonia Bookshop in Great Western Road. It has more variety than a music hall, more good works than the Salvation Army, the customers tend to raise the ire a bit mainly because they seem to think of bookshops as being a cross between a betting shop and pawn brokers.

On the south side of the city Adams books is worth the journey. The other shops in central Glasgow are alright if you have a long time but not much hope if you are in a rush. In the directory part of this book Glasgow and Paisley are listed together, with Greenock and Helensburgh under separate alphabetical listing, this guide though is based on a geographical encompassing, and on the type of customers that all these shops have in common.

I had come out of McClarens in Helensburgh feeling very pleased, as I had just bought a golf book which although I had no idea

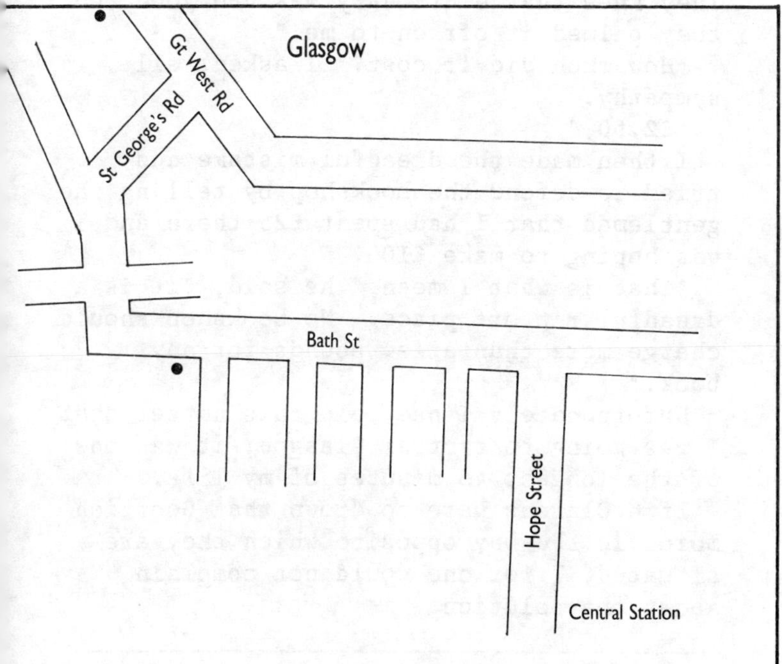

how much I was likely to get for it, I was fairly sure it would be five or six times what I had paid, which was £25.00. On the train on the way back to central Glasgow (a forty five minute journey) a gentleman opposite me asked where I had bought the book, I told him. He then asked how much I had paid for it, I told him.

"I always knew they were robbers in that shop", he said.

Always keen to hear scandal of any kind I asked for more details.

"I went into that bookshop once...(he said it as if wild horses would not drag him back in again)... and they sold me a dictionary. The very first time I used it, it didnae have the word I was looking for. They knew that dictionary was nae good and they palmed it off on to me."

"How much did it cost?" I asked, all sympathy.

"£2.50."

I then made the dreadful mistake and tried to defend the bookshop by telling the gentleman that I had spent £25 there and I was hoping to make £100.

"That is what I mean," he said, "it is a dreadful rip off place. No bookshop should charge more than a few pounds for any book."

Unfortunately I had told this nutter that I was going to central Glasgow; it was one of the longest 45 minutes of my life.

If McClarens were to drown that Scottish moron in the bay opposite which they are situated, I for one would not complain about the polution.

There are two other lesser shops in Inverness and there is a bookshop in Dingwall north of Inverness which I had assumed was closed, but is not. There are bookshops on the islands of Orkney, the Hebrides, Iona and the Isle of Lewis, however the logistics and cost of getting to these solely for the bookshops is somewhat prohibitive (considering most of these are officially only open during the Scottish summer months). I did try at Christmas time and failed completely. The weather was so bad that there were no sailings to any of them. But to solve this problem I have enrolled in a course in sailing and I shall be visiting them all in the summer, including an alleged shop in Campbeltown which even though it is close to Glasgow as the crow flies is a swine of a place to get to by road.

Travelling south from Inverness it is worthwhile stopping at Blair Atholl and Dunkeld especially during the summer when both these establishments go in for sensible opening hours (i.e. Sundays). The two shops in Perth tend to have somewhat more restrained opening times and are only worth going to if you have to pass through the place. It is however worth trying the Bridge of Allen Bookshop which occasionally opens on a Sunday and is more interesting than the name might suggest.

It is also more than worthwhile stopping off at the Stirling Bookshop on the way to Glasgow.

I keep hearing that there is a secondhand bookshop in Kelso, but I also keep hearing that it has closed down. The gentleman who runs GT books in Edinburgh did briefly open up a shop there but he has also told me that he had to close it because 'it was like trying to sell dentures to sharks'. However other people claim that there is a secondhand bookshop. Given how difficult it is to get to Kelso I shall carry on believing that there is not, even in the teeth of the evidence.

WALES

LAND OF OUR FURTHEST WHOLELY LAND

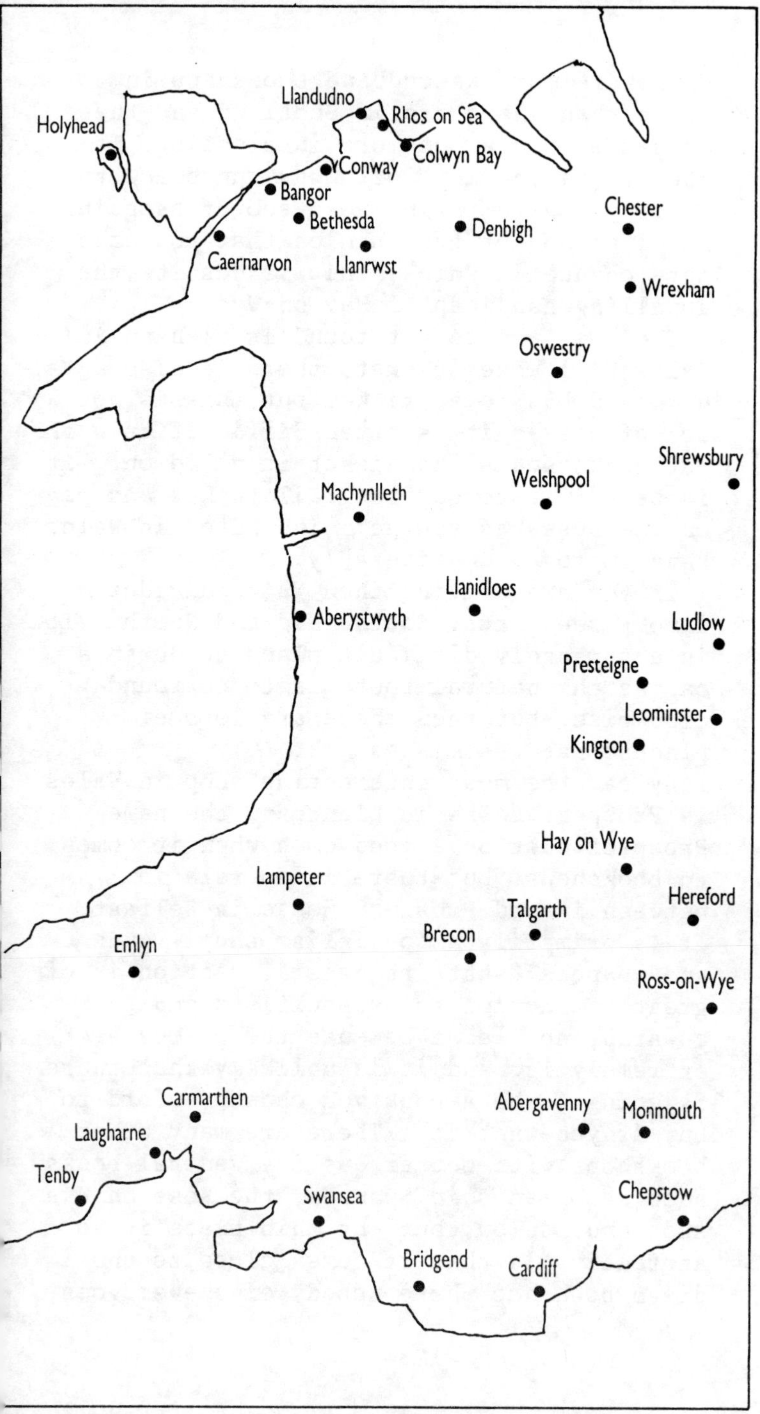
Holyhead
Llandudno
Rhos on Sea
Colwyn Bay
Conway
Bangor
Bethesda
Caernarvon
Llanrwst
Denbigh
Chester
Wrexham
Oswestry
Shrewsbury
Welshpool
Machynlleth
Llanidloes
Aberystwyth
Ludlow
Presteigne
Leominster
Kington
Hay on Wye
Lampeter
Hereford
Talgarth
Brecon
Emlyn
Ross-on-Wye
Carmarthen
Abergavenny
Monmouth
Laugharne
Tenby
Swansea
Chepstow
Bridgend
Cardiff

There are more secondhand bookshops in Wales than there are in Scotland and these days they are a lot more interesting. It used to be the icy north was the place to go if you were trying to discover bargains but I am now of the opinion that you stand more chance in Wales, this is despite the appalling handicap of Hay on Wye.

The best way to get round is with an All Wales Rail Rover ticket, there is also a combined bus rover ticket but this is not a lot of use as it is often difficult to work out which buses the ticket is valid on. It is best just to buy the rail ticket and pay on the buses as you go. The buses in Wales have improved considerably.

If you are driving then Wales divides into three parts: South, Mid and North. It is a strangely difficult place to do in a car as the natural route is to go round clockwise, but then there are lots of places that get missed out.

By far the most interesting shop in Wales is Prospect Books in Llanrwst, the name Prospect must be a good omen when it comes to bookshops, but there is no relation between it and Prospect House in Belfast. It is primarily a specialist shop - guns and weapons - but its general section is of great attraction to us pacifists and cowards, not least because the prices are extremely low and it is unlikely that there is going to be a book you cannot afford to buy if you want it. There are many other bookshops with better quality general books such as Dylan's in Swansea, the Ross on Wye shop and Ludlow, but why this place is so attractive is that it comes close to the dream bookshop where nobody else ever goes, it is not exactly easy to get to, you have to change at Llandudno Junction and the trains are not over frequent but it is almost on a natural route that leads to Blaenau Ffestinog where there is a Welsh language shop which has cheap English books and I am unreliably informed that there is a second bookshop in BF.

The best place to base yourself for North Wales is Chester, primarily because of the restaurants which far excel anything anywhere else in Wales. My favourite is the Abbey Walls, which is egregiously expensive and unlike any other veggie I have seen in that it has extremely good service.

Crewe is more strategically placed than Chester but the fish and chip shop by the station, its one culinary delight, does not manage to compete with anything Chester has to offer and the hotels are so bad that I preferred sleeping on Crewe station. The hotels in Chester tend to be expensive vis a vis those of The North Wales coast, but the advantage of Chester is that you can go East, North, South and West all in one day and return.

Chester's secondhand bookshops are nowhere near as high key as the location, but is a major contestant in the POCS contest. It is however an easy place to walk round and to get to by train.

The bookshop that is almost worth avoiding is Bookleafs in Saltney on the outskirts of Chester. They seem to feel that everyone who goes in a secondhand bookshop is a mug and likely to pay their prices without quibbling.

The two shops in Colwyn Bay if linked

with the shop in Rhos Point distinctly have the feel that they could be worthwhile as does the shop in Conway, which is best approached from Llandudno Junction rather than from Conway (where British Frail only stops to demolish the odd castle).

Well worth avoiding is the Llandudno Bookshop which is a follower of the James Joyce school of literature (I am an artist, you do all the work and I get all the money). It is because this shop is so nearly interesting that it is so irritating. The books are indeed well chosen but they are arranged so that you have to devote a lifetime to studying them. To add physical insult to mental injury the shop has the secondhand bookshop world's most irritating habit: lunch.

The owner does not seem to get any pleasure out of announcing that this shop is now closed. Something which happens with more frequency in this shop than any other in Britain. It is such a regular event for him that it has lost all its joy. Perhaps if he hired a lady from a charity shop she would do it with more elan. Where the other shops in this part of the world are accommodating to tourists (the one in Conway opens on a Sunday and the one in Rhos Point in the evenings), this one behaves as if it were a part of the sons of Glendower intent on preserving the Welsh spirit of bloody mindedness... I meet worms of bookdealers who claim that I have it very wrong about this shop, that there are many bargains to be had, that the owner is very polite and knowledgable, and that there is system to the books i.e. the interesting ones (to Dealers) are all on the ground floor or near the desk. I would be happy to concur in this belief if only I could get into this shop. If, as I recommend, you stay in Chester then by the time you have got to Llandudno this shop is ready to announce it is closing for lunch. If you stay in a hotel in Llandudno (a major contestant in the cheapest hotels in Britain contest) then you have to wait until 10.30 for it to open. This I maintain is cruelty to dumb book collectors. Those of us whose job it is to eat worms do not complain about getting up early, but we do, justifiably I feel, complain about the worms not poking their heads out.

The shop in Bangor has improved and now makes it worthwhile going in this direction, from there it is best to head south to Machynlleth (pronounced Mahunlith) from there to Aberystwyth, where I have allegedly missed one low key shop. It is in Aber (as those of us who cannot cope with Welsh names call it) that the problems of getting round Wales begin. By train you can only go east, but by car it is best to go south to Carmarthen, Swansea and Cardiff. From then it is best to go to Abergevenny and Ross on Wye.

In this part of the world there is a great whirlpool which seasoned navigators attempt to avoid by carrying on via Herefore to Ludlow and Shrewsbury, but such is its fame that despite multifarious warnings it swallows several victims every year. It survives on a diet of hot air and innocent sprats.

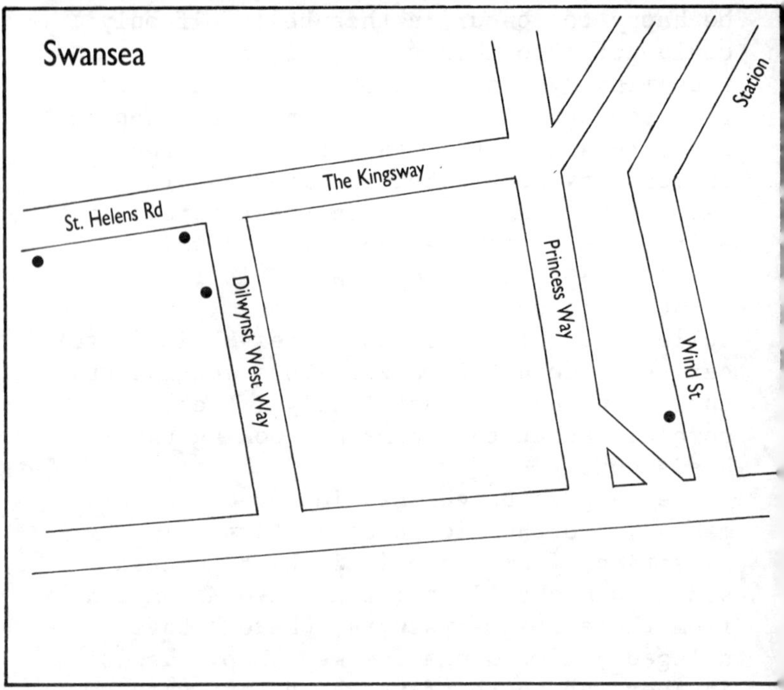

HAY ON WYE

THE TRIUMPH OF HYPE OVER EXPERIENCE

The worst bores are the ones who nearly have something interesting to say, a close second are the ones who whilst you are standing there, glazed out of your mind, launch into a sub plot before you realise what has happened and you then have to wait for them to finish that before they can get back to the main plot and finish boring you properly.

They are closely followed by the ones who disagree with you when you describe something as being boring.

Most people would not raise an eyelid if you described a book as being boring, after all it is possible to make the most interesting seeming subject deadly by writing about it for too long, but if you described a secondhand bookshop as being boring then many people would beg to differ.

For how can it be that a place which contains on average 5,000 books, each of which must have been of interest to at least one person - the author - and have been bought by one other - usually the author's mother - how can it be that at least 10,000 votes of interest can be so casually dismissed.

And what would the average reasonable person think of somebody who declared an entire town of secondhand books to be one of the most boring places ever created. A place which claims to have over one million secondhand books - and presumably two million votes of interest - how could any reasonable person dismiss it as being "boring".

Well I will not bore you any longer: I'm your man. Hay on Wye is a boring drump: It is the boring dump of boring dumps: It is the Everest, the Niagara, the Gobi and the Tierra del Fuego of Dumps. If T S Eliot had lived nowadays he would not had to have written The Wasteland: Instead he could have published a guide to Hay on Wye.

The Bible was the first book ever printed (I will not bore you with all the caveats), I would not be surprised to hear that there are more copies of it than any other book in the world, but the number of people who are interested in buying bibles is diminishing every day. How I know this is that I collect a particular type of bible, quite simply because they are one of the cheapest books to buy. If bibles were popular then the price would increase to a level at which I would be too mean to pay. The fastest way to depress a bookseller is to tell him you have a bok to sell: this raises his spirits and then you can terminally depress him by saying it is a bible. There are many people who collect bibles but the number who actually read them does seem to be declining. Indeed I do not think I know anybody who has actually read it all the way through. This may well be a reflection on the ignorant people with whom I associate, but I like to believe that it is an indication that they have more interesting things to do.

There is one book that prisoners sentenced to solitary confinement always ask for: it is the Bible. The reason they choose this above all other tomes is that it is the only book to which they are legally entitled. They ask for it not to read it, but so that they will have something in which to roll their cigarettes. Bibles often come made of India paper and this is good for the purpose. The prisoners are in no danger of being discovered because the warders seldom read books of any kind. Occasionally prisoners succumb to the boredom and they begin to read the good book and this explains why so many prisoners become Born Again Christians. Not through real choice but lack of opportunity to become anything else.

They have the books but there is no differentiation between any of them, they are wonderful until you start reading them and then you discover that they are only good for burning. This then is level one of boredom. **The good book as fag paper.**

Nobody can maintain an interest in any single subject for more than twenty minutes. For people who do not regularly go into secondhand bookshops the whole place is a single subject. Those people who go in frequently are able to divide the place into different subjects, they look at the Art books for fifteen minutes and then they change to History. They are dividing the stock into two interests. This amount of time interest applies to any subject whatsoever. If I began to lecture you on the relevance of epaulettes as virility symbols then I would maintain your interest for twenty minutes unless you were interested in the psychology of fashion, for the ordinary person, most of whom never go in secondhand bookshops, all books are of equal interest, after twenty minutes terminal boredom sets in.

The editors of The Reader's Digest condensed books know this, that is why they try to make the chapters shorter and have a change of focus every twenty minutes of reading time. It makes no difference what books you have in a secondhand bookshop you are only going to be able to interest most people for twenty minutes, after that you are boring them to death: This then is the second level of boredom THE READER'S DIE GEST.

The fastest way to bore a collector is to have all the books they want at prices they know they can never afford. The essence of collecting of any kind is finding the objects at prices you can afford, or even more tantalisingly at prices you can nearly afford. It is a paradox that if the books were affordable they would not be there because somebody would have bought them, but it is also possible to price something in such a way that the collector is actively deterred by even attempting to look further at those books, which are only available by gross over pricing. This is usually done in ignorance. The knowledgable dealer does indeed try for higher prices all the time but he knows what the average price level is. Thus, if a book has been sold previously for £25 he may attempt to ask £30 for it. What is upsetting to the collector is when some ignoramus asks £75 for a book, showing that he is completely ignorant of the average price level. It is also true that a dealer will examine the ignoramus' stock carefully because ignorance works both ways: those people who grossly overprice books are often the same ones who underprice them. The primary joy of collecting is the hunt. Collecting of all kinds is simply Big Game hunting by other means. If you could go into a bookshop and buy all the books you were looking for at one fell swoop there would be absolutely no fun in it, this is why all collectors rise to the level they can nearly afford. Thus millionaires collect Impressionist paintings because that is the level they can sometimes buy at, and people on social security collect comics because that is the level they can nearly afford. In the days when impressionist paintings were the price of comics no millionaire would ever have purchased one. Thus it is possible to bore with the price. Even when the price is right it is possible to bore collectors by making the effort involved far too difficult, or expensive...

In London there is a gentleman who collects old Tram tickets, he haunts the secondhand bookshops looking for tram tickets that have been used as bookmarkers. He does not buy the book if it has a tram ticket but simply removes and ticket and adds it to his already extensive, but by no means expensive, collection. This innocuous pursuit would not be irritating were it not for the gentleman's personal habits. Not content with liberating the tickets he enquires of the bookshops if they have bought any interesting books recently - interesting in this sense means ones with tram tickets - he further expects bookshop owners to remove the tickets from books and save them for him. The notion that he might make some trifling contribution to the provision of this service does not occur to him. Indeed should you suggtest that the tram ticket has a market price he becomes quite irritated and replies that it only has such because he has created the whole subsection of tram ticket collecting and further that he is performing a service by telling you of the rarity of particular tram tickets as he stashes them away in his wallet.

That you are not interested in hearing the history of tram tickets does not deter him. That you have informed him, as I have, that if you saw a tram ticket in a book you would take particular pleasure in burning it seems to encourage him to ask if you could make a note of which tram ticket it was that was burnt.

One day whilst I was trying to extract £120 out of a collector for a particular book, he came into the premises I was using at the time, and with that air of eternal optimism with which the true collector is always recognised he asked if the book had any tram tickets in it.

I informed him that this book was almost unique, that the basement of the shop from which I had purchased it seemed to contain nothing but books with tram tickets in them. That there had been more tram tickets than I knew existed in the world. That I would have brought all the tram tickets I could have managed had I been able to carry them, but that because of my ignorance of tram tickets which I hastened to add, he could in no way be held responsible for I did not know which were the valuable tram tickets and thus had left them so that he could enjoy the pleasure of getting them himself. He asked me where I had seen these tram tickets. I informed him that I was not certain of the exact shop but that it had been one of the ones in Hay on Wye.

"I could not go that far for a tram ticket!"

I truly wish I could have emulated the venom he put into that phrase 'tram ticket'.

I could also see that I had presented him with a serious dilemma, after what was the longest period I had ever seen him keep his mouth shut, about two and a half seconds, he said:

"Promise you won't tell anybody about this," as he furtively produced a list from inside his cavernous raincoat, "but these are the tram tickets I am seriously looking for, were any of the ticket in Hay on Wye on this list?"

I studied the list carefully, and informed him that I could not be 100% certain but I had a vague feeling that the tram tickets on his list and the ones in Hay on Wye were almost identical. Even before I had finished telling this lie I regretted it for he seemed about to keel over with shock.

"I wish you had not told me that," he said, "you realise that I cannot possibly go and get those tickets."

"Why ever not?"

"Well if I had the complete set of tram tickets it would disappoint all the bookshop owners in London who collect them for me. I am certain that for some of them it is the only thing that keeps them happy."

This then is the third level of boredom: THE ANAL LIST.

To a dealer the number of copies of a particular item is no deterrence, indeed s/he is likely to be particularly grateful if there are multiple copies. An experienced dealer will know that it is unlikely to effect the genuine scarcity of the book overall. Overpricing does not bore dealers, because it only means ignorance and then it is worthwhile wading through the stock. What bores bookdealers is seeing the same books time and time again, but even these books can be used as an indicator of ignorance. What really bores dealers, even me, is having to spend all day not buying a book. It is true that the more professional the dealer, the less the number of books they buy, but the dealer who buys no books whatsoever is never going to make any money whatsoever. Thus to bore a dealer two types of irritant are needed: Firstly that the shop should be impossible to get into either because it is miles from anywhere or not on any natural route; and secondly that the chance of buying a book on which you can make a serious profit is somewhere between slim and negligible. Dealers even more than collectors live in hope, primarily because they are disappointed so often. They only give up on a place when it has disappointed them time and time again and again, until it has reached an almost mystical level of te dium.

Hay on Wye is unique in Britain, and possibly the world, it is the repository of repositories of the good book as fag paper. It is the grave yard of grave yards of The Readers Die Gest, it is the cess pit of cess pits for the anal list, but above all it is the Te dium of Te diums, for dealers.

- **DO YOU** have the eye for the great works of English Literature? The ones that nobody ever reads other than for University Courses or Quiz Shows?
- **COULD YOU** find a place in your heart, and our library, for the books that nobody else is ever likely to want?
- **IS YOUR** taste so excruciatingly good that nobody else ever agrees with it?
- **DO YOU** have the ability to make even interesting books tedious?

IF THE ANSWER TO ALL THESE QUESTIONS IS YES, THEN YOU COULD BE THE PERSON WE ARE LOOKING FOR.

We would expect you either to be a provincial secondhand bookshop owner with about as much interest in other peoples' opinions as Saddam Hussein, or more extreme still, a member of the PBFA obsessed with the one part of a book that the author had nothing to do with - the dustwrapper.

The job we offer entails working with the highest classes of society, the ones who never read books. The books they are looking for are the ones you see people photographed against in the pages of financial magazines, shortly before they are arrested for fraud. They are the ones that nobody has ever read, but that journalists defend to the death in the hope that they too will have similar sales one day.

If you qualify, send a Curriculum Vitae and mark the envelope: CLOTT. (Candidate Librarian on The Titanic).

E N G L A N D

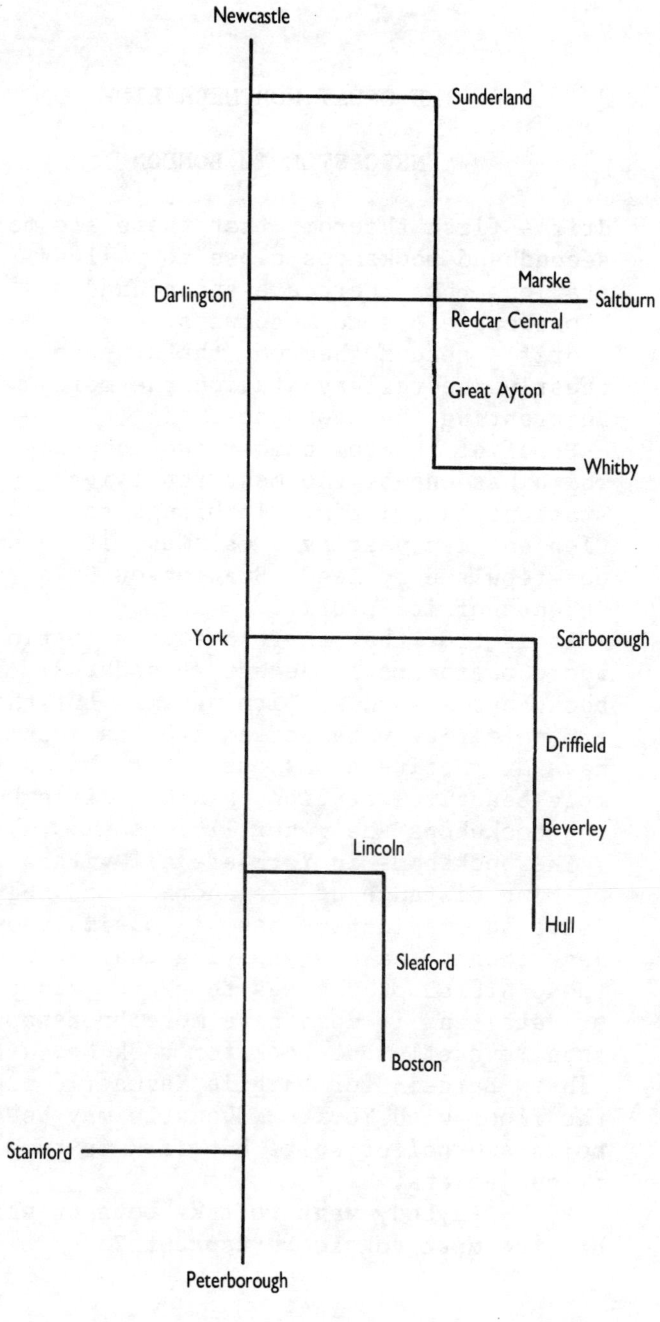
Newcastle
Sunderland
Marske
Darlington
Saltburn
Redcar Central
Great Ayton
Whitby
York
Scarborough
Driffield
Beverley
Lincoln
Hull
Sleaford
Boston
Stamford
Peterborough

THE GREAT NORTHERN LINE

NEWCASTLE TO LONDON

drif's first theorom, that there are more secondhand bookshops close to railway stations than there are secondhand bookshops close to motorways.

drif's second theorom, that the more ghastly the railway station the more interesting the bookshops.

Proof of theorom number two is Newcastle which has one of the most repulsive stations in Britain. It brings to mind the Elephant Man wearing a walkman, it is only out-repulsed by Leeds Station or BT's defence of its profits.

It is true that there are ugly stations where there are no decent secondhand bookshops - such as Birmingham - but there are no cities with attractive stations that have attractive bookshops. York has a far more beautiful station than Newcastle but the bookshops are generally dismal.

The bookshops in York are all within walking distance of one another and they issue an imaginative map (it claims they have twenty dealers implying that most of these are shops whereas they are mainly private) and it does have more bookshops than Newcastle but book for book Newcastle wins. Bargain for bargain Newcastle wipes the floor with York. Newcastle may be boils and boiler suits but York is twee and tweed jackets.

RC: "Anybody want to take bets on which has the most veggie restaurants?"

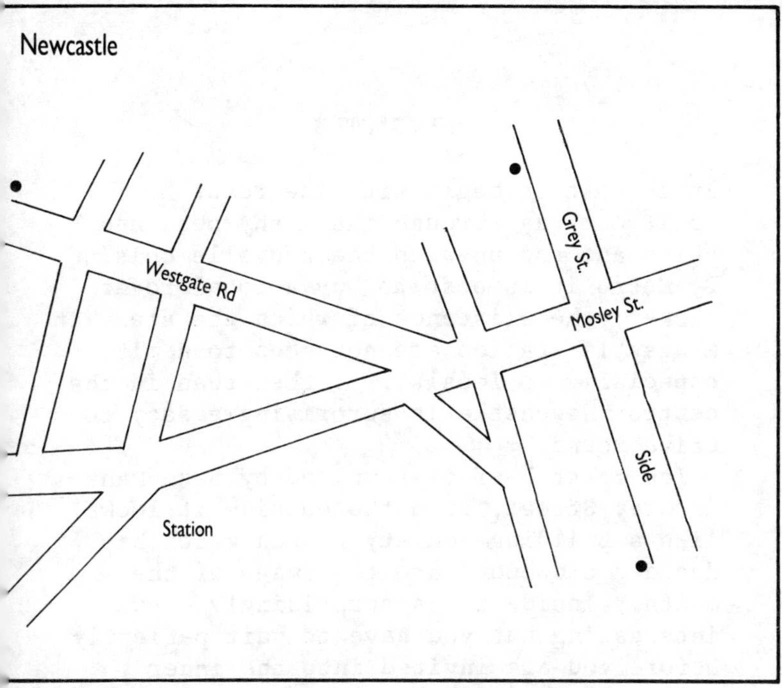
Newcastle
Westgate Rd
Grey St.
Mosley St.
Side
Station

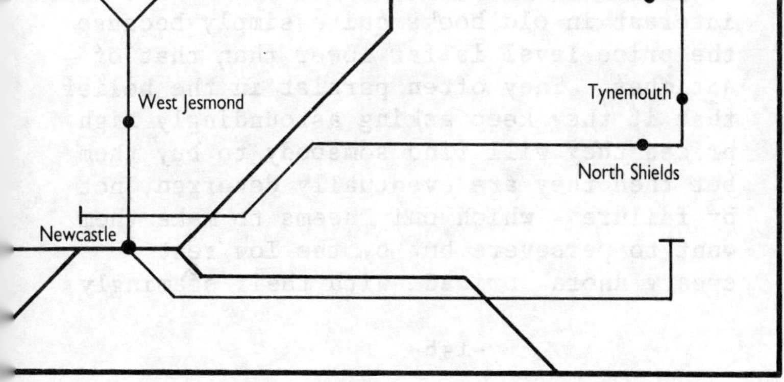
Newcastle
Whitley Bay
Tynemouth
North Shields
West Jesmond
Newcastle

NEWCASTLE

It is best to begin with the roast beef, work your way through the mushy peas and chips and end up with the nouvelle cuisine. By Metro it is best to buy a local rover ticket, the existence of which the staff at Newcastle station are not keen to admit, especially to locals... Other than in the centre, Newcastle is surprisingly easy to drive round.

The roast beef is supplied by Steedmans in Grey Street, from the outside it looks like a Building Society branch which has decided old books are the image of the month. Inside it is surprisingly interesting but you have to wait patiently before you are invited into the inner sanctum. Some of the books merit it, but alas they do not provide mortgages.

From Steedmans you can either go to Davis's in Westgate Road, which is mainly new books and remainders can be worthwhile, or more profitably to:

Berwick Books in Jesmond which is an antique shop with a far better than average stock of secondhand books for an antique shop. Antique dealers usually lose interest in old books quite simply because the price level is far lower than that of antiques. They often persist in the belief that if they keep asking astoundingly high prices they will find somebody to buy them but then they are eventually deterred, not by failure - which only seems to make them want to persevere but by the low rent sweaty anorak brigade with their seemingly inane enquiries as to whether they have a first edition of 'On The Road'. It completely confuses their rationale to discover that a modern book can be worth more than £100.

From Berwick it is best to go round to Olivers in Whitley Bay, you can also get off the metro at Monkseaton where there is a small but interesting record and bookshop, and then walk to Olivers. Monkseaton and Whitley Bay are essentially one and the same place, but the natives behave as if they are not only miles apart but have nothing to do with Newcastle. I treat anywhere that is on the metro as being Newcastle: officially it has some bizarre name like Tyne and Wear (they didn't dare call it wash 'n' wear because few people around here do) but how you can prove that Whitley Bay is Newcastle is that when you breathe in it has exactly the same odour as central Newcastle, that of rusty cans of diarrhoea.

Tynemouth has it too but at least you can go to the bookshop there on a Sunday.

The gentleman in Keel Row Books in North Shields has all the talents in abundance which most people who dream of retiring and opening a secondhand bookshop usually only possess singularly. He is able to get more books into a small space than any other shop I have seen, the books are ones that most professional bookdealers would consider unsaleable. He has perfected the art of deterring collectors from buying books that they are keen to own. He should start a course entitled "HOW NOT TO RUN A SECONDHAND BOOKSHOP".

Paradoxically North Shields Books is run

by somebody who does not specifically wish to be a bookdealer. His main ambition is to sell old records but he cannot get enough of these and so he has to fill the spare space with books. This confirms me in my belief that the best people to do things are those that are trying to make money and not the ones who do it for love, or even worse, to promote culture. I think that we should have the same system for politicians. That we should hold elections, let them campaign as much as they like and then on polling day we should inform them that they are exactly the wrong people to be in charge of our destinies simply because they so much want to be. We should then go out and ask the first person in the street and the person who is most convinced that he did not want the job should be made to do it. If this bookshop is anything to go by it is a lot better than having people who want to do it running the show, such as the lunatic in Keel Row Books.

However, there is one bookshop in Newcastle where this belief falls down completely. It is the Newcastle Bookshop, par excellance, it serves nothing but nouvelle cuisine (well in Newcastle it counts as nouvelle cuisine). My only dislike is that you cannot go to this shop first without wasting time, but then it does give you the chance to savour getting into it later in the day. In my opinion it is a great secondhand bookshop, that is, it does things of which I am in favour. It opens hours that you do not need a computer to remember, and you distinctly get the feeling that they would not complain if you were to ask to be let in out of those hours. It has a reserve stock, something of which I am even more in favour. The reason is that there are lots of people who go in secondhand bookshops who have absolutely no idea how to handle the books and some have strange notions that the rest of us wish to hear their comments on the prices, like antique dealers they believe that all old books should be worth money and that modern books are relatively worthless, unless they are trying to sell them of course.

The books in Mr. Mills upstairs room are all modern art, design, photography and trade catalogues. What those of us used to such things call taste freak wear, I can always spot a taste freak, they are the ones who go white when I pull a book off the shelf by the top of the spine, and then tell them that I find the sound of books being torn deeply satisfying. If that doesn't work I ask in my loudest voice how come such modern books have such high prices. I for one would certainly never pay such prices, and I am deeply grateful to Mr Mills for supplying so many taste freaks for me to upset.

It is not everywhere that lets me do this. In the Charing Cross Road there is one alleged secondhand bookshop which does not even entertain getting its new books out of the window for me, they claim I only wish to leer at the photographs of naked ladies which they seem to specialise in - I have never understood this, how come it is wrong for me to look at these books but alright for them to sell them? For a long time I was convinced that it was a new bookshop but then I spoke to other dealers and they informed me that it not only had a reserve stock of art books but that it issued a catalogue. Once I heard this I went straight round and asked to see the back room, but the staff at Zwemmer's had clearly been primed for they denied that they had any secondhand books, let alone a back room. Other than calling them liars there is not much you can do in a situation like this, so I called them liars. They took umbrage at this truth telling on my part, and I am now barred from the front of the shop and thus will never get the opportunity to be barred from the back...

I am beginning to suspect that the art in art bookshops consists of being the right type of person, thus if you have to ask to see the books you are not the right type of person. I am deeply grateful to Mr Mills for letting me feel that I am the right type of person, even if it is only for one day a year.

There has been a slight change in Hexham since I was last there and I am not sure if there are now two bookshops or just one, but the one I used to like called Hencotes Antiques and Books has certainly changed hands.

In Sunderland a newly opened secondhand bookshop has sprung up since last I was there, but Sunderland still has the world's worst remainder shop with secondhand books (by the bus station), and there is a bizarre bookshop called the Durham Book Centre - you wait until you get inside it gets much worse - which only officially opens on a Saturday. It is vaguely connected with the bookshop in Alston which only opens during the summer. Alston does not appear on any sensible map. It is midway between Carlisle, Newcastle and Glasgow. This may not be an exact geographic location but that is sure as hell the way it feels.

From Darlington there is an arm of the railway line which goes through Middlesborough and Stockton, both have part time bookshops - Middlesborough by stock, Stockton by time. This line then divides and you can either go to Redcar, which I like, and Saltburn which I distinctly like, the other way passes through, but not close enough to, Stokesley with stops at Great Ayton, Lealhome and Whitby (the Whitby shop also has a sub branch in Robin Hoods Bay). It is an epic journey by train but I cannot honestly say it is worthwhile just for the bookshops. It seems to me much more profitable to go to Redcar & Saltburn.

YORK

Now that the bookshops in Durham are so hopeless, and the one in Darlington has closed down the next in line after Newcastle is York, where with one notable exception they are universally depressing. It is like a hospice for bookfairies. These are the books that are selected for Public School prizes, they are all extremely worthy and all the books that people put on their lists to be read some century or other, but there is no air of excitement to them. They may be proud of their Viking heritage, their great cathedral and their splendid railway station, but if you nutted one of the bookshop owners I feel certain that you would end up with a hall mark on pate.

At York you have to decide whether to go south with the mainline or east with the sidetrack. South is about as interesting as the Gobi Desert, but without the warmth. The shop on the outskirts of Doncaster is a major candidate for one of the worst in Britain, the one in Newark has closed down, there is nothing in Grantham and only T V Coles counts as a proper shop in Peterborough.

It is best to go to Scarborough and on the way stop off at Malton which on a good day can be better than York.

Helmsley has two bookshops both of which are very right and proper, and bookfairies would be very proud of them, but us oiks feel there is more scope and hope in Scarborough. It is certainly an appropriate place to start a day. The local council has appropriated Dracula, with poetic imagination they ignored that he actually came ashore at Whitby, whilst ignoring another immigrant who genuinely has a place in Whitby and now has another in Scarborough, the existence of which the local tourist office denies because they cannot abide the name: Mrs Lofthouse. They may have a point. As a name for a secondhand bookshop it is totally inappropriate. It is neither awful enough to be memorable or memorable enough to be awe full. It sounds like it should be selling biscuits. The shop is a bit like those boxes of broken biscuits that they used to sell cheaply, it has a wonderful glass top and is very dark inside. It has broken bits of everything but nothing whole of anything and is slightly unsatisfying. I bought the best there was in it and it cost £5 per pound. It appears that I have mislaid a shop in Scarborough. Besides the one behind the old cinema, with antiques and the one on the other side of town which does paperbacks. Lack of Garlick.

Dracula should have come ashore at Scarborough; it is a much easier place to leave than Whitby, you can either go to York or south to Hull, an almost unique city in Britain: It does not have a proper secondhand bookshop; there is a shop specialising in paperbacks by the station but what those of us who know about such things call a secondhand bookshop it is not. If Scarborough can get away with appropriating Dracula, Hull should get away with Frankenstein's monster, where he would feel very much at home.

The line between Scarborough and Hull is a thin one but not quite anorexic. In Bridlington the gentleman is part of the campaign for real kilts, by the time you have left you will feel like joining the campaign for real dirks. His anecdotes are in their anecdotage, the one saving grace is that Bridlington has more charity shops than he has books. The shop in DRIFFIELD is a strange combination of SF and Military which is more than you can say for DRIFFIELD which does not know whether it should be twinned with Ambridge or Toytown.

The three sisters of Beverley are like the play and the singing group. It is difficult to remember the name of the third one. The place looks like it would inspire Jane Austen to write another book: Covert & Covetousness. Somehow it is not the type of place you expect to see on the East

Yorkshire moors and the bookshops have lots of the books you would want but not at the prices you would want to pay. The third shop looks like a novel by Ethell M Dell and is in an Antiques Arcade by Eastgate Books which has general books and specialises in Sarawak? Alex Alec mainly goes in for literature but not to be outdone has an eclectic general stock.

Cottingham; it sounds like a place that would be buried in the footnotes, but it is actually as close as HULL gets to having a secondhand bookshop midway between the heaven of Beverley and social disadvantage, as we politically correcters say, of Hull.

* * * * *

For the benefit of those of you who open books at random what I am trying to do in this section is list shops in towns where you do not have to sit and calculate with a computer when they are going to be open, so thus you should be ale to turn up on the Scarborough/Hull line and find more than fifty per cent of the shops open without having to think about them, this allows for bookdealers' notorious unreliability, half day closings and holidays. Much to my relief when I checked the computer Scarborough/Hull is officially surprisingly free of inhabitants - this is possibly one of the reasons I like it so much. Scarborough Books and the shop in Bridlington also open on a Sunday during the summer.

the missing
LINCS

There was once a film called 'The Land Time Forgot', Lincolnshire could have had a starring role, the one thing you cannot do here is forget the land. But British Frail has not forgotten some of the stations, and to make sure that you don't, it makes the trains wait at them for extraordinarily long times. There is no need to go on the Trans-Siberian Express whilst we still have trains in Lincolnshire. It takes about the same time to get from Moscow to Vladivostock as it does to get from Newark to Cleethorpes, but the fare is slightly less on the Trans-Siberian Express.

Even in a motor car it is a long way, the roads all seem to go in the opposite directions to the towns. They seemed to have been laid out by somebody who was not sure which way round to put them.

I have tried cycling it. It was like doing the Tour de France, blindfold. Nothing changes in it. At first you think it is going to be wonderful because it will be reasonably flat, but after about three minutes you begin to dream of hills, and a wind that is not against you.

Lincoln is a good taste of what things are like generally. It does have secondhand books; the same ones every year.

The first shop on the hill towards the cathedral is called Readers Rest. It does not mean that you would take a rest after going halfway up the hill, what it means is that you would take a rest from ever reading again after looking at these books, as the hill they are half way up is the one to total boredom. As I have explained earlier the worst bores are the ones who nearly have something interesting to say, and this bookshop does look as if it was going to be interesting but I think you might have more luck trying to get something interesting out of Mr Major.

If there were prizes for bookshops then this one would get the Betty Trask award for novels written in the traditional Romantic manner, there is the other possibility that it has been carefully preserved by The National Trust as an example of what a secondhand bookshop looked like in the 1950's.

The second shop Harlequin is even further up the hill to total boredom. It has not quite reached the pinnacle but this is not for want of trying. It goes in for the more traditional pantomime, not least the interminable intermissions. This is roast beef with a vengence, the four course lunch stuck there in the middle of the day, instead of gravy they have jugs of dust that they pour all over the books every morning, they even have the ability to make relatively new books look as if there are a hundred years of purchase deterrant behind them.

The difference is notable if you go to Sleaford which although it does not have the world's greatest stock, has the ability to make boring books interesting. How you do this is with price. By making deadly books deadly cheap you can persuade the type of people who find Harlequin rivetting to buy your books, you can then concentrate on trying to attract the more interesting books and wait patiently for more interesting people to turn up to buy them. The price of a book is in itself no indication as to its interest. High price books are simply those that several people agree are interesting. The reason I like the shop in Sleaford is that it has books that I find interesting and at a price that I am willing to pay.

Harlequin has books that I want but at prices I would never consider paying, and from the look of things nobody else does either.

The other good news about Lincolnshire is Mr Redmond of Billingborough. At first this does not look like a bookshop, and indeed it is a private house, but on Saturday and Sunday the stables at the rear are officially open for oats.

It is not quite hay, but it is not quite silage either and at the prices offered it is possible to buy bulk. The other good news is that it does open during the week if the owner is there.

RC: "What a creep, all the bloke did was compliment him on his suit, what other moron would wear a suit when the temperature was 90 in the motor car."

STAMFORD

DEFINITELY NOT A RAFFLE

Because it is to the West of the A1 and the London/Newcastle rail line it is hard to conceive that Stamford is in Lincolnshire, but from the point of view of book collectors it is the capital. Since the demise of the legencry Abe Schein it has been trying to live down its past and has gone in for rebirthing. There is no actual difference and they all have that 1000 yard stare but at least they tried.

If you arrive by train then the first port of call is Robert Humm's which specialises in Railways but quite often has books which could be of interest to the general collector, the specialist stock tends to be at prices that would make British Frail look cheap but the non specialists are an away day bargain.

The railway side of the bridge leads to St. Mary's Hill which has a newsagent with books at the rear, some of which you would gladly put behind you. But other people claim that I am somewhat prejudiced about this shop and that many bargains are known. Further along and at the rear of the George Hotel by the car park is a small shop which I find more attractive.

RC: "It specialises in food!"

And it has a general stock upstairs which looks like it could repay much visiting.

If you now cross the bridge and attempt to go straight ahead although the streets won't let you and then turn right into the main street, on the right is Cheyne Row which has one of the smallest stocks with a large reward in Britain. In the next street parallel is a charity bookshop, for and on behalf of cats. Like cats it is indifferent to the mere whims of human beings and comes and goes as it pleases.

At the far end of the main street and right is Staniland' the epitome of roast beef. The shop itself is newly refurbished and the same size as everything else in Stamford put together but it is the books which reek of Olde England. It is not so much the actual choice as the prominence which they are given, thus it would be possible for a nouvelle cuisine shop to have exactly the same books but price them to make the place more interesting.

I firmly believe that this type of bookselling is on the way out. But in the same way as there are still households which eat roast beef every Sunday lunchtime so there are bookshops which keep attempting to do the only thing they know how. It is the prominence which is given to certain types of books as if somehow there still was a carriage trade who understood and know about books... the largest number of customers in secondhand bookshops these days are simply people trying to buy books more cheaply than the publishers of new books.

RC: "Belt up! When are we going to have some gossip, you should have been a theologian. You have not put the boot in for pages yet."

Included in Lincolnshire by popular demand and because nobody knows where it really is: UPPINGHAM, RUTLAND.

UPPINGHAM

GOLDMARK BOOKS

Those of you with a delicate disposition and a liking for olde worlde bookshops should be a trifle circumspect when entering Mr Goldmark's seemingly idyllic emporium in sedate but stately Uppingham. I did not notice anything amiss on my last visit but then I am not exactly renowned for my sensitivity.

In the name of security, Mr Goldmark has installed close circuit TV cameras, these cameras are of a much higher order than normal - such is the degree of clarity that those of you worried about your image would do well to check whether you have scrubbed your fingernails well enough recently. There are some cameras that are obvious and others which are hidden, but as usual Mr Goldmark has gone one step further than your average peeping tom, he has installed a sound system - such is its delicacy that no matter how discreet your attempts to cover it up Mr Goldmark can hear you fart. I have no doubt that if the buggers who create these things invent a device where you can smell what is going on in another room, Mr Goldmark will be among the first to whom they will attempt to sell it.

Mr Goldmark's enthusiasm to partake of the private aspects of his customers' lives is such that he now spends his days watching and listening to a bank of televisions which he has in his upstairs office. Should you peruse a book just a little too avidly Mr G will descend and attempt to further lure you into parting with the readies, after all he has to pay for the TV and sound system somehow.

Mr Goldmark claims that he will completely disregard any remarks that are made about him personally. I presume that what he means is that he will disregard any unflattering remarks, the chances of him disregarding a flattering remark are about the same as Mr Maxwell disregarding a pension fund. Mr Goldmark's desire and ability to get himself into the newspapers on the flimsiest of premises is only exceeded by my own.

Oh how I wish I had known of Mr G's peccadillos when I was in Uppingham, I would have turned up with a prepared script for the bald headed overweight deep brown noser, with his polo neck jumpers which make him look ike a walking advert for durex he always seems prepared for any perversion - I would not have been content with picking my nose, scoffing at his classifications, deriding his egregiously overpriced books, I would have taken the opportunity to see if my underwear was in a fit state to have an accident in, then I would have held my annual smegma count and next I would checked whether his erotica section was accurately described. Normally I do not like to do it, but in Mr G's shop I would feel no compunction about coming between books.

A friend of mine's ambition was to have sex with head librarians, maybe I could pervert him and turn his interests to bookshop assistants, they are almost as unattractive... I did nearly seduce a young lady in a bookshop once but just as she was about to acquiesce I saw a book that I had been looking for for five years. I met her a few years later - she told me she worked in a hotel with a five inch pile carpet - I asked if there were any books?

What I would tell Mr Goldmark, in my prepared rant is that he is a pervert, a voyeur, a dirty old man, a disgusting hypocrite, that he is worse than a flasher - at least they have the courage to do it in front of their victims and not skulk in some cupboard - it is a despicable act to spy on somebody when they are totally unaware of it. It is indeed true that they have closed circuit televisions in supermarkets, but there you are fully aware of them and they cannot overhear your every muttering. One of the reasons that they do not have more CCTV's in supermarkets is that the staff, no matter how honest, cannot stand being watched all day and who can blame them? Who would like their employer to know every word that was said about them, indeed who would like their friends to know every word that was said about them behind their back. One other reason that they do not have more is that the security men whose job it is to watch them end up spending their entire time looking for the ladies with the biggest tits.

It is not good enough to say that we should not say things about people that we would not say to their face. Civilisation consists of being polite to people you loathe, of taking an interest in things you despise and of doing things you detest. Who could bear to listen to all the things that are said about them by somebody else?

For three years I attended a psychiatrist, whom I thought took great interest in me, and I would like to thank the lady for she was indeed a real help. The reason I never went back to her was that I overheard a phone conversation she had with another person in which she told them that she could not stand me, that I was the most intolerable patient she had ever had.

RC: "You told me you left that shrink because she said you were giving her nightmares."

In all the time I had been going to her it had not once occurred to me that she did not like me. It could well be true that I am so thick skinned that a rhinoceros with hydraulic attachments would be unlikely to dent my carapace, but it was my fault entirely for listening to a conversation when I should not have been doing so. If you eavesdrop on people you cannot complain about what you hear.

RC: "Trust you to nause it, there'll be no chance of two's up on the video now."

THE WEST

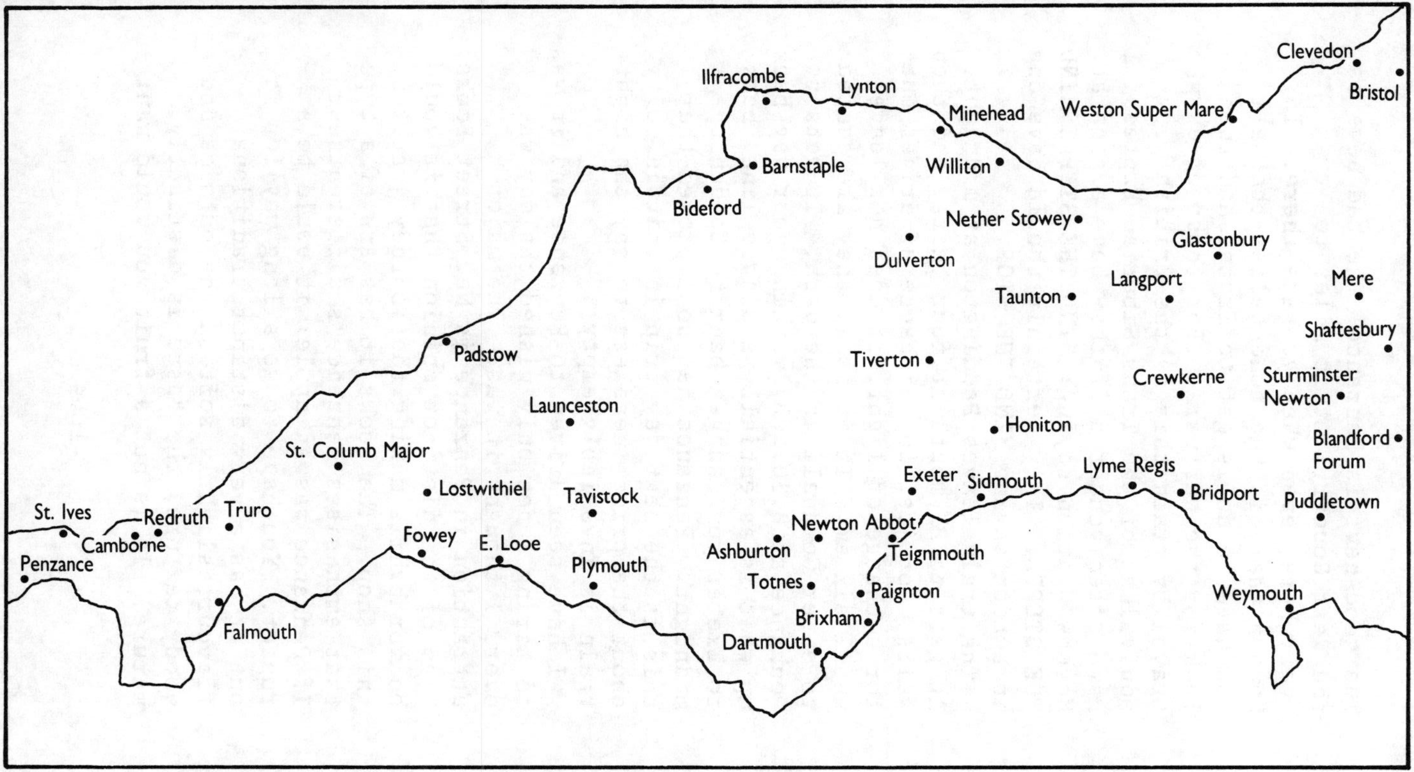

Clevedon
Bristol
Ilfracombe
Lynton
Minehead
Weston Super Mare
Barnstaple
Williton
Bideford
Nether Stowey
Dulverton
Glastonbury
Taunton
Langport
Mere
Shaftesbury
Padstow
Tiverton
Crewkerne
Sturminster Newton
Launceston
Honiton
Blandford Forum
St. Columb Major
Exeter
Lyme Regis
Lostwithiel
Sidmouth
Bridport
Tavistock
Puddletown
St. Ives
Redruth
Truro
Newton Abbot
Camborne
Fowey
Ashburton
Teignmouth
E. Looe
Penzance
Plymouth
Totnes
Paignton
Weymouth
Brixham
Falmouth
Dartmouth

The good news is Penzance, the bad news is the West Country: it is miles to everywhere, even when you are there. In London there is the fond belief that all you have to do is get to Exeter and then look for the car park. For those of us who travel by train this is the British equivalent of the Trans-Siberian Express. I have often wondered if they have a sign at Moscow Station saying: MIND THE STEPPE MIND THE STEPPE. They certainly should have one in London saying MIND THE STOP.

The train leaves Paddington at midnight, it gets to Plymouth at four thirty and then waits, not just for a change of driver but for a change of light, it does not leave until six am. It is as if they are scared to enter Cornwall in the dark. It gets to Penzance at 8.30. By working your way back up what is essentially a single line back to Exeter you can get back to London by midnight. Penzance has so improved that this is the best day trip in Britain, pity about the price (needless to say the night train is invariably empty).

I have been driven to Penzance and it was so tiring I not only wished the day was over, I thought it was. The major attraction in Penzance is New Street Books. I am of the distinct opinion that it would be worthwhile making the journey just for this shop. The books it has are of a type that emphasises Penzance's differentness. If Penzance was an apple: it would be a russet. You have to go a long way for it but it has a very distinct traditional flavour, slightly soft on the outside and a woody texture, the taste is distinctly mature. It is not a fruit you would want to eat a lot of and it is one where a little goes a long way.

The taste of maturity has come to Penzance with the arrival of its latest course: New Street Books. This is no Cornish pastie.

RC: "When you do your veggie guide are you going to compare all the meals to books?"

The art of making a good meal consists not just in taking seemingly ordinary ingredients and making them into something greater than was there, but in the whole service and lay out and presentation... the best meals are those where you want more.

The New Street Bookshop has books that make studying the menu worthwhile. I dread to think what it must be like during the summer when I imagine people go in asking if they have any good Catherine Cookson paperbacks but the owner is so polite that I doubt if he would help sponsor my scheme to buy Lands End and put up signs saying Coach Parties Welcome (so that they would drive straight over the cliff). How people can go round in groups of more than four is beyond me, especially in secondhand bookshops...

Penzance Rare Books is also worth making the detour to, and would almost be if it were not for New Street, but the two together make Penzance more worthwhile than an annual dinner. There are also two other takeaways and the POCS.

From Penzance it is best to go to Falmouth which has also improved but not quite up to the scale of Penzance, the shops are much more tourist orientated and some open on Sunday which is useful. The south coast of Cornwall is distinctly better than the North, the middle has bookshops but they take some getting to - and I have not. Foye and Looe are better than Lostwithierl and Tavistock.

In theory Plymouth is a good place to base yourself but in practice it does not seem to work out. Its the type of place John Major would describe as interesting.

RC: "What have you got against Mr Major?"

drif: "If you could measure personality like IQ his would be so far down the scale you would have to take to pot holing to register it."

Exeter is a better bet than Plymouth simply because it is so easy to get away from. The bookshops make Plymouth look interesting, the shop in Newton Abbot is not run along monastic lines, but it is not exactly Ellis Peters either, the shop in Paignton is a drif special which leads to Totnes.

Totnes; its the way Hampstead dreams of being, filled with the beautiful people, who are just the same as every body else, without their mascara. It is all, new age, wholemeal and earth shoes and that is just the car park. The bookshops specialise mainly in Literace, there is a super-abundance of the POCS and it is worth a morning.

The bookshops in the Barnstaple area are only worth going to if you are in the area, with the exception of the one in Braunton just to the north of the town. A far more interesting route is the one east out of Exeter to Honiton, which now has the addition of Mr Colycot who used to be Honiton and Virginibus which used to be in

Greek myths (it has now taken over the old Brockwell shop), together with the 3 other establishments of lesser quality. This makes Honiton well worth a detour, it is odd that Honiton which is essentially a one street town should have so many secondhand bookshops, and Exeter which is a city should have only two owned by the same people.

BBC cricket commentators always refer to the groin as being "the upper leg region" there can be no doubt that Honiton is the generative part of the west country, even BBC commentators would have difficulty thinking of a suitable ephemism for Exeter. I think the closest they could come is describing it as 'the arsehole'.

The line that leads to Salisbury is slow and infrequent (this is presumably why it is on the network South East, not even British Frail would have the gall to ask Intercity prices for it. I often wonder if they stopped trying to run a railway and tried providing a housing service for tramps like me who spend our lives on trains whether they may not actually run a better transport system. Certainly if they charged for seats by length of time occupied they would make a fortune. The towns on this line do not have the world's best bookshops but taken together they do become more than interesting. My own favourite is Shaftesbury (Gillingham Station) which is more like a time machine than a secondhand bookshop.

The other line out of Exeter goes through Taunton which must be the most stable city in Britain, mainly because most of the residents are asses.

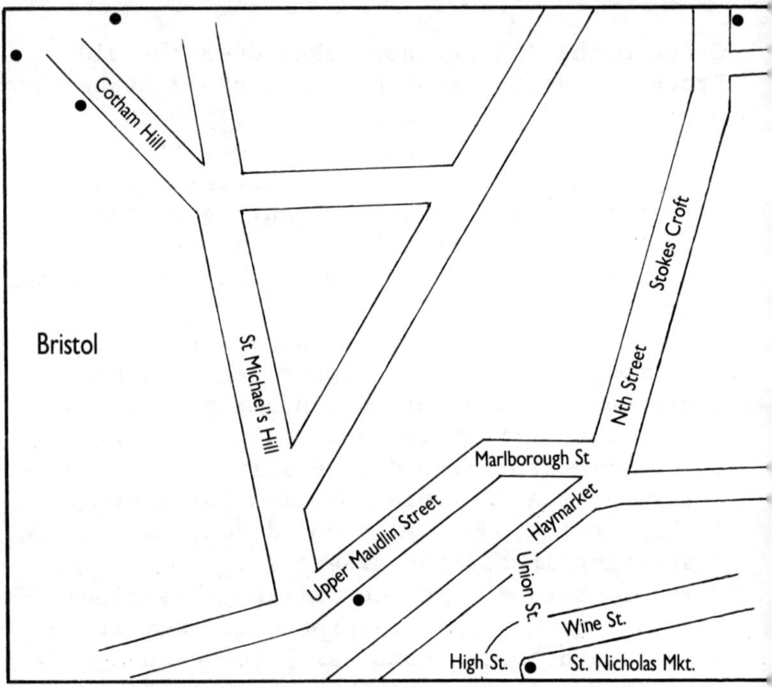
Bristol
Cotham Hill
St Michael's Hill
Stokes Croft
Nth Street
Marlborough St
Upper Maudlin Street
Haymarket
Union St.
Wine St.
High St.
St. Nicholas Mkt.

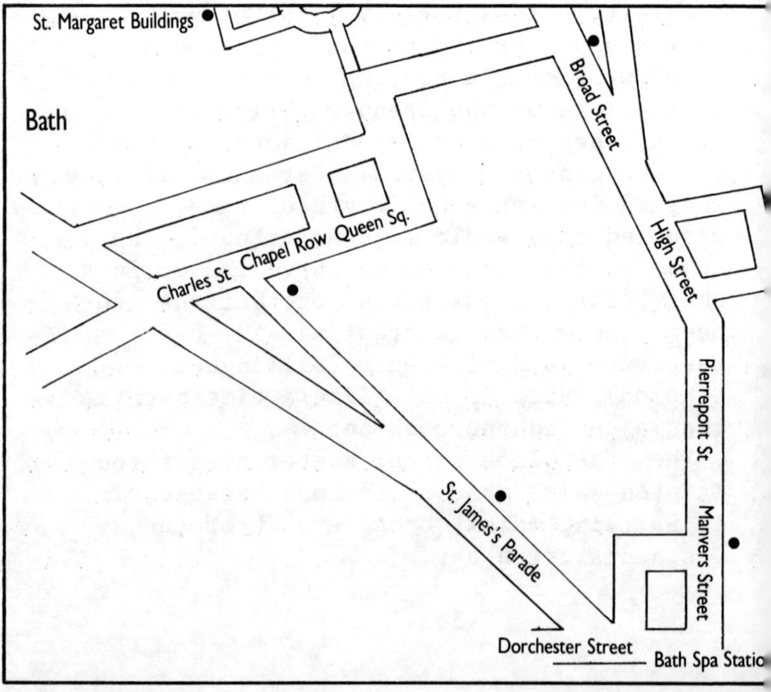
St. Margaret Buildings
Bath
Broad Street
High Street
Queen Sq.
Chapel Row
Charles St
Pierrepont St
St. James's Parade
Manvers Street
Dorchester Street

Weston Super Mare sounds like another hoarse joke, but the bookshops are actually worth looking at, the hotels are unbelievably cheap which is possibly why there is much POCS. It is far cheaper to stay in Weston and travel to Bath and Bristol than it is to stay in either of the latter.

The Bristol bookshops are more likely to procure results than those in Bath, they tend to be darker, which is strange because the ones in Bath could save a fortune on electricity and they could have their own self-selecting device, for their little eyes open up more than you could believe when a tourist walks in the shops.

Bradford on Avon is a surprise candidate in the 'strange place to have five secondhand bookshops' contest. They are not quite as good as Honiton but it is just as odd.

Not the least odd is 'Books and Prints' which is almost as full of itself as it is of books. They have decided to be a high turnover shop in a low population town. I don't think they could do any better by being in Bath which is an appallingly expensive place, but even though Bradford on Avon is on the rail line about once a week, it is not on what I would call a natural route of any kind.

CARLISLE

PRESTON

LIVERPOOL

MANCHESTER

BIRMINGHAM

OXFORD

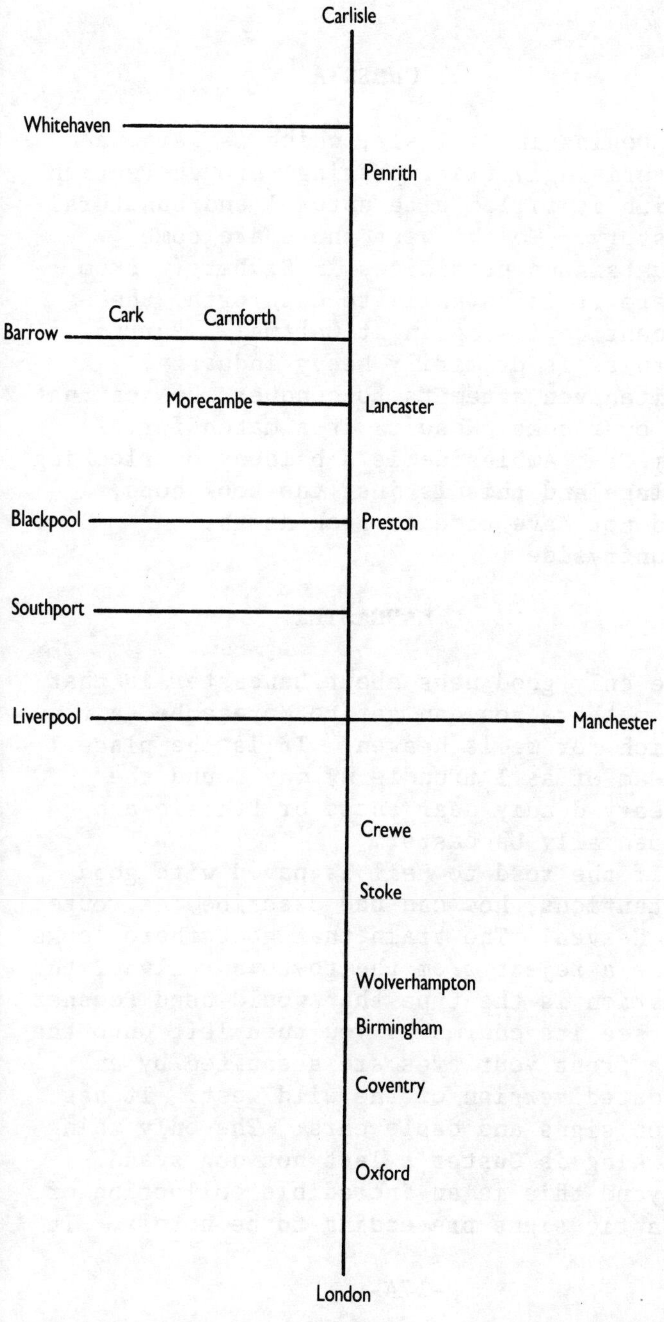
Carlisle
Whitehaven
Penrith
Cark
Carnforth
Barrow
Morecambe
Lancaster
Blackpool
Preston
Southport
Liverpool
Manchester
Crewe
Stoke
Wolverhampton
Birmingham
Coventry
Oxford
London

CUMBRIA

It begins in Carlisle, which is large and surprisingly flat, passing through Penrith which is filled with natural and unnatural history. To the west there are some mountainous precipices in Sedberg. From there it is downhill to Carnforth, the ascent begins again at Cartmel. Barrow in Furness is primarily heavy industry, Whitehaven attempts to conquer the sea that it overlooks, Keswick is a match for all comers. Ambleside is a balcony overlooking a lake and this is just the bookshops, I did not have time to look at the countryside.

LANCASTER

The only good news about Lancaster is that from there you can get to Morecambe, a town which for me is heaven. It is the place I dream of as I trundle my way round the dreary deadly dear shops of Britain and especially Lancaster.

If the road to Hell is paved with good intentions, how can one describe the route to Heaven? The train that goes there looks like a reject from the toytown railway, the station is the type that would need Pevsner to see its charms as you turn left onto the sea front your eyes are assaulted by an updated version of the wild west. It has neon signs and cable cars. The only thing lacking is Custer's last hot dog stand. Beyond this is an incredible collection of plastic signs pretending to be hotels. It has been designed by Satan, just keep your eyes straight ahead, for just one mile...

Then you come upon it: Heaven, disguised as a knitting wool shop. There are just a few books in the window but these exist to confuse more than inform, and when you enter there are hardly any books at all, you have to go through a door and up some stairs and then it is it: the drif special of drif specials.

For most bookdealers the books in this shop are the world's greatest collection of dogs, they would travel as far to avoid them as I would to get near to them. They think I am barking mad to find this shop so wonderful. For them this is the dog bookshop of dog bookshops but this is precisely why I like it so much. What is a dog to them is a best friend to me. These are the books that I slavver over. These are the tomes which I like to get my Rotweiler teeth into. If there were more shops like this I would become as sleek as a greyhound. The Saint Bernard in me would guide everybody through this pass. I do not need the pack to tell me how to follow the trail to this shop, within 100 miles I know I am on the right scent, in it I am a poodle. Out I am a bitch. Forcing me to go to other shops in this area like McCormacks in Lancaster or Halewoods in Preston is cruely to dumb animals. It may be the books most people would put in a kennel, but it is the way I would like my home to be. This shop has more breeding than Crufts, more friendship than Patience Strong - (it does have quite a few Patience Strong's as well). The only thing more gentle than its bark is its bite.

PRESTON

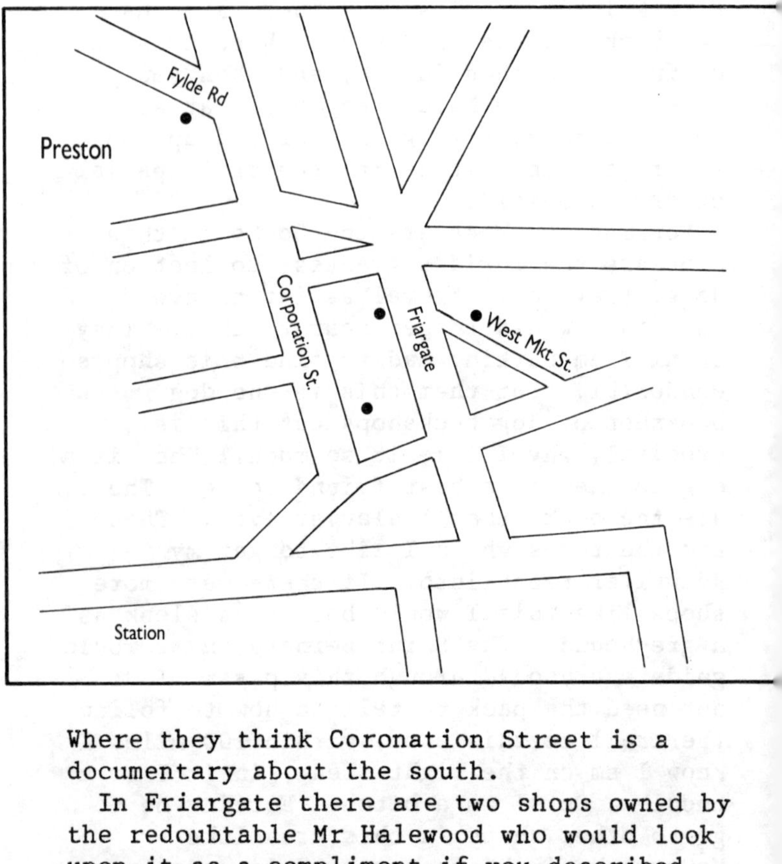

Where they think Coronation Street is a documentary about the south.

In Friargate there are two shops owned by the redoubtable Mr Halewood who would look upon it as a compliment if you described him as being boorish, the good news is that he is not much in evidence these days: the bad news is that his offspring have taken to parodying him. The shop and stock also have an element of parody about them as if the dancers in a working mens' club were attempting to perform a ballet. It is a bit like finding your olive is not pitted when you expected it to be, somehow it is extra hard because of the surprise. For those of you who are prepared to jump through the appropriate hurdles there are reserve stocks upstairs and at the back, like dried prunes.

A far more interesting experience is Great Grandfathers in Leyland just to the south of Preston. Do not be deterred by the dreadful name, which conjures up maiden aunts who have decided to start selling books because they had nothing better to do. It is very professionally run, and extremely varied but most of all the books have a very genuine feel to them, they are no more or less than they pretend to be. The prices have a certain smoothness but that is because this shop is an unpeeled grape.

The shop in Wigan opened and closed in a blaze of disinterest but I have heard of another shop opening around here somewhere. There are also shops in Lytham St Annes both of which make Oxfam look like high culture, and there is nearly a drif special in Blackpool.

SOUTHPORT

I like it; its beautiful. I even like the charity shops.

RC: "I will go an' get the death by boredom signs, he is always hopeless when he is trying to praise somewhere. If I was the shops in Southport I would bung him to start slagging the places off."

The Southport Liverpool line is like a see saw: there are ruffians at one end trying to bounce the thing up and down as much as they can and at the other there are polite well spoken children scared out of their wits but unable to get off.

The first thing to remember is that Southport and Stockport are two completely different places, and Southport is the pretty one. If there were beauty contests for towns Stockport would start espousing feminism.

On entering Broadhurst's you honestly feel that you should doff your trilby and check that your cuffs are the right length. At first it is not obvious that it is a secondhand bookshop. You have to ascend the stairs and it is like ascending to paradise, even the books are well dressed and polite. At first they do have a slightly uniform quality but closer inspection proves that they are all individuals and some unique ones at that. It looks like Moss Bros but it comes up like Saville Row and as they say in Saville Row the quality remains long after the price is forgotten.

Kernaghans is not quite Saville Row but it is not quite as downmarket as Marks & Spencers either, but it does have more books than M & S has branches and whilst the same item may come in different sizes, unlike most large shops it has discovered how to make a place interesting. Well padded is the term they use in tailoring.

Parkinson's is the Army Surplus stores, it is filled to overflowing with technical hardware but also has some very serviceable clobber, and there is one day when it wipes the floor with the other shops: it goes in for Sunday best...

HAZLEDENE BOOKS
LIVERPOOL

THE JOHN LODWICK STORY

One of Hazledene Books specialities is surrealism: they do not sell it: they just practice it.

In the window is a sign saying 'no students, collectors only'. The unwritten subtext is no dealers either.

The last time I stood outside this shop it was indeed an almost unique occasion; it was open at 3pm on a Tuesday afternoon. I am so used to just looking through the window of this establishment, which used to proudly proclaim that it was subsidised by the Arts Council that I did so again out of habit. It contained among other items three books by one Iain Sinclair, a gentleman whose previous claim to fame is that he used to be one of my chauffeurs. I don't think I can be held responsible for people going down in the world once they have left my employ, but I would like to say that if his poetry is anything like his driving I for one shall not be using it.

The three books were Whitechappel Scarlett Tracings, (that believe it or not is one book), The Kodak Mantra Diaries and Brown Clouds (well what can I say?) Some malevolent masters of the wooden spoon claim that I appear as a character in WST, admittedly heavily disguised, as a skinhead who etches his name into books in a handwriting "like poor quality knitting".

I went in and as usual omitted to mention

that I was a bookdealer, I was very much looking forward to being asked to leave when I did deign to tell him and when he asked me to leave I would ask how I could be welcome as a piece of fiction but not in real life? But for the moment I intended to savour the irony of the situation.

I kept smiling to myself as I perused the shelves, it was the only sound in that undim cavern but my titterings were brought to a halt when I got to some books by a Mr John Lodwick. They seemed somehow familiar, and when I opened them there on the fly leaf were strange indentations reminiscent of an archaeological dig, deep dry rivers etched by somebody whose handwriting looked like poor quality knitting. Above that were erudite descriptions in an extremely neat hand, one that I knew well for I had once tried to forge it onto a book called Brown Clouds.

Using my superior powers of deduction I worked out that the owner of this shop had bought these books from Mr. Sinclair who had bought them from me.

How I knew this was that I had spent a considerable length of time trying to locate these particular books, and I had had to explain to almost every dealer I had contacted who Mr Lodwick was.

A very polite but nervous gentleman had rung me up and asked in a timid voice whether I had heard of John Lodwick. I claimed to know him well, as I searched through the reference books. The relief in the gentleman's voice was a pleasure to behold and he informed me that he was looking for any novels by JL. I told him that there would be no trouble whatsoever in locating them and that he should look upon them as being his. He was so grateful that he informed me that I was the first person not to have treated his request with derision and that he looked forward to hearing from me.

As soon as he put down the phone I rang Iain Sinclair and asked who the hell John Lodwick was - if you work as a chauffeur for me you have got to be able to do more than just drive, but please, no more poets.

I could hear him rifling through the reference books and eventually he came up with an obscure tome on British Novelists 1945-1985 The Great Years, and told me that JL wrote twelve novels, a travel book and a military history; that he had been in the British Army during the second world war and had died in a car 'accident' with five other people whilst under the influence of drink. As far as I could work out he sounded like one of my ex chauffeurs... I told Mr Sinclair that I was now looking for all of the Lodwick books.

I learnt long ago not to depend solely on people who write books called Brown Clouds to supply me with my desires and I rang all the post war fiction specialists I could think of. Those that did not laugh, or inform me that nobody was looking for Mr Lodwick told me that they had never heard of him, as if that somehow settled the issue. The only shop which had heard of him was Rota's where they gave me a good description of his works, they said they were a low rent version of Simon Raven.

Eventually my favourite shop in Edgware came upwith three titles. I quoted them off to the gentleman from Worthing and a few days later a cheque was in the post for one of the books, as he politely informed me he could not afford them all at one time at the prices asked, but he could just afford one a month.

I am fairly good at finding books, I will rephrase that, I am a lot better at finding books than I am at finding chauffeurs, but so far I have not found a system of informing people that I am no longer looking for a particular author or book. Over the next few months I was offered several works of Mr Lodwick, my customer was keen to buy them but at the current rate it would have taken two years to pay; by the time I had the complete works I was wondering if he was going to be alive long enough.

I now had so many books by John Lodwick that visitors assumed I was an avid admirer and would ask me what they were about. I was thus reduced to reading one. I chose the autobiography called the Cradle of Neptune in the hope that it would tell me all about his other works but alas it only went up to the age of sixteen when he was expelled from Dartmouth for stealing a postal order.

When Iain rang and told me he had six John Lodwicks I informed him I had lost all interest in being a bookdealer, my ambition now was to become an historian. I had only to find a third book in the same vein as Mr Lodwicks and the Archer Shee case, and I would be able to write the definitive history of organised crime against the post office at Dartmouth.

Mr Sinclair informed me that he would be putting his Lodwicks in his next catalogue, which he did, and they all sold, and people kept ringing me up and offering Iain's Lodwicks at vastly inflated prices. So as not to upset them and to ensure that they would keep looking for other books in the future I bought them. I had no hope that the man in Worthing would be able to buy them, by the time he was rich enough I would be renowned as a major historian.

What I did was sell all the Lodwicks to Mr Sinclair who then advertised them in his next catalogue. He was inundated with orders, and he then rang me instructing me to find more John Lodwicks. Together we had created a market in John Lodwicks. So far the gentleman had only paid for two and now dealers all over Britain were dealing in them.

Dealers were now declining to offer me John Lodwicks on the grounds that I was not a good enough customer, however I had returned to looking for them because they were a good source of cash, from Mr Iain Sinclair who was getting multiple orders, not least from a certain shop in Liverpool calld Hazledene Books at whose shelves I was now looking and admiring the gall of their prices; they were almost half as much as mine.

This then was the situation. Mr Sinclair is welcome as a dealer provided he only sold books to Hazledene Books, he was not welcome as a dealer if he attempted to buy books from Hazledene Books. Mr Sinclair and I trade books with one another as if they were tennis balls. The only net agreement is can we make a profit out of them, who we sell them to is irrelevant. Mr Sinclair is however welcome in Hazledene

Books as a writer.

I am welcome in Hazledene Books as a character in a book and presumably I would be welcome if I was selling books, however I am not welcome if I attempt to buy books to sell.

Now my question is this: What about the gentleman in Worthing, the poor innocent who single handedly, and I think still unbeknownst to him, created an entire John Lodwick industry, would he be welcome in Hazledene Books if by some great stroke of good fortune a kind person was to tell him that they had some John Lodwicks in stock, and if he had enough time to make a trek to Liverpool from Worthing. I don't think it could be done in one day, even if you got there he would be unable to get back, and if having got himself to Liverpool he then had the even greater fortune to find the Hazledene Bookshop open, and then if he had the courage to enter this shop, a feat which many Liverpool Irish slummies have vowed never to attempt, would he be welcome? Now think carefully, the sign in the window says 'No students, collectors only'. And remember this shop is seen by the Arts Council as an outpost of civilisation in the cultural desert of Merseyside, that theoretically it is the job of establishments such as this to keep the beacon of culture flashing, would the gentleman from Worthing be made welcome? The answer is no, not just because the owner of the Hazledene Bookshop is a miserable old git, but because the gentleman from Worthing was a student of the Open University, who was writing a thesis on John Lodwick, whom he had considered a much under-rated writer, and whom he had commissioned just after the war to write the history of the regiment of which he, the gentleman from Worthing was Colonel; and it was this book which began Lodwick's literary career.

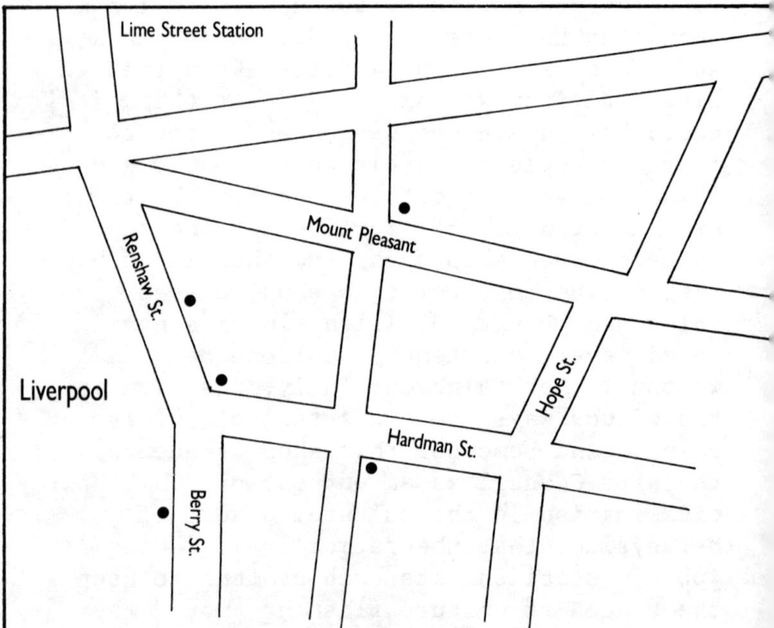

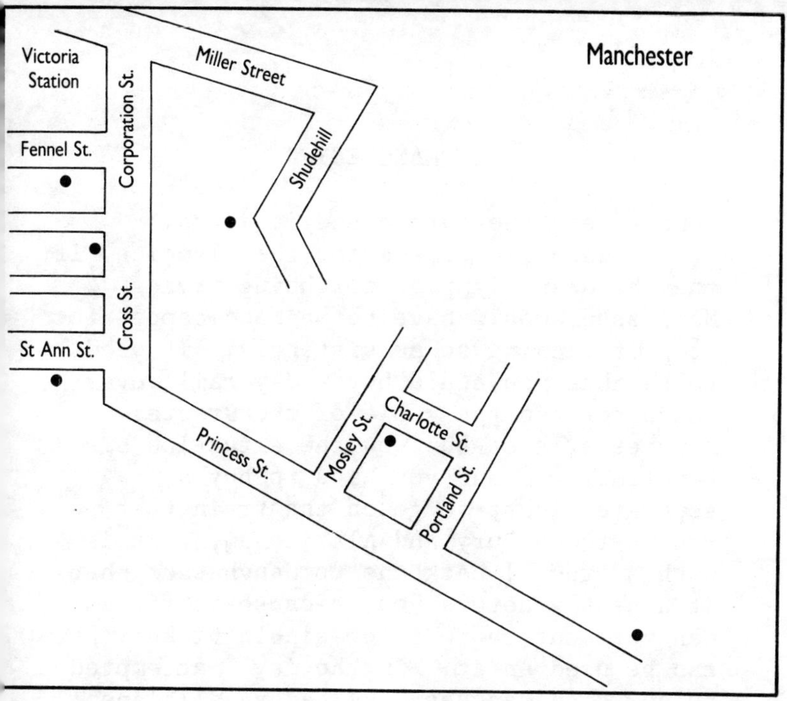

Manchester
Victoria Station
Miller Street
Corporation St.
Fennel St.
Shudehill
Cross St.
St Ann St.
Charlotte St.
Mosley St.
Princess St.
Portland St.

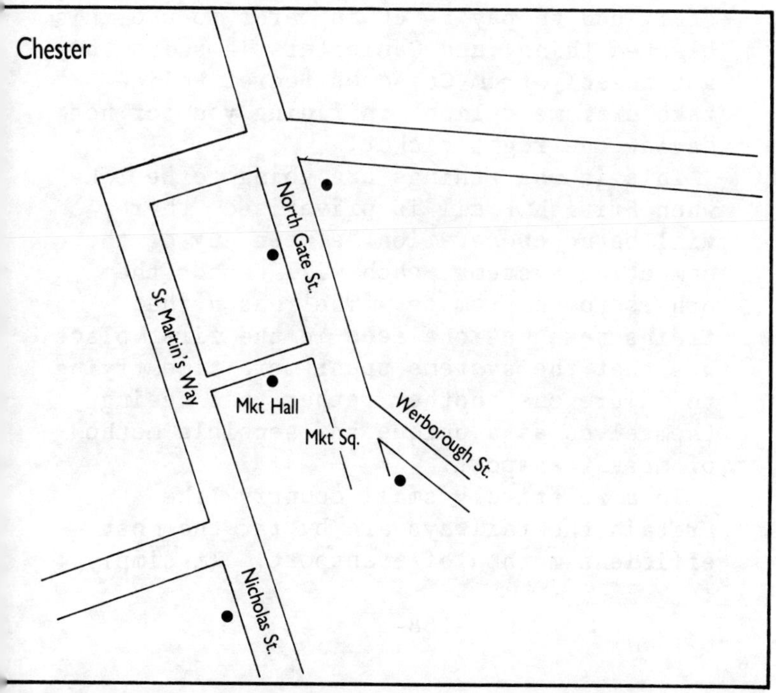

Chester
North Gate St.
St Martin's Way
Mkt Hall
Mkt Sq.
Werborough St.
Nicholas St.

MANCHESTER

I have seen the future and it jerks.

Manchester is trying for the Olympics. If they held an olympics for being trying, Manchester would have to be handicapped to stop it winning so consistently. It used to be that you could buy a day rail rover which covered the whole of the Greater Manchester area but now the situation has been improved and you have to buy a separate ticket to go on the train that runs between Bury and Altrincham, this is such a crucial backbone to Manchester that it honestly deters you, because as far as I can work out there is no single ticket that can be used on it. On the day I attempted to go round Manchester I had an all line rover, and a Greater Manchester rover and I still had to pay £4.60 in fares to use this blasted thing, and Gauleiters in suits they got cheaply from Ceascues Secret Police take extreme delight in fining you for not having the right ticket.

This is what things are going to be like when British Frail is privatised, there will be no cooperation between any of the competing systems, each will expect the others to compromise. The reason that trains were nationalised in the first place was that the systems spent more time trying to injure one another rather than seeing themselves as a unique and sensible method of mass transport.

In a relatively small country like Britain the railways are by far the most efficient method of transport. It simply is not possible for everybody to have a motor car, which most people drive to work then drive home and take to one place at weekends.

The most important part of a tall building is the lift, even the Reichmann brothers who built Canary Wharf got that right. It is the transport system which controls all the other features of the building. Once you have a common transport (and what are lifts but railways that go upwards?) then you can allow other people to get to each floor in any method they cloose. If they want to walk they can do so, if they wish to land a helicopter on the roof they can do so, but nobody would dream of allowing everybody to have their own personal method of getting up the building.

Lifts are 'free' in that the people who use them do not pay for them directly. It is the people who want people to use them who pay for them. When people rent a floor of an office building they also rent the use of the lift, nobody would dream of charging the people who are coming to the particular floor for the use of the lift. The distance you travel on lifts is never taken into consideration, the people at the top need the people at the bottom just as much as the people at the bottom need the ones at the top.

In the same way as it is the people on each floor who pay for the lift so it should be that the people who occupy the cities should pay for the railroads. It is they who benefit most when people visit them, it is they who want other people to come to them. Asking the people whom they want to spend money on before they even get a chance to see what it is they are going to buy is madness.

From now on I shall be boycotting all private railway schemes and Manchester's in particular... that will teach them to upset me.

STOKE ON TRENT

THE INCONTINENT SPECIAL

I once met a London tax driver whose solution to the city's appalling transport problems was to drain the Thames and make it into a motorway from Heathrow to Essex, which is where most taxi drivers live. I wish I had kept his phone number and then I could have asked about Stoke's problems. There are five bookshops: Hanley, Burslem, Wolstanton, Newcastle and New Milton. Walking is too long, driving is too impossible because of the one way streets and there are no railway lines that go to each place. It is better to go to Leek, the shops may not be great but you can at least walk to them, they are not taking the piss like the ones in Stoke.

BIRMINGHAM

THE BLACK COUNTRY

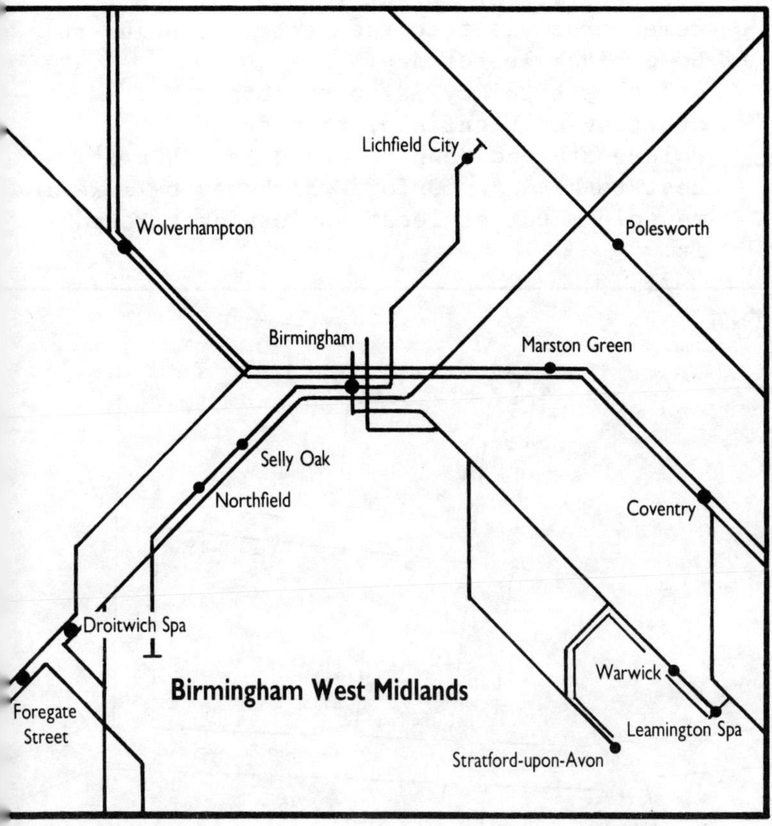

The reason the Race Relations Board does not object to it being called the Black Country is that anybody who travels through it is bound to end up being sympathetic to the residents.

The only ray of sunshine is from the railway lines which radiate rather than convect. You can buy a rover ticket either daily or weekly and the whole place is quite efficient to get round, but just remember a visit to the centre is going to be a black letter day.

The best policy is to surround it, starting at Lichfield, then on to Polesworth and down to Coventry. Then it is best to head for Oxford which may be like a mausoleum but at least you can walk round it.

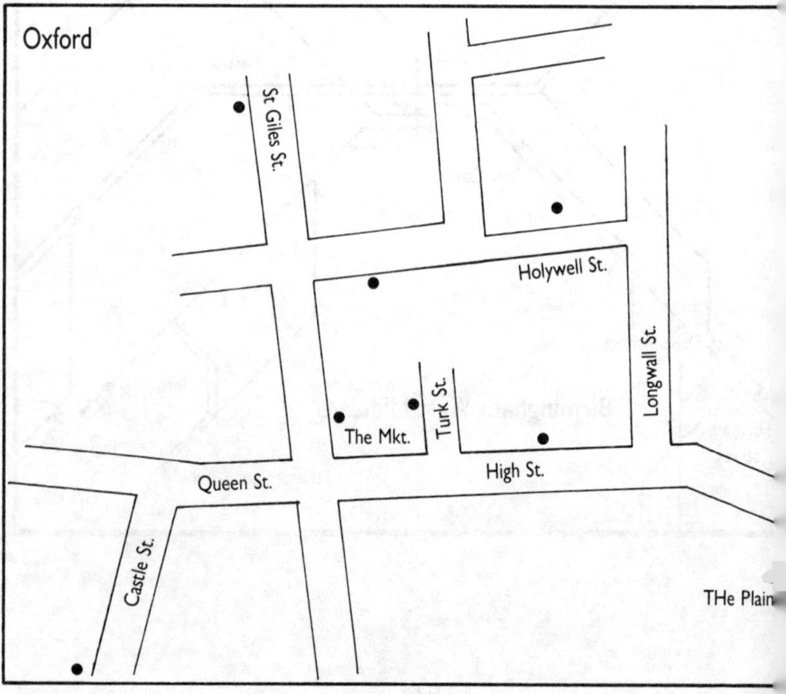

HARROGATE TO LONDON

THE BLACK BONE OF ENGLAND

A Spine Chiller

You can tell that Harrogate is a prosperous place, it has almost as many charity shops as Wimbledon. In Wimbledon they have tennis, but in Harrogate they have balls. The amounts they ask for a thing would make you consider emigrating to the south; Wakefield for instance, where books are so cheap the people in Harrogate would accuse them of being illegal immigrants.

As long as you have money and time Harrogate can be quite pleasant, but then what isn't? But the really good news about Harrogate is that unless you turn up in a limousine they completely ignore you, it is an experience that is almost worth travelling by British Rail for.

Whereas in Leeds they almost nail you to the floor if you wear a tie, the Mr Miles shop by the town hall tries its best to persevere with solid roast beef traditions but now has to allow in so much riff raff on its shelves that it can almost be worth a look.

There is a university in Leeds, the main purpose of which is instructing the locals in which ticket is valid on the buses. It tries hard but it fails miserably. The shops out by Hyde Park seem almost like an oasis by the time you have worked out how to get there.

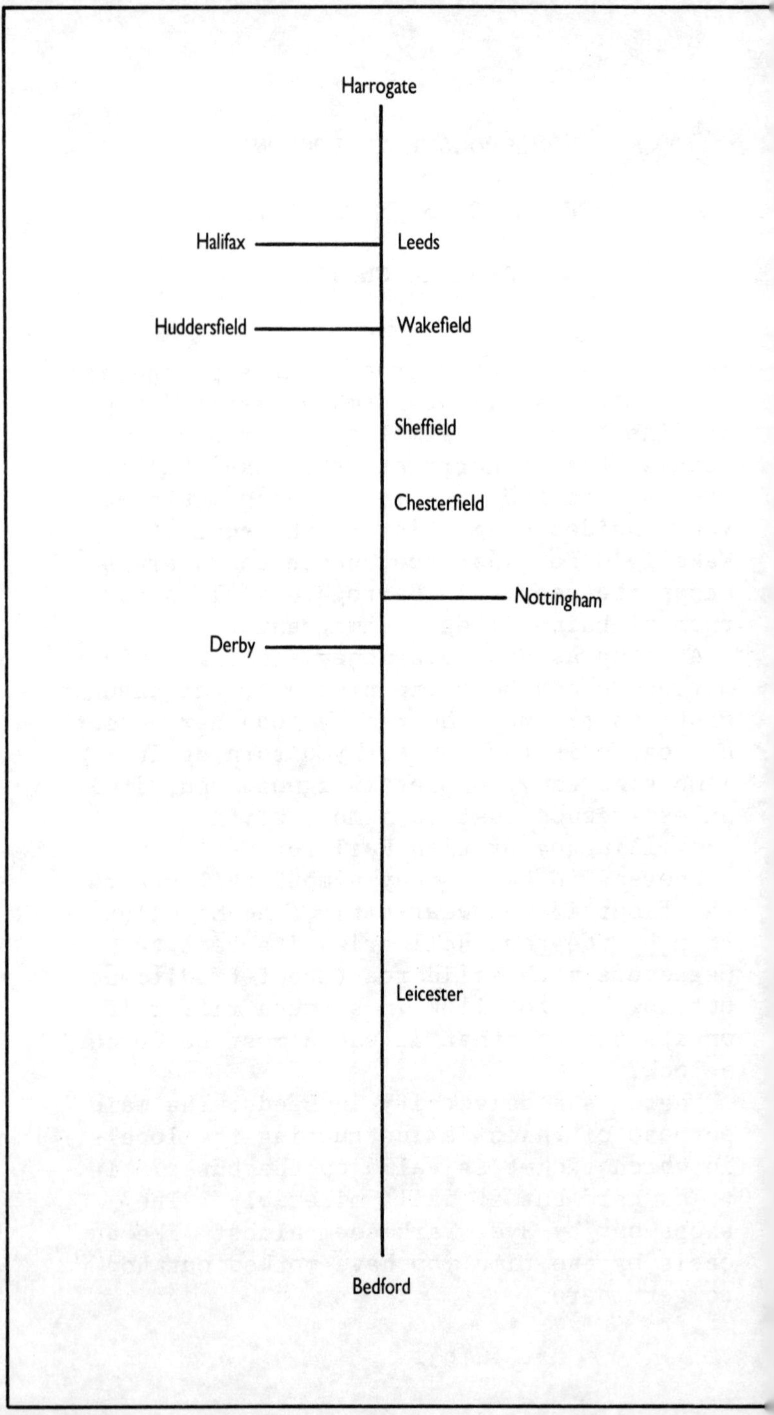
Harrogate
Halifax
Leeds
Huddersfield
Wakefield
Sheffield
Chesterfield
Nottingham
Derby
Leicester
Bedford

In Halifax they have the Three Piece Hall (and another shop has allegedly opened just to the north of it, it looks like Britain's one attempt at Italian architecture and is occupied by a specailist in military history). The second shop is occupied by a specialist in havoc making, it is not so much the books as what he does with them. Bookshops are notorious for accidently placing books in the wrong section but none can compete with this shop; if he had three ducks on his wall he would get them in the wrong order.

Holmfirth has the sigh a mees twins, in Daisy Lane Books they have television cameras watching you. I don't mind doing screen tests, but I would like to know what it is I am appearing in.

In Toll House Books I found one book I was distinctly keen to buy, but it was unpriced. The assistant had to go off in search of the owner, who very reluctantly returned to what she considered to be the low level task of pricing. She looked at me as if I was the type of person who rubbed the prices out of books and gave the shop a second chance. As I had not done so on this occasion I was very offended. She then spent a long time looking me up and down and I much appreciated her, what I took to be, admiration. I was wearing my Prince of Wales check jacket, my moleskin plus fours, my bright yellow stockings and my ratting cap, apparel which I consider to be de rigeur in the north. I was expecting a comment on the tartan tie but instead she said: '£45'.

I did not take kindly to this the last time I had bought this book in a bookshop (classified in a previous edition of drif's guide as being one of the most expensive in Britain) it had cost £20.

I gave her my most rehearsed riposte, it is famed not so much for the words but as the tone in which it is said, it sounds as if I am auditioning to become a castrati.

"I can't afford that," I said.

To which she replied:

"I don't expect that YOU can afford it, but you should not say so in that tone of voice."

She was right, I should have used another tone. This question of which tone to use when you are trying to negotiate is extremely difficult to get right. It is almost as difficult as knowing which is the right tie to wear with a Prince of Wales jacket, but not quite as important.

In the end it is best to be lighthearted, quite simply because so many bookdealers take pricing so seriously.

In Sheffield you do not get the feeling that you would end up as a true castrati if you did make an offer for a book. They would not use the knives for which they are famous. It would more than likely be a broken bottle.

Despite the atmosphere and sound system of a Glasgow nightclub, Rare and Racy remains the most interesting shop. They have books which it might just be worth knifing people for, but I do not think they have books that are worth putting up with the sound system.

Alan Hills is slightly more sedate, but those of us who wear tartan ties welcome less clashes, from external stimuli. I think he works on the basis that the prices are going to be shock enough.

After this pair the shops in the Sharrowvale Road area re not only non musical they are most attractive to the deaf and the dumb.

In YSF books I was asked if Billericay was a place of any account. I left for the Porter Bookshop without saying a word.

It takes a day to do all the shops in Sheffield and it takes a day to do all the shops in Leeds, but I think I would prefer Sheffield. You do get the feeling that they would not be averse to the use of the broken bottle, but in Leeds they feel this would be an extreme extravagance on a foreignor (somebody who does not come from Yorkshire).

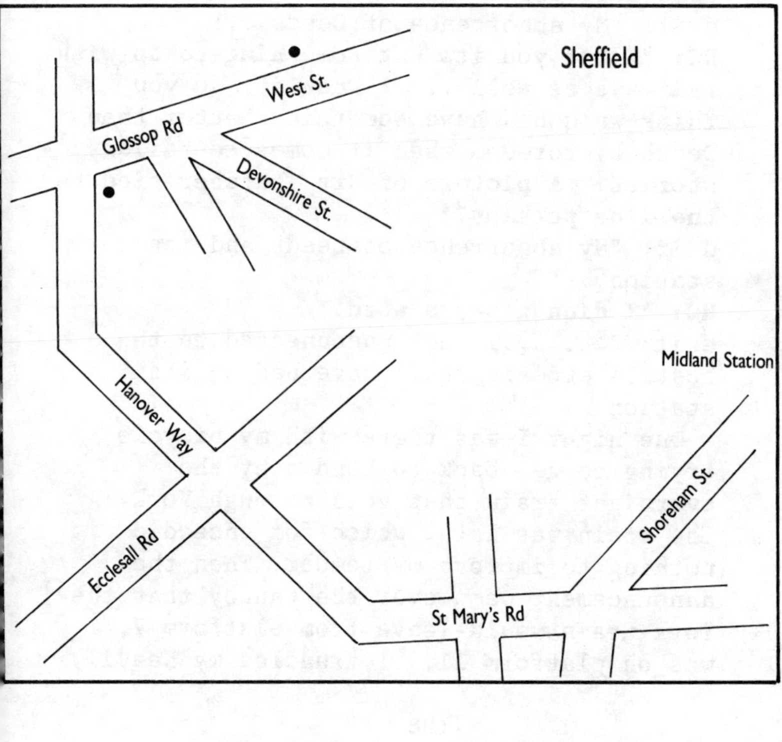

My Abhorrence of Leeds

RC: "I'll go and get the Death by Boredom signs".
drif: "Whadayamean?"
RC: "Everytime you use that MY, I can tell its going to be long and deadly, I bet you this story has got nothing to do with bookdealing. See you are not saying a word. I can always tell, give me time and I will be able to work out how long and dreary it is going to be as well."
drif: "........."
RC: "Well get on with it, there is no need to sulk, if you don't tell it now you will more than likely claim it happened somewhere else."
drif: "My abhorrence of Leeds..."
RC: "I bet you its got something to do with railways as well ... I knew it, do you think we could have something better than Death by Boredom when it comes to railway stories? A picture of Mrs Thatcher tied to the line perhaps?"
drif: "My abhorrence of Leeds and its station..."
RC: "I didn't say a word."
drif: "......is not unconnected to the hostile experiences I have had on its station.

One night I was there with my bicycle trying to get back to London by the overnight train that goes through York. The train was late, which for once did nothing to improve my temper. Then the announcement came over the tannoy that the York train would leave from platform 7, I was on platform 11. I trundled my heavily laden bike to the lift, went down to the underground passage which would have made Hades look like heaven and got the lift up to platform 7. I was stood there breathing wearily when a British Rail employee accosted me with the immortal words: 'Where did you come from?'

I was not exactly certain if I had heard him correctly not just because the natives of Leeds speak a different dialect, but because he raised his voice with every word. When I did not answer at all he seemed to begin changing colour rather than language.

I honestly could not work out what this question meant. I could see that I was not expected to give a philosophical answer, but I certainly could not work out what answer was expected. In a mannerism I often use with my chauffeur I breathed out, heavily, this seemed to infuriate him even more. He now began bouncing up and down on the platform, and other porters were beginning to form an audience. Seeing that I was getting my just desserts I asked in my best Bertie Wooster come Kantian voice:

"Well it depends what you mean, do you mean where did I come from in the cosmos, do you mean where was I born, or do you mean where did I come from today?"

This seemed to have the desired effect, he almost hit the roof. Ever since I have wondered if that is why they have them so high in railway stations.

He screamed at me in a voice that could have been used in psychiatric training sessions: "Where did you come from just now?"

"Ah now we are getting somewhere," I

said. "It is always best to frame your questions with appropriate parameters."

This particular choice of word may have been inappropriate, he looked as if, if he had a parameter he would have framed me with it. He stamped the floor, turned the colour of W C Fields' nose and screamed in a voice that I hoped would halt the train in York;

"Where did you come from just now?"

I could tell by his incandescence, that he was deadly earnest, and if he got any more serious he would certainly have been dead. I put on my reasonable dealing with the lower orders voice:

"I came from platform 11"

(on reflection it sounds like an SF novel, but none of the people there went in for that type of fantasy).

"And how did you get here?"

This was a question that I felt deserved a witty reply, but unfortunately I started laughing before I could give one.

He began roaring at me again, in a voice that was a cross between a lion clearings its throat and niagara. The amount of spittle bore more resemblance to the latter.

By now the more junior staff were alongside him possibly in a hope that they would get a chance to use their lessons in mouth to mouth ressucitation, or taking lessons in applying British Frail's citizens charter.

"How did you get from platform 11 to platform 7?" This more reasonable tone arose because by now a more senior British Frail official had joined the proceedings.

"I used the lift."

"You admit it then, you admit it."

"And who gave you permission to use the lift?"

This was the more senior official but the obsolescent bundle of rage was being kept on for special effect.

Now that it had dawned on me what all this was about I could not stop laughing. I think if I had been applying for a post in the diplomatic corps it might have reduced my chances but on Leeds station at ten o'clock on a blustery evening I was not overperturbed.

"Who gave you permission to use the lift?" (it was the highly trained manager).

"Come come, surely this is not what all this is about?"

But it was and they were in more than deadly earnest. I breathed out again. The porter, who when he retired could have hoped for a job in the everlasting light bulb industry, again took up the cudgels:

"And what does it say on that lift?"

I put on my quizzical look and said "Miss Otis regrets?"

"Can't you read, what it says is no UNAUTHORISED PERSON TO USE THIS LIFT."

I did not believe that this was what this entire confrontation was about, but eight British Frail porters, a senior railwayman and one manager felt otherwise. It was then that for the first time in my life I attempted to claim some literary talent. I normally describe myself as being a compiler of guide books, but on this occasion I felt that poetic licence was entirely justified.

"Oh well in that case I am qualified to

use the lift which says No Unauthorised Persons; I am an author."

I was the only one to smile, but not for long for then another voice behind me said:

"We have had enough of your sarcasm, come along with me."

It was a British Transport Policeman. He did not take too kindly when I burst out laughing, and when we reached his office he said after much disparagement of my reprehensible behaviour.

"I can either arrest you for misuse of British Rail property or, you can agree to be cautioned. Which is it going to be?"

I could not keep a straight face, I thought about it and declined to say anything. I stood there in dumb insolence refusing to talk or even utter a syllable.

The policeman disappeared and a few minutes later returned with reinforcements and I was led off to an interrogation room which much to my joy had a long shelf like seat where I stretched out and promptly went to sleep.

I was awoken by the policeman bouncing into the room, with a face that was a good impersonation of the non philosophical railway porter and he expostulated in a voice that implied he had never heard of such horror.

"You never told us you were under investigation for murder!"

Refreshed from my sleep and with my comprehensive experience of the wonder that for want of a better term is called British Justice I could see exactly what was going to happen. I would get off the murder charge but I would get life for using the lift...

RC: "Well what about the rest of the story?"
drif: "Excuse me, are you the same person who was complaining earlier about the interminable length of my anecdotes?"
RC: "Well you can't just leave it like that?"
drif: "I thought you were the one who was not keen that I should relate these stories at length."
RC: "Being arrested for murder is hardly an anecdote, is it?"
drif: "You are the one who is always urging me to keep to the bookdealing."
RC: "Well you mean it was NOT a bookdealer you murdered?"

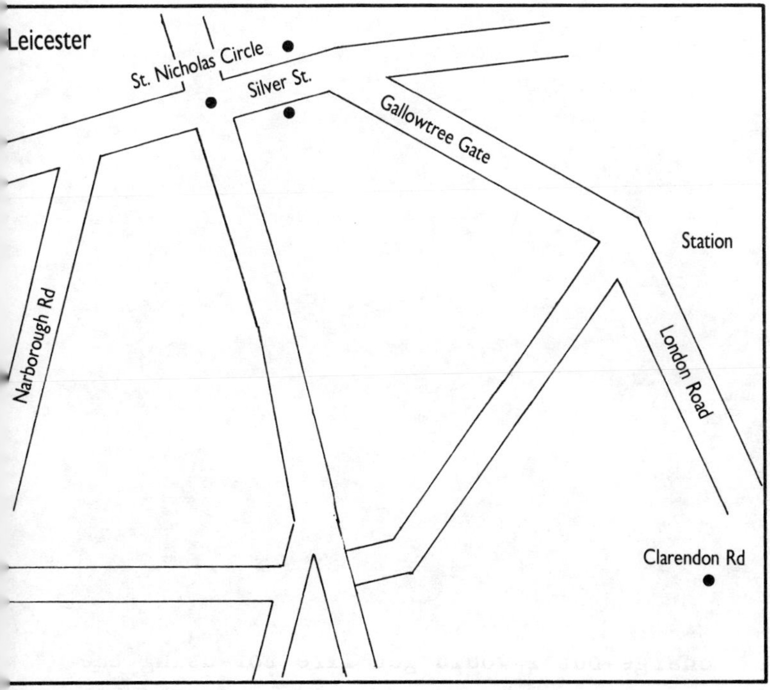

THE NETWORK SOUTHEAST

Network South East

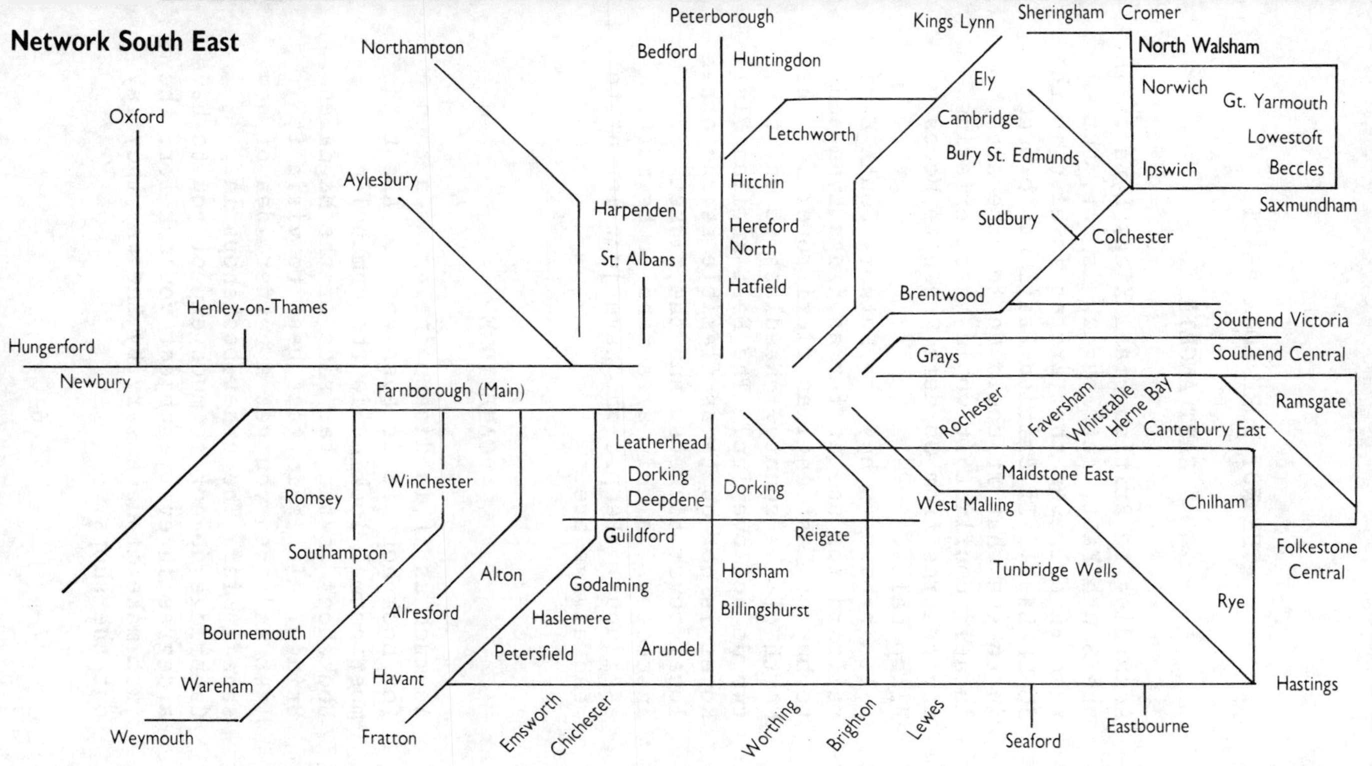

THE NOT WORK SOUR FEAST

EAST ANGLIA

According to British Frail Kings Lynn is in the South East, but Ipswich is not, but then BR believes that Exeter is also in the South East. If British Frail was brought in to see what it could do for the arab israeli conflict it would start offering day returns from Golders Green to Mecca Bingo halls.

It is best to buy the Network South East railcard for use as far as Kings Lynn and to buy an East Anglian flexi rover for the North of the county. Needless to say the two do not overlap. The East Anglian Flexi Rover is not quite as flexible as the other local rover tickets, and the ticket inspectors in this area tend to be more assiduous. People who have just learnt to read always are.

CAMBRIDGE

As much as it is disappointing as a town, for bookshops it is even worse. About the most normal looking is the Unmaudlin Bookshop* on the far side of the Magdalen Bridge. It is in fact best to visit it last and then you get a better idea of how sane it is. The other bookshops in Cambridge do not so much expect you to have a degree in every subject you ask for, they just make it necessary by the way they lay out the shops.

The only other shop where I can cope is The Haunted Bookshop in St Edwards Passage; it specialised in childrens books.

It is no accident that Hoaxfam have chosen Cambridge for their purpose built charity bookshop, this is not an institution I expect you to avoid, I would very much recommend it.

Having massacred the junk shops of Britain this Holier than Thou bunch of hypocrites is now intent on wiping out the secondhand bookshops.

RC: "You have already had a go at that mob."

drif: "If they can have alleged charity shops in every town in Britain then the least I can do is have another go at them."

As I was saying, not only do they have the resources to purchase a shop in the heart of Cambridge when other bookshops are closing down, they spend money on making it look like something from the inside of Homes & Gardens. They sure as hell did not get their fittings from Hoaxfam. They then charge more than any other secondhand bookshop would possibly dare, in ignorance, it is appalling to think how much they would charge if they knew some of the values of the books. They are not in the business of encouraging book collectors, indeed they see such things as being entirely frivolous, it is the ignorance with which they price the books which is the main grounds for objection. They get the stuff for free, they get the premises rate free, they get the staff for free and then they charge the most they can think of. Unless we hurl bricks through the windows now, we will be the ones whom

Hoaxfam and its ilk will be helping. They do it in the name of charity; if they had an ounce of charity in them they would stop.

From Cambridge it is best to go to Ely which has the most strange hours in Britain and then on to Kings Lynn which has one of the strangest bookshops in Britain. The Tower Bookshop in Tower Street is a strange combination of comic shop and drif special. It is one of those shops where you have to look at the price of all the books because they are so oddly priced. Even more odd is the selection. It is known that there are regional differences in food likes and dislikes. People in the north of England like orange cheese, in the south they like yellow. This bookshop would lead you to believe there are also differences in book likes and dislikes.

I like the shop in Fakenham but what I don't like is that it is almost impossible to get to and back by public transport. Its easy enough getting there but getting back is much more problematical, but it is almost worth being stranded on the edge of civilisation for this bookshop. The Tin Drum has style, plus it also has a very helpful owner, it is not until you meet him that you realise how miserable some of the others are.

It is a shop which takes an entire day to go through properly, but a day here would be filled with hope - the most essential quality that a secondhand bookshop can have.

The shop in Holt is currently subject to much change; it has gone into partnership with Mr T Hull of Norwich who has closed his establishment here.

The shop in Sheringham is a drif special not least in that it opens late and on Sundays during the tourist season. The shop in Cromer is smaller and slightly less flexible.

Even if you do not do well in Fakenham, Sheringham or Cromer you will do well by just avoiding the bookshop in Walsingham. It is not the books which are bad, but the owner. I have a vague suspicion that he is funded by Atheists to make Christians look bad; I didn't think the name of Christians could get any worse until I met him. Talk about talk, if you were deaf, dumb and blind he would do his best to make your life miserable.

Such is my horror of the above bookshop that I have not gone near the one in North Walsingham because in some way I feel that they are vaguely related.

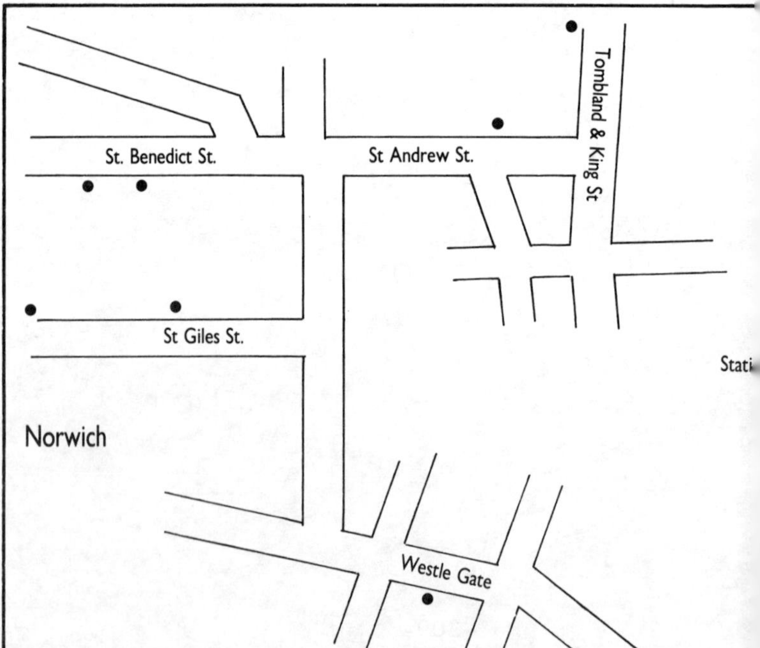

Tombland & King St
St. Benedict St.
St Andrew St.
St Giles St.
Stati
Norwich
Westle Gate

Norwich is a good place to base yourself, especially if you do not have a motor car, (the local council seem to hate them even more than me). The hotels and retaurants tend to be needlessly expensive but the bookshops make up for it. By far the most interesting bookshop in Norwich is Tombland and not just because of the name. They have the ability to make roast beef books into nouvelle cuisine.

The Scientific Anglian which could be a pleasant dessert has a taste like school tapioca. The other shops are very much in between.

Tristram Hull is now closed and moved to Holt. Peter Crowe's shop is the ABA at rest and Ellis continues with the good work of disguising remainders as secondhand books.

For the epitome of roast beef it is best to go to Great Yarmouth and then to continue down the coast. This part is filled with solid English puddings other than Mr Rolph in Lowestoft who is like the opposite of a greenhouse plant. There is a second shop in Lowestoft which I have not visited. I got stuck listening to one of the shorter anecdotes of the gentleman in Southwold, a place where the entire population is rehearsing for a part in the local production of the Rhyme of the Ancient Mariner.

In a valiant attempt to dislodge the East Anglians out of their complacency, the gentleman who owns Westleton Books in the village of the same name has taken to quietly trying to disturb their psyche. The books in this shop have an extremely UNSETTLING effect on the mind. THOUSANDS

NOW LIVING WILL NEVER DYE, DROWNED IN A FAR COUNTRY, THE PIE THAT CAME IN FROM THE COLD, THE BOOK OF COMMON PAYERS.

Even British Frail admits that Colchester is in the Network South East, when it comes to Kent British Frail has to admit that all of it is in the South East, but to compensate for this they now have teams of flying inspectors. Their brains are completely in the air. You are now supposed to have a ticket which specifically says where you are going, that you have a ticket which actually costs more than they are attempting to charge for the full fare is irrelevant, thus if you buy a return ticket to Ramsgate, you also have to state which way you are going either via the coast or Canterbury. You are not allowed to choose the route. This sounds like a joke until you hear that they charge you £10 for simply changing your mind.

Canterbury is not so much the roast beef as the strawberries and cream. It is great but the thing you remember most is the cost.

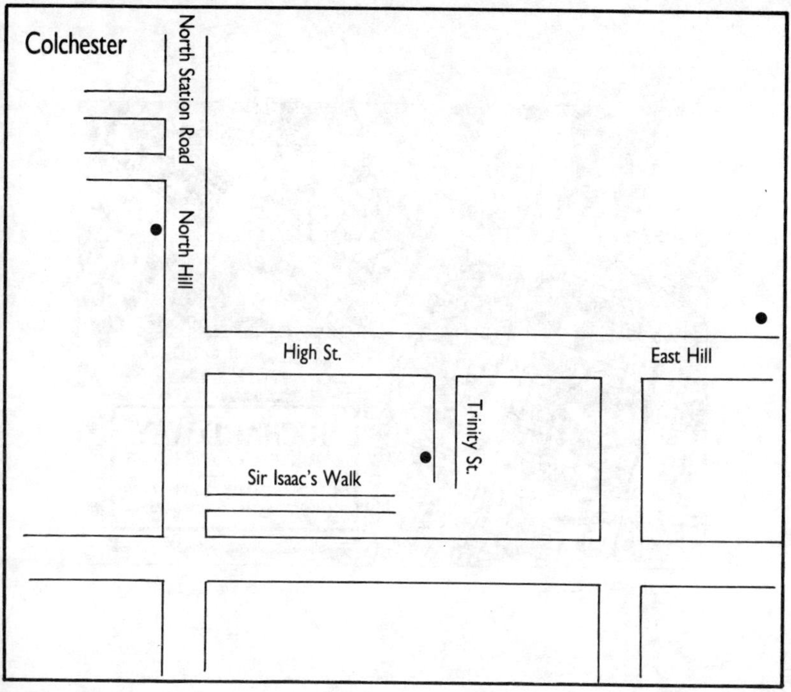
Colchester
North Station Road
North Hill
High St.
East Hill
Trinity St.
Sir Isaac's Walk

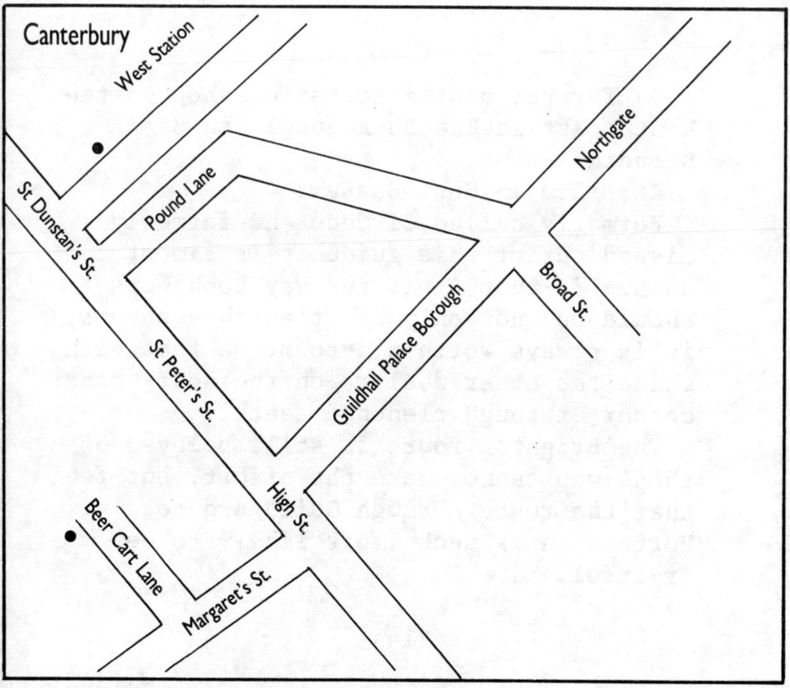
Canterbury
West Station
Northgate
Pound Lane
St Dunstan's St.
Broad St.
Guildhall Palace Borough
St Peter's St.
High St.
Beer Cart Lane
Margaret's St.

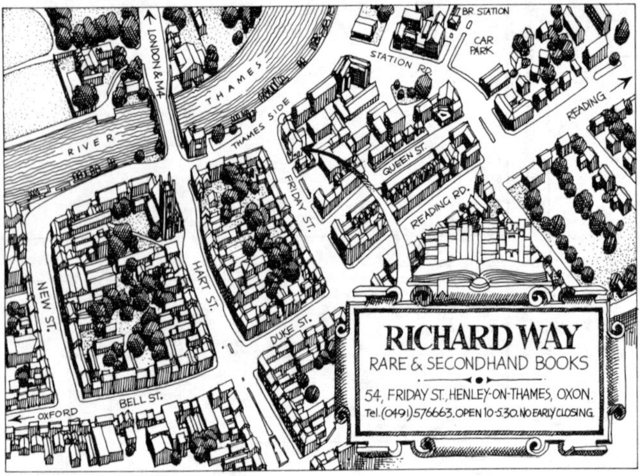

By far the most interesting shop on the Kent coast is The Book Jungle in St Leonards.

RC: "Its in West Sussex."

Formerly called Cirdeco and formerly missed out of this guide it is almost unique in that it is the way bookshops should be, not only is it worth a detour, it is always worth a detour. A fact with which the other dealers on the south coast concur, through clenched teeth.

The Brighton route is still beloved of those who cannot make the effort, but feel that the route through Guildford to Portsmouth is much more likely to be fruitful.

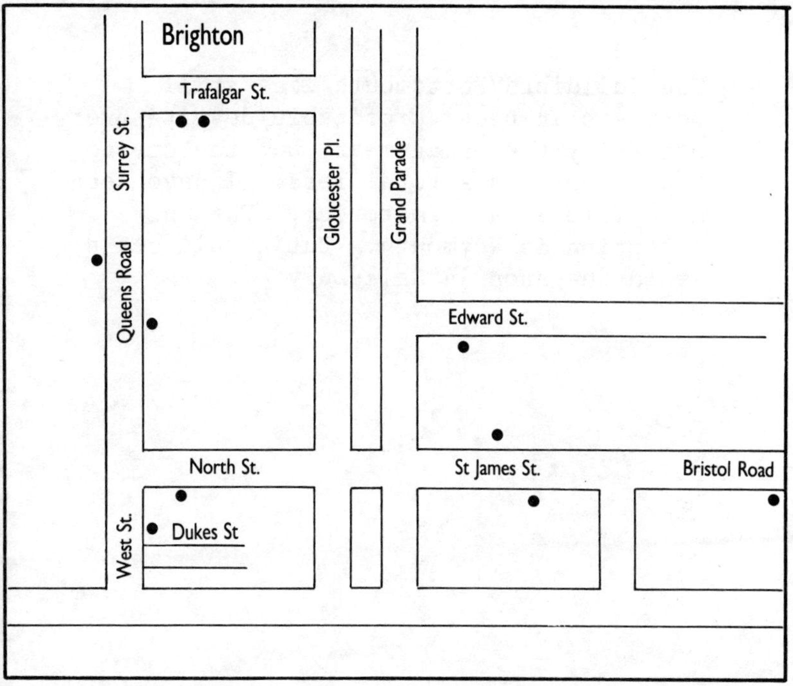
Brighton
Trafalgar St.
Surrey St.
Queens Road
Gloucester Pl.
Grand Parade
Edward St.
North St.
St James St.
Bristol Road
Dukes St
West St.

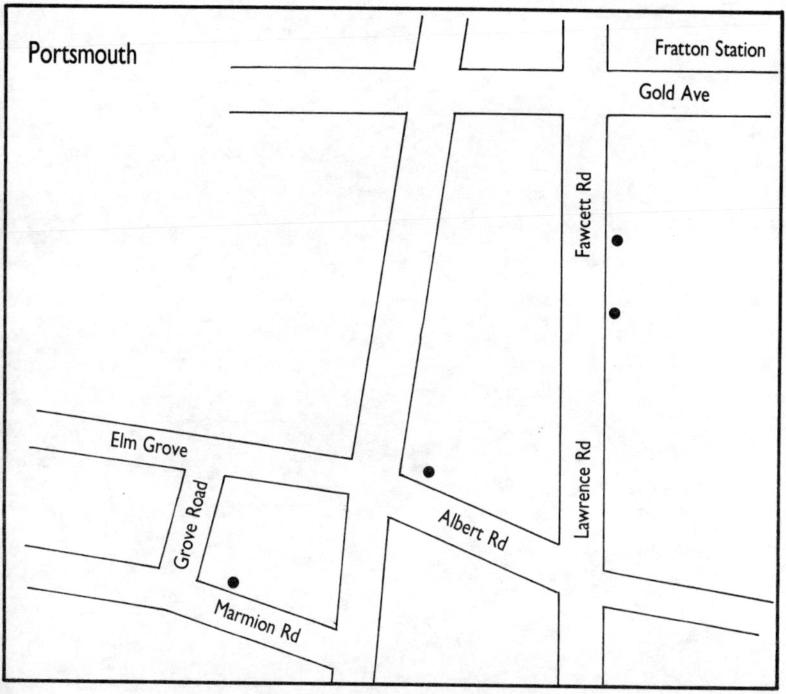
Portsmouth
Fratton Station
Gold Ave
Fawcett Rd
Elm Grove
Grove Road
Albert Rd
Lawrence Rd
Marmion Rd

The Guildford/Portsmouth line still persists in being profitable despite every effort by the management, but the one to Bournemouth is a total loss. I have seen more life in a crematorium. The only exception is Weymouth. But at all costs, avoid the shop in Salisbury.

LONDON

DO YOU SOMETIMES FEEL YOUR LIFE IS ALMOST A COMPLETE WASTE? THAT THINGS ARE NOT GOING QUITE THE WAY YOU HAD HOPED? THAT NOTHING SEEMS TO TURN OUT THE WAY YOU HAD PLANNED? WELL NOW AT LONG LAST HELP IS AT HAND. WE CAN SHOW YOU HOW TO WASTE YOUR LIFE COMPLETELY.

Although we have been in the business for many years, it is not until now that we have been able to speak of our true nature - but this has not stopped many uninformed people from spreading false stories. It is to counter these vicious untruths that we are speaking out for the first time. Now a leading publisher can enable you to share some of the greatest secrets of the universe: How to do nothing and be proud of it: How to continue to do nothing when other people try to make youdo something: How to do nothing using vast amounts of other peoples' money, when you have been paid to do something: How to be indifferent to complaints that you are doing nothing: How to claim that you will do something and still do nothing. Never in the long story of civilisation has there been such a revelation, this is no idle boast, the very mention of our name will be more than enough to convince of the sincere truth of our claim, for we are: **LONDON TRANSPORT** (the world's greatest time wasters).

L O N D O N T R A N S P O R T
WE MAKE A SIMPLE JOUNREY AN EPIC ADVENTURE

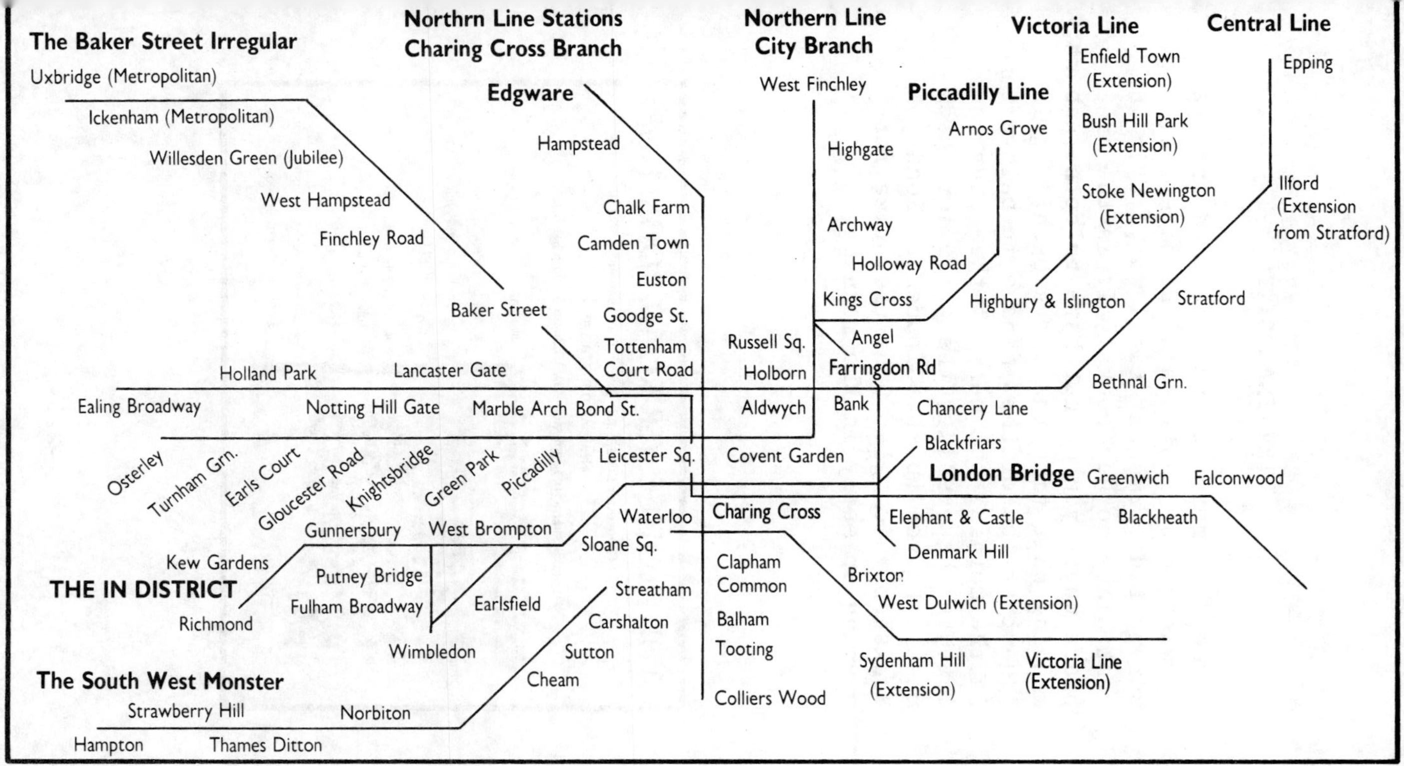
The Baker Street Irregular
Uxbridge (Metropolitan)
Ickenham (Metropolitan)
Willesden Green (Jubilee)
West Hampstead
Finchley Road
Baker Street
Northrn Line Stations
Charing Cross Branch
Edgware
Hampstead
Chalk Farm
Camden Town
Euston
Goodge St.
Tottenham
Court Road
Northern Line
City Branch
West Finchley
Highgate
Archway
Kings Cross
Russell Sq.
Holborn
Aldwych
Angel
Farringdon Rd
Bank
Piccadilly Line
Arnos Grove
Holloway Road
Victoria Line
Enfield Town
(Extension)
Bush Hill Park
(Extension)
Stoke Newington
(Extension)
Highbury & Islington
Central Line
Epping
Ilford
(Extension
from Stratford)
Stratford
Bethnal Grn.
Chancery Lane
Holland Park
Lancaster Gate
Ealing Broadway
Notting Hill Gate
Marble Arch
Bond St.
Leicester Sq.
Covent Garden
Blackfriars
London Bridge
Greenwich
Falconwood
Osterley
Turnham Grn.
Earls Court
Gloucester Road
Knightsbridge
Green Park
Piccadilly
Charing Cross
Elephant & Castle
Blackheath
Waterloo
Gunnersbury
West Brompton
Sloane Sq.
Denmark Hill
Kew Gardens
Putney Bridge
Clapham
Common
Brixton
THE IN DISTRICT
Streatham
West Dulwich (Extension)
Fulham Broadway
Earlsfield
Richmond
Carshalton
Balham
Tooting
Wimbledon
Sutton
Sydenham Hill
(Extension)
Victoria Line
(Extension)
The South West Monster
Cheam
Colliers Wood
Strawberry Hill
Norbiton
Hampton
Thames Ditton

TERMINAL CITY

London has more secondhand bookshops than anywhere else in Britain. Despite the unreported permanent civil war, it is the best place to buy books. It is the one place where you do not have to bother about knowing what time the shops open. It is true that few of them manage it before ten in the morning but many of them stay open late in the evening, the prize for which must be given to the Gloucester Road Bookshop which also wins the prize for opening up early in the morning.

It is best to purchase an off peak all zone travel card (covering you for travel on the tube, buses and British Frail lines within the M25) which currently costs £3.40 per day. Travelling in a motor car is lunacy, the reason most London taxi drivers are completely demented is that they have to drive round working out which is the fastest way to go as opposed to the shortest route, they also have to cope with one way streets and that wonderful piece of Newspeak; ROADWORKS AHEAD (if we had drifspeak it would be; ROAD DOES NOT WORK AHEAD.

The one book that licensed taxi drivers always have is a street atlas and this is the one piece of taxi driver behaviour that you should emulate. If you are not familiar with London then relying on my or anybody else's directions is not going to work. If you ask a Londoner they will tell youthat there is also a South Bank, they conceive of the North Bank as being Central London. Most of them are not even aware that there is an East and West Bank. Londoners are the ones who think the river is straight.

The directions I give in the directory are all from tube stations, but just trying to negotiate your way out of tube stations requires highly complex maps itself. I use Leicester Square tube almost every day (for Charing Cross Road, Charing Cross tube is not as near as Leicester Square) and I have never worked out which name is the exit I need to come out closest to the bookshops, how I remember it is that it is the one by the newsagent.

Instead of naming exits London Underground should put up photographs showing where the exit comes out.

Where possible I have tried to indicate when there are several exits, but without an AtoZ you are bound to get lost. But do not be dismayed; it happens to us Londoners all the time.

LONDON

FARRINGDON ROAD

In Farringdon Road there is a newly built office block which if it is to stand a chance of winning one of these prizes so beloved of architects could only enter the contest: Best Building with Down's Syndrome.

I don't doubt that the sires of this monstrosity feel that their baby is the most beautiful in the world, even if she is a little handicapped, or that they cherish the architect's equivalent of baby's first photograph. The artist's impression especially commissioned to commemorate how truly beautiful their offspring was, showing purposeful executives in dark blue chalk stripe striding past revolving doors, leaving their liveried chauffeurs to park the limousine, young men in Armani suits holding the doors of Porsches for power dressed blondes and delicate office girls in pastel shades nibbling sushi. A black man would be chatting happily to a child by the fountain and a cycle messenger dressed for the Tour De France would be disappearing into the distance.

The only person capable of capturing an accurate portrait of Farringdon Road on a

Saturday morning is Heironymous Bosch. Ever since I can remember the road in front of that building has been badly scarred by groups of people who could make it look perfectly formed and truly beautiful.

Men in heavy duty anoraks that would be useful if you were crossing Antartica - but their trainers belie the possibility - stand around practising shoulder lifts, with their hands in their pockets. Adolescents dressed in clothes even Oxfam would be uncharitable about try to look what they feel is normal. Fully paid up members of the indoor revolutionary party kitted out by Army surplus stores of the people's republic of dementia try to look sane. Boiler suited behemoths wonder if they should hold the annual ceremony of scraping the Anorak (this tends to be the female element who are on the whole a lot cleaner than the male). Those that do wear suits look as if they bought them from the KGB surplus stores, come rain or shine they are there every Saturday morning. Only the weather changes not the faces or the apparel.

They stand together but somehow apart as if they were waiting for a job interview, each a rival but each sharing the same aim.

In the road are five long tables covered in canvas, the grime of which must be an inspiration to many habituee of the Farringdon Road. For no discernible reason they seem to assemble in front of one particular stall and some of the more youthful and brave furtively lift the cover, looking like schoolboys scared to be seen going into the girls' changing room. They remember the last time the master caught them. George finds them out every time.

If anything he is more indescribably dressed than any of them, he is their role model, but somehow they fail to carry it off precisely because they are trying, whereas he is trying to look like nothing. He actually dresses as if he does not want you to see him. A short stocky man he has almost succeeded in hiding himself. He is the type of person automatic doors fail to open for. An invisible Napoleon.

Then it happens he stands at one end of the table and like a magician pulls the cloth away. The scrum vie to find out what is underneath. They are crammed so close together that it would make London Underground green with envy., they elbow, they barge, they take flying leaps, knees are brought into play. It is as if that table had on it one loaf of bread and they were there on behalf of the starving. Nobody wants to leave without at least a crumb.

In front of another table, a group of slightly less malnutrished ones are trying hard to look unconcerned and unconnected with the marauders, they do not wish to be seen even contemplating such lower class antics... they seem slightly more prosperous, they smoke cigars, have had haircuts this year and it is possible to see the colour of their Tee shirts. But when George performs his canvas pulling trick they show that the officer class is not to be outdone by impoverished oiks. That insouciant stance is a feint to ensure that their rivals do not learn that there are more and better loaves on this table.

The same people who were great friends a few seconds ago are now the greatest foes. All have perfected the technique of hitting whilst lifting, gouging whilst grabbing, pulling whilst punching. One even leaps onto the table and declares independence but George with all the majesty of a High Court judge pulls him off and the proceedings continue.

There is one man standing on top of yet another table directing his soldiers further into the battle, showing them where the enemy is weak.

It is at the third table that the generals congregate, they disdain the minor skirmishes which they look upon as being training for junior troops, for the real battle is to come, those frantic confrontations are but dim memories. They pass judgment as if they were Blucher or Ney.

George stands by his supply wagon and as if deciding how to ration one loaf amongst these generals used to better fare, he pulls out a book, but this is no tally, this is no register, this is no dole and more strangely still he is asking them to offer money for it. He is holding an auction, of a book, an old book. They appear to be trying to crush him from all sides at the same time. It looks like a form of group frottage, the more robust their behaviour the more lively George the emperor gets. Occasionally he issues reprimands, and sometimes orders demotions, but his heart is not in it, he revels in the aggression for it is he that controls it. If they don't push him enough he brings out yet more tempting prizes.

The perversion in which these people are engaged is known as book collecting. They are buying old books, the reason they are emasculating one another, threatening to tear limb from limb, swearing, leaping on tables and bullying, is that they are trying to get the books first. Whoever thought that books brought about civilised instincts had never been to the Farringdon Road on a Saturday morning.

Every week the almost identical mob appear. Occasionally a few strangers arrive but they soon suffer shell shock. They were ignorant of the fact that to be a book collector in the Farringdon Road you have to have practised karate, studied military tactics and read Machiavelli, and that is for the cheap table.

The ersatz venom of book reviews engaged in by Sunday Newspapers is but a pale simulacrum of what actually happens every Saturday in Farringdon Road. There it is hand to hand fighting, you have to look your enemy in the eye as you gouge him or her in the groin. It is battle to the death.

One of the most interesting feature of the people you see at George's (only an outsider would call it Farringdon Road) is that you seldom see them anywhere else. You do see some of them behind the counters of secondhand bookshops or manning book stalls but you do not see them buying elsewhere. They are never any real competition in shops, perhaps shops are too gentle for them.

Every week George goes through this performance, that is when he is not holidaying in the Bahamas, or attending to his accounts in the Channel Islands, for George has these addicts thoroughly sussed. He buys books wholesale and he sells them retail, but unlike most dealers what George does is only look at unit price. Thus he buys a tea chest for £100 and if it has 200 books he sells them for £1 each, many is the book that is in these tea chests that is 'worth' £10 and George sells it for £1. He is famous for doing this on an even bigger scale. The tales of books bought for £10 and sold for £1000 afterwards are by no means legend. This is why the knives are out every Saturday morning. The people who go to George's somehow behave as if George were ignorant of the 'real' value of these books but how do you think George managed to get hold of them so consistently if he is so ignorant?

George is notorious for buying teachests at auction, and many is the bookshop owner who has sent tea chests full of books to auction hoping that George will be the bidder or at least the underbidder. But George spots it every time, he can tell the difference between a genuine seller of tea chests and one sent in by the trade. Try as they might no trade chest has ever landed up in George's hands other than at a price he was happy to pay.

George is a pusher, the people who buy his books are addicts, they are hooked on the 'treasure in the attic' syndrome so beloved of journalists that all you have to do is hunt down some forgotten treasure and thousands of pounds will be yours. This ethos fostered by endless newspaper articles and inane radio and television programmes about items bought for a few shillings and sold at auction for many thousands, this permeates what passes for a mind in George's customers.

Many of George's bovver boys do have ibraries which are ostensibly worth thousands, but only because they never attempt to sell them. In the same way as they pounce on the books they pounce on the informatino tha the book they have bought is worth £50. They ignore the fact that there is no such thing as worth, there is only what you can get, and most of them never attempt to sell anything.

There are some who do, and it is possible to spot George's books in the Charing Cross Road or Bloomsbury and at many a PBFA bookfair. Strangely these books belong to people who describe themselves as being collectors and that they are simply disposing of surplus requirements. You can recognise the books by that same ragged look that George's customers have.
George's stall is the closest that there is to a wholesaler of secondhand books.
People unfamiliar with the ways of bookdealers such as bank managers, journalists and strangely, solicitors, have the vague notion that there is some warehouse where you can go and spend £1,000 on a lot of books and then price them up at £2,000. You can go anywhere and spend £1,000 and you can price them at £2,000 but the crucial part of the exercise is getting the £2,000 for them.

Many is the redundant moron who spends his money at auction in the belief that if somebody else is paying £1,000 for these books he too must be able to get more than that for them. Britain is littered with shops that contain nothing but the far fetched fantasies of their owners... The only wholesaler in Britain is George and how he can buy books for £1,000 and sell them for £2,000 is that he has all these idiots believing that they will get great treasures from him. George has understood, and I very much doubt if he read it in a book, that the man who makes the most money in a goldrush is the man who sells the shovels.

Waterloo station is named after the battle, what they should do in honour of George is name a battle after him. Saddam Hussein might well be able to withstand the full military might of the Western World but I am certain that he would show the white flag if they invited him to George's.

THE CHARING X ROAD

The Charing Cross Road is synonymous in the public mind with books, more especially secondhand books, but as so often in life the public is wrong. The truth is tha there are more new bookshops, more clothes shops, more hamburger joints, more kebab takeaways, more ticket touts and more down and outs than there are secondhand bookshops in Charing Cross Road.

It is true that the Charing Cross Road contains more secondhand bookshops than anywhere else in Britain (including Hay on Wye), and it is also true that the shops are more diverse than anywhere else in Britain (and especially Hay on Wye), but what is not quite appreciated in the public mind is how much the number and quality of the shops has declined in recent years. To this extent the Charing Cross Road is a microcosm of what is happening to secondhand bookshops in the rest of Britain.

There are now roughly 26 establishments in the Charing Cross Road - an area in which I include Cecil Court - which could be described as having secondhand books. However, for many of these the secondhand element is minor. Places such as Foyle, which if not a candidate for the worst secondhand bookshop in Britain contest is certain the worst in the Charing X, and Zwemmers have so little interest in the secondhand side that one wonders why they actually bother, but no matter how bad the stock, the image still persists that they are major buyers and sellers of secondhand books.

The truth is that there are only six establishments which sell general secondhand books in the Charing X Road, the others all sell books of a highly specialised nature, such as art, music, Greek, Crime fiction and occult, not only do they welcome the ordinary public or general secondhand book collectors it is my belief that most of the owners of these establishments would be able to intimidate Mrs Thatcher were she mistakenly to dare enter the portals.

The reason that there appear to be slightly more general secondhand shops is that in the Charing X there is a curious phenomena viz that almost all of the owners of the shops have two establishments, either directly alongside, or separately.

The most obvious example is in the section between Shaftesbury Avenue and Leicester Square Tube. Here just three owners have six secondhand shops. This is because they were able to negotiate a reduction in rents from the Building Association which owns the building and which had formerly belonged to the GLC which created a policy of letting out this section to bookshops (but not specifically secondhand). There are two reasons why these shops are keen to have double premises, firstly the Charing X Road is an extremely good site (relative to other positions in Britain, you would have extreme difficulty failing in the Charing X although it has happened); and secondly by ensuring that only they have the shops which are at relatively moderate rents they ensure that newcomers will start with one hand tied behind their back.

The shops that are currently in the Charing X Road live almost solely on the image which has been created over the years. They like to believe that they are good booksellers, but like the image this is the exact opposite of the truth. On the whole most of the shops and their assistants are rude, ignorant, arrogant and uninterested. This is because no polite, knowledgeable, interested, ordinary human being could ever survive such a hostile environment.

The customers in the Charing X have been conditioned by hopelessly inaccurate books - if 84 Charing X Road was such a great shop how come it had to close? And inane adverts - the chances of your finding a book on the phone in the Charing X are about the same as BT admitting that it was embarrassed by its profits. They (the customers) march into the shops expecting instant service, total knowledge and that the assistant will just hand over the book they are looking for. The whole idea of browsing in bookshops is now a thing of the past (I think thanks to that inane advert).

There is another group which is a regular visitor to the Charing X shores, and these are the people selling books. What is most strange about this species is how seldom they bring in interesting books and how often they have drearily high expectations. Even drearier is how often the shops buy these books after much discussion.

Lest the picture I paint should seem too gloomy I should point out that there is another group that does quietly thrive and politely flourish in the Charing X, these are the genuine collectors, they go their gentle way picking up bargains all the day, for they have discovered the surprising truth that the bookshops in the Charing X are cheaper, more varied, and have a faster turnover than any of the others in Britain.

SEVEN EASY & EFFICIENT WAYS TO UPSET A CHARING CROSS ROAD BOOKSHOP ASSISTANT.

1. Ask if this is the bookshop about which the unforgettable book (whose name you cannot quite remember(was written by the delightful American lady who was so egocentric that she never guessed that the bookshop in question loathd her, as did the New York bookshops. That was why they would not look for the common books she wanted.
2. Say how interesting it must be to work in a secondhand bookshop and that you wish you could spend your time talking with the assistants about Shelley, Shakespeare & Sholokov. Express sympathy because they are forced to listen to pop music, discuss nightclubs, dream of parties and have to keep looking at the clock.
3. First ask if they buy books (imply that they usually steal them), then take in an old book, a family bible is best, and test their honesty. Say that it was bought by your great grandfather (omit to mention that he did this yesterday) and that you have taken it to experts and had it 'valued'. See if the value that Sotheby's guarantee it is worth is the same as that which the bookshop offers for it. If there is a discrepancy between what the pinstriped hungover old Etonian who has been working in Bond Street for three weeks since leaving his crammers under a cloud, and the assistants who have been

in the secondhand bookshop for ten years, carefully explain why they have never progressed beyond being a bookshop assistant. This is best done in a haughty tone.

4. Ask the assistants if they know anything about books; if they make the mistake of saying, a little, ask which was the edition of the poems of Acton Ellis and Currer Bell which sold eight copies, if they do not answer immediately ask if this is genuinely a secondhand bookshop.
5. March straight up to the desk, stopping all conversations ask for directions to the Phoenix Theatre. Express extreme displeasure if you are not given a synopsis of the show.
6. Find a paperback with a printed price of 40p then point out that they have written £3 on it, offer to pay 20p since it is an old book.
7. Ask for a highly specialist book, it is best to choose one that your grandfather had on his shelves. When they have to admit they do not have it, ask where you can find a sensible bookshop, then when they give you the address express extreme irritation that it is not within walking distance. Imply that you are used to better service than this, ask for the address to be written down, with its openings hours, phone number and the location of the nearest tube. Be firm, ask them to draw a map, then tell them that you have a copy of this book and would they like to buy it before you offer it to a properly managed secondhand bookshop.

Renowned American authoress seeks mature Englishman to help fulfil fantasies; view possible partnership on sequel to unforgettable romance. Must be good listener and steeped in knowledge of old bookshops, prepared to travel entire length of Charing X Road and know how to use phone. Lifelong reward for successful applicant. Apply with photo: H.H., New York"...

HH: JR, you sound exactly what I want, a typical Englishman with his ear to the secondhand bookshops. JR have you ever thought of becoming a writer? I couldn't do better than a fly fisherman for what I have planned next, especially one so neatly dressed and literate. JR I know how it feels to be lacking the necessary resources, but I wanna tell you I never let it stop me. Now here's the plan. I want you to contact the bookshops in the Charing X Road and let them know I am going to sell my entire library, this is why I need a real man, it will be like an auction for the copyright to the bible, but JR, I want you to go about it modestly. I don't want you to get sidetracked, find out how much we can get cash, up front. We will sort out the shares later. Byeeee." (Boy am I glad I'm not paying for the phone calls).

..."Listen JR there can't be only four secondhand bookshops in the Charing X Rd, you can't be looking right... no, I don't mean your tweed jacket, you gotta use your imagination, invent things a little, invent them a lot, how do you think I wrote a bestseller. Well what you could do is tell them all the books are signed, the Shakespeare, the Keats, the Dickens, no JR by me not those DWEMS and tell them the original manuscript is in my own fair hand. What do you mean they want you to take the books in? JR have they been taking you in? Have you explained to them how much stuff there is. Why my most famous book is 156pp long. JR I cannot believe this, without me those bookshops would be nothing. JR I don't know how to tell you this, but I had an intimate relationship with a Charing X Rd bookshop... what do you mean that's why the others are not keen now.

JR, when I said Charing X Road I meant it, never put any more effort into a thing than you need to, who the hell has heard of Cecil Court. It sounds like another British politician being arrested for homosexuality, and it is just as seedy looking. I don't care if it has twenty secondhand bookshops, it does not have a name. JR, names are crucial, and what do you mean the modern first edition specialist said it was not his type of material, what sort of fantasies does he have in his basement. JR, you were a British officer, right? You have been to public school, right? And you have fought a war, right? So how can you be nervous about going into these shops?

Listen JR, just give me your telephone credit card number and I will sort it out myself."

JR: "Good morning is that the publishers, I have just had a splendid idea for a book. I have been going round the secondhand bookshops in Charing X Road and the Cecil Court, and it turns out that they are deliberately not living up to their image, not only that there are only half a dozen general bookshops the other twenty call themselves specialists, and all of them are the exact opposite of the way they are shown on television, or in books, indeed they all seem to make a point of appearing extremely rude, ignorant and obsessed by pop music. Worse than that they appear to be intent on making money. They recently negotiated a deal with the housing association that they would only have to pay half the market rent, and that was the ones who had two shops each. They offer derisory sums for the books that are brought in all day long because people who sell them have spent their lives believing the media which says the Charing X Road booksellers are experts. Indeed, at times there are more people trying to sell to the shops then there are people trying to buy. But you should see some of the people who do buy; they look like my idea of a secondhand bookdealer. They quibble over fifty pence books, they refuse to pay more than half price for newly published books and some of the books are on sale before they are officially published, can that be right? And then there are dealers who do nothing but hang round these shops waiting to buy the books that are put out too cheaply. By accident I talked to one, he said that he makes more money in the Charing X Road than he does traipsing round the whole of Britain; that was all he thought about - money.

What do you mean you have already been

offered this book, you are the first publisher I have spoken to. Of course I am certain, and no my name is not HH... but how can she possibly know anything about it, what is this book going to be called... FLY FISHING IN THE CHARING CROSS ROAD?

INDOOR REVOLUTIONARIES

If it is the gentle world of old style book collecting where some skill and patience is needed to sort the chaff from the wheat then you cannot do better than a branch of the indoor revolution.

They may propound the total overthrow of Capitalism, they may pay lip service to terrorists, they may condemn individualism as being a bourgeois affectation, but when it comes to selling secondhand books it is often hard to find better bargains.

Porcupines, the name seems designed to deter, is in the basement of Houseman's in the Caledonian Road. There cannot be a revolutionary moment worldwide which does not know of Houseman's. Not for them the unspoken ambiguities of a Shropshire lad, this is the place with all the written answers. If a Palestinian wishes to unmask an Israeli double agent, he asks him the route from Kings Cross to Houseman's... Editions of chairman Mao's little Red book used to contain erratum slips with Houseman's address on them. The more violent the revolutionary, the more likely it is that they have made the trek from Kings Cross to Houseman's, only the toughest survive intact. The Peruvian shining path guerrillas are so called because they experienced the dark shadows of life in Kings Cross. If you are serious about holding a revolution then the first prerequisite is to get some literature into Houseman's.

It is perhaps because they spend so much time being politically correct that bookshops such as Porcupines often have books which are highly attractive to us rightwingers. In Houseman's anybody who does not wear a black tee shirt or read the guardian is defined as a rightwinger.

Not all leftwing bookshops are as interesting, pleasant, lucrative or as tolerant as this one, but it is easy to spot those that are not keen on anybody of the incorrect political persuasion. After years of deliberation, endless committee meetings, and by the time everybody else had forgotten its existence, it was they who granted political asylum to the Cold War.

THE GLOUCESTER ROAD BOOKSHOP

If a group of librarians got together to make a horror film, I have no doubt that the Gloucester Road Bookshop would be very close to the end result.

For librarians the first abomination would be that there is nobody in charge of saying "We will be closing in five minutes" indeed it is not even an ambition to which any junior library assistant could aspire for the Gloucester Road bookshop seldom seems to sleep. The hours it is open are enough to give stacks full of librarians insomnia.

The books are those beloved of librarians, the type that seem to be chosen by a committee which has been informed that interest in books on underwater diving is up, but that we should not forget the junior reader; then they buy a book on how to blow bubbles...

The stock is like Woman's Hour on steroids or Radio 4 on Ecstasy. It is the Pathe News on LSD, it is the bastard offspring of a member of the literace and a megalomaniac.

There is a possibility that one of the reasons the GRB seldom seems to close is that they are scared that yet more books will breed during the night. There seems to be some dreadful alien force at work spreading into every empty space until the books have now taken over completely, there is hardly any space left for human beings. The tomes spring out of walls like street corner yobboes, they lie on their backs like drunken hacks from the Spectator, it is only the press of customers feet which keeps a path beaten through this jungle.

This shop has been a silent witness to an heroic act of bravery far beyond the call of duty. Whilst under constant barrage, these fighters withstood innumerable onslaughts, with the stiff upper lip they took everything that was thrown at them. They were not heard to utter a single word of complaint. Then one day they all did the sensible thing, they saw that the battle had been lost, that even were they to be given fresh recruits or leaders with greater metal there was nothing that could be done, other than what had previously been unthinkable, they surrendered. Never have so few bookshelves done so much.

The other possibility is that when GBR is officially closed, it is a centre for a new type of therapy - a cross between the Bates method and the Alexander technique - the students have to dance on tip toe through the shop and not touch any of the books. They are given one book to find by thought and in the dark. The latter is no handicap because you can't see most of the books when the lights are on anyway.

Most men when they open a woman's magazine turn to the problem page. In the GRB there is no need to indulge in such furtive behaviour, the largely female staff have decided that waiting for men to read their problems is too slow, so they have launched a policy of broadcasting. It is like Forum Magazine on a ghetto blaster. It was not until I went into this shop that I discovered how to cure thrush with carrots. I am not complaining, far from it, I find it deeply reassuring. I go in bankrupt, friendless and suffering from piles (through sitting on the doorsteps of other less reliable bookshops) and they put everything into proportion for me.

Sometimes the staff in this shop stimulate me into having a Pavlovian reaction to become a librarian manque. I am desperate to tell them to shut up. In pubs and wine bars they have happy hours to encourage custom. What the GRB could do is have a silent hour.

It is possible that the whole thing is a psychological boot camp. First they wear you down by not having any change in the exterior environment, then they shout things at you but you are supposed to take no notice and say thing, then they put things in the 'wrong' places to disorientate you and to see if you are concentrating. I am not sure if you get extra marks if you find something in the wrong section but it can certainly be very profitable. I found a book called Green Memories in the natural history section. It is about golf. Perhaps what the books and the shop (and the therapy) are trying to show is that if you persevere long enough you will get all the things you want in the end.

They certainly seem to have got what they wanted they are about to open up another branch.

BLOOMSBURY

THE RESTHOME FOR BOOKFAIRIES

I am deeply grateful to the Bloomsbury Bookseller Association for appointing me Public Relations Officer for the area. My initial thoughts are that we have a splendid opportunity to establish a thriving booksellers row for serious book collectors.

My suggestions for increasing the awareness amongst serious collectors are the following:

1. That we should announce that Sir William Rees Mogg has put up his failing bookshop Pickering & Chatto for sale and that as soon as he can find a mug big enough to buy it he will be moving to the Museum Street area. There is no actual

proof that he is intending to do so, but then there is no proof that he was ever an antiquarian bookdealer yet thousands of people believed it. We only have his word and that of umpteen journalists, and the strange fact that any story about Sir WRM always includes photographs of him against a stack of books.

2. The calibre of the customers in Bloomsbury is not quite as high as the bookshops. There is something inappropriate about their dress. I suggest that we should institute the Eric Korn Memorial Prize for best dressed customer.

3. Now that most of the booksellers in Bloomsburys are ex ABA or ex PBFA we should accuse those organisations of being instrumental in the practice of auction rings. Most journalists love a piece of scandal, especially one they do not understand, and under the rules of fair play they always have to get a second opinion before they can unfairly condemn somebody. In Museum Street we are uniquely placed to be that second opinion, they will not have to walk more than two minutes from the Russell Hotel to talk to us.

4. Most of our books are of a higher quality than those in the Charing X Road but it would not get us very far to claim so, what we need is something better than a trashy book about us, or an inane TV advert filmed in a Bloomsbury Bookshop, what we need is really something bigger than either of these two. what I suggest is that we hold a party for the Queen Mother and ask

her which books she would most like in the world, then when she turns up to collect them we should also give her the bill. If the impudence does not kill her, the price will. Our name will be inextricably linked with Royal Bookselling ever after.

These four simple solutions will, I hope, increase our public awareness of the delights that can be obtained by serious book collectors in Bloomsbury.

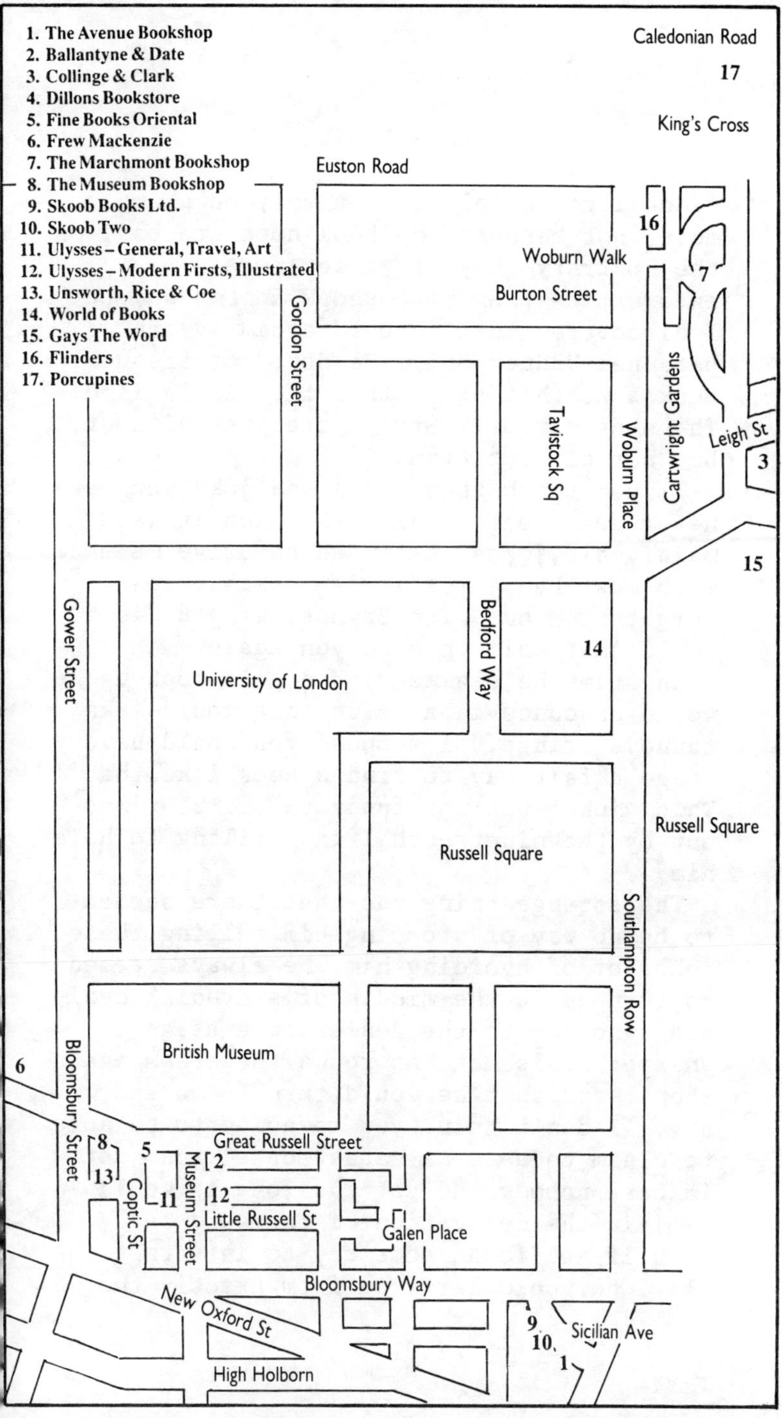

1. The Avenue Bookshop
2. Ballantyne & Date
3. Collinge & Clark
4. Dillons Bookstore
5. Fine Books Oriental
6. Frew Mackenzie
7. The Marchmont Bookshop
8. The Museum Bookshop
9. Skoob Books Ltd.
10. Skoob Two
11. Ulysses – General, Travel, Art
12. Ulysses – Modern Firsts, Illustrated
13. Unsworth, Rice & Coe
14. World of Books
15. Gays The Word
16. Flinders
17. Porcupines
Caledonian Road
King's Cross
Euston Road
Woburn Walk
Burton Street
Gordon Street
Tavistock Sq
Woburn Place
Cartwright Gardens
Leigh St
Gower Street
Bedford Way
University of London
Russell Square
Russell Square
Southampton Row
British Museum
Bloomsbury Street
Great Russell Street
Museum Street
Coptic St
Little Russell St
Galen Place
Bloomsbury Way
New Oxford St
Sicilian Ave
High Holborn

BRYN & BYE

I don't go to Bell Street very much any more, not because the bookshops are bad, on the contrary they are a lot more interesting than most shops in London, but I discovered that I could avoid my own personal Widmerpool. He does not frequent bookshops that are within the circle line. The shops in Bell Street are just without, but not without Bryn.

If you think that was a bad joke you have never heard one of his. I think it was mainly his jokes that used to drive me mad, with most bad jokes it is possible to forget them but with Bryn's, if you did he would just tell them to you again.

Any time he saw me with a golf book he would announce in a voice that would make tannoys cringe, 'I suppose you would have to go a fair way to find a book like that.' This 'joke' was not funny the first time, but by the nineteenth I was willing to hole him.

The strange thing was that there seemed to be no way of stopping him telling these jokes or of avoiding him, he always seemed to turn up in the middle of a crucial deal and announce to the dealer in a stage whisper 'this cat has found the cream again then', and then he would turn to me and say, 'I don't think you re going to be able to claim today as a catastrophe' and just in case nobody had got the joke he would explain the derivation of the word cat. Even if you found some way to interrupt the flow, he would carry on from exactly the

Archive Bookstore
for
Antiquarian & Secondhand
Books on all subjects
&
Sheet Music
for all instruments & moods
& scores, band parts, chamber sets & songsheets,
teaching material, out-of-print & the unusual
We value, buy, collect and sell.
At your service
MON-SAT 10-6PM
071-402 8212
(3 MINS MARYLEBONE OR
EDGWARE ROAD STATION)
BOOKS MUSIC
BELL STREET
83 BELL STREET
MARYLEBONE
LONDON NW1 6TB

place where he had started, once you had stopped... midword. It isn't that I dislike him, it is just that my life is not going to be long enough.

One night I was attempting to get to Penzance from Peterborough and had to arrange to get myself to Birmingham for the early morning train that only comes during summer on Saturdays, needless to say not many people know about this train, and when I got on, apart from a few somnolent tourists on their way to the Cornish Riviera it was almost empty. It was even devoid of drunks which made it more than worth travelling on. I had just begun to fall asleep as the train left New Street when who should start coming down the aisle but Bryn.

'Fancy meeting you here!' he said, 'It must be fate.' The only good news was that I had no books with me, the bad news was that I had to explain all the trains I had got on to get to this one. I asked where he was going and when I found his destination was Penzance I told him mine was Bristol. I then had to give him an itinerary of all the bookshops I intended to visit there, together with their merits and foibles. He said that if I had come via London Paddington it would have been much better from some points of view. I agreed with him but said it was a dreadful mistake on my part. I had five hours to wait and reflect on that statement at Bristol Station, but I can assure you it was a lot less wearing than having to endure Bryn's jokes all the way to Penzance.

It occurred to me that I was going about

things the wrong way, maybe I should not just keep trying to avoid him but instead I should flatten him with my jokes, and the next time I met him in Edgware I tried just that...

"How many black kids does it take to change a light bulb?"

Bryn shook his head, repeated the question several times to himself then asked me to repeat it to him, just to make sure that he had not got it wrong and then said, in a voice that would have cleared drains it was so deep:

"I don't know, how many black kids does it take to change a light bulb?"

"Two, one to change the light bulb and one to hold the ghetto blaster."

I admit this was not a great joke, but it did make some of the people in the shop laugh, including Bryn, but when the titters had died he said:

"Oh yes, that was a very good joke, but can you just explain one thing to me which I don't quite understand, what is a ghetto blaster?"

He had all the buttons, but they were sewn on wrong, and I am not just referring to his clothes, which I used to very much admire, he dressed like a thirties band leader on his way home from a rough night's work at the Cotton Club. His heavy duty utility shirts were always without collars, his dark black suits were of a type an undertaker would describe as being dated, they certainly never seem to go with his brown coordinated shoes... he never wore cufflinks which made his shirts look strange, but somehow he always seemed to look slightly stylish. If I had worn these clothes, people would have accused me of being scruffy. One of my greatest outgoings in life is drycleaning. I am thinking of buying a drycleaners, there is a distinct possibility that I would never bump into Bryn again.

Bryn was a genuine collector, all he ever did was collect things, not just books but thirties records as well. The rumour was that he had a huge house in Hertfordshire that was just filled with 78s, he only collected books as a sideline. He might not have been able to find the cufflinks but he sure as hell could find the books, he always seemed to be at the table that had just unloaded a thousand duff tomes and one absolute gem, and this he would be holding up asking if you thought it was worth 20p. This was a book on Artificial Cranial Deformation which I had recently sold for £150 and was now looking for another copy, but because Bryn was a genuine collector I had never discovered a way of doing business with him.

The last time I saw him was actually one of the few occasions when I remember it as being a pleasant experience, and I think this is why I have not been keen to see him again. Bryn always swore that the shops in Bell Street produced more bargains that anywhere else in London, and he should know he definitely seemed to get more out of them than me.

But one day I did manage to find something in Bell Street with which I was extremely pleased, and I was just in the middle of negotiating the terms of payment when Bryn walked in. I was desperate that he should not see this book. It was a catalogue of old Gramaphones. I hid it under a pile of other things I had bought, tried to work out how I could get rid of him. I did not have to actually listen to the jokes as I had heard them all before, as long as you laughed in the right place he would never notice that you were not concentrating. Eventually I suggested that we should go for a coffee together and that if he would like to go across the road and order them I would join him in a few minutes.

I bought the catalogue, and arranged with the dealer that I would pick it up later and then went over to see Bryn. I took several books with me because I knew a postmortem would ensue. He duly started going through the books, and I explained to him that these were all books that I was looking for on behalf of customers. He had just begun telling me one of his appalling jokes to do with a gutta percha binding, when a gentleman in another seat leant over and said:

"I've got a book at home, its an old book, lot older than those."

Bryn ignored him and carried on telling me that "when you gotta to percha a book you gotta percha it rightaway.

"This book I've got, man in the museum said he had never seen one like it."

Bryn smiled at me, but still continued with the joke. There was more, but fortunately I have forgotten it.

"Really old it is, more valuable than any of the books you got there, if I sold it I would be the richest person in our street."

By now I was unsure which was more annoying, not being able to hear Bryn's joke which I would have to endure come what may, or this old idiot going on about a book that was clearly going to be a family bible. When he attempted his spiel again Bryn said in a voice that the queen could not have bettered for cool interest...

"I am extremely keen to hear your interesting story, and I would very much like to give it my concentration in full, but unfortunately I must tell you that I have come a long way to talk to my friend, and I will talk to you as soon as I have finished talking to him."

It takes one to deal with one. But Bryn was not finished (I should have guessed by now). As the man slunk away, Bryn turned to me and said in his best voice,

"That's the type of behaviour I expect to see in West End cafes, not ones in Bell Street."

I have been frequenting West End cafes ever since.

HOW NOT TO RUN A SECONDHAND BOOKSHOP

For longer than I care to remember there has been a beautiful chandelier shop in Kensington Church Street, just by the part as you come round the one way street from Notting Hill Gate.

It looked more like a museum than a shop, there was a second branch further down the road but itlooked even less like a commercial establishment.

Another strange feature of this 'shop' was that they occasionally used to put out books for sale; there were not a lot of them just half a table full, but usually priced very unattractively. The three vols book club editions of The Lord of The Rings, modern Lloyds Registers and Gideon Bibles, but if you looked carefully into the 'shop' there were piles of books on the floor.

To find out what these were like I bought one of the books outside, and rang a bell to gain entrance. A very surly young man came to the door and asked me what I wanted. I offered some money for the book, and he tutted when I did not proffer the right amount and told me to pay it the next time.

From then on I kept looking in the window of this shop and seeing if there was an opportunity to proffer the money, but none seemed to come, but after a while another pile seemed to appear in the middle of the floor.

One day I saw a lady dusting the chandeliers in the shop with the books. I knocked on the door and offered her the money for the previous book.

"What kept you so long?" she said, "you had the book six months ago."

"I do not live round here," I said.

"A likely story."

"Is there any chance of my seeing the books on the floor?"

"No."

But despite her disavowels I was having a good look at them and I was very keen. When she saw that I was giving them the once over she ushered me out of the shop. Nothing happened for about three, five, seven years. The shop just got dustier, I got more haggard and the books that were put outside got worse.

Several people of my acquaintance did manage to talk their way into this shop but I did not hear of anybody who came out with anything serious.

Then about a year ago, books started flooding onto the table outside, they were genuinely interesting books. It is hard to explain this but they had style of their own. This sounds a stupid thing to say about old books, but these were old books of a particular type.

In the window were more books which were even more curiously priced, thus they would have a three volume set of Shakespeare for £15 each volume or an odd volume of an early first edition of Dickens at £25.

I could not see any indication of the prices of th books outside but there was a sign on the window saying ring bell of shop down the road. I took some books and rang the bell. I don't know if there are manuals of how long one should wait before ringing a bell the second time, but the man who appeared at the door was definitely of the opinion that I had rung it too early.

"Yes, what do you want?"

"I would like to buy some of the books please?"

"What books?"

"The ones that are outside of the shop up the road."

"Well why not pay for them up the road?"

"There is a sign in the window saying pay for them here."

"But can't you see this is a chandelier shop, we don't sell books."

"Yes, but there are books on the table outside the chandelier shop up the road and there is a sign saying pay here and I would like to see some of the books in the window."

"Well, nobody else has offered me any money."

I immediately stored this away in my collection of good potential cliches.

He looked me up and down and said:

"I will go and find somebody who can deal with the likes of you."

He disappeared, and I sat and admired the chandeliers. Museums are a total waste of time and they only ever have the finest things; in a shop you got to see the bad as well as the good. It is easier to make an appraisal when you are seeing the worst things. If you stand the the B & A you only ever see things that are so exquisite that you have no way of forming a relative opinion.

About five minutes later another man came into the shop from the back and said:

"Can I help you sir?"

"Yes, I would like to pay for these books."

"Where did you get them?"

I did not relish going through this process all over again, but fortunately he disappeared before I had to. I am glad it was a chandelier shop and that I had not seen so many chandeliers at close quarters, but in comparison to books I did notice you did not get as many in.

A third man entered and asked if he could heop me. I carefully explained I had come about the books.

"I'm awfully sorry sir, but you have come to the wrong place."

"But I thought this was a branch of the chandelier shop up the road and it says ring the bell here."

"I think there must be some mistake."

"Well come and look in the window."

"I cannot leave the shop sir, I am on my own."

I knew I was extremely bad at recognising people, but I did not think I would have mistaken this black gentleman for the person who had first spoken to me.

Just then another person came to the front door carrying some books. He rang the bell, and I waited. He looked at me as if I was a complete moron, after thinking about it for a few moments I realised he was right and I went and answered the door.

"I just want these three books from up the road, they are £3 each", he said and gave me £10.

"How did you find out they were £3 each?" I enquired.

"Look inside the front end paper and there they are marked," he said.

I did and he was right, but the reason I had not spotted it before was that what they actually said was £3.3.0.

"I have not got any change."

"Don't worry you can keep the money."

...

RC: "How long is this bleeding tripe going to go on for?"

drif: "About another five pages."

RC: "Well why didn't you tell me to go and get the Death by Boredom signs."

drif: "I think it is an interesting story."

RC: "It might well be, but the appalling way you are writing it is ruining the whole thing, when are we going to have some jokes?"

drif: "I can't think of any jokes."

RC: "You don't mean it is all going to be like this, how long does it go on for?"

drif: "About another seven pages."

RC: "I will go and get the Death by Boredom signs."

drif: "That's unfair, I find this interesting."

RC: "I'll get two sets."

drif: "It is not boring, this is a story about some people who had a wonderful collection of books for sale and how they fouled it up."

RC: "Rivetting."

drif: "Well just because you are not interested does not mean everybody won't be."

RC: "So you are not going to let me put the Death by Boredom signs up?"

drif: "No."

RC: "What about the Nearly Death by Boredom signs.?"

drif: "Listen, if you don't want to read, don't read it, I'm not forcing you."
RC: "We may not have to read it, but we pay for it."
drif: "When did you last pay for anything."
RC: "How about a sign saying Normal Service will be Resumed as soon as possible?"
drif: "Shut up."
RC: "I don't know why you are suddenly going off at a mad tangent now that you are coming to the end of the book."
drif: "What do you mean the end, this is just the outline"...

DR. IFFIELD'S UNIQUE
BOOKDEALERS MARRIAGE AGENCY

Are you tired of one night stands in dowergetic hotels? Blind dates in dumb towns? Do you feel you have outgrown penpals interested only in your wrapping? Or wearied of suits keen only on your money? Are you afraid you might get left on the shelf?

WELL AT LAST, THE WORLD'S ONLY MARRIAGE AGENCY FOR SECONDHAND BOOKSHOPS IS HERE TO HELP YOU.

Gentlemen, don't be bashful, whether you are looking for unmarried slim country girls (do not miss our Miss Dorchester) or seeking buxom home counties widows keen on dogs (ask for Mrs Reading).

ladies, would you like to meet a merchant navy officer who has not come to the end of the line (Mr. Dover) or perhaps you run to rough trade (Hull); whatever your desires we are here to help you.

We have clients all over the country just desperate to establish a long term relationship, from untried virgins in Milton Keynes, to motherly matrons in Grantham. From tee totallers in Warrington to bon viveurs in Hounslow.

Are you a sophisticated Metropolitan type, possibly gay? We have just the Haring for you. Into S & M then why not try Whipps Cross. If you are keen on Royalty and water sports we will fix you up with Miss Bognor Regis.

All advertisers guaranteed genuine by
Dr. Iffield: The Sleeping Partner.

DIRECTORY

ALPHABETICAL TOWN INDEX

ABERDEEN, Scotland

ADELPHI BOOKS **0224 898779**
24 Adelphi, Union St., Aberdeen AB1 2DL
Mon-Sat, 9.30-5
Med size R stk, low key, keen on Theology. TWC. P. diff. Adelphi is an alleyway on rhs of Union St, about 1/2 mile. Anorexia Nervosa.

THE OLD CLOCK REPAIR SHOP **0224 627695**
197 King St., Aberdeen.
Mon-Sat, 10-5
Med size drif special. Kuti. Farts. Awyw. Nsoc. Res stk. T. Small discussions. P.poss. Scotrail Aberdeen, oos into hideous shopping centre, turn right into Union St and left at King St. SIOL near Safeways.

OXFAMS WORST BOOKSHOP **0224 642490**
27 Rosemount Viaduct, Aberdeen.
Mon-Sat, 10-4.30, Wed 10-12
Bl av cal, cnd. Av prices. No T. P.poss. Directions as Rosemount.

ROSEMOUNT BOOKSHOP **0224 639355**
3 Gilconston Steps, Skene Sq., Aberdeen AB2 4UW
Mon-Sat, 10-5, L 1-2
Med size R/C stk. Av cal, cnd & prices. T. BR Aberdeen, oos into shopping ctr turn left into Union St and right into Rosemount Viaduct. Third right at Gilgamaston Park which becomes Raeburn Place and left at bottom.

G R WINRAM **0224 630673**
90 Leadside Road, Aberdeen AB2 4TU.
Mon-Sat, 10-5.30, L 1-2 Rel.
Med size R/C stk, v independently minded. Av cnd & prices. Bgns known. TWC. P.poss. Scotrail Aberdeen, oos into hideous shopping ctr, cross Union St to Rosemount Viaduct & continue for 1/2 mile & turn left at Leadside Cres. which leads into Leadside Road.

ABERFELDY, Scotland

THE STRATHTAY BOOKSHOP **0887 29519**
8 Dunkeld St., Aberfeldy, Perthshire PH15 2DA
NV. Rumoured to be awful. No railway station.

ABERGAVENNY, Wales

H K LOCKYER **0873 5825**
Monk Street (No no.), Abergavenny, Gwent NP7 5PN
Mon-Sat, 9.30-5.30, REL
Lg R/C/D stk. Roast Beef & Nouvelle Cuisine. Emphon HSF. WAD. P.diff. BR: Abergavenny, oos down drive turn right into town & right past bus stn, SIOL.

ABERYSTWYTH, Wales

YSTWYTH BOOKS **0970 617511**
7 Princess Street, Aberystwyth, Dyfed, Wales SY25 1DX
Mon-Sat, 10-5.30, clsd Wed.
New bksp with upstairs rm of s/h R/C stk, excessively gd cnd. Emphon student/academic & Welsh. Av cal & prices. TWC. DOSO. P.diff. BR: Aberystwyth oos, turn left, turn right at roundabout and left into Queen Street which leads into Princess Street. SIOR.

Rumours of a second low key shop, address unknown.

ACOCKS GREEN

MAXWELLS BOOKSHOP **021 7068379**
22 Shaftmoor Lane, Acocks Green, West Midlands B27 7RS
Mon-Sat, 10.30-4.45.
Med size R/C stk av cal, cnd and prices. Keen on technical subjects.

ADARE, Eire

GEORGE STACPOOLE **061 86409**
Adare, Co Limerick.
Summer Shop. Spec in Lace and Antiques with small HSF stk. NV.

ALDEBERGH

TREWINS BOOKS **098 684649**
178B High Street, Aldebergh, Suffolk IP15 5AN
Mon-Sat, 10-2 and 2-5, clsd Wed
Small R/C stk av cal, cnd and prices. T.

ALRESFORD

LAURENCE OXLEY 0962 732188
17 Broad Street, Alresford, Hampshire SO24 9AW.
Mon-Sat, 9-1 & 2-5
Med/lg R/C stk, solid roast beef. Av cal, cnd & prices. BR: Winchester (NAST 10 miles).Etf.

ALSTON

INCREDIBLE'S 091 5674389
Front Street, Alston, Northumbria
Sat & Sun, 11-4
Bric a Brac shop with v lg R/C stk. WAD. V int bks. P.poss. BR: Haltwhistle & cab. NAST 12 miles.

ALTON

ALTON SECONDHAND BOOKS 0420 89352
11 Normandy Street, Alton, Hampshire.
Mon-Sat, 9.30-5.30, 9-5 Wed & Sat
Med/lg R/C stk. B&MC cum drif special. Av cnd & prices. TWC. P.poss. BR: Alton, oos down drive & turn left into town, SIOL.

ALTRINCHAM

ABACUS BOOKS 061 8285106
34 Regent Road, Altrincham, Manchester.
Mon-Sat, 10-5, Wed 4
It is imposs to decide if this is a new bksp with s/h bks or a s/h bksp with new bks. TWC. P.poss. BR: Altrincham, Oos turn left & second right. SIOR.

GROSVENOR BOOKS 061 9287950
31 Grosvenor Road, Altrincham, Manchester.
Mon-Sat, afternoons
Newly listed R/C stk slightly low key but with hope. TWC. P.poss. BR: Altrincham, Oos turn right & keep Station on right & straight ahead.

AMBLESIDE

THE LITTLE BOOKSHOP **05394 32094**
1 Cheapside, Ambleside, Cumbria LA12 OAR
Mon-Sat, 9-5, clsd Thurs
Med size R/C stk, av cal, cnd and prices. ETF in centre of town.

ARUNDEL

THE ARUNDEL BOOKSHOP **0903 882680**
10 High St, Arundel, West Sussex BN18 9AB
Mon-Sat, 9.15-5.15, L 1-2.15, some Suns am
Lg R/C/D stk, av cal, cnd and prices. BR: Arundel, oos ahead to Castle and SIOR.

ASHBURTON

ASHBURTON RARE BOOKS **0364 53341**
20 West Street, Ashburton, Devon.
Mon-Sat, 10-5
Med size R/C stk, av cal, cnd & prices. T. Etf. About to Close.

THE DARTMOOR BOOKSHOP **NOW CLOSED**
2 Kingsbridge Lane, Ashburton, Devon.
Mon-Sat, 9.30-5.30
Med size R/C/D stk, ab av cal, cnd and prices. Emphon Local Hist. GIOPIC.

ASHBY DE LA ZOUCHE

CROFT BOOKSHOP **0530 417034**
1A Mill Lane Mews, Ashby de la Zouche, Leics LE6 5HP
Mon-Sat, 10-5, L: 12-1, clsd Wed
Med size R/C average stk, av cnd & prices. Not an average talker. BR: Burton (NAST 15 miles). Find car park by Leisure Centre, Mill Lane is nearby.

AXMINSTER

THE OLD CURIOSITY SHOP **0297 33010**
7 South Street, Axminster, EX13 5AD
Mon-Sat, 8.30-5.30, Wed 1pm
Small R stk in rear of curio shp, av cal, cnd and prices, too small and low key, but worth a look if you're in the area early enough. BR: Axminster, oos turn left into town, and right at South St. SIOL.

AYLESBURY

THE BOOKSHOP SQUARE EDGE **0296 89480**
38 Kingsbury, Aylesbury, Bucks HP20 2JE
Mon-Sat, 10.30-5.30
Med size R/C stk, av cal, cnd and prices. TWC. BR: Aylesbury, oos into town centre and SIOL in second square.

PETER EATON'S **0296 641393**
The Lilies, Weedon, Aylesbury, Bucks HP22 4AS
Mon-Sat, 10-5
Extremely lg R/C/D stk. Almost solid roast beef. Needs an entire day!

BAKEWELL

ALAN HILL **0629 814841**
3 Buxton Road, Bakewell, Derbyshire SK17 6EW.
Mon-Sat, 10-5.30
Med size R/C stk, av cal, cnd & prices. T. Etf.

BANGOR, N Ireland

THE OTHER BOOKSHOP **0247 458778**
4 Dufferin Ave, Bangor, N.I.
Mon-Sat, 10-5
Med size R/C stk, av cal, cnd & prices. Keen on pbks. TWC. P. poss. NIR: Bangor, oos turn left & SIOR.

Almost identical to THE OTHER BOOKSHOP, 30 Dufferin Ave, no phone.

BANGOR, Wales

BANGOR BOOKS **0248 352659**
122 High Street, Bangor, Gwynned, LU57 3AN
Mon-Sat, 9.30-5.30, clsd Wed.
Med size R/C bks, av cal, cnd & prices. WAD. P.diff. BR: Bangor, oos turn left & follow signs saying Caernarvon (not City Centre) turn left at bottom & cont SIOR.

BARNARD CASTLE

CURLEWS **0833 31090**
41 Galgate, Barnard Castle, Durham DL12 8EJ.
Mon-Sat, 9.30-5.30
I found the veggie, I found the antq shp with some bks, I found the rmndr shop at the bottom of the hill but I did not find out about this place until after I got back to London and they do not answer the phone!

BARNSTAPLE

TARKA BOOKS **0271 74997**
5 Bear Street, Barnstaple, Devon EX32 7BU.
Mon-Sat, 10-5
Med size R/C stk, av cal, cnd and prices. BR: Barnstaple, over bridge into Boutport Street & right nr mkt where there is also a bookstall occasionally.

BARROW IN FURNESS

MOSTLY BOOKS **0229 836808**
247 Rawlinson Street, Barrow in Furness, Cumbria LA14 1DW.
Tues-Sat, 11-5, clsd Thurs
Med size R/C/D stk, spec in technical bks of an artistic nature. BR: Barrow, oos ahead, turn right into town & second left.

BASILDON

Rumours of shop. That cannot be true, there is not even a rumour of civilisation in Basildon.

BATH

ASPIDISTRA **0225 461948**
46 St James Street, Bath, Avon BA1 1UG.
Mon-Sat, 10.30-4
Med size R/C stk, keen on Art. Av cal, cnd & prices.

DEREK & GLENDA WALLIS **0225 424677**
6 Chapel Row, Bath, Avon BA1 1HN.
Mon-Sat, 10-5.30
Lg R/C/D stk, av cal, cnd & prices. Emphon Childrens and Ill.

BANKES BOOKS **0225 444580**
5 Margarets Buildings, Bath, Avon BA12 1LP.
Mon-Sat, 10-5
Med/lg C/D stk, ab av cal, cnd & prices.

BATH OLD BOOKS **0225 422244**
9C Margarets Buildings, Bath, Avon.
Mon-Sat 9.30-5
Med/lg C/D stk, ab av cal, cnd & prices.

PATTERSON & LIDDLE **0225 426722**
10 St Margarets Buildings, Brock Street, Bath BA1 2LP
Mon-Sat, 10-5
Newly opened C/tourists shp. Solid roast beef. Emphon bindings & bookfairy stk.

CAMDEN BOOKS **0225 461606**
146 Walcot Street, Bath, Avon, BA1 5BL.
Mon-Sat, 10-5
Med/lg C/D stk, ab av cal, cnd & prices. Emphon Art.

BATH BOOK EXCHANGE **0225 66214**
35 Broad Street, Bath, Avon BA1 5LP.
Mon-Sat, 9-5, L: 12.30-1.30
Small/med size low key R stk. Emphon pbks and remndrs.

GEORGE BAYNTUN **0225 466000**
Manvers Street, Bath, Avon BA1 1JW
Mon-Fri, 9-5.30, L: 1-2
Med size spec in decorative bindings. Bks to be photographed against. In the basement is P R R Rainsford which spec in art bks but apptmt required.

BATLEY

VINTAGE MOTOR SHOP **0924 470773**
498 Bradford Road, Batley, Yorks WF17 5JY
Thurs-Sat, 11-5
Lg Spec Motoring shop. Primarily new bks & motor manuals. NV.

BATTLE

BATTLE ANTIQUES **NO PHONE**
91A High Street, Battle, Sussex TN33 0AQ.
Mon-Sat, 10-5
Antq shp with s/h bks. NV.

BECCLES

BESLEY'S BOOKS **0502 715762**
4 Blyburgate, Beccles, Suffolk NR34 9TA
Mon-Sat, 9.30-5, clsd Wed, sometimes clsd for L
Med size R/C stk, ab av cal & cnd, av prices. Etgow. P.diff. TWC. BR: Beccles, oos ahead into town & turn right at T junction. SIOR.

RICHARD WILDMAN **0234 43905**
20 Mill Street, Bedford MK40 3HD
Tues-Sat, 12-6
Med size R/C stk, av cal, cnd & prices. BR: Bedford, oos ahead, right & left at bottom & continue past AA office.

THE EAGLE BOOKSHOP **0234 269295**
103 Castle Road, Bedford, MK40 3AD
Mon-Sat, 10-5
Newly opened R/C stk, ave cal, cnd & prices. TWC. P.poss. From Wildmans, oos turn left & cont past roundabout.

BELFAST, N Ireland

ARCADE BOOKS 0232 438474
10-12 Gresham Street, Belfast, BT1 1TN.
Mon-Sat, 10-5, Rel
Med size R/C stk, Irish drif special, av cal, cnd & prices. TWC. From Knows Horrenda, oosh, turn right & second left.

BOOKFINDERS 0232 328269
47 University Road, Belfast, BT1 1ND.
Mon-Sat, 10-5.30
Med size R/C stk, emphon Irish. Ab av cal, cnd & prices. TWC. P. poss. From Prospect House continue south.

THE BOOKSTORE 0232 242046
73 Union Street, Belfast, BT1 2JG.
Mon-Sat, 10-5, Unr
Small/med low key R stk, bl av cnd & ab av prices. No T. P. poss. From Knows Horrenda oosh, turn right & third right.

KNOWS HORRENDA BOOKSHOP* 0232 244137
25 Lower North Street, Belfast, BT1.
Mon-Sat, 10-5.30
Med size R/C stk, primarily rmndrs & pbks. Av cal, cnd & prices. TWC.

LEAVES BOOKSHOP 0232 664600
84A Stranmillis Road, Belfast, BT9 5AD.
Mon-Sat, 10.45-4, Sat 10-5
Med size R/C stk, av cal, gd cnd, av prices. Small res stk. TWC. P.poss. NIR: Botanic Gardens, oos, turn left & right & left at main road, & bear left at Stranmillis.

MEWS ANTIQUES & BOOKS 0232 751319
260 Antrim Lodge, Belfast BT15 2AT.
Tues-Sat, 10.30-5
Antq shop with small but v. int stk of R/C bks. TWC. P.poss. NIR: York Road, oos ahead & right into Queen St, left into Limstone Rd & right into Antrim Rd. SIOL.

PROSPECT HOUSE 0232 245787
93 Dublin Road, Belfast, BT2 7HT.
Tues-Sat, 11-5
Med/nrly lg C/D stk, emphon Irish, Ab av cal, cnd, av Irish prices. T. WaD. Etgow. Res stk. As Roma Ryan.

ROMA RYAN **0232 242777**
73 Dublin Road, Belfast BT2 7HF.
Mon-Sat, 11-5.30
Med size C/D stk, emphon Irish & Prints. Av cal, cnd & prices. T. P. poss. From Town hall, turn left into Bedford Ave & continue, SIOR.

WAR ON WANT **0232 232064**
1 Rugby Avenue, Belfast BT7 1RD.
Mon-Fri, 10.30-4.30. EC Sat
Med size R stk, bta Charity shop. Etgow. P.poss. From Well Read oosh, turn left & left & SIOL.

VOLUME ONE **NO PHONE**
Unit 10, The Haymarket, Royal Avenue, Belfast BT1 1DT
Mon-Sat, 10-5
Med size R/C stk, drif special, av cal, cnd & prices. TWC. P.poss. From Arcade oosh, turn left & left into arcade.

WELL READ **NO PHONE**
171 Ormeau Road, Belfast.
Mon-Sat, 11-5, Unr
Small/med size R stk, appalling cnd, appalling bks, appalling manners, appalling damp. Well worth avoiding. From Belfast Central oos, turn left & left at main road & keep walking - 1 mile. SIOR.

WORLD OF BOOKS **0232 454272**
329 Woodstock Road, Belfast BT6 8PT
Mon-Sat, 10-5.30. Wed -5
Med size R/C stk, emphon pbks. Nsoc. P.poss. NIR: Belfast Central, oos turn right & right at Woodstock Link & bear left, SIOR.

BERWICK UPON TWEED

D & K MACNAUGHTON **0289 331502**
11 Church Street, Berwick upon Tweed, TD15
Mon-Sat, 10-5 Rel
Med size R/C stk. NPLOTCGI. Av cal, emphon Scottish & local history. Roast beefish, av prices. TWC. P.poss. BR Berwick, oos turn right, left & right into town through arch & left at church. SIOL.

BETHESDA, Wales

A E MORRIS **0248 352695**
40 High St, Bethesda, Gwynned, LL57 3AN
Mon-Sat, 9.30-5, clsd Wed
Med size R/C stk, slightly roast beef/Helen Hanff/Bookdealer/ Silverfish special. T & D. P.poss. Etf. BR: Bangor NAST (5 miles)

BRYN BOOTS **0248 602134**
11 Ogwen Terrace, Bethesda, Gwynned, LL57 3AY.
Tues-Sat, 10-5
Boot shp with small res stk of bks upstairs. Etf.

BEVERLEY

EASTGATE BOOKSHOP **0482 868579**
11 Eastgate, Beverley, Hull HU17 ODW.
Mon-Sat, 10-5
Med size R/C stk, av cal, cnd & prices. Res stk of bks on Borneo. BR: Beverley, oos ahead, turn left at T junction. There is a bkstl in the Antiques Mkt next to the above shop.

ALEX ALEC SMITH **0482 869453**
31 Highgate, Beverley, Hull HU17 ODN.
Tues-Sat, 10-5
Med size R/C stk, ab av cal & cnd. Av prices. Keen on Lit. Parallel to above shop.

BEXHILL

SAM ROBINSON **CLOSING**

BIDEFORD

RAINBOW **023 7478592**
19 Market Place, Bideford, Devon.
Mon-Sat, 10-5, L: 1-2 exc Wed
Med size R/C stk, av cal, cnd & prices. NV.

SCUDDERS **023 727567**
11 Bridge Street, Bideford, Devon EX39 2EU
Mon-Sat, 9.30-5.30
Antique shp with BTA stk of bks.

BILLINGBOROUGH

ALAN REDMOND BOOKS **0529 240215**
25 High Street, Billingborough, Lincs NG34 OQB
Sat-Sun 10-6
Med size R/C stk, av cal, cnd & prices.

BILLINGSHURST

BOOKS AND THINGS **0403 815131**
58-62 High Street, Billingshurst, W. Sussex RH14 9NY
Mon-Sat, 9.30-5.30
New bksp with upstairs room, low key R/C stk. BR: Billingshurst, oos turn right into town & right at T junction & SIOL.

BIRKENHEAD

THE WIRRAL BOOKSHOP **051 6380160**
325 Borough Road, Birkenhead, Merseyside
Fri-Sat only, 10.30-5
Med size R/C stk, silverfish drif special. NV but doorstepped. BR: Birkenhead Central, Oos, turn left and follow deathway. SIOL.

SPEAKS VOLUMES **051 6476076**
48 Grange Road West, Birkenhead, Merseyside L41 4DA.
Mon-Sat, 10-5
Med size Charity bksp NPLOTCGI. No T. Med size R stk, only worth a trip if you are going to Wirral Bksp. BR: Birkenhead Central, oos ahead into Borough Rd, turn right at traffic lights & first middle left (you'll see).

BIRMINGHAM

TAPLINS BOOKSHOP **021 7796505**
62 Station Road, Marston Green, West Midlands B37 7BI
Tues-Sat, 10.30-5
Med size R/C stk, ab av cal, cnd , av prices. BR: Marston Gn, oos & right, SIOL.

STEPHEN WYCHERLEY **021 4711006**
508 Bristol Road, Selly Oak, Birmingham B29 6DB
Mon-Sat, 10.30-5.30, clsd Wed
Med size C/D stk, av cal, cnd, ab av prices. Res stks. TWC.

BIRMINGHAM BOOKSHOP 021 4728556
567 Bristol Road, Selly Oak, Birmingham B29 6AF.
Mon-Sat, 10-5
Med/lg R/C stk, av cal, cnd & prices.

BEECH BOOKS 021 5599822
286 Oldbury Road, Rowley Regis, Birmingham B65 OJN.
Mon-Thurs 11-4.30, Fri-Sat 11-5
Med size R/C stk, av cal, cnd & prices.

BLITZGEIST 021 4264122
189 High Street, Harbourne, Birmingham B17 9QD
Mon-Sat, 10-6
Med/lg R/C stk, ab av cal, cnd, av prices. T&D.

SIMMONS BOOKSHOP 027 5024622
37 Lower High Street, Wednesbury, West Midlands WS10 7AQ
Mon-Sat, 9-5, Thurs 2pm
Med size R/C stk, emphon pbks but worthwhile stk hdbks. Res stk. TWC. P.diff. BR: Wolverhampton (NAST 5 miles) Easy bus. Etf.

CLENT BOOKS 021 5500309
52 Summer Hill, Halesowen, West Midlands.
Mon-Sat, 10-4
Med size R/C stk, av cal, cnd & prices.

BISHOP'S CASTLE, Wales

YARBOROUGH HOUSE BOOKSHOP 0588 638318
The Square, Bishop's Castle, Wales SY9 5BN.
Tues-Sun 10-5, clsd Wed
Med/lg R/C Literace, but WAD. V gd cnd & prices. Etf in Centre of town. P.poss. BR: Shrewsbury (NAST 20 miles).

BLACKHEATH (see London)

BLACKPOOL

CHEVET BOOKS 0253 751858
157 Dickson Road, Blackpool, Lancs FY1 2EU.
Mon-Sat, 10.15-6.15, Sundays in summer
Med size R/C stk, NSOC but not low key enough to be a drif special. BR: Blackpool, oos at right hand corner & right & SIOR.

BLACKROCK, Eire

CARRAIG BOOKS **882575**
73 Main Street, Blackrock, Co Dublin.
Mon-Sat, 9-5.30
Med/lg C/D stk. Emphon Irish, ab av cal, cnd, bl av prices. WaD. Some general bks, Etgow. P.diff. IR: Dun Laochaire, oos to left, turn right & left into main st, keep on left & SIOR.

INDOOR MARKET BOOKS **PHONE UNKNOWN**
Indoor Market, 19 Main Street, Blackrock, Co Dublin.
Mon-Sat, 10.30-5.30
Bta (Irish division) bkstl in mkt with res stk elsewhere. IR as above.

BLAENAU FFESTINOG, Wales

SIOP LYFRAU'R HEN BOST **0766 831802**
45 Stryd Fawr, Blaenau Ffestinog, Gwynned, LL41 3AA.
Mon-Sat, 10-5
Med size R/C stk, low key, principally Welsh bks. TWC. P.poss. BR (Bf) oos turn right, SIOL.

BLAIR ATHOLL, Scotland

ATHOLL BROWSE **079 681530**
by Blair Atholl Stn, Blair Atholl, Perthshire PH18 5SG.
Open until late every day in summer, 1-5 in winter, Rel
Small R/C stk, av cal, cnd and prices. TWC. P.poss. Scotrail Blair Atholl, etf.

BLAKENEY

ELKIN MATTHEWS **0263 740475**
Cley Road (No no.), Blakeney, Norfolk NR25 7NL
not open regular hours - BTR
Med size C/D stk, av cal, cnd & prices.

BLANDFORD FORUM

SECOND READING BOOKSHOP — **NOW CLOSED**

DORSET BOOKSHOP — **0258 52256**
69 East Street, Blandford Forum, Dorset DT1 7DX
Mon-Sat, 9.30-5.30, Wed 1pm
New bksp with R/C stk, av cal, cnd & prices. Etf. BR: Dorchester (NAST 15 miles).

BOOKS AND BYGONES — **0258 456407**
69 Salisbury Street, Blandford Forum, Dorset DT11 7DX
Mon-Sat, 10-4.30
Antq shop with bta stk of bks. Etf.

BOROUGHBRIDGE

BATES AND HINDMARCH — **0423 324258**
Bridge St (No no), Boroughbridge, N. Yorks.
Mon-Sat, 10-5, clsd Thurs but BTR
Small C bookfairy stk, ab av cnd & prices. BR: Harrogate (NAST 10 miles) Etf by bridge in antq shp.

BOSCASTLE

Rumours of a summer shop.

BOSTON (Lincs)

PILGRIM BOOKS — **0205 356931**
7 Red Lion Street, Boston, Lincolnshire
Wed 9-4, Sat 9-5, V.Rel
Med size R/C stk, av cal, cnd & prices. Oos head for Church. Turn left at Bank St and cut through Woolworths. SIOR.

BOURNEMOUTH

HOLDENHURST BOOKS — **0202 397718**
275 Holdenhurst Road, Bournemouth, Dorset.
Mon-Sat, 10-5.30, clsd Wed
Med size R/C stk, av cal, cnd. Emphon Motoring & Transport. T. P.poss. BR: Bournemouth, oos turn left into Holdenhurst Rd & cont for 1 mile.

BOOKS & MAPS
WE BUY RARE & SECONDHAND BOOKS
• LEATHER BINDINGS • PAPERBACKS • MAPS
• POSTCARDS • FINE ILLUSTRATED BOOKS
• CHILDRENS BOOKS • OBJECT D'ART
• AUTOGRAPHS & MANUSCRIPTS
FROM A SINGLE BOOK TO A COMPLETE LIBRARY!
FREE VALUATIONS
TRADE ENQUIRIES WELCOME
BOURNEMOUTH (0202) 521373
OPEN MON-SAT 9-5.30
SHOP: 1 JEWEL BOX BLDS, CARDIGAN RD, WINTON, BOURNEMOUTH

YESTERDAY'S BOOKS **0202 302023**
65-67 Bennet Road, Charminster, Bournemouth, Dorset BH8 8RH.
Mon-Sat, 9.30-5.30
Med size R/C stk, av cal, cnd & prices. Keen on Africa. T. P.poss. From Holdenhurst oosh, turn left & cont for 1 mile (follow signs for Winton Charminster) & Bennet Rd is on left.

BOOKS & MAPS **0202 521373**
1 Cardigan Road, Winton, Bournemouth, Dorset.
Mon-Sat, 9.30-5.30
Newly opened. R/C stk, ab av cal, bl av cnd, ab av bullshit. T&D. P.poss. From Yesterday's bks go back down Bennet Rd, turn left & follow signs for Winton (1 mile) & right & Cardigan Rd is on right.

H & S ROWAN **0202 398820**
459 Christchurch Road, Boscombe, Bournemouth, Dorset BH1 4AD.
Mon-Sat, 9-6
Med/lg R/C/D stk, av cal, cnd & prices. TWC. P.diff. BR: Bournemouth, oos turn right towards sea front & left at roundabout.

SIDNEY WRIGHT **0202 397153**
12-13 Royal Arcade, Bournemouth, Dorset BH1 4EZ.
Mon-Sat, 9-5.30
Med size R/C stk, Stokers Special. Av cal & prices. TWC. P.poss. From Rowans, oosh on right & arcade is on left, 1 mile.

ASHLEY BOOKSHOP **0202 302499**
308 Ashley Road, Bournemouth, Dorset BH1 4LH.
Mon-Sat, 10-5.30, Rel
V lg R/C stk, ab av cal, cnd, av prices. TWC. P.diff. From Wright, turn left into Christchurch Rd & left at first major junction. SIOR in old church opp Sainsbury's.

TUCKTON BOOKS **0202 434751**
122 Tuckton Road, Southbourne, Bournemouth BH6 3JX.
Mon-Sat, 9.30-6
Recently changed hands. Previous owner has moved to Winton. Med size R stk, bl av cal, cnd, av prices. TWC. BR: Christchurch & bus (NAST).

BRACKLEY

THE OLD HALL BOOKSHOP **0280 704146**
32 Market Place, Brackley, Northamptonshire NN13 5DP
Mon-Sat, 9.30-5.30, L: 102
Lg R/C stk, ab av cal, cnd, av prices. Keen on Lit. Etf.

BRADFORD

THE SILVERFISH SPECIAL BOOKSHOP **NO PHONE**
Southgate (No no), Bradford, Yorks.
Usually open Fri & Sat, but temperamental
Small/med low key R/C stk, too bad to be a drif special and too smelly. BR: Bradford Interchange, oos down drive & ahead into Bridge St which becomes Sunbridge & left past Sunwins.

BRADFORD ON AVON

BOOKS & PRINTS 0225 868300
Dutch Barton, Church Street, Bradford on Avon, Wilts BA15 1LN
Mon-Sat, 10.30-5.30, Thurs 8pm
Lg R/C/D stk, recently changed hands. Emphon Lit & Hist. Fast t/o. WAD. P.poss. BR: Bradford on Avon, oos turn left out of drive into town over bridge & first left & SIOR in small detached cottage.

EX LIBRIS 02216 3595
1 The Shambles, Bradford on Avon, Wilts BA15 1TS
Mon-Sat, 9-5.30
New bksp with rear rm of s/h bks, av cal, cnd & prices. TWC. P.diff. BR: Bradford on Avon, oos down drive, turn left, up hill & turn right into paved alley.

THE ROUNDABOUT SHOP 02216 3241
1 & 2 Silver Street, Bradford on Avon, Wilts BA15 1JX
Mon-Sat, 10-5
Newsagent with small stk of R/C bks, av cal, cnd & prices. T & D. P.diff. BR: Bradford on Avon, oos down drive, turn left SIOL over bridge.

WHITEHILL BOOKSHOP 02216 2402
15A Silver Street, Bradford on Avon, Wilts BA15 1JZ
Primarily Sats, 11-4.30
Small R/C stk, av cal, cnd & prices. TWC. From EX LIBRIS oosh, turn left & cont up hill.

CANAL BOOKSHOP 0225 723812
Avon Cliff, Bradford on Avon, Wilts.
Mainly seasonal
Spec in Canals. New & s/h. BR: Bradford on Avon, oos turn right & follow Frome Rd, turn right onto Canal at Canal Tavern (1 mile approx).

BRAITHWAITE

BOOK COTTAGE **NOW CLOSED**

BRAUNTON

BOOK CELLAR **0271 815061**
East Street (No no.), Braunton, North Devon.
Mon-Sat, 10-5, clsd Tues
Med size R/C stk, well worth a look. Av cnd & prices. T. BR: Barnstaple (NAST 3 miles). Etf.

BRECON, Wales

D G & A S EVANS **0874 2714**
7 The Street, Brecon, Wales LD3 7LL.
Mon-Sat, 9-5, Wed 9-1, L: 1-2
New bksp with low key R stk, av cnd & prices. TWC. P.poss. Etf by car park. BR: Hereford (NAST).

BRENTWOOD

THE BOOKEND **NO PHONE**
38 Kings Road, Brentwood, Essex.
Mon-Sat, 10-5, Thurs 1pm
Med size R/C stk, av cal, cnd & prices. T. BR Brentwood, oos up hill & keep to left. SIOR.

BRIDGEND, Wales

BRIDGEND BOOK BARN **745540**
39 Market Street, Bridgend, South Glamorgan
Mon-Sat, 10-5.30, Rel
Med size R/C stk, vg cnd, more int than av bks, av prices. Etgow. P.diff. BR: Bridgend, oos ahead down hill & cont where cars cannot & turn right.

BRIDGENORTH

BOOKSTACK **0746 7670891**
2A Castle Terrace, Bridgenorth, W Midlands WV16 4AH.
Mon 10.30-5, clsd Tues & Thurs, Wed & Fri 10.30-4.30, Sat 9.30-4.30, Sun pm
Med size R/C low key, av prices. BR: Wolverhampton (NAST 18 miles).

BRIDGE OF ALLAN, Scotland

BRIDGE OF ALLAN BOOKS **0786 834483**
2 Henderson Street, Bridge of Allan, Stirlingshire FK9 4HT
Mon-Sat, 10-5.30, some Sundays
Med size C/D stk, emphon History, esp Scottish. VG cnd, av prices, TWC, P.poss. Scotrail B of A, oos turn right into town, SIOR.

BRIDLINGTON

JL BOOK EXCHANGE **0262 601285**
72 Hildethorpe Road, Bridlington, Yorks YO15 3BQ
Summer 8.30-8.30 every day, Winter Mon-Sat 9-5
Small R stk, av cal, cnd & prices. Oos, turn right and left into town.

BRIDPORT

PIC'S BOOKSHOP **0308 25689**
11 South Street, Bridport, Dorset DT6 3NR
Mon-Sat, 9.30-5, Thurs 1pm
Med size R/C stk, av cal, cnd & prices.

Rumours of second shop.

BRIGHTLINGSEA

VICTORIA BOOKS **0206 302374**
22 Victoria Place, Brightlingsea, Essex CO7 9BX.
Mon-Sat, 10.30-4.30, clsd Tues
Med size R/C stk, av cal, cnd & prices. Etf. BR: Colchester

BRIGHTON - see map

THE TRAFALGAR BOOKSHOP **0273 684300**
44 Trafalgar Street, Brighton, E Sussex BN1 4ED.
Mon-Fri, 10-6, Sat 5pm
Med/lg R/C/D stk, av cal, cnd & prices. Emphon Sports espec horseracing.

DEJA VU **0273 600400**
31 Trafalgar Street, Brighton, E Sussex BN1 4ED.
Mon-Sat, 11-6
Med size Spec in Occult & Esoteric. Ab av cal, cnd & prices.

WAX FACTOR 0273 673744
24 Trafalgar Street, Brighton.
Mon-Sat, 9.30-5.30
Record shp with some bks on pop music & Occult. Also pbks. - too deafening.

COURTHOUSE BOOKSHOP 0273 600365
181 Edward Street, Brighton, E Sussex BN2 2JB.
Mon-Sat 10.30-4.30
Small R/C stk, av cal, cnd & prices.

BRIMSTONES **PHONE UNKNOWN**
St James's St (No no), Brighton, E Sussex.
Mon-Sat, 9.30-5.30
Newly opened, R/C stk. Av cal, cnd & prices. Keen on Crime Fiction. T. P.diff. The reason I do not have the number in the street OR the phone number is that the member of staff couldn't see any reason why she should give it to me. From Courthouse Bks oosh, turn left, left & left.

TALL STOREY'S 0273 697381
88 St James Street, Brighton, E Sussex BN2 1TP.
Mon-Sat, 10-6
Med/lg R/C stk, res D stk primarily left wing.

KEMPTOWN BOOKS 0273 682110
91 St Georges Road, Brighton, E Sussex BN2 1EF.
Mon-Sat, 10.30-5.30
New Bksp with small C stk. Emphon artistic.

HOLLEYMAN & TREACHER 0273 28007
21A-22 Duke Street, Brighton, E Sussex BN1 1AB.
Mon-Sat, 9-5.30
Lg R/C/D stk, av cal, cnd & prices.

COLIN PAGE 0273 25954
36 Duke Street, Brighton BN1 1AG.
Mon-Sat, 10-5.30
Med/lg R/C/D stk, ab av cal, cnd & prices. T.

N F BROOKES 0273 23105
12A Queens Road, Brighton BN1 3WA.
Mon-Sat, 9.30-5.15, Sun 11-1.30
Lg R/C stk, emphon rmndrs & foreign languages. Av cal, cnd & prices.

BRISTOL

BRISTOL BOOKS **0272 634716**
5 North Street, Bedminster, Bristol BS3 1EN.
Mon-Sat, 10-6
Small/med size R/C stk, emphon pbks. Av cal, cnd & prices.

BRISTOL BOOKS **0272 245548**
180B Cheltenham Road, Montpelier, Bristol BS6 5RB.
Mon-Sat, 10-6
Med size stk, emphon pbks. Av cal, cnd & prices.

THE WISE OWL BOOKSHOP **0272 262783**
26 Upper Maudlin Street, Bristol, BS2 8DJ.
Mon-Sat, 10.30-5.30
Med/lg R/C stk. Emphon Occult & Performing Arts. Av cal, cnd & prices.

COTHAM HILL BOOKSHOP **0272 732344**
29A Cotham Hill, Bristol BS6 6JY.
Mon-Sat, 9.30-5.30
Med/lg R/C/D stk, av cal, cnd & prices. Emphon Art and Batsfords.

PATTERSON & LIDDLE **0272 731205**
2C Chandos Road, Bristol BS6 6PE.
Mon-Sat, 10-6
Med size R/C/D stk, av cal, cnd & prices. Emphon railways.

JOHN ROBERTS **0272 268368**
43 Triangle West, Bristol BS68 1ES.
Mon-Sat, 9-5
Med size R/C stk, av cal, cnd & prices.

BEWARE OF THE LEOPARD BOOKS **0272 257277**
Stall 77, St Nicholas Market, St Nicholas St, Bristol BS1 1LJ
Mon-Sat, 10-4
BTA stall in mkt. Av cal, cnd & prices. TWC.

A R KEMMISH **PHONE UNKNOWN**
Stall 71,St Nicholas Market, St Nicholas St, Bristol BS1 1LJ.
NFDA.

GOLDNEY BOOKS **0272 237408**
18 Clifton Road, Clifton, Bristol BS8 1AQ.
Mon-Sat, 10.30-5.30, Thurs 7pm
Newly opened Bijou/Gallery style shop. Emphon Ills & Childrens, ab av cal, cnd & prices.

WELLINGTON BOOKS 0272 739848
4A Waterloo St, Clifton, Bristol BS8 4BT.
Mon-Sat, 10-6
Newly opened C/D stk, av cal, cnd & prices. TWC. From Goldney bks oosh, turn right, follow road round to Clifton & turn left.

BRIXHAM

THE BOOK WARREN 08045 58531
9a Bolton Street, Brixham, Devon.
Mon-Sat 10-4.30, clsd Wed in winter
Med size R/C stk, low cal, cnd & prices. Br: Paignton (NAST 5 miles).

BROADSTAIRS

ALBION BOOKSHOP 0843 62876
29 Albion Street, Broadstairs, Kent CT10 1IX
Mon-Sat, 9.30-5.30, L: 1-2
Lg R/C stk, av cal, cnd & prices. BR: Broadstairs, oos turn left towards sea front & left at bottom, shp is in alleyway on right.

BROADWAY

STRATFORD TREVERS 0386 853668
45 High Street, Broadway, Worcestershire WR12 7DP
Mon-Sat, 9.30-5.15, L: 1-2.15, Sun 2.15-5.30
Med/lg C stk, ab av cal, cnd & prices. BR: Evesham (NAST 10 miles).

BROMLEY (see London)

BROXBOURNE

CRAFT BARN **PHONE UNKNOWN**
Chime Garden Centre, Old Naleing Road, Broxbourne, Herts NFDA.

BUDE

Rumours of a low key but Int shop.

BUNGAY

SCORPIO BOOKS **0986 5743**
1 Nethergate, Bungay, Suffolk NR35 1HE
Thur,Fri,Sat 10-5, L: 1-2
Med size gen stk, spec in Aviation, Military & Jazz. Etf.

BURFORD

THE COTSWOLD BOOKSHOP **099382 3308**
High Street, Burford, Oxfordshire OX8 4QA
Mon-Sat 9-dusk
Med size R/C stk, av cal, cnd & prices.

QUILL BOOKS **099 382 ????**
24 High Street, Burford, Oxfordshire OX14 4RR
Mon-Sat, 10.30-5.30, clsd Wed 1-2
Newly opened. Med size R/C stk, emphon Modern Lit. TWC. P.poss. BR: Evesham, (NAST 15 miles).

BURNTWOOD

ANTIQUES, BOOKS, CURIOS **0543 682217**
Church View, Burntwood, Walsall, W. Midlands WS7 5DP.
Wed & Sat 10-4.30, or by appointment
Med/lg R/C stk, low key, low prices. A drif Anorexia Nervosa special. BR: Lichfield (NAST 4 miles). Etf. In old part of Burntwood by church. P.poss.

BUSHMILLS, N. Ireland

CAUSEWAY BOOKS **02657 31033**
Main Street, Bushmills, County Antrim.
Mon-Sat, 10-5
Med size R/C stk, slightly low key, nrly good enough to be a drif special. TWC. P.poss. Etf in High Street. NIR: Coleraine (NAST 8 miles but buses good).

BURTON ON TRENT

THE NEEDWOOD BOOKSHOP **0283 41641**
55 New Street, Burton on Trent.
Mon-Sat, 9.30-5 V.rel
Med/lg R/C stk, slightly Roast Beef/Bookfairy, but well worth a look if you are in the area. BR: Burton, oos turn right & right & third right.

THE BRIDGE END BOOKSHOP **0283 46743**
198 Bearwood Hill Road, Burton on Trent.
Mon-Sat, 9-5, clsd am Thurs
Med size R/C stk, a drif special. Silverfish special. Av prices. BR: Burton, oos turn right & follow signs for A50 over bridge and SIOR.

BURY ST EDMUNDS

BURY BOOKSHOP **0248 703107**
28A Hatter Street, Bury St Edmunds, Suffolk LF33 1NE
Mon-Sat, 9.30-3, Rel
New bksp with med size R/C stk, av cal, cnd & prices. BR: Bury, oos ahead into town centre, cross Mkt Sq, turn left & second right.

BUXTON

HALL BANK BOOKSHOP **0298 70889**
9 Hall Bank, Buxton, Derbyshire SK17 6EW
Mon-Sat, 10.30-5.30, Sun 2-4.30, BTR in winter
Med size R/C stk, av cal, cnd & prices. BR: Buxton, oos down drive, turn left, follow rd round to right & take right hand fork up hill.

THE SMALLEST BOOKSHOP **NO PHONE**
Old Court House, George Street, Buxton, No postcode.
Mon-Sat, 10-5
Small R/C stk, at rear of sweet shop. NV.

CAERNARVON, Wales

THE BALCONY BOOKSHOP **0286 671152 (HM)**
The Old Market Hall, Palace St, Caernarvon, Gwynned, Wales
Mon-Sat, 10.30-5, clsd Thur
Med size R/C stk, low key. BR: Bangor (NAST 10 miles) + bus, at stop turn left towards castle & second right.

CAISTOR

PLOUGH BOOKS **0472 852073**
19 Plough Hill, Caistor, Lincolnshire LN7 6UB
Tues-Sat, 10.30-5, Sun 11-4
Med size R/C stk, av cal, cnd & prices. NV.

CAMBOURNE

VICTORIA GALLERY **0209 719268**
28 Gross Street, Cambourne, Cornwall TR14 8EX
Mon-Sat, 10-5, clsd Wed
Antique shop with med size BTA R/C stk. Main stk is now at New Street Books, Penzance. BR: Cambourne, oos ahead into town at crossroads SIOR.

CAMBRIDGE

ALISTAIR AND GARON **0228 62086**
70 King Street, Cambridge CB1 1LN.
Mon-Sat 9.30-6
Record shop with small/med stk of R/C bks. Av cal, cnd & prices. BR: Cambridge, oos ahead & turn right into town, turn right at bus stn and come back on yourself.

THE BOOKROOM **0223 69694**
13A St Elegius Street, Cambridge CB2 1HS.
Mon-Fri, 9.30-5
Med size C stk, av cal, cnd & prices. I can never find it.

C. DAVID **0223 354619**
3 St Edwards Passage, Cambridge CB2 3PJ.
Mon-Sat, 9.30-5 Rel
Med/lg C/D stk, av cal, cnd & prices. BR: Cambridge, oos ahead, right at T junction, left at Main Sq & ahead into passage.

THE HAUNTED BOOKSHOP **0223 312913**
9 St Edwards Passage, Cambridge CB2 3RJ.
Mon-Sat, 9.30-5.30, L: 1-2
Med size C/D stk, ab av cal, cnd, av prices. Emphon Childrens. As above.

GREEN STREET BOOKSHOP **0223 67876**
3 Green Street, Cambridge.
Mon-Fri, 9.15-5, Sat 9.30-4.30
Med/lg C/D stk, emphon Student/Acad. Ab av cal, cnd & prices. From Haunted bksp turn right back to Main Sq & left.

OXFAM BOOKSHOP **NO PHONE**
28 Sidney Street, Cambridge.
Mon-Sat, 10-4, Rel
Purpose built s/h bksp which has the highest av prices in Cambridge. From Green St bksp go back to Main Street & turn left.

DEIGHTON BELL 0223 353939
13 Trinity Street, Cambridge CB2 1TJ
Mon-Sat, 9.30-5.30
Med/lg C/D stk, ab av cal, cnd & prices. Emphon Lit, Bibliography, Antqrn and Charm! From Oxfam oosh, turn right & left.

QUINTO **NOW CLOSED**

THE UNMAUDLIN BOOKSHOP 0223 62457
12A Magdalene Street, Cambridge.
Mon-Sat, 10.30-6, Sun 2-5
Med size R/C stk, av cal, cnd & prices. From Oxfam, cont North over bridge, SIOL.

CANTERBURY

PAUL HOLCOMBE 0227 457913
5 North Lane, Canterbury, Kent CT2 7EB
Mon 11-4, Tues clsd, Wed 10-4.30, Thur clsd, Fri & Sat 10-5, Sun 12-4
Lg R/C stk. Emphon Scientific and Engineering. Av cal, cnd & prices. BR: Canterbury West, oos ahead, turn left & left.

THE CHAUCER BOOKSHOP 0227 453912
6 Beer Cart Lane, Canterbury CT1 2NY
Mon-Sat, 9.30-5.30
Med size R/C/D stk, av cal, cnd & prices. BR: Canterbury West oos ahead, left into town & right at Margaret St & right.

DAVID MILES 0227 464773
37 Northgate, Canterbury, Kent CT1 1BL
Mon-Sat, 10-5
Lg C/D stk, ab av cal, cnd & prices. Emphon Childrens & Ills. BR: Canterbury West, oos ahead, left into High St & left at Cathedral St & cont. SIOL.

BELL HARRY BOOKSHOP **NOW CLOSED**

STEPHEN THOMPSON **NOW CLOSED**

CARDIFF, Wales

CAPITAL BOOKSHOP 0222 388423
27 Morgan Arcade, Cardiff CR1 2AF
Mon-Sat, 10-5.30 Rel
Med/lg R/C, nrly D stk, keen on Welsh, av cal, cnd & prices, TWC. P.imposs. BR: Cardiff oos ahead past bus stn, turn right & left into St Mary St & Morgan Arcade is on right.

SECOND READING 0222 461404
Dickens Arcade, 9-11 Castle Street, Cardiff CF5 1FN
Mon-Sat, 10-5.30
Med size R/C stk, NSOC, av cal & prices. Almost a drif special, tends to attract nutters. From Capital turn right into Hill St & arcade almost opp & find establishment labelled Emporium, shop is upstairs. There is also a bkstl downstairs in bsmt.

ROATH BOOKS 0222 490523
189 City Road, Cardiff, Wales.
Mon-Sat, 10-5.30
Med size R/C stk. B&MC, driff special. Etgow. P.poss. From St Mary St cont towards Castle into High St & turn right into Queen St & cont, Newport Road & third left. SIOR. (not poss in motor car).

PONTCANNA OLD BOOKS 0222 641047
1 Pontcanna Street, Cardiff, CF1 9HQ
Mon-Sat, 10-5.30
Med size R/C/D stk. Av cal, cnd & prices. Emphon Mil Hist & Welsh. T. Etgow. P.poss. From High St turn left at Castle, over bridge & right into Cathedral Road & first left. SIOR in second parade of shops. Also has stall in Jacobs Well Market where a second stall is open Thurs & Sat.

CARLISLE

BOOKCASE 0228 445560
17 Castle Street, Carlisle.
Mon-Sat
Med/lg R/C stk, av cal, cnd & prices. Oos turn left & cont. towards Castle, SIOR.

CARMARTHEN, Wales

CARMARTHEN BOOKS 0267 2356676
1 St Mary Street, Carmarthen, Dyfed SA31 1TN, Wales
Mon-Sat, 10-5, V.Rel
Med size R/C/D stk. Av cal, NSOC, av prices. Bgns known, almost WAD. Emphon Welsh (res stk). TWC. P.not easy. BR: Carmarthen, oos, turn right left over bridge and right up hill into town. Turn left at top & right & shop is beautifully signposted by Guild Hall.

CARNDOMAGH, Eire

ARCADE BOOKS, CARNDOMAGH
NV. But rumoured to be quite int. But it takes a full day to get there & back.

CARNFORTH

THE CARNFORTH BOOKSHOP **0524 734588**
38/42 Market Street, Carnforth, Lancashire LA5 9JE.
Mon-Sat, 9.30-5.30
Lg R/C stk, av cal, cnd & prices. Oos down drive, turn right & SIOL.

CARSHALTON (see London)

CARTMEL

PETER BAIN SMITH **044 854359**
Bank Court, Cartmel, Cumbria LA11 6QB
Everyday 11-6. Winter clsd Mon & Tues.
Med/lg R/C stk. Keen on Childrens. Etf. BR: Cark & Cartmel, oos turn left & right into village & right at main road (not towards Holkham Hall).

CASHEL, Eire

THE BOOKSHOP **062 61605**
Ladyswell Street, Caskel, Tipperary.
Mon-Sat, 10-5
Med size R/C stk, drif special. NV. Etf in Cashel, IR: Tipperary (NAST 20 miles).

CHANNEL ISLANDS

THESAURUS **0534 37045**
26 Burrard Street, St Helier, Jersey, Channel Islands.
Mon-Sat, 8.30-5.30
V lge R/C/D stk, ab av cal & cnd. Av prices. Bgns known. WAD. T & D. P.poss (aeroplanes only). NV.

THESAURUS (St Peter's Port) **NOW CLOSED**

CHARD

THE CHARD BOOKSHOP **NOW CLOSED**
2 Pig Lane, Holyrood Street, Chard, Somerset TA20 2AH
Tues-Sat, 9.30-6, btr
Small/med R/C stk, av cal, cnd & prices. Keen on Asia. Bookfairy. Etgow. P.poss. BR: Crewkerne (NAST 10 miles), etf.

CHELTENHAM

HEYNES BOOKSHOP **0242 515423**
49 Clarence Street, Cheltenham, Gloucestershire.
Mon-Sat, 10-5
Med/lg R/C stk. NSOC. Av cal, ab av prices. Etf on one way system by bus stn in centre of town.

MICHAEL REYNER **0242 512806**
11 St Lukes Road, Cheltenham, Glos.
Thur-Sat, 10-5
Med size R/C stk. Emphon Cricket. Av cal, cnd & prices. BR: Cheltenham, turn right into Lansdowne Rd & cont along Montpelier Terrace, turn left at Eagle Star bldg & first right.

ALAN HANCOX **0242 513204**
101 Promenade, Cheltenham, Glos.
Mon-Sat, 9.30-4.45, L: 1-2.15, Wed 1pm, Rel
Med/lg R/C stk, ab av cal & cnd, av prices. Keen on Lit & Arts. Currently subject to massive changes. On opposite side to bus stn to Heynes.

CHEPSTOW, Wales

GLANCE BACK BOOKS **NO PHONE**
17 Upper Church St, Chepstow, Gwent, Wales NP6 5EX.
Mon-Sat, 10-5.30, Sun in summer
Lg R/C stk, av cal, cnd & prices. T. Etf at far end of town.

CHESHAM

FORUM BOOKS **PHONE UNKNOWN**
Church St (No no), Chesham, Hertfordshire.
Tues-Sat, 10-5.30
Newly opened med size low key R stk, av cnd & prices. NFDA. Tube: Chesham, oos down drive, turn left into paved zone & right.

CHESTER

STOTHERT'S **0244 340756**
4 Nicholas Street, Chester, CH1 2NX
Mon-Sat, 9.30-5, L 1-2
Med size R/C stk, slightly Roast Beef. Keen on HSF. BR: Chester, oos turn right & left onto Ring Road SIOR - 1 mile.

TEG'S BOOKS **0244 311017**
4 Odeon Buildings, Northgate Street, Chester
Mon-Sat, 10-5
Med size R/C stk, ave cal, cnd & prices. Emphon pbks. Newly opened. From Stothert's into centre of town & turn left towards town hall & go past.

WORDS & MUSIC **0244 311910**
1 City Wall's, Northgate Street, Chester
Mon-Sat, 9-6
Small/med R/C stk. Emphon Lit. Av prices, TWC. P. v.diff. TWC. From Teg's oosh, turn left & right into Rufus Court & up steps.

EARLS EYE BOOKS **0244 319688**
B15 Chester Market.
Mon-Sat, 10-6.
Bookstall.

BOOKLEAFS **PHONE UNKNOWN**
26B High Street, Saltney, Chester CH4 8SE
Mon-Sat, 10-5, Sun 11-4
Lg R/C stk, almost a drif special but charges almost as much as me. TWC. BR Chester (NAST 3 miles), oos follow signs for Wrexham, then Saltney, under Bridge and past first major road on right. SIOR.

SPCK 0244 323753
7-11 St Werburgh Street, Chester CH1 2EJ
Mon-Sat, 9-5 Rel
New bksp with BTA SPCK s/h stk. Not great on its own but combined with the other Chester shps it is WAD. BR Chester, oos turn right, left at Shopping St under subway, straight ahead until T junction, turn right into St Werburgh St, SIOL (by cathedral).

CHESTERFIELD

ALAN HILL 0246 231158
8 Falcon Yard, Chesterfield, Derbyshire, S40 1PF
Mon-Sat, 9.30-5.30
Med size R/C/nrly D stk, ab av cal, cnd, av prices. TWC. P.diff. BR: Chesterfield, oos head for crooked spire on far side of Market Place, enter Falcon Yard and SIOL.

CHRYSALIS 0246 69950
309 Chatsworth Road, Chesterfield, Derbyshire.
Tues-Sat, 10-5
Newly opened antq shp with BTA med size R/C stk. Variable prices. TWC. P.poss. From Alan Hill oosh, turn right, left into Market Place & cont straight ahead for about 1/2 mile.

TILLEY'S 0246 454270
29/31 South Street, New Whittington, Chesterfield, Derbyshire S43 2AA
Mon-Sat, 9.30-5, L: 1.30-3
Med/lg Spec in Modern Mags. Ab av cal, cnd & prices. TWC. BR: Chesterfield (NAST 5 miles). Look for signs for New Whittington.

CHICHESTER

THE CHICHESTER BOOKSHOP 0243 785473
39 Southgate, Chichester, W Sussex PO15 1DP.
Mon-Sat, 9-5
Lg R/C/D stk, av cal, cnd & prices. BR: Chichester, oos into town and SIOR.

ST PETERS BOOKSHOP 0243 778477
St Peter's Arcade, West Street, Chichester, PO19 1QI.
Tues-Sat, 10.30-5.30, L: 1.30-2.30
Small/med size R/C/D stk, av cal, cnd & prices. BR: Chester, oos into town & SIOR on far side of cathedral.

CHILHAM

THE FORGE BOOKSHOP **0227 730267**
The Street, Chilham, Kent.
Mon-Sat, 9.30-5.30
Small R/C stk, av cal & cnd. Keen on Gardening. BR: Chilham, oos ahead, turn left towards village and left at sign post.

CHIPPING CAMDEN

DRAYCOTT BOOKS **0386 841392**
1 Sheep Street, Chipping Camden, Glos GL55 6DS.
Mon-Sat, 10-5, L: 1-2
Med size R/C stk, more int than av. Etgow. P.poss. BR: Moreton in Marsh (NAST 10 miles) Etf off main street.

CHIPPING SODBURY

BAILEY'S BOOKSHOP **0454 513399**
15 Horse Street, Chipping Sodbury, Wilts BS17 6DA.
Mon-Sat, 9.30-5, clsd Wed
Med size R/C stk, av cal, cnd & prices. BR: Bristol Parkway (NAST 10 miles) etf.

CHORLTON CUM HARDY

See MANCHESTER

CHORLTON ON MEDLOCK

McGILLS BOOKSHOP **PHONE UNKNOWN**
184 Oxford Road, Chorlton on Medlock, Manchester M13 8QQ
Mon-Sat, 10.30-5.30
Med size R/C stk, av cal, cnd & prices. Emphon students bks.

CINDERFORD, Wales

THE CINDERFORD BOOKSHOP* **NO PHONE**
Market Square, Cinderford, Wales.
Mon-Sat, 10-5
Small R stk. A drif special. Av cal, cnd. TWC. P.poss. Etf. BR: Chepstow (NAST 10 miles).

CIRENCESTER

THOMPSON'S BOOKSHOP **0285 655239**
Dunstall House, Park Street, Cirencester, Glos GL7 2BX
Tues-Sat, 10-5
Med size R/C stk and Spec Architecture. Ab av cal, cnd & prices. BR: Kemble, (NAST 5 miles), etf.

CLARE

TRINDERS BOOKSELLERS **0787 277130**
Malting Lane (No no), Clare, Suffolk CO10 8NW.
Sats only 10-1 & 2-5
Small R/C stk, av cal, cnd & prices. TWC. P.poss. Etf. BR: Sudbury (NAST 5 miles), etf.

CLEETHORPES

LAFAYETTE BOOKSELLERS **0472 699244**
6 High Street, Cleethorpes, Sth Humberside DN35 8JN.
Tues-Sat.
R stk, av cal, cnd & prices. T. BR: Cleethorpes, oos turn right & left & first right.

PIK A BOOK **PHONE UNKNOWN**
203 Grimsby Road, Cleethorpes, Sth Humberside DN35 7HH.
Mon-Sat, 10-5
Small R stk. Av cal, cnd & prices. From Lafayette cont West about 1 mile.

CLEOBURY MORTIMER

M & M BALDWIN **0299 270110**
24 High Street, Cleobury Mortimer, W Midlands DY14 8BY.
Wed 2-6, Sat 10-6 L: 1-2, Fri in summer 10-6, L: 1-2
Med size Spec in Canals & Ind. Hist. Ab av cal, cnd & prices. T. BR: Ludlow (NAST 10 miles), etf. V. attractive.

CLEVEDON

CLEVEDON BOOKS **0272 872304**
Cinema Building, Old Church Road, Clevedon, BS21 5NN
Tues-Sat 10.30-5.30, clsd Wed, L: 1-2.45
Med size R/C stk. Emphon Prints.f Bl av cal, cnd & ab av prices. Out to lunch. BR: Bristol, (NAST 15 miles) etf.

COCKERMOUTH

WINKWORTH **0900 824984**
102 Main Street, Cockermouth, Cumbria, CA2 9LX.
Mon-Sat, 9-5
New bksp with med size R/C stk. Keen on Local Hist. Av cal; cnd & prices. BR: Whitehaven (NAST 10 miles), etf.

COGGESHALL

ELKIN MATTHEWS **0376 61730**
16 Stoneham Street, Coggeshall, Essex CO6 1TT.
Mon-Sat, 9-4.30, L: 1-2, clsd Wed
Med size C/D stk. Emphon Childrens & Ills. Ab av cal, cnd & prices. WAD. BR: Kelvedon (NAST 5 miles), etf.

JOHN LEWIS **0376 61518**
35 Stoneham Street, Coggeshall, Essex CO6 1TT.
Hours unknown, btr
Med size Spec stk. C stk of Maritime bks. As above.

COLCHESTER

CASTLE BOOKSHOP **0206 577550**
37 North Hill, Colchester, Essex CO1 1QR.
Mon-Sat, 9-5, V.Rel
Lg R/C/D stk, av cal, cnd & prices. TWC. BR: Colchester, oos turn right & up hill into town, SIOR.

ALPHABETS **0206 572751**
13 Trinity Street, Colchester, Essex CO1 1JN.
Mon-Sat, 10-5, clsd Thurs
Med size R/C stk. Bl av cal & cnd, av prices. TWC. From Castle Bks, oosh, turn right & left with traffic & first right opp Courts.

GREYFRIARS BOOKS **0206 563138**
92B East Road, Colchester, Essex CO1 2QN.
Mon-Sat, 9.45-5.30
Med size R/C stk, av cal, cnd & prices. From Castle Bks, oosh right and follow traffic to left & straight ahead downhill, SIOL.

COLERAINE, N.Ireland

THE IRISH DRIF'S SPECIAL **0265 54024**
Mac's Market, Railway Place, Coleraine.
Mon-Sat, 10.30-5
Med size R/C stk, silverfish special. Nsoc, but can be worth wading through. T & D. P.poss. NIR: Coleraine, oos, turn left into town & SIOL.

THE COLERAINE BOOKSHOP **0265 52557**
5 Stone Row, Coleraine.
Mon-Sat, 10.30-5.30
Med size R/C/D stk, bta cal, bta cnd, bta high prices. TWC. P.poss. Etgow. WaD. NIR: Coleraine, oos turn left.
There are also some low key bks in the War On Want charity shop opp Macs Market.

COLNE

COLNE BOOKS **0282 870952**
Shackleton Hall, Colne, Lancaster B88 OLG
Mon-Sat, 9-5.30, clsd Tues
Small/med R/C stk, av cal, cnd & prices. Slightly paperbacky. BR: Colne, oos up hill, SIOL.

COLWYN BAY, Wales

BAY BOOKSHOP **0482 531642**
14 Seaview Road, Colwyn Bay, Clwyd LL29 8DG
Mon-Sat, 9.30-5, clsd Wed in winter, REL
Med/lg R/C/D stk, slightly Roast Beef. Res stk. Etgow. T. P.diff. BR: Colwyn Bay oos turn left into parade of shops, SIOR.

COLWYN BOOKS **0482 530683**
66 Abergale Road, Colwyn Bay, LL29 7PP
Mon-Sat, 10.30-6, clsd Wed
Med size R/C stk, slightly low key. Av cnd & prices. Keen on Theology. TWC. Etgow. P.diff. BR: Colwyn Bay, oos straight ahead 200 yds turn left & SIOR.

CONWY, Wales

THE BOOKSHOP **0492 592137**
21 High Street, Conwy, Gwynned LL32 8DE
EVERY DAY IN SUMMER 10-6, Tues-Sat 10-5, Wed 1pm.
Med size R/C stk, av cal, cnd & prices. T. BR: Conwy (not recommended - use Llandudno Junction) into town, turn right.

There is also an antq shp at the bottom of the road & turn right, SIOL. Has some int bks.

CORK, Eire

LEE'S BOOKSTORE **010021 272307**
10 The Quay, Cork, Eire.
Tues-Sat 10-5.30, L 1-2
Med size R/C stk, av cal, cnd. Ab av prices. TWC. P.Poss. IR: Cork, oos turn left & left over bridge & right by quay.

COTTINGHAM

THE COTTINGHAM BOOKSHOP **0482 845567**
Cotta House, 169/171 Hallgate, Cottingham, HU17 4BB.
Mon-Sat, 10-5
Med size R stk. Ab av cal, cnd & prices. BR: Cottingham, oos turn right at Church Rd, and cont, SIOL in arcade.

COVENTRY

GOSFORD BOOKS **0203 220813**
116 Gosford Street, Gosford, Coventry, CV1 5DL.
Mon-Sat, 10-5.30
Med size R/C stk, av cal, cnd & prices. T. P.diff. BR: Coventry, oos follow signs for town centre, turn right at statue of covered Lady Godiva & cont, SIOR.

LUCKMAN'S ANTIQUES **0203 223842**
40 Far Gosford Street, Coventry, CV1 5DW.
Mon-Sat, 11-6
A d'ranged shop. He would like it to be a bksp & I would like it to be a bksp but at the moment what it is is a place that sells pornography, junk & some bks. From Gosford Bks oosh turn right, SIOL 1/2 mile.

ARMSTRONG'S BOOKS & COLLECTIBLES **0203 714344**
163 Sovereign Road, Earlsdon, Coventry, W. Midlands.
Mon-Sat, 10.30-5.30, L: 1-2 Unr
Med size R/C B&MC & Bullshit Special. T & D. P.poss. From Gosford, oosh turn left back to Lady Godiva, and cont to ring road, go under and keep straight & turn left past school & then under tunnel & ahead.

COWES, ISLE OF WIGHT

THE NEVER OPEN BOOKSHOP **0983 293598**
65 High Street, Cowes, Isle of Wight.
Mon-Sat, 10-5. BTR
Med size R/C stk, av cal, cnd & prices.

CRANBROOK

THORNTON'S **0580 712965**
The Street, Cranbrook, TN17 2JD.
April-Oct Tues-Sat 11-6, Fri-Sat winter, 10-5.30
Med size R/C stk, keen on Gardening. Av cal,, cnd & prices. Seasonal.

CRAYFORD, KENT (see London)

CREWE

COPNAL BOOKS **0270 580470**
16 Meredith Street, Crewe CW1 2PW.
Mon-Sat, 10-5.30, clsd Wed
Med/lg R/C stk, Stokers Special. Av cal, cnd & prices. TWC. P.poss. BR: Crewe, oos turn left & right at traffic lights, cont for one mile, keeping railway on right & past Asda look for car park. Street is behind.

CREWKERNE

THE BOOKSHOP **0460 76579**
17 Falkland Square, Crewkerne, Somerset TA18 7JB.
Mon-Sat, 10-5.15+
Lg R/C stk, consists of several D's sharing. Variable. TWC. P.poss. BR: Crewkerne, oos turn right into town & look for shopping precinct on right. SIOL.

OSCAR'S ANTIQUES **0460 72718**
13 Market Square, Crewkerne, Somerset.
Mon-Sat, 10-5, Unr
Antq shp with med size R/C stk at D prices. NSOC. Stokers Special. Av cnd & prices.

COACH HOUSE BOOKS **NOW CLOSED**

CRIEFF, Scotland

STRATHERN ANTIQUES **0764 4344**
2 Comrie Street, Crieff, Perthshire PH7 4AY
Mon-Sat, 10-5. L 1-2, clsd Wed
Antique shop with bta stk of bks. TWC. P.poss. Etf. Scotrail Perth NAST (7 miles).

CRIEF CINEMA BOOKSHOP **NOW CLOSED**

CROMER

BOOKWORMS **0263 515078**
9 New Street, Cromer, Norfolk NR27 9HF.
Mon-Sat, 10-5, Sun 2-5, clsd Wed
Small/med size R/C stk. Ab av cal, cnd. Av prices. BR: Cromer, oos turn left, straight ahead towards seafront & left.

CROMFORD

SCARTHIN BOOKS **0629 823272**
The Promenade, Scarthin, Cromford, DE4 3QF.
Mon-Sat, 10-6, L: 1.30-2.30, Sun 12-6
Lg R/C/nrly D stk. NSOC. No T. BR: Cromford, down path, turn right into town & shop is beyond pond on left.

DARLINGTON

VOKES AND SON **0325 359790**
No longer a bookshop. Now moved to 185 Grange Road, Darlington, Durham.

DARTMOUTH

CHANTRY BOOKSHOP 0803 832796
11 Higher Street, Dartmouth, Devon TQ6 9RB.
Mon-Sat, 10.30-5, clsd winter
Primarily a print shp with small R/C stk of bks. Helen Hanff Special. Etf on hill in centre of town. BR: Paignton (NAST 10 miles).

DAWLISH

THE OLD BOOKSHOP 0626 866026
Strand Hill, Dawlish, Devon EX7 9HR.
Mon-Sat, 10-5, Sundays in summer
Med size touristy shop. TWC. P.poss. BR: Dawlish, oos turn left & right at bottom, follow road round & left & come back on yourself.

DEAL

THE GOLDEN HIND 0304 375086
85 Beach Street, Deal, Kent CT14 6JR.
Mon-Sun, 10-5.30
Med size R/C stk, av cal, cnd. Non av prices. BR: Deal, oos & right & left to seafront & SIOL.

DEEPING ST JAMES

BRIDGE BOOKSHOP 0778 343175
106 Church Street, Deeping St James, Peterborough PE6 8HE.
Mon-Sat, 10.30-5.30, clsd Thurs, Sun pm
Med size R/C stk, av cal, cnd & prices. Keen on Local Hist. Etf. BR: Peterborough (NAST 10 miles).

DERBY

LAURA'S BOOKSHOP 0332 47094
58 Osmaston Road, Derby DE1 3HZ.
Tues-Sat, 10-5.30, clsd Wed
Med/lg R/C stk, ab av cal, cnd & prices. WAD. BR: Derby, oos ahead, turn right into London Road, cross roundabout & turn left back on yourself.

TEMPLE GALLERY **0332 293752**
348 Abbey Street, Derby, Derbyshire.
Mon-Sat, 10.30-6
Med size R/C stk, av cal, cnd & prices. Also does prints. Etgow. From Lauras, oosh turn right, right at roundabout & follow main road round to Abbey Street.

DEVIZES

D'ARCY BOOKS **0380 726922**
The Chequers, High Street, Devizes, Wilts SN10 1AT.
Mon-Sat, 10.30-5.30
Med/lg R/C stk, ab av cal, cnd & prices. BR: Swindon (V NAST 15 miles) etf in centre of town.

DINGWALL, Scotland

DINGWALL ANTIQUES **GIOPOC**

DONCASTER

ATHENA BOOKS **0302 322913**
34 Imperial Crescent, Doncaster, DN2 5BW.
Mon-Sat, 9-5
Med/lg Spec in Military Hist. Ab av cal, cnd, av prices. TWC. P.poss.

DORKING

T S HILL BOOKS **0306 886468**
122 South Street, Dorking, Surrey RH24 2EU.
Mon-Sat, 10-5, clsd Wed
Med size R/C stk, av cal, cnd & prices. TWC. BR: Dorking oos turn left & right at T junction & keep to left for one mile.

DOUGLAS (see Isle of Man)

DRIFFIELD

THE DRIFFIELD BOOKSHOP **0377 44210**
21 Middle Street Nth, Driffield, Yorks YO25 7SW.
Mon-Sat, 10-5.30, Thurs 6.30, Fri 10-8
Med size R/C/D stk, Emphon Mod Lit and S.F. Ab av cal, cnd & prices. Oos, turn right into town, SIOR at far end.

DROITWICH

GRANT BOOKS **0905 778155**
Victoria Sq (No no.), Droitwich, WR9 8DE.
Med size Spec in Golf. Ab av cal, cnd & prices. Has some general bks. BR: Droitwich, oos into town & look for main square, shop is in upstairs office.

SEDGEBARROW BOOKS **0527 72489**(hm)
Droitwich Market Hall, Droitwich, Worcs.
Tues, Fri & Sat, 9-4.30
Bta R Mkt stall. Etf in centre of town.

DUBLIN, Eire

CATHACH BOOKS **0103531 718676**
10 Duke Street, Dublin 2.
Mon-Sat, 9.30-6
Med/lg Spec in high cal Irish bks. Ab av prices. TWC. P.diff. From Hanna oosh turn left, turn left, and left into Duke St.

CATHAIR BOOKS **0103531 6792406**
1 Essex Gate, Dublin 8.
Mon-Sat, 9.30-6 REL
Med size Spec in Irish bks, ab av cal, NSOC, ab av prices. T. Helpful. P.diff. From Webbs oosh, turn left & left at second set of lights & first right.

CHARTERS **0103531 723297**
70 Middle Abbey Street, Dublin.
Mon-Sat, 10-6, Sun pm
New bksp with bsmt of R/C stk, primarily Irish. Bl av cal, ab av prices. TWC. P.diff. From Connolly Stn ahead into Talbot St, left at O'Connell & first right into abbey.

COLLECTORS CORNER **NO PHONE**
38A Talbot St, Dublin
Mon-Sat, 10-6
Low key pbk shop with some hardbacks. The most int of which are in the window. IR: Connolly, oos & ahead.

DANDELION BOOKSHOP **0103531 784759**
80 Angier Street, Dublin 2.
Mon-Sat, 10.30-6.30 REL
Lg R/C stk, primarily rmndrs & pbks. But some int hardbacks. Etgow. From Stokes, oosh, turn right & left & continue for 1/2 mile. Shop is on right.

DUFFY & CO **PHONE UNKNOWN**
4 Leinster Street South, Dublin 2.
Mon-Sat, 10-5
New rmndr & s/h, but S/h better than you might at first expect. Directions as for Hannas.

GREENE'S BOOKSHOP **0103531 762554**
16 Clare Street, Dublin 2.
Mon-Fri, 9-5.30, Sat 9-1 REL
Med size R/C stk, emphon Irish. Ab av prices. TWC. From Duffy, oosh turn left & follow road round to right.

FRED HANNA **0103531 771255**
27 Nassau Street, Dublin 2.
Mon-Sat, 9-5.30
New bksp with med size Spec stk of Irish bks. Ab av cal, cnd & prices. TWC. P.poss. IR: Nassau St, oos turn left & left at Trinity College & right into Nassau St.

THE MEETING ROOM **NO PHONE**
7 Bedford Row, Dublin 2.
Mon-Sat, 9-7, REL
Sm/med size R/nearly C stk. Emphon pbks but worth a look for the hardbacks. Av cal, cnd & prices. TWC. P.diff. From Cathair, oosh down steps, straight ahead to O'Connel St, turn left, cross bdge & turn right by quay & SIOL in side street.

RATHMINES BOOKSHOP **0103531 961064**
211 Lower Rathmines Road, Dublin.
Mon-Sat, 10-9, Sun 1-6, REL
New bksp with sm R/C stk, av cal, cnd & prices. TWC. Included because it opens after 7 and Sundays (v rare in Eire). From Dandelion Bks oosh, turn right & cont for 1 1/2 miles. SIOL.

STOKES BOOKS **0103531 713584**
19 Market Arcade, South Great George St, Dublin 2
Mon-Sat, 10.30-5.30
Med size C/D stk of Irish bks, some general, gd cnd. Ab av cal, cnd & prices. TWC. From Cathair oosh, turn right, right & left at top & first right at crossroads & shop is in arcade on left. There is also a small low key establishment called Bygones.

THE WINDING STAIR BOOKSHOP & CAFE **0103531 733292**
40 Lower Ormond Quay, Dublin 1
Mon-Sat, 10.30-6
Lg R/C stk, emphon Irish bks. But more gen that most Dublin bksps. TWC. P.poss. WAD. From The Meeting Room oosh, turn left onto Quay & cross Halfpenny Bridge & SIOL.

WEBBS **0103531 777255**
5-6 Crampton Quay,Dublin 2
Mon-Sat, 9-5.30, REL
S/h & rmndrs, emphon Irish. Av cal, cnd & prices. T. P.poss. Directions as Meeting Room but further down quay.

DUFFTOWN, Scotland

DUFFTOWN BOOKSHOP **0340 20027**
5 Balvenie Street, Dufftown, Banffshire AB5 4AB
Fri & Sat 10-5 (more in summer)
Med/lg R/C stk, v gd cnd, v high prices. Wide range of subjects. Res stk. Etf by Clocktower. BR Elgin (NAST 20 miles) NPLOTCGI. Twc. P.poss.

DULVERTON

ROTHWELL AND DUNWORTH **0398 23169**
2 Bridge Street, Dulverton, Somerset TA22 9HZ.
Mon-Sat, 10-5, L: 1-2, exc Thurs
Med size R/C/D stk. Emphon HSF. Also bookstall in Dulverton.

DUNDEE, Scotland

MURRAY'S BOOKSTALL **NO PHONE**
Den's Road Market, Dundee
Mon-Fri, 10-5
Bta stall in junk market. Keen on penguins. WAD. P.poss. Scotrail Dundee, oos over footbridge ahead and right through pavel area to Wallgate and on other side turn right into Victoria Rd and left into Den's Road. There are other lesser book stalls in this market.

COLLECTORS CORNUCOPIA **NOW CLOSED**

DUNKELD, Scotland

DUNKELD ANTIQUES & BOOKS **035 028832**
The Old Kirk, The Terrace, Dunkeld, Perthshire PR8 OAD.
Open every day until late even in winter
Much bta C/D stk, emphon Scottish & sporting. T&D. P.poss. Scotrail Dunkeld, oos follow signs to village, etf over bridge.

DUN LAOGHAIRE, Eire

NAUGHTON BOOKSELLERS **0103531 2804392**
8 Marine Terrace, Dun Laoghaire, Co Dublin.
Mon-Sat, 9.30-5.30. REL
Med/lg R/C/D stk, primarily Irish but not The Dublin Dulysses. WAD. P.poss. IR: Dun Laoghaire oos to left & follow Sea front road.

DURHAM

UNIVERSITY BOOKSHOP **091 3842095**
55/57 Saddler Street, Durham DH1 3ET.
Mon-Sat, 9.30-5
Med size R/C stk, Acad orientated. Av cal, cnd & prices.

EASTBOURNE

CAMMILA'S BOOKSHOP **0323 36001**
57 Grove Road, Eastbourne, East Sussex BN21 4TX.
Mon-Sat, 10-6
Lg R/C/D stk. Bl av cal & cnd. Ab av prices.

RAYMOND SMITH **0323 34128**
30 South Street, Eastbourne, East Sussex BN21 2PL.
Mon-Sat, 9-5.30, clsd Wed
R/C stk, av cal, cnd & prices.

EAST GRINSTEAD

THE CAFE BOOKSHOP **0342 322669**
27 High Street, East Grinstead, RH19 3AW.
Mon-Sat, 9-5.30
New Bksp with small low key R stk. Bl av cnd & prices. TWC. Too small. BR: E Grinstead oos, turn left into main street. SIOL.

EAST LOOE (see Looe)

EAST MOLESEY (see London)

EDGWARE (see London)

EDINBURGH, Scotland

BOOKFARE **031 225 9237**
8 Victoria St., Edinburgh EH1 22HG
Mon-Sat, 10.30-5.30
Med size C nearly D stk. Good cnd. Keen on Penguins. TWC. P.diff.f BR: Waverley, oos up to bridge and turn left towards Castle.

BROUGHTON BOOKS **031 557 8010**
2a Broughton Place, Edinburgh EH1 3RX
Tues-Fri, 11-6, Sat 10.30-5.30
Med/lg R/C stk, ab av cal, cnd, av prices. More int now that you can see what he has got. TWC. P.poss. From Waverley turn right into Princes St, continue Leith St and left Broughton St (about 1 mile).

CASTLE BOOKS **031 556 0624**
20a Canongate, Edinburgh EH8 8DG
Mon-Sat, 11-5.30
Med size C stk. Bookfairy cal & prices. Not bookfairy cnd. TWC. P.diff. Turn left from South Bridge towards Holyrood House, SIOL.

JAMES A DICKSON **031 225 6937**
12 Forrest Road, Edinburgh EH1 2QN
Mon-Sat, 9.30-5.30
New spec. Theological stk, av cal, cnd & prices. TWC. P.diff. From Tills go North, follow road round to left & turn second right.

DUNDAS BOOKSHOP **031 556 4591**
23A Dundas Street, Edinburgh EH3 6QQ
Tues-Sat, 12-5.30
Small/med R/C stk, av cal, cnd & prices. T. P.diff. Etgow (Scottish version). From Waverley turn left into Princes St & second right & continue.

GRANT & SHAW **031 229 8399**
62 West Port, Edinburgh EH1 2LD
Open if they are there even if it does not look like it.
A Samuel Becket special. Spec in Antqrn espec Scottish. Ab av cal, cnd & prices. T & D. P.diff. DOSO (several times). Oos (Waverley) turn left & right towards the mound, onto George IV Bridge, right at Victoria St & continue to far side of Grass market. SIOL.

G T BOOKS 031 556 8032
8 Drummond Street, Edinburgh EH8 9TV
Mon-Sat, 9.30-7
Med size R/low key C stk, almost a drif special (but too many Remainders). Bl av cnd & prices. Etgow. P.diff. From Thin's continue South & turn left.

MCNAUGHTON'S BOOKSHOP 031 556 5897
3a & 4a Haddington Place, Leith Walk, Edinburgh EH2 4AE
Tues-Sat, 9.30-5.30
Med/lg C/D stk, ab av cal, cnd & prices. Netgow. P.poss. From Waverley Stn turn right into Princes St & follow through for 1 mile, SIOL.

ANDREW PRINGLE 031 556 9698
7 Dundas Street, Edinburgh EH3 6QG
Mon-Fri, 10-5.30, Sat 10.30-4
Med/lg C/D stk archetypal. Bookfairy. Gd cnd. Ab av cal & prices. TWC. P.diff. DOSO. From Waverley turn left into Princes St and second left, SIOR on first floor.

OLD GRINDLES BOOKSHOP 031 229 7252
3 Spittal Street, Edinburgh EH3 9DY
Mon-Sat, 9-9
Med/lg R/C/D stk. Av cal, cnd & prices, emphon Lit espec Scottish. TWC. P.poss. Scotrail Waverley, oos into Princes St turn left at Lothian Road and fourth left at Bread St, SIOL.

REID & REID 031 225 9660
134 St Stephen Street, Edinburgh EH3 5EE
Mon-Sat, 11-5
Small stk of Bookfairy bks in antique shop. TWC. P.poss. From Waverley turn left into Princes St, right into Frederick St which becomes Howe St & left into St Stephen St (approx 1 1/2 miles).

SECOND EDITION 031 556 9403
9 Howard St, Edinburgh EH3 5JP
Mon-Fri 12-5.30, Sat 9.30-5.30
Lg C/D stk, ab av cal & prices, av cnd. TWC. WAD. P.poss. As Broughton Bks but follow road through for 1 mile, SIOL.

JAMES THIN 031 556 6743
53 South Bridge, Edinburgh EH1 6QC
Mon-Sun, 9am-10pm
New bksp with med size R stk. Res stk of C/D bks (by application). Av cnd & prices. TWC. P.diff. Scotrail Waverley, oos into Princes St & turn right over North Bridge.

THRIFT BOOK CENTRE **NO PHONE**
26 Lochrin Buildings, Edinburgh
Mon-Fri, 10.30-3.30, Sat 10-1
Small low key Charity bksp, av cal, cnd & prices. No T. NEB.

TILL'S BOOKSHOP **031 667 0895**
1 Hope Park Crescent, Edinburgh
Mon-Fri, 12-7.30, Sat 11-6
Med size R/C stk, primarily pbks & movie posters. Vg cnd, av prices, TWC, P.poss. From Thin's continue South until Hope Park Terr, turn right & right into Buccleuch St & SIOR of next block.

EGHAM (See Englefield Green)

ELGIN, Scotland

SPEY BOOKS **NOW CLOSED**
105 High Street, Elgin
Tues, Fri & Sat, 10-5
Spec in Scottish & Nat Hist. DOSO. Scotrail Elgin, OOS turn left, turn right towards church & attempt to walk straight ahead until you get to the second shopping street. Shop is on first floor.

There is a junk shop with bks on the way to Spey Bks from the Stn.

ELHAM

ELHAM VALLEY BOOKSHOP **0303 840359**
St Mary's Road (No no), Elham, Kent
Tues-Sat, 10-5
Newly opened R/C stk, av cal, cnd & prices. T. A bit like a charity bookfair, complete with tea & cakes. N etf, on Main Street. P.poss. BR: Folkstone (NAST 10 miles).

Second shop now opened.

ELY

THE ELY BOOKSHOP **0353 661824**
11A St Mary's, Ely, Cambridgeshire CB7 4GS.
Mon-Sat, 10-3, clsd Tues (longer in summer)
Med size R/C stk, av cal, cnd & prices. BR: Ely, oos towards cathedral, past it and left.

EMSWORTH

MARY HUBBARD **0243 377394**
10 South Street, Emsworth, Hampshire PO19 7EH.
Mon,Thurs-Sat, 10-5.30
Small R/C stk. Av cal, cnd & prices. BR: Emsworth, oos, turn right into town.

THE BOOKSHOP **0243 372617**
The Square, Emsworth, Hampshire PO30 7EJ.
Mon-Sat, 10-5.30, L: 1-2.15, clsd Wed 1pm
New Bksp with small R stk, bl av cal, cnd & prices. From Hubbard, oosh turn left & left.

ENFIELD (See London)

ENGLEFIELD GREEN

BLACKLOCKS **0704 434856**
8 Victoria Street, Englefield Green, Surrey TW20 0JJ.
Mon-Sat, 9-5
Small R/C stk, av cal, cnd & prices. Etf. BR: Egham (NAST 3 miles).

EPPING (see London)

ETON

ETON ANTIQUE BOOKSHOP **0753 855534**
88 High Street, Eton, Berkshire SL4 6AP.
Mon-Sat, 10-5.30, Sun 12-6
Med size C/D stk, av cal, cnd, ab av prices. BR: Eton & Windsor, oos over bridge.

EVESHAM

BOOKWORMS **0386 45509**
81 Port Street, Evesham, Worcestershire.
Tues-Sat, 9.30-5
Med size R/C stk, av cal, NSOC, av prices. Etf.

Second shop recently opened. NFDA.

EXETER

EXETER RARE BOOKS **0392 431587**
12A Guildhall Shopping Ctr, Exeter.
Mon-Sat, 10-5, L: 1-2
Med size C/D stk, av cal, cnd & prices. Oos turn right into town etf.

DICKENS CENTENARY BOOKCASE **0392 431587**
City Arcade, Fore Street, Exeter.
Mon-Sat, 10-5
Med size R/C stk, av cal, cnd & prices. From above oosh right & right and look for alleyway on left.

EYE

FAITH LEGG **0379 871439**
The Guildhall Bookroom, Church St, Eye, Suffolk IP35 7BD.
Fri-Sat, 10-5
Med size, gen stk, plus Spec in Embroidery & Crafts. Etf. BR: Diss (NAST 5 miles).

FAKENHAM

THE TIN DRUM BOOKSHOP **0533 548236**
32 Oak Street, Fakenham, Norfolk NR21 9DY.
Mon-Sat, 10-6, Wed 1pm
Lg R/C/D stk, NSOC. Av prices. BR: Kings Lynn, (V NAST 20 miles). Etf to left of square.

FALMOUTH

BROWSER'S BOOKSHOP **0326 313464**
11 St Georges Arcade, Falmouth, Cornwall
Mon-Sun, 10-5, REL
Med nrly lg R/C stk. Literace. Mainly aimed at journalists. T. P.v.diff. BR: Falmouth, oos down ahead turn left & follow signs into town & cont along main street, SIOL in arcade.

BOOKMART **0326 211252**
94 High Street, Falmouth, Cornwall TR1 3AD
Mon-Sat, 10-5, REL
Med size nrly lg R/C stk. Literace. With occasional sparks of Mantovani. TWC. Av cnd, cal & prices. From Browsers oosh, turn left & left and cont across junction. SIOR.

TONY POWELL **NO PHONE**
2 Old Brewery Yard, High St, Falmouth, Cornwall
Mon-Sat, 10-4, UNR
Small B&MC. Low key, av cnd & prices. FARTS.

FARNBOROUGH

E S WICKS **0252 544876**
48 Peabody Road, Farnborough, Hampshire.
Mon-Sat, 9-5, Fri & Sat 5.30. Rel
Med/lg R/C stk, av cal, cnd & prices. BR Lamphill, oos turn left & right at parade of shops.

FARNBOROUGH BKSP & GALLERY **0252 518033**
28 Guildford Road, West Farnborough, Hampshire GU17 6PU.
Mon-Sat, 10-5
Med size R/C stk, av cal, cnd & prices. TWC. P.poss. Follow signs for Farnborough from Lamphill.

FARNHAM

BYGONES **0252 737865**
5A Castle Street, Farnham, Surrey GU9 7HT.
Tues-Sat, 10-5
Med size R/C/D stk, av cal, cnd & prices. TWC. Oos ahead left at T junction & first right.

COBWEBS **0252 734531**
29 The Woolmead, East Street, Farnham, Surrey.
Mon-Sat, 10-5
Lg R/C stk, ab av cal, cnd & prices. Oos ahead & right at T junction.

FAVERSHAM

THE FAVERSHAM BOOKSHOP **0795 532873**
1A Gatefield Street, Faversham, Kent ME13 8NX.
Mon-Sat, 10-5.30, L: 1-2, clsd Thurs, no L on Sats
Med size R/C stk, av cal, cnd & prices. Keen on Kipling.

PERIWINKLE PRESS **0795 426242**
119 West Street, Faversham, Kent. NV.

FELIXSTOWE

THE TREASURE CHEST **0394 270717**
70 Hamilton Road, Felixstowe, Suffolk IP11 7AF.
Mon-Sat, 9-5.30
Med/lg R/C/D stk. Av cal, cnd & prices. TWC. Oos, turn right into town & SIOL.

FOLKESTONE

G & D J MARRIN **0303 53016**
149 Sandgate Road, Folkestone, Kent CT20 2DA.
Mon-Sat, 9.30-5.30, L: 1-2.30
Med size R/C/D stk, av cal, cnd & prices. Emphon Local Hist and World War 1. BR: Folkestone Central, oos turn right and keep to right towards shopping ctr & turn right and SIOL.

FOWEY

BOOKENDS **072 6833361**
4 South Street, Fowey, Cornwall PL25 1AR.
Mon-Sat, 9.30-6, L: 1-2
Small/med size R/C stk, av cal, cnd & prices. BR: St Austell (NAST 10 miles). Etf.

FRAMLINGHAM

MRS T BELL **0728 723046**
19 Market Hill, Framlingham, Suffolk IP13 9BB.
Mon-Sat, 9.45-1, 2-4.30, clsd Wed
Med size R stk, av cal, cnd & prices. T. Etf.

FROME

THE OLD CURIOSITY SHOP **0373 64482**
15 Catherine Hill, Frome, Somerset TA11 1BZ.
Mon-Sat, 10-5, L: 1-2, clsd Thurs
Med/lg R/C/D stk. Roast beef, NSOC, av prices, P.poss.

GALWAY, Eire

BYRNES SECONDHAND BOOKSHOP **091 61766**
61 Dominick Street, Galway.
Mon-Sat, 10.30-6. REL
Med size R/C stk, ab av cal (for Eire) low prices (for Eire), v. Int (for Eire). T & D. P.diff. Oos, turn left, left into square & right on other side, left into Main St & follow through & cross bridge. SIOR.

WITCH BOOKS & ANTIQUES **091 68388**
Lower Dominick House (No no), Galway
Mon-Sat, 10-5.30
Antq shop with genuine collection of C/D bks almost unique in Eire. T & D. Ab av prices. From Byrnes, cont along, SIOL.

KENNY'S BOOKSHOP & ART GALLERY **091 62739**
High Street (No no), Galway.
Mon-Sat, 9-6, REL
V lg Spec in Irish & some other Lit. bunch of rip-off artists. T & D with free photographs. P.imposs. IR Galway, oos then left & left into square, right on other side & follow until road forks, take left, SIOL.

GIGGLESWICK

POST HORN BOOKS **072 823438**
Giggleswick (that believe it or not IS the complete address)
Tues-Sat, 10.30-5.30
Med size R/C stk. Av cal, cnd & prices. NV.

GLASGOW, Scotland

ADAM BOOKS **041 649 1314**
13 Battlefield Avenue, Langside, Glasgow G42 9HT
Mon-Sat, 10-5.30
Med size R/C stk. Av cal, cnd. Scotrail Mount Florida, OOS down ramp & turn right & first left.

CALEDONIA BOOKS **041 334 9663**
483 Great Western Road, Glasgow G12 8HL
Mon-Sat, 10.30-6, Rel
Med/lg R/C/D stk, emphon Lit & Social History. Av cal, ab av cnd, av prices. T. P.poss. Tube: Hillhead, OOS turn left.

DOWANSIDE BOOKS 041 945 2787
Dowanside Lane (no no.), Glasgow G12 9BZ
Mon-Sat, 10-5.30
Small/med R/students type bks. Av cal, av cnd & strange prices. TWC. P.diff. Tube: Hillhead, OOS cross road & Dowanside Lane is to right.

GILMOREHILL BOOKS 041 339 7504
43 Bank Street, Glasgow G12 8NE
Mon-Sat, 10.30-5.30
Med sized R/C stk, keen on rmndrs. Av cal, cnd and prices. TWC. P.poss. From Caledonia, OOSH, turn left, & first left into Bank St.

COOPER HAY 041 226 3074
203 Bath Street, Glasgow G2 4HZ
Mon-Fri, 10-5.30, Sat 10-1, Rel
Med/lg, high cal C/D stk. Emphon good cnd, Scottish Lit, Art, Bibliography, Miniatures, Bindings. P. poss. T. BR: Glasgow Queen Street, OOS to right, turn right up steps & left into Bath St & continue 1/2 mile.

VOLTAIRE & ROUSSEAU 041 339 1811
12 Otago Lane, Glasgow G12 8HP
Mon-Sat 11-6+
Lg R/C stk. Nsoc. From Gilmorehill OOSH, turn first left into Cowan St. & right into Otago St & left into Otago Lane.

WORDSWORTH BOOKS & CARDS 041 887 7303
4 Johnson Street, Paisley, PA1 1XG
Mon-Sat, 10.30-5.30, Rel
Small/med sized R/C stk. A drif special. TWC. P.poss. Scotrail: Gilmour St, OOS turn right & fourth left (third past Town Hall).

GLASTONBURY

DEJA VU 0273 600400
17 High Street, Glastonbury, Somerset.
Mon-Sat, 10.30-5
Med size Spec in Occult & Esoteric. Av cal, cnd & prices. BR: Swindon (NAST 15 miles) Etf.

HADDONS BOOKSHOP 0458 31753
30 Benedict Street, Glastonbury, Somerset.
Mon-Sat, 9-5.30
Med size R/C stk, av cal, cnd & prices. Etf.

SPECIALIST PAPERBACK COLLECTORS in "Monarch" by Haddons.

GLENROTHES, Scotland

MITCHELL'S BOOKSHOP **0592 758737 (Hm)**
26 Woodside Way, Glenrothes, Fife KY7 5AJ
Mon-Sat, 9-6, Wed 9-12, Thurs 9-8
Med sized low key R stk with definite potential to become a drif special. Res stk at rear. Low prices. T & D. P.poss. Scotrail: Kirkcaldy and take bus (frequent) etf.

GLOSSOP (see Manchester)

GLOUCESTER

THE BOOKSHOP **0452 331011**
26 Westgate, Gloucester.
Mon-Sat, 9-5.30
V lg R/C/D stk, egregiously priced. Ab av cal, cnd & prices. BR: Gloucester oos ahead into town & turn right.

QUAYSIDE BOOKSHOP **0452 300422**
2 Severn Road, Gloucester GL1 2LE.
Everyday, 10.30-5.30
Med/lg R/C stk, ab av cal, cnd & prices.

GODALMING

THE EUREKA BOOKSHOP **0843 426968**
19a Church Street, Godalming, Surrey GU1 1EL.
Mon-Fri, 10.30-3, Wed 1pm, Sat 10.30-5.30
Small R/C stk, av cal, cnd & prices. BR: Godalming, Oos ahead & SIOR.

NSF **NO PHONE**
9 Queen Street, Godalming, Surrey.
Mon-Sat, 10-4
Med size R stk. Emphon pbks. Av cal, cnd & prices.

Third shop recently opened.

GOODRINGTON

BIDDY'S BOOKSHOP **0803 556151**
99 Dartmouth Road, Goodrington, Paignton, Devon.
Mon-Sun, 10-4.30, much more in summer
Med size R/C stk, low key. Good cnd. Av prices. BR: Paignton, follow signs for Brixham 2 miles on left.

GOSFORTH

ARCHIE MILES **094 05792**
Beck Place, Gosforth, Cumbria CA20 1AT.
Tues-Sat, 10-6, Sun 2-6. BTR in winter
Med size C/D stk, ab av cal, cnd & prices. TWC. Etf. BR: Sellafield (NAST 3 miles).

GOSPORT

RICHARD MARTIN **0705 520642**
25 Stoke Road, Gosport, Hampshire PO12 1LS.
Tues-Sat, 10-5, Sun 2-6
Med size C stk. Emphon Maritime. Av cal, cnd & prices. Etf. BR: Portsmouth (NAST 3 miles).

GRAYS

KENDON'S (BOB GILBERT) **0375 372187** (hm)
10 London Road, Grays, Essex.
Sats 9.30-5, some Thurs pm
Med size R/C stk, av cal, cnd & prices. Oos, turn left into town & left at end of paved area.

GREAT AYTON

THE GREAT AYTON BOOKSHOP **0642 723358**
17 High Street, Great Ayton, Nth Yorkshire.
Tues-Sat, 10-5.30, Wed 2pm, Sun 2-5.30
Med size R/C stk, av cal, cnd & prices. Etf.

GREAT YARMOUTH

DAVID FERROW **0493 843800**
77 Howard Street Sth, Gt Yarmouth, Norfolk NR30 1LN.
Mon-Fri, 9.30-5.30, L: 1-2.30
Med/lg R/C/D stk, av cal, cnd, ab av prices. Oos, turn right & right at car park sign.

GREENOCK, Scotland

WESTWORDS **0475 892467**
14 Newton Street, Greenock, Strathclyde
Mon-Sat, 10-5.30
Med size R/C stk, low key, av cnd, low prices. Almost a drif special, but fails because Greenock is not easy to get to and is so depressing. Scotrail: Greenock West, OOS turn right & right into Newton St.

GUERNSEY (see Channel Isles)

GUILDFORD

THOMAS THORP **0483 62770**
170 High Street, Guildford, GU1 3HP.
Mon-Sat, 9-5.30
Lg New bksp with med size R/C stk which seems to be decreasing fast. BR: Guildford oos turn right & left over bridge & look for signs saying "Bus Stn" & then uphill & shp is ahead.

THOMAS TRAYLEN 0483 572424

49-50 Quarry Street, Guildford, Surrey GU1 3AA

Mon-Sat, 9-5

Lg C/D stk, ab av cal, cnd & prices. Emphon Roast Beef. From Thorp's, oosh turn left downhill & left.

HADDINGTON, Scotland

JEAN LAWSON 062082 5851

3 Lodge Street, Haddington, E. Lothian EH41 3PX

Tues-Sat, 10-5, L 1-2, clsd Thurs

Med size R/C stk, av cal, vg cnd, av prices. DOSO. Scotrail: Musselburgh & take bus (NAST - 10 miles) etf alongside High Street.

HADLEIGH

THE IDLER 0473 827752

71 High Street, Hadleigh, Suffolk.

Mon-Sat, 9.30-5.30, Wed 1pm

Small stk, av cal, cnd & prices. Etf.

HALESOWEN

see BIRMINGHAM

HALESWORTH

SHOP NEWLY OPENED NFDA.

HALIFAX

THE COLLECTOR 0422 363895

36 The Colonnade, Piece Hall, Halifax HX1 1RS.

Mon-Sat, 10-5.30, clsd Wed, Thurs. Open Sunday pm

Med size Spec in Military Hist. Ab av cal, cnd, av prices. Oos, ahead into market.

WEST RIDING BOOKS **NO PHONE**

12 The Piece Hall, Halifax HX1.

Thurs-Sun, 10.45-6

Med size R/C stk, slightly low key.

THE SHOP FOR THE DERANGED LADDER CARRIER **PHONE UNKNOWN**
Piece Hall, Halifax.
Lg R/C/nrly D stk. NSOC. Permanently expanding. Av prices.

HAMPTON (see London)

HANLEY (see Stoke on Trent)

HARBOURNE (see Birmingham)

HARPENDEN

BOOK CABIN **058 2768581**
379 Luton Road, Harpenden, Herts AL5 3NF.
Mon-Sat, 9.30-5
Med size C/D stk, av cal, cnd & prices. Emphon Antqrn. WAD.
BR: Harpenden, oos, down drive turn left & right & continue.

HARROGATE (see map)

RIPPON BOOKSHOP **0423 501835**
6 Station Bridge, Harrogate, Yorks.
Mon-Sat, 10-5, Unr
Med size R/C stk, Roast Beef, Emphon Yorkshire. TWC. P.diff.
BR: Harrogate, oos turn left & left & SIOR upstairs.

THE HARROGATE BOOKSHOP **0423 500479**
29 Cheltenham Crescent, Harrogate, Yorks.
Mon-Sat, 10-5.30, Rel
Med/lg R/C/D stk, solid Roast Beef, but with Juniper sauce.
Emphon Music. WAD. Vetgow and v helpful. Oos turn right & second left & keep to right, SIOL.

J E COURTNEY **0423 500341**
5 Mount Parade, Harrogate, Yorks.
Tues-Sat 10-5.30
Small C Spec stk, emphon Maritime. Av cal, ab av cnd, av prices. TWC. P.poss. From Harrogate Bksp oosh, cont downhill, turn left & straight ahead.

BOOKSTOP BOOKSHOP **0423 505817**
11 Mayfield Grove, Harrogate, Yorkshire.
Mon-Sat, 10-5.30, Wed 1pm
Med size R/C stk, slightly Lit. Keen on pbks, but worth a look. P.poss. BR: Harrogate, oos turn right & cont for 1/2 mile.

HASLEMERE

THE HASLEMERE BOOKSHOP **0428 652952**
2 Causewayside, Haslemere, Surrey GU27 2JJ.
Mon-Sat, 9-5.15
New Bksp with med size R/C stk. Av cal, cnd & prices. BR: Haslemere, oos turn left, follow road round & left into town. SIOL.

HASLINGDEN

HASLINGDEN BOOKSHOP **0706 831170**
99 Deardengate, Haslingden, Rossendale, Lancs.
Mon-Sat, 10-5.30, clsd Wed
Med size R/C stk, av cal & cnd. Keen on Motor Racing. TWC. P.poss. BR: Oswaldwistle (NAST 7 miles) Etf by crossroads.

HASTINGS

HOWES BOOKSHOP **0424 423437**
Trinity Hall, Braybrooke Terr, Hastings, E Sussex TN14 1EG
Mon-Fri, 9.30-5, Sat 9.30-1
V lg R/C/D stk. Ab av cal and cnd. Av prices. TWC.

JOHN WILBRAHAM **0424 446413**
16 George Street, Old Town, Hastings TN34 3EE.
Mon-Sat, 9.30-5.30, L: 1-2, clsd Wed, Rel
Med size R/C/D stk, av cal, cnd & prices. Emphon Antqrn.

OLD HASTINGS BOOKSHOP **0424 425989**
15 George Street, Old Town, Hastings TN34 3EG
Mon-Sat, 10-4, clsd Wed
Med size R/C stk, av cal, cnd & prices.

TAMARISK **0424 420591**
80 High Street, Hastings, E Sussex TN34 3EL.
Sat only 10-5
Med size R/C stk, Emphon Lit and Music. Av cal, cnd & prices.

BOOK JUNGLE **0424 421187**
24 North Street, St Leonards, E Sussex TN36 OEX.
Mon-Sat, 10-5.30
Med/lg R/C/D stk, slightly low key but v. fast turnover. WAD. Much frequented by the other shopkeepers in Hastings. BR: St. Leonards, Warrior Square, Oos, straight ahead towards Seafront & turn right into North Street. SIOR.

SPRINGFIELD BOOKSHOP, London Road, St Leonards. Recently changed hands.

HATFIELD

OLD CATHAY FINE BOOKS **0707 274200**
43 Park Street, Old Hatfield, Hertfordshire AL9 5BA
Mon-Sat, 10.30-5.30, L: 1-2.30
Newly opened. Med size C/D stk emphon A&C Black, P G Wodehouse, Iain Fleming and Thrillers. Fine cnd, ab av cal & prices, but bgns known in Non Spec fields. TWC. P.poss. BR: Hatfield, oos straight ahead then cont down path & turn left. SIOL.

HAVANT

BOOKENDS **0795 470094**
2 North Street, Havant, Hampshire PO9 1PR.
Mon-Sat, 9-5
Med size R/C stk, av cal, cnd & prices. TWC. BR: Havant, oos turn left and right and SIOL.

HAWES

KIT CALVERT **0969 667667**
Market Place, Hawes, Nth Yorkshire.
Mon-Sat, 10-5, Sun 2-5, BTR in winter
Med size R/C stk, ab av cal, cnd & prices. Etf. BR: Penrith (V NAST 25 miles), etf off main street.

HAY ON WYE

THE CHILDREN'S BOOKSHOP **0497 821083**
Toll Cottage, Pontvaen, Hay on Wye, HR3 5EW
Mon-Sat, 9.30-5.30 & Sun pm
Med size R/C stk of Childrens bks, Av cal, cnd & prices, Etgow. TWC. P.poss. ETF on road into Hay from Hereford.

THE RECYCLED BOOKSHOP **0497 821450**
2 Broad Street, Hay on Wye, HR3 3DB
Wed-Sat, 10-5.30, Rel
Med size, nrly Spec in Psychology & Psychotherapy bks, a small amt of gen. FARTS & SMELLS. TWC. Etgow if you can talk psychobabble. P.poss.

WEST HOUSE BOOKS 0497 821225
20 Broad Street, Hay on Wye, HR3 5DB
Mon-Sun 10-5.30, clsd Tues in winter
Med size R/C stk, Helen Hanff Special. Keen on Cookery, Childrens, Photography & Dictionaries. TWC. Av cnd & prices.

ADDYMAN BOOKS 0497 821136
39 Lion Street, Hay on Wye, HR3 5AA
Mon-Sat, 10-6, Sundays in summer
Med R/C stk, NSOC but more int than most in Hay. WAD. P.poss. Av prices. TWC.

THE POETRY BOOKSHOP 0497 820305
22 Broad Street, Hay on Wye, HR3 5BQ
Mon-Sat, 10-5.30, L: 1-2 Rel
Med size Spec in Poetry, has expanded out of the thin 20th Century into the thick 19th Century. Ab av cal, cnd & av prices. T. Etgow. P.poss. WAD.

RICHARD BOOTH 0497 820322
44 Lion Street, Hay on Wye, HR3 5AA
Mon-Sun, 9-5.30, 9 in summer
Egregious, enormous, excruciating, unfortunately unmissable. V lg R/C stk, NSOC, wayward prices. TWC. Mr Both has as many other locations in Hay as he has bankruptcies.

ROSE'S 0497 820013
14 Broad Street, Haye on Wye, HR3 5DB
Mon-Sat, 10-5, clsd Wed, L: 1-2 (more summer,less winter) btr
Med size spec in Childrens bks, R/C nearly D stk, av cal, cnd & prices. TWC.

THE TWO FACED BOOKSHOP 0497 821341
The Pavement, Hay, HR3 5BU
Mon-Sun, 9-6
Lg R/C/D stk, Literace. TWC.

MARK WESTWOOD 0497 820068
High Town (No no), Hay on Wye, HR3 5AE
Mon-Sat, 12-5 Unr
Small/med size Spec in Scientific & Antqrn. Ab av cal, bookfairy. TWC.

HAY ASSOCIATES 0497 820875
14 High Town, Hay on Wye
Mon-Sun, 10.30-5.30
Lg R/C/D stk, ab av cal, cnd, av prices. Bookfairy.

J GEOFFREY ASPIN 0497 820437
27 Castle Street, Hay on Wye HR3 5DF
Mon-Sat, 1-5 Unr
Med size Spec in Antqrn & Theology. Helen Hanff Spec. TWC.

BOZ 0497 821277
13a Castle Street, Hay on Wye, HR3 5DF
Mon-Sat, 10-5, L: 1-2 (less in Winter)
Med size R/C/D stk, keen on Kitchens & 19th Century Lit.

HAY CINEMA 0497 820071
Castle Street, Hay on Wye, HR3 5DF
Every day 10-7
V lg R/C/D stk, interminably deadly. Res stk of Deadliness upstairs. TWC.

HEBDEN BRIDGE

BOOKS & COLLECTORS CENTRE 0422 844600
16 Market Street, Hebden Bridge, W Yorks HX7 6AA
open every day bar Christmas day 10-5.30
Med/lg R/C stk slightly low key. Int & worth perusing but dedication needed. BR: Hebden Bdg, oos down drive turn left into town & SIOR past Tourist Ctr.

HATCHARD & DAUGHTERS 0422 845717
56 Market Street, Hebden Bridge, W Yorks.
Thurs & Fri, 1-5
Med size R/C stk, more int than av, etf in centre of town.

HELENSBURGH, Scotland

McCLAREN BOOKS 0436 76453
91 West Clyde Street, Helensburgh, Dumbartonshire G84 8BB
Mon-Sat, 9.30-5, L 1-2, clsd Wed (winter, more in summer)
Med sized C/D stk, emphon Shipping. Espec Sailing, ab av cal, cnd, av prices. Bgns known. WAD. TWC. P.poss. Scotrail: Helensburgh Central, OOS turn right & left & right at Sea front.

HELMSLEY

RIEVAULX 0439 70912
18 High Street, Helmsley, Nth Yorks YO6 5AG.
Tues-Sat, 10.30-5.30, Sun 2-6
Med size C/D stk, ab av cnd & prices. Etf.

HELMSLEY ANTIQUARIAN & S/H BKS **0439 70014**
The Old Fire Station, Borogate, Helmsley, Nth Yorks YO6 5BN.
Mon-Sat, 10-5.30, sun in summer 12-5.30
Med/lg R/C stk, av cal, cnd & prices. TWC. BR: Malton (NAST 15 miles) Etf.

HENLEY ON THAMES

THE ATTIC **0491 579107**
4 Station Road, Henley on Thames, RG9 1AY.
Mon-Sat, 9.30-6, Sunday 11-5
Med size R/C stk, av cal, cnd & prices. BR: Henley, oos, SIOL.

RICHARD WAY **0491 576663**
54 Friday Street, Henley on Thames RG9 1AH.
Mon-Sat, 10-5.30
Med size R/C/D stk. Ab av cal, cnd & prices. Emphon Rowing.

RICHARD J KINGSTON **0491 574535**
95 Bell Street, Henley on Thames, RG9 2BD.
Mon-Fri, 9-5.30, Sat 9.30-5
Small/med size R/C stk, av cal, cnd & prices. TWC. BR: Henley oT, oos turn left & right & right.

HEREFORD

CHAPTERS **PHONE UNKNOWN**
17 Union Street, Hereford.
Mon-Sat, 9-5
Med size Charity Bksp with av cal cnd and prices. OOs, turn left & right into town, & head for cathedral.

THE HEREFORD BOOKSHOP **0432 357617**
24 Church Street, Hereford HR1 2LR.
Mon-Sat, 9.15-5.30
New Bksp with upstairs rm of R/C stk. Av cal, cnd & prices. From above, oosh, left & left.

Third shop is now closed.

HERNE BAY

PENDEES **0227 374778**
29 High Street, Herne Bay, Kent CT6 5LJ.
Mon-Sat, 9-6, Thurs 1pm
Med size R/C stk, bl av cal, cnd, av prices. BR: Herne Bay, oos ahead to main road & right.

HERTFORD

OXFAM BOOKSHOP 0992 583221
9 Station Road, Hertford.
Mon-Sat, 10.30-4.30
Small R stk, av cal, cnd & prices. BR: Hertford, oos ahead. SIOL.

CASTLE BOOKSHOP 0992 586537
25 Castle Street, Hertford SG14 1HH.
Mon-Sat, 10-5, clsd Thur
Med size R/C stk, av cal, cnd & prices. From Oxfam Oosh, turn left & left & continue.

HEXHAM

HENCOTES BOOKS & ANTIQUES 0434 605971
8 Hencotes, Hexham, Northumberland NE46 OEJ.
Mon-Sat, 9.30-4.30, Thurs 3pm
Med size low key R/C stk, low prices. BR: Hexham, into town, keep to left of cathedral, past Green turn right. Changed hands, now owned by shop underneath.

TURN OF THE CENTURY ANTIQUES 0434 603988
8 Market Street, Hexham, Northumberland NE46 1HU
Tues, Wed, Fri & Sat, 11-5
Small R/C stk keen on Domestic. Av cal, cnd & prices. To right of church in centre of town.

HINCKLEY

THE READERS RETURN 0455 61107
32-34 New Buildings, Hinckley, Leicestershire.
Mon-Sat, 10-5.30, clsd Wed
Med size R/C stk, bl av cal, cnd, av prices. Etf.

HINDHEAD

BEACON HILL BOOKS 0428 606783
Beacon Hill Road (No no.), Hindhead, Surrey GU26 2AH.
Mon-Sat, 9-5
Med size R/C stk. Emphon Nat Hist. Primarily rmndrs.

HITCHIN

ERIC T MOORE **0462 450497**
24 Bridge Street, Hitchin, Hertfordshire SG5 2DC.
Mon-Sat, 9.30-5.30, L: 1-2.15
Med/lg R/C stk, av cal, cnd & prices. OOs, turn left, cont for 1 mile, second roundabout.

HOLBEACH

P J CASSIDY **0406 26322**
1B Boston Road, Holbeach, Lincolnshire PE12 7LR.
Mon-Sat, 10-6
Med size R/C/D stk. Strong on Local Hist. Av cal, cnd & prices. T. Etf. BR: Spalding (NAST 10 miles). NV.

HOLMFIRTH

DAISY LANE BOOKS **0484 688409**
Towngate (No no), Holmfirth, Yorks HD7 1HA.
Mon-Sun, 9-5.30, 10-4.30 in winter
Med/lg R/C stk, av cal, bl av cnd, av prices. T. BR: Huddersfield (NAST 10 miles). Etf by bus stn.

THE TOLL HOUSE **484 686541**
32-35 Huddersfield Road, Holmfirth, Yorks
Mon-Sat, 9-5
Med/lg R/C Literace/Tourist stk. Av cal, ab av prices. TWC. P.diff. From Bus stn go over bridge & turn left.

HOLT (Norfolk)

SIMON GOUGH **0263 712650**
5 Fish Street Hill, Holt, Norfolk.
Mon-Sat, 9.30-5.30
Med/lg C/D stk, ab av cal, cnd & prices. Emphon HSF. Etf.

HOLT, Wales

CASTLE BOOKSHOP **0829 270382**
Castle Street, Holt, LL13 9YW.
Mon-Sat, 10-6, winter 5pm
Med size RC stk, Emphon Art. Av cal, cnd & prices. Etf.

HOLYHEAD, Wales

ANGLESEY BOOKS 0407 760988
1 Thomas Street, Holyhead, Wales LL65 1ZZ
Mon-Sat, 10-4.30, Tues 1pm
Med size Spec in Mountaineering bks. Some gen. Av cal, cnd & prices. T & D. P.poss. BR: Anglesey, oos turn right into town & SIOL in first side street.

HONITON

HONITON OLD BOOKSHOP 0404 47180
51 High Street, Honiton, Devon
Mon-Sat, 10.30-5.30 Rel
Med size R/C/D stk, ab av cal, ab av cnd, av prices. Etgow. WAD. P.poss. BR: Honiton, Oos, turn left at bottom of steps & right at T Junction.

G M WOODHEAD 0404 42969
53 High Street, Honiton, Devon.
Mon-Sat, 10-5, L: 1-2.15, clsd Sat pm
Antq shp with Lg R stk, Silverfish special. TWC. P.poss. Dir as above.

ABINGDON HOUSE 0404 47180
136 High Street, Honiton, Devon.
Mon-Sat, 10.30-5.30
BTA bkstl R/C stk in Antq Mkt. Res stk upstairs. P.poss. Dir as above.

GRAHAM YORK 0404 42074
132 High Street, Honiton, Devon.
Mon-Sat, 9.30-5.30 Rel
BTA bkstl in Antq Mkt. TWC. At T junction turn left SIOL.

VIRGINIBUS 0404 43460
174 High Street, Honiton, Devon EX14 8LA.
Mon-Sat, 10-5.30
Med size C/D stk. Libricide. Lthrwr. Bookfairy. Ab av cal, cnd & prices. TWC. P.poss. Dir as above (formerly Brockwells, but bears no resemblance now).

HORNCASTLE

JABBERWOCKY 0507 522112
14 St Lawrence Street, Horncastle, Lincolnshire LN19 5BJ
Mon-Wed, & Sat 10-5
Med size R/C stk, bl av cal, cnd & prices. BR: Lincoln, (NAST 15 miles) etf.

TIM SMITH'S BOOKS 0507 527139
12 North Street, Horncastle, Lincs.
Mon-Sat, 10-5, clsd Wed
Med size R/C stk, av cal, cnd & prices. Directions as above.

HORSHAM

THE HORSHAM BOOKSHOP 0403 54847
4 Park Street, Horsham, W. Sussex RH12 1DG.
Tues-Sat, 9.30-5.30
Med size R/C stk, av cal & cnd. Ab av prices. BR Horsham, oos turn left & left at T junction & left.

MURRAY & KENNET 0403 54817
102 Bishopric, Horsham, W. Sussex RH12 1QH.
Mon-Sat, 9-5.15, L: 1.30-2.15, clsd Thurs
Med size R/C stk, ab av cal & cnd. Av prices. Emphon Mod 1sts. From Horsham Bksp turn left & right & through paved zone.

HOWDEN

HOWDEN BOOKSHOP 0430 432071
5B Vicar Lane, Howden, Humberside DN14 7BP.
Mon-Sat, 9-5
New bksp with med size R/C stk, av cal, cnd & prices. TWC. P.poss. BR: Howden oos turn right towards village, turn right into village & look for lane on right.

HUDDERSFIELD

ROBLINS 0484 516793
18 Westgate, Huddersfield, HD1 1NN.
Mon-Sat, 9.30-5.30
Med size R/C stk, emphon pbks. B&MC special. Av cnd & prices. NFDA.

HULL

KAYE BOOKS **NOW CLOSED**

THE SHOP WITH NO NAME **NOW CLOSED**

SHERIDAN'S 0482 28759
19 Anlaby Road, Hull, HU1 2PJ.
Mon-Sat, 9-5.30
Med sized stk, primarily Scholarly & Student pbks. Ab av cal, cnd, av prices. TWC. P.poss. BR: Hull, oos turn right & right.

HUNGERFORD

BLAKEWAY BOOKS 0488 683581
13 Bridge Street, Hungerford, Berkshire RG17 0EH.
Fri & Sat, 10-5, also seems to be open most weekdays.
Med size R/C stk, av cal, cnd & prices. Etf.

HURSTPIERPOINT

CHIMERA BOOKS 0273 832255
17 High Street, Hurstpierpoint, W Sussex BN6 9SB.
Mon-Sat, 9-5.30
Med size, Spec in Oriental Art. Ab av cal, cnd & prices.

HYTHE

THE OLD GALLERY BOOKSHOP 0303 269339
125 High Street, Hythe, Kent.
Mon-SAt, 10-5
Med size R/C stk, keen on Mil Hist, Local Hist & Transport. BR Folkstone (NAST). Etf.

ICKENHAM, Middlesex

see LONDON

ILFRACOMBE

FITZJOHN'S BOOKS 0271 866888
44 Fore Street, Ilfracombe, Devon.
Mon-Sat, 10-5
Med size R/C stk, emphon Rmndrs. Av cal, cnd & prices. BR: Barnstaple (NAST 10 miles). Etf.

ILKLEY

THE GROVE BOOKSHOP **0943 609335**
10 The Grove, Ilkley, W. Yorks LS29 9EG.
Mon-Sat, 10-5
New bksp with small s/h R/C stk, av cal, cnd & prices. NV. BR: Ilkley, oos turn right.

INVERNESS, Scotland

THE INVERNESS BOOKSHOP **0463 239947**
10 Bank Street, Inverness, IV1 1QY
Mon-Sat, 10-5.30
Lg C/D stk, emphon Scottish, Mountaineering & Lit. Ab av cal, cnd & prices. No T. Res stk. TOPS. P.poss. BR: Inverness, OOS turn right & left at river bank.

BOOKS ETCETERA **0463 712040**
8 Inverness Market, Inverness.
Mon-Sat, 10-5
Small R stk of Hardbacks, primarily pbks. Av cal, cnd & prices. T. P.diff. Scotrail: Inverness, OOS,and into market almost opposite.

HIGHLAND ANTIQUES **0463 231316**
15 Tomnahurich St., Inverness IV3 5DA
Mon-Sat, 10-5
Antique shop with small but select stk of HSF bks. Av cal. TWC. P.poss. As Inverness Bksp, OOSH & turn left & right over bridge, SIOL.

IONA, Scotland

THE IONA BOOKSHOP **06817 304335**
The Old Printing House Bdg, Iona, Argyll, PA76 6SL.
Shop open 7 days a week in summer, closed winter
I have tried several times to get to this shop but it is not possible to do it in less than 2 days. My dream is to have a photograph of myself taken outside it. I will have another go next year. Can be done in 1 day from Oban during the summer.

IPSWICH

CLAUDE COX **0473 254776**
3 & 5 Silent Street, Ipswich, IP1 1TF.
Mon-Sat, 10-5, clsd Wed
Med/lg R/C/D stk. Ab av cal. Emphon Antqrn & Printing. BR Ipswich, oos ahead to black glass monolith & keep to right. SIOL.

ISLE OF MAN

GARRETS ANTIQUARIAN BOOKS **0624 629660**
9 Duke Street, Douglas, Isle of Man.
Tues-Sat, 10.30-4.30
Small R/C stk, av cal, cnd & prices. T. Etgow. P.diff. Etf in basement of Gents' Outfitters. Res stk.

DON MULRYAN **NOW CLOSED**

HAMLEYS **0624 897670**
Building 258, Jurby Airport, Jurby, Isle of Man.
Wed,Thur,Sat & Sun, 10-4.30
V lg warehouse. V low prices. WAD. Etgow. P.poss. Etf by hotel.

THE GOLDEN PAST **0624 842170**
18A Michael Street, Peel, Isle of Man.
Mon-Sat, 1.30-4.30, clsd Thur
Antq jewellery shp with bks. Av cal, cnd & prices. TWC. P. poss. Etf.

ISLE OF WIGHT

See individual towns: Cowes, Newport, Ryde, St Helens, Totland, Ventnor, Yarmouth.

ISLEWORTH, Middlesex

See LONDON

JERSEY

see CHANNEL ISLANDS

JESMOND, Tyne & Wear

See NEWCASTLE

KENDAL

KIRKLAND BOOKS **0539 740841**
68 Kirkland, Kendal, Cumbria.
Mon-Sat, 10-5, clsd Thurs
Med size R/C stk, av cal, cnd & prices. Oos, turn left & right at Junction & left & cont over bridge.

KESWICK

APPLEBY'S **07687 74054**
5 St John's Street, Keswick, Cumbria CA12 5AU.
Mon-Sat, 9-5.30, clsd Wed in winter
New shop with med size R/C stk. Av cal, cnd & prices. Keen on Cricket. BR Kendal, (NAST 10 miles), etf.

KING'S LYNN

TOWER BOOKSHOP **NO PHONE**
Tower Street (No no), King's Lynn, Norfolk.
Mon-Sat, 10-5
Med/lg R/C stk, emphon comics but some other int bks. Ab av prices. No T. P.diff. BR: King's Lynn, oos turn left & right & look for tower.

THE DIAMOND BOOKSHOP **0553 775230**
1 The Diamond, King's Lynn, Norfolk.
Sats 11-3, btr
Med size R/C stk, av cal, cnd & prices. Keen on Music. BR: King's Lynn, follow signs for London Rd and The Diamond is 2 miles outside of town.

KINGSBRIDGE

ROOM AT THE TOP **0548 856364**
The Shambles, Market Arcade, Fore Street, Kingsbridge, Devon
Mon-Sat, 9-4, Thur & Sat 12pm.
Med size R/C/nrly D stk. Av cal, cnd & prices. BR: Plymouth (NAST 15 miles) Etf upstairs of Market Hall.

KINGTON

CASTLE HILL BOOKS **0544 231195**
12 Church Street, Kington, Herefordshire HR5 3AZ
Mon-Sat 10-5.30, Sunday 2-5 in summer
Med size R/C stk, ab av cal, cnd & prices. NV. Etf.

ARROW BOOKS **0544 230729**
17 Duke Street, Kington, Herefordshire.
Mon-Sat 10-5, clsd Wed
Small/med R/C stk, slightly Roast Beef. Av cnd & prices. BR: Leominster (NAST) Rumoured moving to somewhere unpronounceable.

KIRKBY LONSDALE

BECKHEAD BOOKS **05242 71314**
10 Beckhead, Kirkby Lonsdale, Cumbria LA6 2AY.
Mon-Sat, 10-5, clsd Wed, less in Winter
Med size R/C stk, NSOC, av prices. BR: Penrith (NAST 10 miles).

KIRKCALDY, Scotland

BOOK ENDS **0592 205294**
449 High Street, Kirkcaldy, KY1 2SN
Tues-Sat, 10-5. Rel
Med size R/C stk, av cal, cnd & prices. Res stk., av cnd & prices. TWC. P.poss. Scotrail: Kirkcaldy, OOS through gardens to Adam Smith Theatre. Turn left into St Bryce Girdle & 3rd right into no entry street, follow through & turn left towards factories.

KIRKWALL, Scotland

A & P STEADMAN **0856 875040**
Unit 1 Halston Ind Est., Kirkwall, The Orkneys.
Mon-Sat, 9-4.45
Med size R/C stk, emphon Local Hist. NV.

M E MCCARTY **NO PHONE**
Anchor Bldgs, Kirkwall, Orkney.
Mon-Sat, 10-5
Small R/C stk primarily bks on Diving. Av cal, cnd &prices. Etf.

LAMPETER, Wales

WEST WALES BOOKS **0570 423778**
Railway Hotel, Tregaron Road, Lampeter.
Mon-Sat, 10-6, clsd Wed. V.Rel
Med size R/C stk, emphon Lit & Students espec Welsh. Etgow. P.poss. BR Carmarthen (NAST 20 miles but buses good). In Lampeter follow signs for Tregaron & where road turns right, SIOL at rear of hotel.

LANCASTER

ATTICUS **0524 381413**
26 King Street, Lancaster.
Mon-Sat, 10-5, clsd Wed
Small/Med R/C stk, av cal, cnd & prices. Emphon student Acad bks. BR: Lancaster, oos turn right & left & right at main road, SIOR.

McCORMACKS **0524 36405**
6 Rosemary Lane, Lancaster LA1 1NR.
Mon-Sat, 10-5, clsd Wed
Med/lg C stk, ab av cal, cnd & prices. BR: Lancaster, oos turn right & left & left at main road & follow signs round to car park. SIOR.

LANCHESTER

THOMAS RARE BOOKS **0207 529066**
9 Station Road, County Durham DH7 0EX.
Tues-Fri, 1-5, Sat 9-5
Small stk, ab av cal, cnd & prices. Bookfairy. NV. BR: Durham, (NAST 10 miles).

LANGPORT

THE OLD BOOKSHOP **0458 252644**
Bow Street (No no), Langport, Somerset TA10 8PQ
Mon-Sat, 9-5.30
Small R/C stk, av cal, cnd & prices. Etf. NV.

LAUGHARNE, Wales

CORRAN BOOKS **0994 427444**
King Street (No no), Laugharne, Dyfed SA33 4SJ.
No times posted, no notice saying when he will be open!

LAUNCESTON

HUTTON BOOKS **0566 776503**
8 Rae Hill, Launceston, Cornwall PL15 9BA.
Mon-Sat, 10-5, clsd Thurs
Med size R/C/D stk, bookfairy. Av cal, cnd & prices. BR: Plymouth (NAST 20 miles) Etf.

LAVENHAM

R G ARCHER **0787 247229**
7 Water Street, Lavenham, Suffolk CO10 9RW.
Mon-Sat, 9-5, Sun 10-5
Med size R/C stk, av cal & cnd. BR: Sudbury (NAST 10 miles). Etf.

LEAMINGTON SPA

PORTLAND BOOKS **0926 338793**
5 Spencer Street, Leamington Spa, Warwicks CV31 3NE.
Mon-Sat, 10-5.30
Med/lg R/C stk, av cal, cnd & prices. TWC. P.poss. BR: Leamington Spa, oos turn left & left & right.

LEATHERHEAD

BOOKWORM **0372 377443**
22 North Street, Leatherhead, Surrey KT22 7AT.
Mon-Sat, 9.30-5.30
New bksp with small R/C stk, av cal, cnd & prices. It is not so much bookworm as silverfish. BR: Leatherhead, oos turn left into town & right, SIOL.

LEDBURY

KEITH SMITH BOOKS **0531 5336**
78B The Homend, Ledbury, Herefordshire HR8 1BX.
Tues-Sat, 10-5
Med size R/C stk, av cal, cnd & prices. TWC. P.poss. BR: Ledbury, oos ahead into town & SIOR.

LEEDS

MR MILES **0532 455327**
12 Great George Street, Leeds LS1 3DW.
Mon-Sat, 9-5.30
V lg R/C/D stk, av cal, cnd & prices. Keen on Acad/Students. Res stk. BR: Leeds, oos ahead cont to Headrow & shop is behind town hall & left.

ALLERTON BOOKS **0532 695012**
11A Headingly Lane, Hyde Park Corner, Leeds LS6 1BL.
Mon-Sat, 9.30-5.30
Med size R/C stk, av cal, cnd & prices. TWC. From Mr Miles oosh turn right & right, keep to right of Pepperpot Bldg, turn left into Woodhouse Lane, SIOL (about 2 miles).

BOOKSIDE **0532 744021**
Midland Back Passage, Midland Road, Leeds 6.
Mon-Sat, 10-6
Med/lg R/C stk, Silverfish/Stoker Special. Av cal, cnd & prices. From Allerton Bks oosh turn right, right into Hyde Park Rd & follow signs from church.

ST MICHAELS BOOKSHOP **0532 746067**
69 St Michaels Lane, Headingley, Leeds.
Mon-Sat, 10.30-5.45
Small R/C stk, keen on cricket, av cal, cnd & prices. From Allerton Bks oosh, left & 5th left (not signposted) & SIOL (about 1 1/2 miles).

ALMAR BOOKS **0532 755611**
10 Commercial Road, Kirkstall, Leeds LS5 3AQ.
Mon-Sat, 10.15-5.30 +&-
Lg R/C stk, Literace, av cal, cnd & prices. From St Michaels Bksp oosh turn left cont to end, turn right into Kirkstall Hill, left Kirkstall Lane & left Kirkstall Rd. (NAST 1 1/2 miles).

There is an Antique stl in Cornmarket, BR: Leeds, oos turn right & cont. NV.

LEEK

THE LEEK BOOKSHOP **0538 573591**
4 Brook Street, Leek, Staffs.
Mon-Sat, 10-4, clsd Thurs
Med size R/C stk, variable quality & prices. TWC. P.diff. BR: Stoke (NAST 10 miles). In Leek locate bus stn & turn left at clocktower, downhill. SIOR past crossroads.

THE VILLAGE BOOKSHOP **0538 372092**
17 Russell Street, Leek, Staffs ST13 5JF.
Mon-Sat, 9.30-5, Thurs 1pm
Med size R/C stk, av cal, cnd & prices. Nfda.

LEEK OLD BOOKS **0538 399033**
43 Bath Street, Leek, Staffs ST13 6JQ.
Mon-Sat, 9.30-4.30, Sat 3.30, clsd Thur Rel
Med/nrly lg R/C stk, slightly more varied & Int than the other two. Keen on Nat Hist. Av cal, cnd & prices. Bgns known. From Village Bksp Oosh, turn right & right at Main St & third left. SIOR.

LEICESTER

CLARENDON BOOKS **0533 701856**
144 Park Road, Leicester, LE2 3AN.
Tues-Sat, 10-5, Sun pm
Med size R/C stk, av cal, cnd & prices. BR: Leicester, oos turn left, cont 1 mile & turn right, SIOL.

BLACK CAT BOOKSHOP **0533 512756**
Silver Arcade (No no), Leicester, LE1 5FB.
Mon-Sat, 9.30-5
Med size R/C stk, av cal, cnd & prices. BR: Leicester, oos turn right into ctr of town & left at Circle.

FOREST BOOKS **0533 627171**
42 Silver Arcade, Leicester LE1 5FB.
Mon-Sat, 9.30-5
Med/lg R/C Stk, av cal & prices. Ab av int. Directions as above.

MAYNARD & BRADLEY **0533 532712**
1 Royal Arcade, Silver Street, Leicester LE1 5XW.
Mon-Fri 9.30-5.30, Sat 9
Med size R/C/D stk, Bookfairy. Emphon Local Hist. From Silver Arcade turn left, SIOR.

TIN DRUM BOOKS **0533 548236**
68 Narborough Road, Leciester LE3 0BR.
Mon-Sat, 10-6
Med size R/C stk, av cal, cnd & prices. GIOPOC. From Maynard & B, oosh, turn right onto main road & cont for 1 mile & left.

LEIGH ON SEA

LEIGH GALLERY BOOKS **0702 715477**
137 Leigh Road, Leigh on Sea, Essex.
Tues-Sat, 10-4.45
Med R/C stk, av cal cnd & prices. TWC. BR: Leigh on Sea, oos ahead into town ctr & turn right.

LEOMINSTER

MAINLY BOOKS **0568 615722**
7 School Lane, Leominster, Herefordshire HR6 8AA
Mon-Sat, 9.30-6
Med size R/C bks and antiques. V. worthy but slightly boring. Av cal, cnd & prices. TWC. BR: Leominster, oos ahead turn left into town, right at main street & first right & right.

There are also 2 bkstls in ctr of town. Etf.

MINSTER ANTIQUES & BOOKS **NOW CLOSED**

LETCHWORTH

DAVID'S BOOKSHOP **0462 673767**
7 Eastcheap, Letchworth, Hertfordshire SG6 3NF.
Mon-Sat, 9-6
Med size R/C stk, bl av cal, av cnd & prices. BR: Letchworth, oos ahead to left & turn right. SIOR.

LEWES

A J CUMMING **0273 472319**
159 High Street, Lewes, E Sussex BN7 1KU.
Mon-Sat, 10-5, L: 1-2
Med/lg C/D stk, ab av cal, cnd & prices. WAD. BR: Lewes, oos turn right up hill & left into High St.

There is also a low key pbk/hardbk shp on right as you come out of stn, but open only during summer. Owned by above.

FIFTEENTH CENTURY BOOKSHOP **0273 474160**
99 High Street, Lewes, E Sussex BN7 1XH.
Mon-Sat, 10-5.30
Med/nrly lg R/C stk. NSOC. Ab av prices. Dir as above.

BOW WINDOWS BOOKSHOP **0273 480780**
128 High Street, Lewes, E Sussex.
Mon-Sat, 9-5
Med size C/D stk. Solid Roast Beef. Dir as above.

LEYBURN

WHITE BOAR ANTIQUES **0969 23901**
Kirkgate, Middleham, N. Yorks.
Mon-Sat, 10-5.30, Sun in summer
Antq shop with BTA stk of R/C bks. Av cnd & prices. Etf. BR: Darlington (NAST 10 miles).

LEYLAND

GREAT GRANDFATHERS **0772 422268**
832 Towngate, Leyland, Lancashire PR5 1LR.
Tues-Sat, 9.30-5.30, clsd Wed
Med/lg R/C/D stk. Av cal, cnd & prices. BR: Leyland, oos turn left & follow road round to left. At roundabout turn right into shopping st & follow road round to left. (NAST 1 1/2 miles).

LICHFIELD

THE STAFFS BOOKSHOP **0543 264093**
6 Dam Street, Lichfield, Staffordshire WS13 6AA.
Mon-Sat, 9.30-5.30
Lg R/C/D stk, ab av cal, cnd & prices. Emphon Childrens and Ills. WAD. Oos, head for Cathedral. Shop is behind cathedral.

LIMERICK, Eire

O'BRIEN BOOKS & PHOTO GALLERY **061 342604**
Bedford Row, Limerick.
Mon-Sat, 10.30-5.30, REL
Med size R/C stk, low key. Emphon pbks but much better than most Irish bksps. T&D. P.poss. IR: Limerick, oos straight ahead, turn left & right & left at Bedford Row.

LINCOLN

READERS REST **0522 543217**
13-14 Steep Hill, Lincoln LN2 1LT.
Mon-Sat, 9.30-5, some Suns
Med size R/C stk, av cal, cnd & prices. BR: Lincoln, oos turn left & right up hill towards cathedral, SIOL.

HARLEQUIN **0522 522589**
20-22 Steep Hill, Lincoln.
Mon-Sat, 10.30-5, L: 1-2.30
Med/lg R/C stk, av cal, cnd & prices. Dir as above.

ELIZABETH NELSON **NOW CLOSED**

LISKEARD

Rumours of shop. NFDA.

LITTLEBOROUGH

GEORGE KELSALL **0706 70244**
22 Church Street, Littleborough, Gtr Manchester DL15 9AA.
Mon-Sat, 10-5.30, clsd Tues
New bksp with med size R/C/D stk, ab av cal, cnd & prices. BR: Littleborough, oos ahead & left.

LIVERPOOL

HENRY BOHN **051 7094501**
32 Berry Street, Liverpool
Mon-Sat, 10-5
Med size R/C stk, av cal, cnd & prices. BR: Lime Street, oos, turn left & straight ahead, shop is on right on corner.

REIDS OF LIVERPOOL **051 7092312**
105 Mount Pleasant, Liverpool L5 5AT.
Mon-Sat, 10.30-6
Med/lg R/C/D stk, av cal, cnd & prices. BR: Lime Street, oos turn left into Renshaw St & left at Mount Pleasant.

HAZLEDEAN BOOKSHOP **051 7088780**
61 Renshaw Street, Liverpool LL1 2SJ.
Mon-Sat, 12-6, totally Unr
Complete and utter creep I refuse to describe this shop. BR: Lime Street, oos turn left into Renshaw St & SIOL.

THE OUT OF PRINT BOOKSHOP 051 7089700
97 Renshaw Street, Liverpool L1 2FP.
Mon-Sat, 10-5
Med size R/C stk, ab av cal, cnd & prices. BR: Lime Street, oos turn left.

ATTICUS 051 7089834
Hardman St (No no), Liverpool
Mon-Sat, 10-5
Small R/C stk, emphon pbks, students. No T. From Out of Print Bksp oosh, turn left & left, SIOR.

ZEBRA BOOKS Anfield opened & closed in a blaze of disinterest.

LLANDUDNO, Wales

DAVID HUGHES 0492 77700
21 Madoc Street, Llandudno, Gwynned, Wales LL65.
Mon-Sat, 10.30-5, L: 1-2.30
Lg R/C stk, ab av int, bl av cnd, ab av prices. Oos ahead and left & continue.

LLANGOLLEN, Wales

MAXINES CAFE 0978 860334
17 Castle Street, Llangollen, Clwyd, N Wales LL20 8NY.
Mon-Sun, 10-5, longer in summer
V lg R/C stk, NSOC. Mainly pbks & multiple copies. Some astounding prices. TWC. P.poss. BR: Wrexham (NAST 10 miles). Etf by bridge.

BROWSERS **NO PHONE**
10 Bernyn Street, Llangollen, Clwyd, N Wales.
Tues-Sat, 10-5
Small R/C stk, av cal, cnd & prices. TWC. From Maxines oosh, turn left & left (100 yards).

LLANIDLOES, Wales

THE GREAT OAK BOOKSHOP 05512 2959
35 Great Oak Street, Llanidloes, Powys SY18 6BW
Fri & Sat 10-6
Med size R/C stk, av cal cnd & prices. Also sells tapes and records. NFDA. NV.

LLANRWST, Wales

PROSPECT BOOKS & PRINTS **0492 640111**
18 Denbigh Street, Llanrwst, Gwynedd LL25 OAA
Mon-Sat, 9-5
Primarily Spec in Guns & Shooting but also has extremely gd R/C stk. WAD. P.poss. BR: Llanrwst, oos turn left into town, SIOL.

LONDON (see end of index)

LONDONDERRY, Northern Ireland

BOOK BARGAINS **0504 46446**
47 Spencer Road, Londonderry.
Mon-Sat, 10.30-5.30, L 1-2. REL
Med/lg R/C stk, drif special, easy perusing, bgns known, keen on Irish. P.diff. NIR: Londonderry, oos and straight ahead uphill towards Radio mast & right & SIOR.

THE UPPER DRECK BOOKSHOP **NO PHONE**
Carlisle Road, Londonderry.
Small low key Samuel Beckett Special, looks like the type of place George Orwell might have been at home in. NIR: Londonderry, oos, turn right & right over bridge & right up hill. SIOR.

LOSTWITHIEL

TARKA BOOKS **0208 873407**
8 Monmouth Lane, Lostwithiel, Cornwall PL22 OBS.
Mon-Sat, 10-5, clsd Wed
New bksp with small rm of s/h bks. BR: Lostwithiel, Oos into town, SIOR.

LOUGHBOROUGH

SPARROW HILL BOOKS **0509 263080**
3 Sparrow Hill, Loughborough, Leics LE11 1BT.
Thurs-Sat, 10-5
Med size R/C stk, av cal, cnd & prices. T. P.poss. BR: Loughborough, Oos ahead into town & right at Sparrow Hill towards church. SIOL.

LOUTH

THE BOOK EXCHANGE **NO PHONE**
48 Queen Street, Louth, Lincolnshire.
Mon-Sat, 10-5
Med size R/C stk, av cal, cnd & prices. TWC. P.poss. BR: Grimsby (NAST). Etf near bus stn.

LOWESTOFT

CURFEW BOOKS **0502 589096**
44 High Street, Lowestoft, Suffolk NR32 1HX.
Mon-Sat, 10-5
Med size R/C stk, av cal, cnd & prices. TWC. P.diff. BR: Lowestoft, oos & into town. Etf.

JOHN ROLPH, THE OLD COACH HOUSE **0502 572039**
Pakefield Street (No no), Lowestoft, Suffolk NR33 OJT.
Tues,Wed,Fri & Sat 11-5, L: 1-2.30
Med size R/C stk, drif special, Anoraksia Nervosa. BR: Lowestoft oos turn right out of town south for 2 miles & left at garage.

LUDLOW

JUDITH ADAMS **0584 872758**
41 Broad Street, Ludlow, Shropshire SY8 1NL
FRI & SAT 10-5
Small Spec stk of C/D bks, Art & Architecture. Av cal, cnd & prices. TWC. P.poss. BR: Ludlow, oos into town, etf.

BOOKS & CHATTELS **0584 876191**
107 Corve Street, Ludlow, Shropshire
Mon-Sat, 11-5, clsd Thur
Med/lg R/C/D stk, Roast Beef. Netgow. P.poss. Etf.

OFFA'S DYKE BOOKS **0584 873854**
5 Bullring, Ludlow, Shropshire SY8 1AD
Mon-Sat, 9.30-5.30, REL
Small/med C/D stk, Literace. Bookfairy. Keen on Art. TWC & D. P.diff. Etf.

20TH CENTURY BOOKS **0584 874441**
132 Corve Street, Ludlow, SY8 2PL
Mon-Sat, 10-5
Small med C/D stk, bookfairy, Literace. Etf.

Another Print & Bksp has recently opened. NFDA.

LYME REGIS

MARINE BOOKSHOP **0297 442088**
Old Bonded Store, The Cobb, Lyme Regis, Dorset DT7 3JF.
Mon-Sun, 10-6
Med size R/C stk slightly low key/touristy. Av cnd & prices. BR: Axminster (NAST 10 miles) Etf on RHS of sea front.

There are a small number of bks in Serendip the new shop in the High Street & there are more bks in the Antq shp at the top of the hill.

LYMINGTON

HUGHES & SMEETH **05906 76324**
9 Gosport Street, Lymington, Hampshire SO14 9OG.
Mon-Sat, 9.30-5
Med size R/C stk, av cal, cnd & prices. TWC. Emphon Maritime. BR: Lymington, oos ahead turn left & SIOL.

TRIANGLE BOOKS **05906 70934**
70 High Street, Lymington, Hampshire.
Mon-Sat, 10-5
Med size R/C stk, ab av cal, cnd. Av prices. From H & S, oosh left & right up hill. SIOR in Antqs arcade.

LYNTON

LYNTON, DEVON there is an antq shop with bks.

LYTHAM ST ANNES

THE BOOKSHOP **0253 728278**
26 St Andrews Street, Lytham St Annes, Lancs.
Mon-Sat, 10-5.30
Med size new bksp with bsmt of s/h R/C stk. Av cal, cnd & prices. BR: Lytham, oos towards seafront & third on left. SIOL.

MACCLESFIELD

BRIDGEWATER BOOKS **0625 424763**
28 Sunderland Street, Macclesfield SK11 6JL.
Mon-Sat, 9-5, clsd Wed
New bksp with small/med size R/C stk. Av cal, cnd & prices. BR: Macclesfield, oos turn left, SIOL.

MACCLESFIELD OLD & RARE BOOKS 0625 610861
124 Chestergate, Macclesfield SK11 6DH.
Mon-Sat, 10-5.30, clsd Tues
Small C/D stk. Bookfairy. Av cal, cnd & prices. TWC. P.diff. BR: Macclesfield oos ahead up hill to right, cont through shopping St to west side of town.

MACHYNLLETH, Wales

DYFI VALLEY BOOKSHOP 0654 703849
6 Doll Street, Machynlleth, Powys, SY20 8NN.
Mon-Sat, 10-6, clsd Thur, L 1-2
Med size R/C stk, ab av int, av cal & prices. T & D. P.poss. BR: Machynlleth, oos down drive, turn left, SIOR.

MAIDSTONE

MAIDSTONE BOOK & PRINT SHOP 0622 662878
28 Union Street, Maidstone, Kent ME14 1ED.
Tues-Sat, 10-6
Med size R/C stk, ab av cal, cnd, av prices. Keen on Childrens. BR: Maidstone East, oos turn right into town & third left. SIOR.

There is also a BTA bkstl in Maidstone Mkt Tuesdays only.

MALDON

ALL BOOKS 0621 856214
2 Mill Road, Maldon, Essex.
Mon-Sat, 10-5, clsd Wed, Sun 2-6
Med size R stk, av cal, cnd & prices. BR Chelmsford (NAST 10 miles) Etf.

MALMESBURY

BATSTONE BOOKS 06666 823072
12 Gloucester Street, Malmesbury, Wilts SN10 OSA.
BTR
Small R/C stk, av cal, cnd & prices. Keen on Occult. BR Swindon (NAST 10 miles) Etf at crossroads.

MALTON

THE SHAMBLES DRIF SPECIAL **PHONE UNKNOWN**
The Shambles, Malton, East Yorkshire.
Mon-Sat, 10.30-5.30, clsd Thurs
V small, poss smallest shp in Britain. V low key, poss lowest in England. V attractive, poss lowest prices in England. BR Malton oos to T junction, turn left & first right, left into Sq & right into alleyway.

There are 3 other places which have s/h bks in Malton, but all v small.

MALVERN

THE MALVERN BOOKSHOP **0684 575915**
7 Abbey Road, Malvern, Hereford, Worcs WR14 3ES.
Mon-Sat, 9.15-5, clsd Wed
Med size R/C stk, av cal, cnd & prices.

PRIORY BOOKS **0684 560258**
Church Walk (No no), Malvern, Hereford, Worcs.
Tues-Sat, 10-5, L: 12.45-2
Med size R/C stk. Av cal, cnd & prices.

KEITH SMITH OF LEDBURY has now opened a shop in Malvern, NFDA.

MANCHESTER

(See also Altrincham & Ramsbottom)

BRIAN BARLOW **061 9629646**
52 Beech Road, Chorlton on Medlock, Manchester M21 1EG.
Mon-Sat, 10-5.30, Wed 1pm.
Med size R/C stk, av cal, cnd & prices. Emphon pbks. TWC. NV.

FENNEL BOOKSHOP **NO PHONE**
Unit 33/34 Corn Exchange, Manchester.
Mon-Sat, 10-5
BTA bkstl in covered Antiques Mkt, ab av cnd, av prices, T. BR: Manchester Victoria, Oos turn right & ahead.

There are also other bkstls in this mkt, including one in bsmt.

MY BACK PAGES **NO PHONE**
Unit 20 Corn Exchange, Manchester.
Mon-Sat, 10-5
Small/med R/C stk, av cal, cnd & prices. T. P.diff. NPL. Dir as above.

FRANKS BOOKSELLERS **061 8327241**
Antique Ctr, Royal Exchange, Manchester.
Mon-Sat, 10-5
Small bkstl, primarily Ephemera, bta. Netgow. TWC. From Corn Exchange turn right & Royal Exchange is on right.

GIBBS BOOKSHOP **061 2367179**
10 Charlotte Street, Manchester M1 4FL.
Mon-Sat, 9.30-5.30 Rel
Med/lg C/D stk, solid Roast Beef. Loaded with rmndrs, but the occasional int bk is thrown up, av cnd & prices. TWC. P.diff. BR: Manchester Victoria, Oos turn right into High St which becomes Fountain St & left Charlotte. (1 mile).

THE GINNEL GALLERY **061 8339037**
16 Lloyd Street, Manchester, M2 5ND.
Mon-Sat, 10-5
Antique (well, 30's) shop with much bta R/C stk of Applied Art & related bks. But '90s prices. TWC. P.diff. BR: Manchester Victoria, Oos turn right into town ctr & right opp town hall.

JAMES P McGILL **061 2329620**
115 Princess Road, Moss Side, Manchester M14 4RB
Mon-Sat, 12-5, Unr
Med/lg R/C/D stk, Samuel Becket Special. Res stk in bsmt. Keen on Irish bks. TWC. P.poss. BR: Manchester Victoria (NAST 3 miles) Bus 108. Etf.

E J MORTEN **061 4457629**
Warburton Street, Didsbury, Manchester M20 0RA.
Mon-Sat, 10-5
Primarily a new bksp with garden shed filled with s/h library bks. The staff are either completely mad or completely rude. TWC. Worth avoiding.

PARAMOUNT BOOK EXCHANGE **061 8349509**
Shudehill (No no), Manchester M4 2AF.
Mon-Sun, 9-7 Rel
Lg R/C stk, primarily pbks & Literace, but can be worth wading through the dross. BR: Manchester Victoria, oos turn left & 2nd right into Schude Hill, SIOL.

MOORLAND BOOKS **0457 871306**

Unit 20 Alexandra Craft Ctr, High St, Uppermill, Oldham OL3 6BY.

Wed-Sat, 11-4, later Sat & Sun

Med size R/C stk in upstairs rm of Antique & Crafts Mkt. Better than it sounds.

BROWZERS BOOKSHOP **061 7980626**

14 Warwick Street, Prestwich, Manchester.

Mon-Sat, 10-5, clsd Wed

Small/med size R/C stk, keen on Rmndrs & Horseriding. Av cal, cnd & prices. TWC. P.poss. MET (see note in guide) Prestwich, Oos ahead through shopping ctr & cross road & slightly to right. There is also a laundrette with some bks but it is well worth avoiding.

ROMILLEY LITTLE BOOKSHOP **061 4274853 (HM)**

1 Hill Street, Romilley, Manchester SK6 2AH.

Opens regularly, once a year.

Med size R/C stk, av cal, cnd & prices. BR: Romilley, etf.

GRENVILLE STREET BOOKSHOP **061 4711909**

105 Grenville Street, Stockport, Cheshire SK3 8ET.

Tues-Sat, 10-6

Med/lg R/C/D stk, Keen on Travel, Victorian atmosphere. TWC. P.poss. BR: Stockport, Oos through barrier, come back on yourself & turn left into what looks like the entrance to a sewer. At top head for roundabout & then turn right into paved shopping street (Castle St). Cont to end & turn right at church. SIOR.

HEATONS BOOKSHOP **061 4315905**

13 School Lane, Heaton Chapel, Manchester.

Mon-Sat, 10.30-4.30

Med size R/C Stk slightly low key, av cnd & prices. TWC. P.poss. BR: Heaton Chapel, Oos turn left & cont across main rd, SIOR.

THE HALE BOOKSHOP **PHONE UNKNOWN**

64A Park Road, Hale, Manchester.

Thur,Fri,Sat 10-6 Rel

Small/med R/C/D stk, ab av cal, bookfairy. Keen on Travel. T. Etgow. P.poss. BR: Hale, oos turn left until you come to a pub called The Bleeding Wolf & turn left & bear left with park. SIOR.

THE GEORGE ST LOFT **0457 863413**
4A George Street, Glossop, Derbyshire.
Wed-Sat, 9.30-5 Rel
Med size R/C stk, NSOC but can be Int. T. Etgow. P.poss. BR: Glossop, Oos turn right & right & left at George St, SIOR.

There is also a bkstl in the Antiques Mkt on the Manchester side of town.

THE ROCHDALE BOOKSHOP **0706 31136**
399 Oldham Road, Rochdale, Manchester OL16 5UN
Sats & occasional other days
Lg R/C/D stk, av cal, slightly Stokers bks, av prices. TWC. Awyw. BR: Rochdale, Oos turn right onto Oldham Rd. SIOL.

THE MARPLE BRIDGE BOOKSHOP **NO PHONE**
42 Town Street, Marple Bridge, Manchester.
Mon-Sat, 10-5, Sunday 2-5, clsd Wed
Med size R/C stk, emphon Fiction. Literace. BR: Marple Bridge, Oos up path & left & right & left towards shops.

THE HIGH STREET BOOKSHOP **NO PHONE**
8 High Street, New Mills, Manchester.
Mon-Sat, 10-4.30, sometimes clsd Wed
Med size R/C stk, emphon pbks. TWC. BR: New Mills, Oos up path & ahead, turn left at shopping street, SIOR.

MANSFIELD

THE BOOKSHELF **0623 648231**
16 Albert Street, Mansfield, Notts NG18 1EB.
Mon-Sat, 9.30-5, clsd Wed
Med size R/C stk, av cal, cnd & prices. NV. NFDA.

MARKET DRAYTON

SECOND CHAPTER **0630 57410**
5 Queen Street, Market Drayton, Shropshire TF9 1PX.
Mon-Sat, 9-6, clsd Thur in winter
Med size R stk, primarily pbks, av cal, cnd & prices. T. P.poss. BR: Shrewsbury (NAST 15 miles). Etf by car park.

MARLBOROUGH

THE ANTIQUE & BOOK COLLECTOR **0672 514040**
Katherine House, The Parade, Marlborough, Wilts SN8 1NE.
Mon-Sat, 9.45-5.30
Med/lg C/D stk, av cal, cnd & prices. BR: Swindon (NAST 10 miles) Etf.

THE MARLBOROUGH BOOKSHOP **0672 5156470**
6 Kingsbury Street, Marlborough, Wilts SN8 1NE.
Mon-Sat, 9.45-5
Print shop with back rm of Sporting & Ills bks. Av cal, cnd, ab av prices. Dir as above.

MILITARY PARADE BOOKSHOP **0672 5156470**
The Parade, Marlborough, Wilts SN8 1NE.
Mon-Sat, 10-5
Small size Spec in Mil. Hist. Av cal, cnd & prices. Dir as above.

MARSTON GREEN

See BIRMINGHAM

MATLOCK

THE BOOKCELLAR **0629 57644**
Dale Road (No no), Matlock, Derbyshire.
Mon-Sat, 9.30-5.30
Med size R/C stk, ab av cal & cnd, av prices. BR: Matlock, oos turn right, SIOL in shopping mall.

JARVIS BOOKS **0629 55322**
57 Smedley Street East, Matlock, Derbyshire.
Mon-Sat, 9.30-5.30
Med/lg stk ab av cal & cnd. Emphon Mountaineering. From above oosh, over bridge, up hill & street is on right near top.

MENSTON

CAMPBELL'S BOOKS **0943 879903**
103 Bradford Road, Menston, W. Yorks LS29 6BU.
Tues-Sat, 10.30-5.30, Unr
Small/med R/C stk, keen on Aviation. Av cal, cnd & prices. TWC. P.poss. BR: Menston, oos turn left & right at end of road. Shop is on corner.

MERE

THE BLUE RIDER **0747 860593**
Salisbury St (No no), Mere, Wilts BA12 6HE.
Mon-Sat, 9.30-5, L: 1-2, clsd Wed
Med size R/C stk, av cal, cnd & prices. T. P.poss. NV. Etf.
BR: Frome (NAST 12 miles).

MIDDLESBOROUGH

There is a small bkstl in Forbes Bldgs at the far end of Linthorpe Rd.

MIDHURST

BROWSE AWHILE **0730 815425**
The Mini Market, Grange Rd (No no), Midhurst GU29 9LT.
Tues-Fri, 11-4, Sat 9.30-5, clsd Wed
Small Bookfairy type stk. Av cal, cnd & prices. NFDA.

MIDDLEHAM

See Leyburn

MINEHEAD

ALCOMBE BOOKS **0643 3425**
26 Alcombe Road, Minehead, Somerset TA24 6AZ.
Mon-Sat, 10-5, exc Wed & Sat
Med size R/C stk, av cal, cnd & prices. BR: Barnstaple (NAST 15 miles) Etf on road to Alcombe.

MODBURY

LAMBS TALES **0548 830317**
63 Brownston Street, Modbury, Devon, PL21 0RQ.
Mon-Sat, 9.30-5.30, L: 12.30-1.30, EC Wed
Small R/C low key, av cnd & prices. TWC. BR: Plymouth (NAST 10 miles) Etf.

MOLD, Wales

ANNIE'S BOOKSTALL 0352 65683
Mold market, Mold, Wales.
Mon-Sat, 10-5
Bta stall with worse than average shop stock. Poor condition, ab av prices. TWC. P.poss. Etf in centre of town. BR: Wrexham (NAST 10 miles).

SCENT WITH LOVE 0352 700374
25 New Street, Mold, Clwyd, Wales.
Tues-Sat, 9.30-4.30. Sats 5
Small low key R stk, av cal, cnd & prices. BR: Wrexham (NAST 10 miles). From bus stn turn right & left at crossroads & SIOR.

MONMOUTH, Wales

BRIAN STEVENS 0600 713701
3 Church Street, Monmouth NP5 3BX.
Mon-Sat, 10-5, L: 1-2, clsd Thurs
Med size R/C stk. Av cal, cnd & prices. BR: Abergavenny (NAST 15 miles) Etf by church.

MONTROSE, Scotland

THE MONTROSE BOOKSHOP 0674 73382
91 Murray Street, Montrose, DD10 8JZ.
Tues-Sat, 10-4, clsd Wed
Med size R/C stk, av cal, cnd & prices. TWC. P.poss. Scotrail: Montrose, OOS turn right & left & left into main street & continue to right, SIOR.

MORECAMBE

COLLECTORS CORNER 0524 420769
124 Heysham Road, Morecambe, Lancashire LA3 1DU.
Mon-Sat, 10-4.30, Rel
Med size R/C stk, drif special. Res stk, av cal, cnd & prices. T. P.poss. BR: Morecambe oos turn left along seafront & cont to Parade of shops on right. SIOR.

MORETON IN MARSH

FOUR SHIRE BOOKSHOP **0608 51451**
17 High Street, Moreton in Marsh, Gloucestershire GL56 OAF.
Mon-Sat, 11-5
Med size R/C stk, av cal, cnd & prices. Keen on needlework. BR: M in M, oos turn right & left at crossroads & SIOL behind Mkt Hall.

MORPETH

APPLEBY'S BOOKSHOP **0670 512960**
60 Newgate Street, Morpeth, Northumberland NE61 1PE.
Mon-Sat, 9-5
New shp with v small low key R stk & Local Hist. Etf.

MUCH WENLOCK

WENLOCK BOOKS **0952 727877**
54 High Street, Much Wenlock, Shropshire
Mon-Sat, 10-5, EC Wed, L 1-2
Med size low key R/C stk, av cnd & prices. TWC. BR: Chester (NAST 10 miles) Etf.

MUSSELBURGH, Scotland

LATTO BOOKS **031 665 2651**
3 Eskside East, Musselburgh, Mid Lothian EH21 7RU
Wed-Sat, 9.30-5. Rel
Small R/C stk & spec stk of Golf. DOSO. P.poss. Scotrail: Musselburgh, OOS turn left to end of road & left & continue until third bridge, cross & shop is slightly to left.

NAILSWORTH

VALENTINES BOOKS **0453 832483**
Old Market, Nailsworth, Gloucestershire GL6 ODU.
Mon-Sat, 9-5.30 L: 1-2
Med size R/C stk, av cal, cnd & prices. BR: Stroud (NAST 10 miles) Etf by bus stn.

NANTWICH

GUILDMASTER BOOKS **0270 629108**
81 Welsh Row, Nantwich, Cheshire.
Open every day 10-dusk
Med size R/C stk, av cal, cnd & prices. Oos, turn right, follow ring road to second bridge & turn left.

NETHER STOWEY

COLERIDGE BOOKS **0278 733338**
11 Castle Street, Nether Stowey, Somerset TA5 1LN.
Tues-Sun, 10-5.30
Small R/C stk, av cal, cnd, emphon Local Hist. NV. BR: Bridgewater (NAST 10 miles).

NEWBURGH, Scotland

THE NEWBURGH BOOKSHOP **NOW CLOSED**

NEWBURY

INVICTA BOOKSHOP **0635 31176**
8 Cromwell Place, Friar Street, Newbury, Reading, RG1 1DT.
Mon-Sat, 9.30-5.30
Med/lg R/C stk, ab av cal, cnd & prices. BR: Newbury, oos ahead, turn left & left. Cont over bridge & shop is in alleyway opp Marks & Spencers.

NEWCASTLE EMLYN, Wales

FRED COOPER BOOKS **0239 711230**
Market Hall (under Clock), Newcastle Emlyn, Dyfed SA38 9AE
Mon-Sat, 9-5, clsd Wed in winter
Stall mainly rmndrs/pbks, but some v cheap hardbacks. TWC. P.poss. Etf. BR: Carmarthen (NAST 15 miles).

NEWCASTLE UNDER LYME

POMES PENNY EACH **0782 630729**
63 High Street, Wolstanton, Newcastle under Lyme ST5 OER.
Mon-Sat, 9.30-6
Med size R/C stk, emphon Lit & Mod 1sts. Ab av cal, cnd, av prices. NFDA.

NEWCASTLE UPON TYNE

AVENUE BOOKS **091 2575836**
Land of Green Ginger, Front St (No no), Tynemouth.
Tues-Sun, 10.30-5, Rel
Med size R/C stk, keen on Nat Hist. Av cal, cnd & prices. T & D. P.poss. Metro: Tynemouth, oos turn left & follow road round to right. Bksp is upstairs in church.

BAY BOOKS **091 2514448**
10A Norham Road, Monkseaton, Whitley Bay, Newcastle.
Mon-Sat, 10.30-5, clsd Tues & Wed
Small R/C stk, primarily pbks but some surprisingly gd hbks. Bl av prices, ab av cnd, WAD. TWC. Metro: Monkseaton, oos turn right & SIOL.

BEWICK BOOKS **091 2812711**
14 Clayton Road, Jesmond, Newcastle NE2 4RP.
Mon-Sat, 10.30-4
Antq shp with bta stk of C/D bks, emphon Lthrwr. T&D. Metro: Jesmond, oos & double back on yourself & SIOL.

DAVIS BOOKS **091 2614580**
140 Westgate Road, Newcastle, Tyne & Wear.
Mon-Sat, 10-5
New rmndr shop with small stk of s/h. Av cal, cnd & prices. TWC. BR: Newcastle, oos straight ahead up alleyway to second block & turn left.

BRIAN MILLS **091 2515380**
1 Side, Newcastle, Tyne & Wear NE1 3JE.
Mon-Sat, 10.30-5.30, V. Rel
Med/Lg R/C/D stk, emphon Design & Applied Art & Local Hist. Ab av cal. WAD. T&D. P.diff. BR: Newcastle, oos turn right & straight ahead towards T junction, 1 block before turn right & follow hill down.

KEEL ROW BOOKS **091 2960664**
11 Fenwick Terrace, Preston, North Shields NE29 0LY.
Tues-Sat, 10.30-5.30
Lg R/C stk, Helen Hanff/Silverfish/B&MC Special. Awyw. Farts & Smells. T&D. Metro: North Shields, oos turn left & right at top & left at church. SIOL.

OLIVER'S BOOKSHOP **091 2513552**
48A Whitley Road, Whitley Bay, Newcastle NE25 2NP.
Mon-Sat, 11-5, clsd Wed, Rel
Med size R/C stk, extremely varied, av cnd & prices. T. P.poss. Metro: Whitley Bay, oos on town side. Straight ahead & turn right at T junction & SIOL. About 1 mile.

NORTH SHIELDS BOOKS **091 2961918**
7 Kirkton Park Terrace, North Shields, Newcastle NE29 1LY.
Tues-Sat, 11-5.30, clsd Tues
Med size C/D stk. V g cnd, av cal. T & D. P.poss. From Keel Row oosh, turn left & SIOR past hospital.

STEEDMANS **091 2326561**
8 Gray Strfeet, Newcastle NE1 6EE.
Mon-Fri 9-5, Sat 12.30pm
Med/lg C/D stk. Roast Beef. V g cnd. Emphon Lthrwr, Platebks & Local Hist. Awyw. Res stk. BR: Newcastle, oos turn right & ahead to T junction & turn left, 1 block before.

NEWENT

COBWEBS **0531 821734**
8/10 Church Street, Newent, Gloucestershire GL18 1PP.
Mon-Sat, 9-5, L: 1-2, clsd Wed
Med/lg R/C stk. Av cal, cnd & prices. BR: Gloucester (NAST 10 miles).

NEW MILTON

BOOKS & THINGS **0425 617521**
99 Old Milton Road, New Milton, Hampshire BH25 6DN.
Mon-Sat, 9.30-5.30, Wed 1pm
Med/lg R/C stk, bl av cal, cnd. ab av prices. Netgow. BR: New Milton, oos turn right into village & right out of town.

NEWPORT (Isle of Wight)

MR MICAWBER **0983 525320**
61 Pyle Street, Newport, Isle of Wight.
Mon-Sat, 10-5.30
New Rmndr shp with smal/med size R/C stk. Av cal, cnd & prices.

NEWPORT, Wales

CARNINGLI CENTRE **NOW CLOSED**

NEWPORT ON TAY, Scotland

MAIR WILKES BOOKS **0382 542352**
3 St Mary's Lane, Newport on Tay, Fife DD6 BAN
Sats only or by appointment, btr
Med/lg C/D stk. High cal, WAD. Emphon Psychology & Scottish History. Etgow. P.poss. BR Dundee, OOS & cross Tay Bridge, turn right at other side & look for church. Shop/office is in Lane alongside.

NEWPORT PAGNELL

KEN'S **0908 610003**
29 High Street, Newport Pagnell, Buckinghamshire ME16 8AR.
Mon-Sat, 9.30-5
Med/lg R/C/D stk. Emphon Ephemera. Ab av cal, cnd, av prices. BR: Milton Keynes (NAST 5 miles) Etf.

NEWTON ABBOT

LINDY'S **0626 63221**
58 Queen Street, Newton Abbot, Devon TQ12 2BZ.
Mon-Sat, 9.30-5, Thurs 1pm
Med/lg R/C stk. Ab av cal, cnd & av prices. Emphon Ephemera, Theology. BR: Newton Abbot, oos ahead into town & follow road.

NORTHAMPTON

WOOTTON BILLINGHAM **0604 34531**
70 St Giles Street, Northampton NN1 4AW.
Mon-Sat, 10-5
Med size R/C stk, av cal, cnd & prices. BR: Northampton oos, turn left & follow road.

OCCULTIQUE **0604 27727**
73 Kettering Road, Northampton NN1 4AW.
Mon-Sat, 10-5
Med size Spec in Occult. Av cal, cnd & prices. Oosh above turn left, left & right & follow one way.

ABINGTON BOOKS **0604 32933**
327 Wellingborough Road, Northampton NN1 4EW
Mon-Sat, 9-5
Med size R/C stk, av cal, cnd &prices. Follow signs for Wellingborough.

NORTH BERWICK, Scotland

THE PENNY FARTHING **0620 4400**
23 Quality Street, North Berwick, East Lothian EH39 4HR
Bike shop with med sized R/C stk. Low key, low prices. TWC. P.poss. Scotrail: North Berwick, OOS turn left & right into town & left at bottom of High St.

NORTHFIELD

NORTHFIELD BKSP & FURNISHINGS **021 4777704**
51-53 Church Road, Norrthfield, Birmingham.
Mon-Sat, 9.30-4.30, Wed 1pm
Med size R/C stk, bl av cal, cnd & prices. BR: Northfield, oos turn right under bridge & continue & right at main road, right at Church road (2 miles).

NORTHWICH

CASTLE BOOK CENTRE **0606 781269**
85 Chester Road, Northwich, Cheshire.
Mon-Sat, 10-5.30, Wed 4.30
Med size R/C stk, av cal, cnd & prices. BR: Northwich, oos turn right into town, SIOR.

NORWICH (see map)

THE TOMBLAND BOOKSHOP **0603 760610**
8 Tombland, Norwich NR3 1HP.
Mon-Sat, 9.30-5
Med/lg R/C/D stk, ab av cal, cnd & prices. WAD.

ST MICHAEL AT PLEA BKSP **0603 619266**
Bank Olain, Norwich NR2 1ER
Mon-Sat, 9.30-5
Small/med size R/C stk. Emphon Local Hist. Av cal, cnd & prices.

THE MOVIE SHOP **0603 615239**
11 St Gregorys Alley, Norwich NR2 1ER.
Mon-Sat, 10-5
Mainly Film bks but some other R/C/D stk. NSOC. Av cal & prices.

HENRY COLLINSON **0603 66348**
Bagley Court, Pottergale, Norwich.
Mon-Sat, 8.30-5.30
Camera shop with BTA R/C stk. Av cnd & prices.

SCIENTIFIC ANGLIAN **0603 624079**
30 St Benedict Street, Norwich NR2 4AC.
Mon-Sat, 10-5.30, clsd Mon & Thur am, later opening winter
Med/lg R/C stk, av cal, NSOC, av prices.

TRISTRAM AND JULIA HULL **0603 624890**
72 St Benedicts Street, Norwich NR7 4AH.
Tues-Sat, 10-5.30, L: 1-2, clsd Thur
Med size C/D stk. EmphonArt & Design, espec Printing. Ab av cal, cnd & prices. Now closed and moved to Michael Gough in Holt.

PETER CROWE **0603 624800**
75 Upper St Giles Street, Norwich NR2 1AD.
Mon-Sat, 9.30-5.30
Lg R/C/D stk, av cal, cnd & prices.

J R & H E ELLIS **0603 623679**
53 Giles Street, Norwich NR2 1NR.
Mon-Sat, 8-5.30
Med/lg R/C stk, av cal, ab av cnd, av prices. Slightly rmndry.

NOTTINGHAM

GEOFF BLORE'S BOOKSHOP **0602 691441**
484 Mansfield Road, Nottingham, NG5 2BF.
Mon-Sat, 10.30-5
Med/lg R/C stk, ab av cal, cnd, av prices. BR: Nottingham, oos turn right & follow signs for Mansfield (NAST 2 miles).

JERMY & WESTERMANN **0602 474522**
203 Mansfield Road, Nottingham NG1 3PS.
Mon-Sat, 11-5
Med/lg R/C/D stk. Ab av cal & cnd, av prices. Dir as above.

MAYNARD & BRADLEY **0602 484824**
30 Friar Street, Nottingham.
Mon-Sat, 9.30-5.30, Sat 9
Med size R/C stk, av cal, cnd & prices. BR: Nottingham, oos turn right, turn right past shopping ctr into ctr of town & turn left.

OAKHAM

COUNTY BOOKSHOP **0572 722403**
343 Northgate, Oakham, Rutland, Leics LE15 6QS
Mon-Sat, 10.30-5
Med size R/C stk, av cal, cnd & prices. BR: Oakham, oos turn left, SIOL.

ORMSKIRK

MERE BOOKS **0695 77570**
48 Southport Road, Ormskirk, Lancashire L39 1QB.
Mon-Fri, 9.30-5.30
Med size R/C stk, av cal, cnd, low prices. BR: Ormskirk oos turn into town towards Gothic Cathedral & right. SIOR.

OSTERLEY

see LONDON

OSWESTRY

NEWGATE BOOKS **0691 650178**
57 Church Street, Oswestry, Shropshire
Mon-Sat, 9.30-5, L 1-2, clsd Tue & Thurs
Bksp & Antiques. Small/med R/C stk, emphon HSF & Roast Beef. TWC. P.poss. BR: Gabowen (NAST 5 miles) into town follow main road round to left.

Alleged second shop - not found - NV.

OTFORD

THE DARENTH BOOKSHOP **09592 2430**
8 High Street, Otford, Kent TN14 5PQ.
Mon-Sat, 9-5, clsd Wed
New bksp with med size R/C stk. Emphon Local Hist. Av cal, cnd, ab av prices. BR: Otford, oos ahead into village. Etf. NV.

OXFORD (see Map)

TITLES **0865 727928**
15 Turl Street, Oxford, OX1 3DQ.
Mon-Sat, 9.30-5.30
Med size C/D stk, ab av cal, cnd & prices.

THE LITTLE BOOKSHOP **0865 591176**
Covered Market, High Street, Oxford.
Mon-Sat, 10-5
Small/med size R/C stk. Bl av cal & cnd, ab av prices.

THE OXFAM BOOKSHOP **0865 310145**
56 St Giles Street, Oxford OX1 3LU.
Mon-Sat, 10-5
Med size BTA charity shop.

WATERFIELDS **0865 721809**
36 Park End Street, Oxford OX1 1HJ.
Mon-Sat, 9.30-5.30
Lg R/C stk, ab av cal, cnd & prices. Emphon Arts.

BLACKWELLS **0865 792792**
48-51 Broad Street, Oxford OX1 3BQ.
Mon-Sat 9-6, tues opens 9.30
Lg C/D stk, v acad. Ab av cal cnd & prices.

THE CLASSICS BOOKSHOP **0865 726466**
3 Turl Street, Oxford OX1 3DQ.
Mon-Sat, 10-5.30
Med size Spec in Classics (i.e. Latin, Greek, Archaeology and Ancient Hist). Av cal, ab av cnd & prices.

THE BOOKSHOP **0865 521075**
Oxford Antiques Centre, 27 Park End Street, Oxford.
Tues-Sat, 10-5.30
Med size R/C stk, av cal, cnd & prices.

NINER & HILL **0865 726195**
43 High Street, Oxford OX1 4AP.
Mon-Sat, 10-5.30
Small/med size C/D stk, ab av cal cnd & prices.

SANDERS **0865 242590**
104 High Street, Oxford OX1 4BW.
Mon-Sat, 9-5.15, L: 1-2.15
Print shp with upstairs room of C bks. Av cal, cnd & prices. Print shop.

THORNTONS 0865 242939
11 Broad Street, Oxford OX1 3DQ.
Mon-Sat, 9.30-5.30
V lg Acad C stk, ab av cal, cnd & prices.

PADSTOW

STRAND BOOKS NO PHONE
4 The Strand, Padstow, Cornwall PI28 8AZ.
Mon-Sat, 9-5, more in summer, Weds 1pm
Med size R/C stk, NSOC, av cal, ab av prices.

PAIGNTON

THE POCKET BOOKSHOP 0803 529804
159 Winner Street, Paignton, Devon TQ3 3BP.
Mon-Sat, 10.30-6, more in summer
Med size R/C stk, ab av cal & cnd, av prices. T. P.poss. BR: Paignton, oos turn left & right into alleyway, follow round to left & cross main rd, turn right & SIOL.

PEEL

See ISLE OF MAN

PENN

THE COTTAGE BOOKSHOP 049 4812632
Elm Road, Penn, Buckinghamshire HP10 8LB.
Tues-Sat, 10-5, L:1-2.15, Rel
V lg R stk. Ab av cal, av cnd & low prices. BR: Beaconsfield (NAST 3 miles).

PENRITH

ST ANDREWS BOOKSHOP 0768 64455
St Andrews View (No no), Penrith, Cumbria CA11 7YF.
Mon-Sat, 9-5, Wed 1pm
New bksp with med size s/h C stk. Av cal, cnd & prices. Keen on Nat Hist. and Ornithology. BR: Penrith, oos turn left & right into town & straight ahead into alleyway by church, SIOL opp.

PENZANCE

ARGANTE **NO PHONE**
1 Princes Street, Penzance, Cornwall TR18 2BS
Currently holding closing down sale, but claims to be re-opening in April. From New Street Books oosh, turn right & left.

THE BOOK CELLAR **0736 60320**
1 Chapel Street, Penzance, Cornwall (Postcode unknown)
Mon-Sat, 10-5
Antique shop with BTA R/C stk. TWC. P.poss. From Argante oosh, turn left & left.

PENZANCE RARE BOOKS **0735 62240**
43 Causeway Head, Penzance, Cornwall TR18 2BS
Mon-Sat, 9-5.30, REL
Med/lg R/C/D stk, av cal, ab av cnd & prices. Etgow. P.diff. BR: Penzance, oos turn right & left up hill to town centre, beyond Market Hall turn right, SIOR. (They also have a pbk branch opposite).

NEW STREET BOOKS **0736 62758**
4 New Street, Penzance, Cornwall TR18 2LZ
Mon-Sat, 10-5, REL
Newly opened C/D stk, amazingly varied. Ab av cal, cnd, av prices. Rest stk. WAD. Etgow. P.diff. BR: Penzance, oos turn right & left into Market Jew St and left 100 yards.

PERSHORE

IAN K PUGH **0386 552681**
40 Bridge Street, Pershore, Worcestershire.
Mon-Sat, 10-5, clsd Thurs
Med size R/C/D stk. Av cal, cnd, ab av prices. BR: Pershore, oos turn left into town (NAST 2 miles). Etf.

There is also a Picture Framers opp with s/h bks and a stl in the mkt.

PERTH, Scotland

PERTH BOOKSHOP **0738 33970**
3A Abbot Street, Perth PH2 OEB
Mon-Sat 10-5, clsd Wed (Winter - only Thurs,Fri,Sat - btr)
Small C stk, emphon Scottish Lit. Erratic hours. Scotrail: Perth, OOS, turn right & right under bridge & right over bridge.

BOOKSHELF **NO PHONE**
67 Princes Street, Perth
Mon-Sat, 10.30-5.30
Med size R/C stk, drif special. Emphon DOGS (both kinds). Av prices. T. P.poss. Scotrail: Perth, OOS turn right & go under bridge & 5th left.

PETERBOROUGH

OLD SOKE BOOKS **0733 64147**
68 Burghley Road, Peterborough PE1 2QE.
Fri & Sat, 10-5
Med size R/C/D stk, av cal, cnd & prices. Etgow. P.diff. BR: Peterborough, oos into shopping ctr, cont through into Westgate St, turn left Park Rd, which becomes Burghley Rd, SIOR in basement.

T V COLES **0733 77268**
961 Lincoln Road, Peterborough, PE4.
Mon-Sat, 10-5, clsd Wed
Med size R/C stk, slightly low key. Keen on Mil. Hist. BR: Peterborough, oos left onto main road & left cont for 2 miles. SIOR.

PETWORTH

BOOKROOM **0798 42073**
Petworth Antiques Mkt, East St, Petworth, GU28 0AB.
Mon-Sat, 10-5.30
Small touristy stk. Keen on Lthrwr, NV. NFDA.

PLYMOUTH

BARBICAN BOOKSHOP **0752 664957**
46 Southside Street, Barbican, Plymouth.
Mon-Sat, 10.30-5.30
Med size R/C stk, bl av cal, av cnd & prices. TWC. BR: Plymouth, oos straight ahead towards seafront, turn left at Town Hall & second right.

CORNERSTONE BOOKS **0752 661165**
New Street Antiques Ctr, The Barbican, Plymouth.
Mon-Sat, 10-5
Med size R/C stk, ab av cal, cnd & prices. From Barbican cont down Southside St & right.

POLESWORTH

G & J CHESTERS **0827 894743**
19 Bridge Street, Polesworth,Staffs R78 1DR.
Mon-Sat, 9.30-5.30, Wed clsd. Thurs until 9pm
Med/lg C/D bks. Ab av cal & cnd, av prices. Emphon Local Topg and Acad. BR: Tamworth (NAST 5 miles).

POOLE

POOLE BOOKSHOP **NO PHONE**
106 Indoor Market, High Street, Poole, Dorset.
Mon-Sat, 9-5
Med size R stk primarily pbks. Low key (i.e. not Penguins). BR: Poole, etf.

Second shop open, details to come

PORTSMOUTH

see SOUTHSEA

PORT STEWART, N. Ireland

NOT JUST BOOKS **026 583 4543**
2 Church Street, Port Stewart.
Sat 11-6, Sun 3-6 & during wk/evenings in summer season, REL
Med size R/C stk. Emphon pbks. Slightly low key. Slightly high prices. But almost unique in Ulster in being open on a Sunday. TWC. P.poss. NIR: Port Rush & Bus NAST 3 miles. Into town along promenade, head for church then do U turn at roundabout & SIOL.

PRESTEIGNE, Wales

TONY BIRD **0544 260316**
2 Hereford Street, Presteigne, Powys, Wales.
Mon-Sat, 10-5
Antique shop with far BTA C/D stk. WAD. P.poss. Discussions. Etgow. BR: Hereford (NAST 15 miles) Etf.

MONCKTON & FRASER **0544 200102**
47 High Street, Presteigne, Powys, Wales.
Mon-Sat, 10-5, Rel
Much BTA Antique shop with int stock of books. NPLOTCGI. WAD. P.poss. Av cnd & prices. TWC. BR: Knighton (NAST 5 miles).

PRESTON

THE BOOKHOUSE **0772 201576**
65/67 Fylde Road, Preston, Lancs PR1 2XQ.
Mon-Sat, 10-5.30
Med size R/C Student/Acad stk. Av cal, cnd & prices. BR: Preston, oos turn right & left with main flow of traffic, follow signs for Blackpool, shop is past roundabout on left.

HALEWOOD & SONS **0772 52603**
68 Friargate, Preston, Lancashire PR1 2AT.
Mon-Sat, 9.15-5.30, Rel
Lg C/D stk, ab av cal, cnd & prices. Res stk. BR: Preston, oos turn right into town & left at Friargate, SIOL with a second shop further down the street on same side.

BOOKS FOR EVERYBODY **PHONE UNKNOWN**
13 Lowthian Street, Preston, Lancashire PR1 2EP.
Mon-Sat, 10-5
Small R stk, keen on Childrens and pbks. From Halewood cross through shopping ctr & find signs on opp side of road pointing to alleyway.

PRESTWICH

see MANCHESTER

PUDDLETOWN

THE ANTIQUE MAP & BOOKSTORE **0305 848633**
32 High Street, Puddletown, Dorset DT2 8RU.
Mon-Sat, 9-5
Med size C/D stk, ab av cal, cnd & prices. Keen on Hardy. Distinctly Bookfairy. You have to ring a bell to get in. BR: Dorchester (NAST 5 miles) Etf.

PULBOROUGH

SUSSEX BOOKS **079 823030**
42A Lower Street, Pulborough, W Sussex RH20 2BW.
Mon-Sat, 10-5.30, clsd Wed pm
Small R/C stk. Touristy. BR: Pulborough, oos turn left into village, straight ahead at fork & SIOL.

RAMSBOTTOM

LITTLE HOLCOMBE BOOKS **0706 825322**
52 Bridge Street, Ramsbottom, Gtr Manchester BLO 9AW.
Mon-Sat, 9.30-5, Wed 1pm
Small size R/C stk, av cal, cnd & prices. Emphon Childrens.
BR: Bury (NAST 5 miles).

RAMSGATE (see map)

WINDMILL BARGAIN BOOKS **0843 591334**
20 Grange Road, Ramsgate, Kent CT11.
Mon-Sat, 9-5.30
Small R stk, av cal, cnd & low prices.

MICHAELS BOOKSHOP **0843 589500**
72 Kings Street, Ramsgate, Kent CT11 8NY.
Mon-Sat, 9.30-5.30
Rmndr Shop with med size R/C stk, av cal, cnd & prices.

THE OLD RAMSGATE BOOKSHOP **About to close**

RAVENSTONEDALE

THE BOOKHOUSE **058 73634**
Grey Garth, Ravenstonedale, Nr Kirkby Stephen CA17 4NQ.
Mon-Sun 9-8
Med size R/C/D stk, emphon Industrial. Av cal, cnd & prices.

READING

VICTORIA BOOKS **NOW CLOSED**

KEEGANS BOOKSHOP, Merchants Place, Friar Street, Reading claims to be a secondhand bookshop. But I say not, my definition of a secondhand bookshop is somewhere where the books have been previously owned by a punter.

REDCAR

REDCAR BOOKSHOP **0642 486122**
39 Lord Street, Redcar, North Yorks TS10 3HN.
Tues-Sat, 10-5, clsd Thurs
Med size R stk, av cal, cnd, bl av prices.

PACE ONE 0642 482365
6 Redcar Lane, Redclard, Cleveland, N Yorks
Mon-Sat, 10.30-5.30
Med size R/C stk primarily pbks & comics but with a selection of worthwhile hbks. Bgns known. TWC & D. P.poss. From Redcard bksp Oosh, turn left & left.

REDRUTH

THE REDRUTH BOOKSHOP 0209 211308
24 Fore Street, Redruth, Cornwall (no postcode)
Mon-Sat, 10-4
Med R/C stk, nrly a drif special, but disqualified because of the prices which are far too adventurous. TWC. P.diff. BR: Redruth, oos turn left down hill, burn right & left into paved area. SIOR through Lorna's Cook Shop.

REIGATE

REIGATE GALLERIES 0737 246055
45A Bell Street, Reigate, Surrey RH2 7AG.
Mon-Sat, 9.30-5.30, Wed 1pm, Rel
Med size R/C stk, av cal, cnd & prices.

RHOS POINT, Wales

RHOS POINT BOOKS 0492 545236
85 The Promenade, Rhos on Sea, Clwyd, Wales.
Summer every day 9.30-5.30, less in winter
Small size R/C stk, ab av cal, bl av cnd, av prices.

RICHMOND (Surrey)

See LONDON

RICHMOND (Yorkshire)

THE BOOKSHOP UNDER THE CHURCH 0748 818703
The Square, Richmond, Yorkshire.
Mon-Sat, 9-5, Sun in Summer
Med size R/C stk, drif special. Av cal, cnd & prices. T. BR: Darlington (NAST 10 miles) Etf.

FIVE OWLS BOOKSHOP **0748 823648**
26 Victoria Road, Richmond, Yorkshire.
Sat 10.30-5, L: (can you believe it!) 12.30-2.30
Med size R/C stk, av cal, cnd & prices. Wins the prize for the most customer orientated bksp in Britain.

RIPON

ST MARGARET'S BOOKSHOP **0765 2877**
10/11 Kirkgate, Ripon, Yorkshire.
Mon-Sat, 10-5, clsd Wed 1pm
New bksp with small R/C stk, av cal cnd & prices. BR: Harrogate, (NAST 5 miles). Etf.

There are also some bks in the Blacksmiths in the Courtyard by cathedral.

RIPPONDEN

THE OLD APOTHECARY BOOKSHOP **0422 822214**
121 Halifax Road, Ripponden, West Yorks HX6 4DA.
Tues-Sat, 9-5, Sat 4pm, clsd Wed
Med size R/C stk, low key, av cnd & prices. BR: Halifax (NAST 7 miles) Etf.

ROBIN HOODS BAY

CURVIN BOOKS **0947 880561**
Chapel Street (No no), Robin Hood's Bay, E. Yorks.
Mon-Sun 10.30-5.30 in summer, Sat & Sun 11-4 in winter
Small low key R stk, av cal, cnd & prices. TWC. P.poss. BR: Whitby (NAST 10 miles) Etf.

ROCHDALE

See MANCHESTER

ROCHESTER

BAGGINS BOOK BAZAAR **0634 811651**
19 High Street, Rochester, Kent.
Mon-Sun 10-6
V lg R/C/D stk. Bl av cal, cnd & prices. TWC.

HEARTS OF OAK BOOKSHOP **NOW CLOSED**

ROMILLEY

see MANCHESTER

ROMSEY

RUSKINS **0794 523881**
27 Bell Street, Romsey, Hampshire SO51 8GY.
Mon-Sat, 9.30-5.30
New bksp with med size BTA s/h stk, emphon F Nightingale.

ROSSINGTON

This shop is so bad that no sane person would go near it.

ROSS ON WYE

ROSS OLD BOOKS **0989 67458**
51-52 High Street, Ross on Wye, Hereford HR8 5HH
Mon-Sat, 10-5
Med/lg R/C/D stk. Fast turnover. Bookfairy. Literace. Nouvelle Cuisine. T & D. P.poss. Etf. BR: Gloucester (NAST).

ROWLEY REGIS (W. Midlands)

See BIRMINGHAM

RUTHIN, Wales

SPREAD EAGLE BOOKS **08242 3840**
3 Upper Clwyd Street, Ruthin, Clwyd, LL15 1HU
Mon-Sat, 9.30-5.30
New bksp with small bta (for New bksp) stk. Emphon Wales. TWC. P.poss. Etf in centre of town. BR: Wrexham (NAST 15 miles).

RYDE

HERITAGE BOOKS **0983 62933**
7 Cross Street, Ryde, Isle of Wight PO3 2AD.
Mon-Sat, 10-5
Med/lg R/C/D stk. Av cal, cnd & prices.

THE RYDE BOOKSHOP 0983 65227
135 High St, Ryde, Isle of Wight PO33 2BJ.
Mon-Sat, 8.30-5.45, Tues 5pm
New bksp with small R/C stk, upstairs. Av cal, cnd & prices. From Heritage oosh, turn left.

RYE

ANTHONY NEVILLE 0797 224552
15 Market Square, Rye, E. Sussex TN31 7LA.
Mon-Sat, 10-5.30, clsd Tues
Med size C/D stk, ab av cal, cnd & prices. TWC. BR: Rye, oos ahead & first left past High St & right.

LANDGATE BOOKS 0797 222280
Hilders Cliff, Rye, East Sussex.
Wed-Sat, 10-5
Med size R/C stk, av cal, cnd & prices. Currently up for sale.

SAFFRON WALDEN

There is an antq shp with bks & an Oxfam bksp. The pair compete to see which can be the worst.

ST ALBANS

OXFAM BOOKSHOP **NO PHONE**
The Street with no name, St Albans, Herts.
Mon-Sat, 10.30-4.30
Med size BTA charity bksp. BR: St Albans, oos up steps & turn right into town. At crossroads go straight ahead & SIOR.

THOMAS THORPE 0727 65576
9 George Street, St Albans, Herts AL3 4ER.
Tues-Sat, 9.30-5.30
Med/lg C/D stk, ab av cal, cnd & prices. Dir as above, but at crossroads turn left & turn right behind Mkt Hall. SIOL.

PATON BOOKS 0727 53984
32-34 Holywell Street, St Albans, Herts AL3 4LR.
Tues-Sat, 9-5
New bksp with lg rm of R/C stk. Av cal, cnd & prices. Dir as above, at Mkt Hall cont straight ahead downhill & SIOR.

ST ANDREWS, Scotland

QUARTO BOOKSHOP **0334 74616**
8 Golf Place, St Andrews, Fire KY16 9JA
Mon-Sat, 10-5.30, L 1-2.15
Med size R/C stk with spec stk of Golf & s/h students bks. T. Etgow. P.poss. BR: Leuchars & bus (NAST - 5 miles). On road into town Golf Place is on left.

BILLSONS **0334 75063**
15 Greyfriars Gdns, St Andrews, Fife KY16 9HG
Mon-Sat, 10-5.30, clsd Thurs
Spec stk of Scottish Antqrn & s/h bks. VG cnd, & prints & maps. TWC. P.poss. From Quarto, OOSH turn right & left & 2nd right.

BOUQUINISTE **0334 76724**
31 Market Street, St Andrews, Fife KY16 9NS
Mon-Sat, 10-5, clsd Thurs
Med size R/low key C stk. Av cnd & prices. TWC. P.poss. From Bouquiniste OOSH, turn left & left into main street & continue. There are also 2 bookstalls in the Market Place.

A & F McILREAVY **0334 72487**
57 South Street, St Andrews, Fife KY16 9QR
Mon-Sat, 9.30-5.30 (Winter -5)
Lg C/D stk, keen on Lit, Mod 1sts & Scottish. Av cal, cnd, ab av prices. Bookfairy. TWC. P.poss. From Bouquniste OOSH turn right & immediately left into Passageway & left.

BOOKO BOOKS **NOW CLOSED**

ST COLUMB MAJOR

COLLECTORS CORNER **0637 880715**
7 Bank Street, St Columb Major, Cornwall TH9 5AT.
Mon-Sat, 10-5
Med size R/C stk, av cal, cnd & prices. BR: St C M, Oos to left (NAST 3 miles). Etf.

ST HELENS (Isle of Wight)

MOTHER GOOSE BOOKSHOP **0983 873897**
Upper Green Rd (No no), St Helens, Isle of Wight PO33 1XB.
Mon-Sat, 11.30-10, L: 1-2.30
Med size R/C stk, av cal cnd & prices.

ST IVES

THE MIRROR AND THE LAMP **NO PHONE**
1 St Andrews Street, St Ives, Cornwall TR26 1AH.
Tues,Wed,Fri & Sat 1-6
Small stk of Poetry & Art.

SALISBURY

D M BEACH **0722 333801**
52 High Street, Salisbury, SP1 2EG.
Mon-Sat, 9-5.30
Med/lg R/C stk, av cal, cnd & prices.BR: Salisbury, Oos down drive, turn right into town & right at major crossroads.

JOHN & JUDITH HEAD **0722 327767**
88 Crane Street, Salisbury SP1 2QD.
Mon-Fri, 10-5
Lg Spec shp in HS&F, ab av cal, cnd & prices. Dir as above.

SALTAIRE

THE BODHRAN **0274 530102**
9 Victoria Road, Saltaire, Yorks BD18 3LA.
Mon-Sat, 10-6, less in winter
Med size R/C stk, av cal, cnd. Keen on Irish. BR: Saltaire Oos up drive & turn right.

What has happened to second shop?

SALTBURN

SALTBURN BOOKSHOP **0287 623335**
3 Amber Street, Saltburn, Cleveland TS10 1DT.
Wed-Sat, 11-5, L: 1-2
Med size R/C stk, low key, av cnd & prices. BR: Saltburn oos to left and head & 2nd right.

SANDOWN

ARMSTRONGS **0983 406226**
14a York Road, Sandown, Isle of Wight.
Summer openings btr.
Small R stk, bl av cal, cnd & prices. Poss the worst bksp in Britain.

SANDWICH

STRAND BOOKS **0304 611948**
21 Strand Street, Sandwich, Kent CT13 9DX.
Mon-Sat, 10-5.30, L: 1-2.15, clsd Wed
Small/med size R stk, ab av prices. Av cnd. BR: Sandwich, Oos over embankment straight ahead into town, SIOR.

SCARBOROUGH

SCARBOROUGH BOOKS **0723 368813**
55 Castle Road, Scarborough, Yorks YO11 1BH.
Mon-Sat, 10-5, Sun in summer
Med size R/C stk. Av cal, cnd & prices. Keen on Esoteric. BR: Scarborough, Oos straight ahead, right at junction & SIOR.

MRS LOFTHOUSE **0947 880561**
2 Queen Street, Scarborough, Yorks.
Mon-Sat, 10-5.30
Lg R/C stk, av cal, cnd & prices. TWC. P.diff. BR: Scarborough, Oos turn right down main street & 4th (ish) left.

There is also an antq shp with bks behind the station, and a pbk shop with some hbks over the bridge on the other side of town. Plus I have allegedly missed one shop.

SEAFORD

THE BARN COLLECTORS MARKET **0323 890010**
Church Lane (No no), Seaford, E Sussex.
Tues,Thur,Sat 10-4.30
Med/lg R/C stk, av cal, NSOC, av prices. TWC. BR: Seaford, Oos turn right & right & shop is in alleyway behind church.

SEDBERGH

R F G HOLLETT & SON **05396 20298**
6 Finkle Street, Sedbergh, LA10 5BZ.
Mon-Sat, 10-5, L: 12-1.15
Med/lg C/D stk, ab av cal, cnd, way ab av prices. Also has res stk. T. I'm too poor to even go through the door.

SETTLE

THE BOOKEND **072 923879**
The Shambles, Market Place, Settle, North Yorks.
Mon-Sat, 10-5.30, L: 1-2, clsd Wed Unr
Small/med low key Stokers bks. Av prices. TWC. P.poss. Etf in bsmt of Mkt Hall.

Second shop in Settle NV - too sober.

SHAFTESBURY

THE BOOK IN HAND **NO PHONE**
17 Bell Street, Shaftesbury, Dorset SP7 8AR.
Mon-Sat, 10-4.30, L: 1-2, less in winter
Med size R/C stk, ab av cal, cnd, av prices. BR: Gillingham (NAST 5 miles) Etf by supermarket car park.
What has happened to second shop?

SHALDON

MAGPIE RARE BOOKS **0626 872 896**
23 Fore Street, Shaldon, Teignmouth, Devon TQ14 ODE.
Mon-Sat, 10-5
Small low key R stk, av cnd & prices. T. P.poss. BR: Teignmouth (NAST 3 miles) Etf.

SHEFFIELD

ALAN HILL **0742 747721**
261 Glossop Road, Sheffield, Sth Yorks S10 2GZ
Mon-Sat, 10.30-5.30
Med/lg C/D stk, av cal, cnd & prices. T. P.diff. BR: Sheffield, Oos turn left onto Ring Rd & follow signs for Glossop. Turn right at Major Crossroads. SIOR.

THE BOOK & ART SHOP **NO PHONE**
204 West Street, Sheffield, Sth Yorks.
Mon-Sat, 10-5.30
Med size R/C stk, keen on Art. Av cal, cnd & prices. T. Dir as above. SIOL.

RARE & RACY 0742 701916
164-166 Devonshire St, Sheffield, Sth Yorks S3 7SG.
Mon-Sat, 10-6
Med/lg R/C/D stk. Av cal, cnd & prices, bgns known. WAD. From Book & Art Shop, Oosh, turn right & right & left. SIOL. They have a second smaller shp at 278 South Road, Walkley.

BIFF BOOKS & RECORDS NO PHONE
11 Commonside, Walkley, Sheffield, Sth Yorks.
Tues-Sat, 11-5.30, Sat 10
Med size R/C stk, emphon pbks & students. From Alan Hill cont north on ring road & turn left at signs for Walkley. SIOR.

BOOK HOUSE NO PHONE
456-458 Glossop Road, Sheffield, South Yorks.
Mon-Sat, 10-5 Unr
Small R/C stk, Sam Beckett Special. Low key. TWC. From Alan Hill, oosh turn left & follow Glossop Rd for one mile. SIOR.

TILLEY'S VINTAGE MAGAZINE SHOP 0742 752442
281 Shoreham Road, Sheffield, South Yorks.
Tue,Fri & Sats only
Primarily Post War Comics & Mags. NFDA.

Y.S.F. 0742 680687
Sharrowvale Road (No no), Sheffield, South Yorks.
Mon-Sat, 10-5
Med size R/C stk, av cal, cnd & prices. From Book House turn left & first right down hill, turn right at bottom following edge of park, right at junction & left & come back on yourself at Junction Rd & ahead into Sharrowvale.

THE PORTER BOOKSHOP 0742 667762
227 Sharrowvale Road, Sheffield, South Yorks.
Mon-Sat, 11-5.30
Med size R/C stk, av cal, cnd & prices. TWC.

SHEPSHED

G K HADFIELD 0509 503014
Ticklow Lane (No no), Shepshed, Leicestershire LE12 9EY.
Mon-Sat, 9-5
Small Spec stk of bks on clocks. New & s/h. BR: Loughborough (NAST 10 miles).

SHERBOURNE

CHAPTER HOUSE BOOKSHOP & GALLERY **0935 816262**
Trendle St (No no), Sherborne, Dorset DT9 3NT.
Mon-Sat, 10-5.30, L: 1-2
Med/lg size R/C stk, av cal, cnd & prices.

BOOKLORE **0939 814191**
2 Hound Street, Sherborne, Dorset DT9 3AA.
Mon-Sat, 9.30-5, Wed 1pm
New bksp with small R/C stk, av cal, cnd & prices.

SWAN GALLERY **0935 814465**
51 Cheap Street, Sherborne, Dorset.
Mon-Sat, 10-5.30
Print Gallery with med size Bookfairy stk of bks, av cal, cnd & prices. ETF in main street.

SHERINGHAM

PETER'S BOOKSHOP **0263 823008**
19 St Peters Street, Sheringham, Norfolk NR26 8QY.
Mon-Sun, 10-6, winter clsd Sun,Mon & Wed
Lg R/C stk, NSOC, av cal & prices. TWC. BR: Sheringham, Oos turn right & second right.

SHREWSBURY

CANDLE LANE BOOKS **0743 65301**
28-31 Princess Street, Shrewsbury, Shropshire SY1 1LW.
Mon-Sat, 9.30-5, L 1-2, Rel
Lg R/C/D stk, emphon Nat Hist, HSF, Solid Roast Beef. I like it but not a lot of other people do. TWC. P.diff. BR: Shrewsbury, oos turn left, follow main road into town & turn left into Market square (signposted tourist office) & cont SIOR.

QUARRY BOOKS **0743 61404**
24 Claremont, Shrewsbury SY1 1RD.
Mon-Sat, 9.30-5.30
Med/lg R/C/D stk. Literace. Gd cnd. TWC. P.poss. BR: Shrewsbury, oos turn left & then right past two of the world's most hideous shopping centres.

SIDMOUTH

SIDMOUTH OLD BOOKS **0395 514461**
12 Temple Street, Sidmouth, Devon EX10 9LY.
Mon-Sat, 10-5
Med size R/D stk, av cal, cnd & prices.

SIDMOUTH ANTIQUE BOOKSHOP **0395 516028**
All Saints Rd (No no), Sidmouth, Devon EX10 8EG.
Mon-Sat, 9.30-5.30
Med size drif special come Stokers Special. Av cal, cnd & prices. TWC. P.diff. From Temple St oosh turn left & right at fork.

SILVER END

BALDWIN'S BOOKSQ **0376 83502**
Boar's Tye Road, Silver End, Essex CM8 8QA.
Sats only, btr other times
Mainly Geological Spec & related bks.

SITTINGBOURNE

see CRANBROOK, KENT

SKIPTON

CHILTON BOOKS **0756 798939**
49 Belmont Bridge, Skipton, Yorks.
Mon-Sat, 10-5, clsd Tues
Med size R/C stk, av cal, cnd & prices. BR: Skipton, Oos turn right & SIOR.

THE BOX OF DELIGHTS **0756 790111**
25 Otley Street, Skipton, Yorks.
Mon-Sat, 11-5.30, clsd Tues & Thur
Med size C/D stk, ab av cal, emphon Ill & Childrens. More than av imagination shown in stk and sometimes in prices. WAD. P.poss. BR: Skipton, Oos turn right cont into town turn left & second right.

SLEAFORD

WESTGATE BOOKSHOP 0529 304276
45 Westgate, Sleaford, Lincolnshire NG34 7PU.
Mon-Sat, 10-5, clsd Thur
Med size R stk, av cal, cnd & prices. BR: Sleaford, Oos turn right & left & left at Mkt Sq.

SNETTISHAM

TORC BOOKS 0485 54188
9 Hall Road, Snettisham, Norfolk PE31 7LY.
Sats 10-6 and BTR
Med size R/C stk, av cal, cnd & prices. BR: King's Lynn (NAST 10 miles) Etf by bus stop.

SOMERTON

SIMON'S BOOKS 0458 72313
Broad Street (No no), Somerton.
Tues-Sat, 10-5.30
Med size R/C stk, av cal, cnd & prices.

SOUTHAMPTON

H M GILBERT 0703 226420
2 Portland Street, Southampton, Hampshire.
Mon-Sat, 8.30-5.30
Lg R/C stk, av cal, cnd & prices. BR: Southampton, Oos cont past Civic Ctr, turn right into Above Bar & third right.

NORTHAM BOOKS **NO PHONE**
30 Northam Road, Southampton, Hampshire SO1.
Wed-Sat, 10-5
Med/lg R/C stk, av cal, cnd & ab av prices. From Gilberts, Oosh turn left, cross Above Bar to Ring Rd, turn left & right at main junction.

SOUTHEND ON SEA

ATTICUS BOOKS 0702 353630
20 Alexandria Street, Southend on Sea, Essex SS1 1BJ.
Sats only
Small/med R/C stk, av cal, cnd & prices.

SOUTH MOLTON

R M YOUNG **0271 890273**
120 East Street, South Molton, Devon, EX36 3BU.
bookrm which opens in summer.

SOUTHPORT

BROADHURST **0704 532064**
5-7 Market Square, Southport, PR8 1HD.
Mon-Sat, 9-5.30, exc Tues
Lg R/C/D stk, ab av cal, cnd & prices. WAD. BR: Southport, Oos turn left & right & left & right. SIOR disguised as new bksp.

BRYAN KERNAGHAN **0704 546329**
53 Wayfarers Arcade, Southport PR8 1NT.
Mon-Sat, 10-5
Med size R/C/D stk, ab av cal, cnd & prices. WAD T. P.diff. From Broadhursts Oosh, turn right & right, cross rd to left & SIOL in arcade.

ANTHONY PARKINSON **0704 547016**
359 Lord Street, Southport, PR8 1NH.
Mon-Sun, 10.30-5
Med size R/C stk, slightly low key, av cal, cnd & prices. From Kernaghan's Oosh, turn left out of arcade & SIOL.

SOUTHSEA

MILLERS BOOK & PRINTS **0705 755796**
55 Fawcett Road, Southsea, Hampshire PO4 ODA.
Tues-Sat, 11-6, clsd Wed
Med size R/C stk, av cal, cnd & prices. BR: Fratton, Oos turn left towards seafront into Fratton Rd, SIOL.

STAR BOOKSHOP **0705 737077**
69 Fawcett Road, Southsea, Hampshire PO4 ODR.
Tues-Sat, 12-6.30, Sat 11-6
Med/lg R/C/D stk, av cal, cnd & prices. Dir as above. WAD.

ADELPHI BOOKS **079 833381 (Hm)**
1 Albert Road, Southsea, Hampshire PO5 2SE.
Tues-Fri, 11.30-4.30, Sat 10-5
Med size R/C stk, av cal, cnd & prices. From Star Bksp, Oosh, turn left & follow road for 1 mile and turn right into Albert Rd, cont 1 mile, SIOR opp Police Station.

BOOK ACADEMY **0702 816632**
13 Marmion Road, Southsea, Hampshire PO5 2AT.
Mon-Sat, 9-5, Rel
Med size R/C stk. Av cal, NSOC, av prices. Res stk of religious bks. From Adelphi, oosh turn left behind Police Stn, cont towards seafront & turn right into Marmion Rd, SIOR at far end.

ASBAH **NO PHONE**
56 Elm Grove, Southsea, Hampshire.
Mon-Fri, 10-4.30 Rel
A charitable charity bksp low key but worth a look. No T. P.poss. From Book Academy, Oosh, turn right & right into main road & left at major crossroads by Telephone Exchange, SIOL.

SOUTHWOLD

PLEASURES **0702 723776**
36 East Street, Southwold, Suffolk IP18 6EJ.
Mon-Sat, 10-5, L: 1-2.30 summer, less in winter
Med size R/C stk, av cal, cnd & prices. T. BR: Halesworth, (NAST 10 miles) Etf.

STAFFORD

ROBERT A PICKEN **0785 53425**
11 Goal Road, Stafford ST11 3AN.
Mon-Sat, 10.30-5.30, clsd Wed, Rel
Small/med size R/C stk, av cal, cnd & prices. BR: Stafford, Oos turn left & follow signs for Stone & shp is opp Prison.

STAMFORD

ROBERT HUMM **0780 66266**
Station House, Stamford, Lincolnshire PE9 2JN.
Mon-Sat, 9.30-5.30
Lg Spec in railways, ab av cal, cnd & prices. TWC. Etf on Station.

STANILAND **0780 55800**
4-5 St George's Street, Stamford, Lincs.
Mon-Sat, 10-5
Lg R/C/D stk, ab av cal, cnd & prices.

ST MARY'S BOOKS 0780 63033
9 St Mary's Hill, Stamford, Lincs PE9 2DP.
Mon-Sun, 8.30-8
Med size R/C stk, av cal, cnd & prices. NSOC.

CHEYNE LANE BOOKSHOP 0780 51079
6 Cheyne Lane, Stamford, Lincs.
Tues-Sat, 10.30-4.30, L: 1-2, clsd Thurs
Small R/C stk, av cal, cnd & prices.

THE GEORGE OF STAMFORD BOOKSHOP 0780 55171
The George Mews, Stamford, Lincs, PE9 2LB.
Tues-Sat, 11-6
New bksp with small R/C stk, emphon Cookery.

STIRLING, Scotland

THE STIRLING BOOKSHOP 0876 81771
30 Spittal Street, Stirling FK8 1DV
Mon-Sat, 10-5, Rel
Lg R/C/D stk. Emphon Scottish History espec Stirlingshire. Ab av cal, cnd & prices. WAD. Etgow. P.poss by Castle. Directions as above.

CORN EXCHANGE BOOKSHOP 0786 73112
53 King Street, Stirling FK8 1DN
Mon-Fri, 10-3, L 1-2, Sat 10-5.
Med size R/C stk. Low key. Nsoc. Bgns known. TWC. P.diff. Scotrail: Stirling Oos ahead to third set of streets.

STOCKPORT

See MANCHESTER

STOCKTON

BARNARD GALLERY 0642 616203
2 Theatre Yard, Stockton, Cleveland TS18 5NL.
Tues-Fri, 10-4, Sat 10-5.30, clsd Thurs
Med size R/C stk, low key. Av cnd, low prices. OOs, turn left into town & right & left past Market Hall into alleyway.

STOKE ON TRENT

ANTIQUARIAN BOOK CENTRE **0782 261352**
30-32 Hope Street, Hanley, Stoke on Trent.
Mon-Sat, 10-5.30
Med size R/C stk, av cal, cnd & prices. Keen on Ceramics & Technical. BR: Stoke on Trent, Oos, left down drive, turn right into town & follow rd through to shopping ctr. Bear left & Hope St is 2nd on right.

THE VILLAGE BOOKSHOP **0782 543005**
56 Millrise Road, Milton, Stoke on Trent.
Mon-Sat, 10-5, clsd Wed
Med size R/C stk, av cal, cnd & prices. T. BR: Stoke (NAST 5 miles) etf in Milton.

BERNARD TAYLOR **0782 824682**
337 Newcastle Street, Longport, Stoke on Trent ST6 3PP.
Wed-Fri, 10-6
Med/lg R/C stk, emphon Technical, Literace & Industrial Hist. Keen on football. Av cnd & prices. TWC. P.diff. BR: Longport, Oos down drive & turn left SIOR 1/2 mile.

POMES PENYEACH **0782 630279**
63 High Street, Wolstanton, Stoke on Trent, ST5 OER.
Mon-Sat, 9.30-5.30, Rel
Med size R/C stk, bookfairy & emphon Mod 1sts & Lit. Ab av cal, cnd. Imaginative prices. TWC. BR: Longport, oos down drive & turn right. Follow signs for Wolstanton 1 1/2 miles.

STOKESLEY

THE STOKESLEY BOOKSHOP **0642 712514**
63 High Street, Stokesley, Cleveland TS9 5BQ.
Mon-Sat, 10-5
Med size R/C stk, av cal, cnd & prices. BR: Middlesbrough (NAST 10 miles), Etf ctr of town.

STORMY DOWN, Wales

BRIDGEND BOOK BARN **NOW CLOSED**
(See Bridgend in Wales)

STORNOWAY, Scotland

THE STORNOWAY BOOKSHOP **PHONE UNKNOWN**
Bells Road (No no), Stornoway, Hebrides.
NFDA
Med size R/C stk, av cal, cnd & prices. NV

STOW ON THE WOLD

BOOKBOX **0451 31214**
Sheep Street (No no), Stow on the Wold, Glos GL54 1AA.
Mon-Sat, 10-5, BTR in winter
Med/lg R/C stk, ab av cal, cnd & prices.

WYCHWOOD BOOKS **0451 31880**
Sheep Street, Stow on Wold, Glos GL54 1AA.
Tues-Sat, 9.30-5, L: 1-2, clsd Wed
Med R/C stk, keen on Nat Hist. Av cal, cnd & prices. TWC.

FOURSHIRE BOOKS **0451 30755**
4 Talbot Court, Stow on Wold, Glos GL54 1BQ.
Mon-Sat, 9.30-5, Sun in summer 11-5
Med size new & s/h bks low key. Emphon Rmndrs. BR: Moreton in Marsh (NAST 5 miles) Etf by Square.

STRATFORD ON AVON

ROBERT VAUGHAN **0789 205312**
20 Chapel Street, Stratford on Avon, CV37 6EP.
Mon-Sat, 9.30-5.30
Med size C/D stk, emphon Shakespeare. Ab av cal, cnd & prices. Etf in ctr of town.

CHAUCER HEAD BOOKSHOP **0789 415691**
21 Chapel Street, Stratford on Avon, CV37 6EP.
Mon-Sat, 10-5.30, Sun 1-5
Med size R/C stk, ab av cal, cnd, av prices. Dir as above.

PAPER MOON BOOKS **0789 297249**
4 Sheep Street, Stratford on Avon.
Mon-Sat, 10-5.30
V lg bkstll. Ab av cal, cnd & prices. Tourist orientated. Now moved to Warwick.

Avoid Stratford on Avon Railway Station.

STROUD

ALAN & JOAN TUCKER **0453 764738**
Station Road (No no), Stroud, Gloucestershire GL5 3AF.
Mon-Sat, 10-5, L: 12.30-1.30, clsd Thurs
New bksp with BTA R/C stk. Av cnd & prices. BR: Stroud, Oos ahead, SIOL.

IMPRINT **0453 759731**
31 High Street, Stroud, Gloucestershire GL5 1AS.
Mon-Sat, 10-5.30
Med size R/C stk, emphon Entertainment. Ab av cal, cnd & av prices. TWC. BR: Stroud, oos ahead, turn right & left after tower & right at top. SIOR.

STURMINSTER NEWTON

STOUR BOOKS **0258 73561**
Bridge Street, Sturminster Newton, Dorset.
Mon-Sat, 10-4.30, clsd all day Tues and 1pm Wed & Sat
Small R/C stk, primarily Childrens and Ill. Av cal, cnd and ab av prices. BR: Dorchester, (NAST 10 miles).

SUDBURY

SUFFOLK RARE BOOKS **0787 72075**
7 New Street, Sudbury, Suffolk CO10 6JH.
Tues, Thur, Fri & Sat, 10.30-4.30
Med size R/C/D stk, av cal, cnd & prices. T. BR: Sudbury, Oos ahead, left into North Street & first left.

SUNDERLAND

DURHAM BOOK CENTRE **091 5674389**
Vine Place, Sunderland
Sats only - other times by request
Med size R/C stk, ab av int. Bl av cnd, av prices. BR Sunderland, oos to right towards Bus stn, turn left & right.

SUTTON

see LONDON

SUTTON IN ASHFIELD

BOOK A BRAC **0627 553667**
110 Outram Street, Sutton in Ashfield, Notts, no postcode.
Mon-Sat, 10-5, clsd Wed, Unr
Small/med R/C stk, av cal, cnd & prices. TWC. P.poss. BR: Nottingham (NAST) Shp is on road heading North out of town.

SWAFFHAM

2 Low Key shps have bks, NV.

SWANAGE

ANTIQUARIAN & SECONDHAND BOOKS **0929 424088**
55 High Street, Swanage, Dorset.
Mon-Sat, 10-5
Med/lg R/C stk, av cal, cnd & prices. TWC. BR: Wareham (NAST 10 miles) Etf.

SWANSEA, Wales

DYLAN'S BOOKSTORE **0792 655255**
Salubrious Passage (No no), Wind Street, Swansea, West Glamorgan, SA1 3RT
Mon-Sat, 10-5
Med/lg C/D stk, ab av cal, cnd & prices. T. Res stk on application. Emphon Welsh & Dylan Thomas. P.diff. BR: Swansea, oos turn left into High St & cont for 1/2 mile. Shop is in alleyway on right past Barclay's bank. WAD.

RALPH ROBERTS **NO PHONE**
12 Dilwyn Street, Swansea, West Glamorgan.
Mon-Sat, 10-5.30
Med/lg R/C stk, low key, NSOC, low prices. TWC. P.poss. BR: Swansea, oos ahead into High St, turn right at paved area which leads to Kingsway & cont for 1 mile. Turn left at roundabout.

ROWLANDS RECORD EXCHANGE **NO PHONE**
11 The Kingsway, Swansea, West Glamorgan.
Mon-Sat, 10-5
Med size Record shp with B&MC type stk. NPIOCGI. Av cal, cnd & prices. As Ralph the Book, but cont along Kingsway.

THE OLD BOOK MART **0792 474919**
27 St Helen's Road, Swansea SA1 4AY.
Mon-Sat, 10-5.30
V lg R/C stk, v gd cnd Readers Digest bks. Emphon Spiritualism & Esoteric. TWC. P.poss. From Rowlands Record Exchange oosh turn left.

SWAY

BEAGLE BOOKS **0590 683421**
1 Middle Road, Sway, Hampshire SO41 6AI.
Mon-Fri, 10-4, clsd Wed, L: 1-2, Sat 9-1
Small C stk, emphon Nat Hist. Av cal, cnd & prices. BR: Sway, Etf.

SWINDON

VICTORIA BOOKSHOP **0793 527364**
30 Wood Street, Swindon, SN1 4AB.
Mon-Sat, 9-5.30
Med/lg stk, Av cal cnd & prices. BR: Swindon, Oos ahead, follow signs for Old Town, etf.

TALGARTH, Wales

THE STRAND BOOKSHOP **0874 711195**
Regent Street, Talgarth, Powys LD3 ODB
Mon-Sun, 10-5, more in summer
Med/lg R/C stk. A drif special with Bookfairy prices. Poss res stk, but pricier, but int bks. TWC. H/bks upstairs of course. BR: Hereford (NAST 25 miles).

TAUNTON

STAPLEGROVE BOOKSHOP **0823 336450**
19 Staplegrove Road, Taunton, Somerset TA1 3PF.
Mon-Sat, 10-5
Med size R/C stk, av cal, cnd & prices. BR: Taunton, Oos, turn towards town & second left into Staplegrove Rd.

ROTHWELL & DUNWORTH **0823 282476**
14 Paul Street, Taunton, Somerset.
Mon-Sat, 11-5.15, Sat 1pm
Med size R/C/D stk, keen on Cricket. In town in front of shopping ctr by car park.

TEALBY

STAFFORDS **0673 83557**
40 Rasen Road, Tealby, Lincolnshire LN8 3XL.
Thurs-Sat, 10.30-5.30
Small Spec in Children's bks & Local Hist. Av cal, cnd & prices. TWC. BR: Mkt Rasen (NAST 5 miles).

TEIGNMOUTH

QUAYSIDE **0626 775436**
43 Northumberland Place, Teignmouth, Devon TQ14 8DE.
Mon-Sat, 9-5.30
New bksp with small R/C stk, low key. Keen on Maritime. Av cnd & prices. TWC. BR: Teignmouth, Oos turn right & left at first roundabout & follow through. There is also a religious shop called Pilgrims Progress in Fore St, but no general bks.

THE BOOKWORM **0626 775177**
26 Regent Street, Teignmouth, Devon.
Mon-Sat, 10-5 & Sun & eves in summer
Med size R stk, slightly low key C stk. Looks hopeful but not renowned for being rewarding. Owner makes up for Teignmouth being a quiet place. BR: Teignmouth, Oos ahead into town & left at clocktower.

TENBY, Wales

ALBATROSS BOOKSHOP **0834 2113**
1 Bridge Street, Tenby, Dyfed, Wales.
BTR. Hours are subject to enormous change
Med size R/C stk, av cal cnd & prices. Emphon Ornithology. NV.

TENTERDEN

TONY NEVILLE **0797 224552**
High Street (No no), Tenterden, E Sussex.
BTR
Spec stk of Art & Architecture bks, av cal, cnd & prices. BR: Tunbridge Wells (NAST 10 miles) etf.

There are rumours of a second shop opening in Tenterden but that is as far as it has got after 3 years.

TEWKESBURY

WAYFARER BOOKS **0684 293337**
19 Church Street, Tewkesbury, Gloucestershire.
Mon-Sat, 10-5
Med size R/C stk, av cal, cnd & prices.

THIRSK

HAMBLETON BOOKSHOP **0845 22343**
43 Market Place, Thirsk, North Yorkshire YO7 1HA.
Mon-Sat, 9.30-5, clsd Wed during winter
New Bksp with med size R/C stk. Keen on Geology. Av cal, cnd & prices.

TIPPERARY, Eire

PENNYFARTHING ARCADE BOOKSHOP **NO PHONE**
52 Main Street, Tipperary.
Mon-Sat, 10-5
Small/med R stk. Drif special. Av prices, almost unique in Irish bksps in that it has a general stk. TWC. P.poss. IR: Tipperary, oos turn left into town, left at Main Street and SIOR.

TIVERTON

THE ANGEL HILL BOOKSHOP **0884 257783**
17 Angel Hill, Tiverton, North Devon.
Mon-Sat, 10-5
Two separate Bookdealers in one premises. 1 emphon Broadcasting, 2 emphon Occult. BR: Tiverton Parkway (NAST 3 miles) Etf.

TODMORDEN

BORDER BOOKSHOP **0706 814721**
63 Halifax Road, Todmorden, Lancs.
Mon-Sat, 10-5, clsd Tues
Med size R/C stk, keen on Cricket, Childrens & Comics. Res stk on request. Av cal, NSOC. TWC. P.poss. BR: Todmorden, Oos downhill to roundabout turn left & SIOL.

PANGOLIN BOOKS 0706 817945
17 Water Street, Todmorden, Lancashire OL14 5AB.
Tues-Sat, 10-5, Mon 12.30. Rel
Med size R/C stk, Literace. Av cal, cnd & prices. TWC. P.poss. BR: Todmorden, Oos downhill to roundabout & cont to left of stream.

Second shop in Todmorden, NFDA.

TORRINGTON

TOR BOOKS 0805 23791
1 South Street, Torrington, Devon EX38 8HE.
Thurs-Sat, 9.30-5
Med size R stk, av cal, cnd & prices. T. BR: Barnstaple (NAST 10 miles) Etf.

TOTLAND (Isle of Wight)

SKLARROF 0983 754960
Craglea, The Broadway, Totland, Isle of Wight.
Mon-Sat, 10-5, Sun in summer, clsd Wed
Med size R/C/D stk, ab av cal, cnd & prices. Emphon M Peeke, Mod 1sts and signed bks. TWC.

TOTNES

PEDLARS PACK 0803 866423
4 The Plains, Totnes, Devon.
Mon-Sat, 9-5
Med size R/C stk, ab av cal & Cnd, av prices. Looks v hopeful. BR: Totnes, Oos turn left onto main road & follow signs for town ctr & turn left at bottom of hill. SIOR.

COLLARDS BOOKSHOP 0548 550246
4 Castle Street, Totnes, Devon TQ9 5NU.
Mon-Sat, 10-5, less in winter
Med/lg R/C stk, ab av cal & av prices. Emphon Detective Fiction. TWC. P.diff. BR: Totnes, oos and directly ahead up hill towards castle.

HARLEQUIN 0803 866406
41 High Street, Totnes, Devon TQ9 5NP.
Mon-Sat, 9-5.30
New bksp with small stk of low key Childrens bks. Av cnd & prices. From Collards, Oosh, turn left & left down hill, SIOR.

THE MAGPIE 0548 830082(HM)
Rotherford Sq (No no), Totnes, Devon.
Mon-Sat, 10-5, clsd Wed & Thur
Antq shp with BTA stk of bks & ephemera. Despite being the least prepossessing it looks the most hopeful in Totnes. TWC & D. P.poss. From Harlequin, Oosh turn right, keep to left going out of town & turn left at The Bull Pub, SIOL.

THE BOOKSHOP BY THE ARCH* 0803 864088
72 Fore Street, Totnes, Devon.
Mon-Sat, 9.30-5.30, EC Thurs
Small/med R/C stk, Literace. Av cnd & prices. TWC. From Pedlars Pack, Oosh turn left & left up hill & SIOL.

TOTTEN

Totten, Hampshire. Shop rumoured to be opening. NFDA.

TRURO

JUST BOOKS 0872 42532
9 Pindar Mews, Truro, Cornwall TR1 2UX.
Mon-Sat, 10-5, clsd Thurs
Med size R/C stk, av cal, cnd & prices. TWC.

TUNBRIDGE WELLS

HALL'S BOOKSHOP 0892 27842
20 Chapel Place, Tunbridge Wells, TN1 1YQ.
Mon-Sat, 9.30-5
Med/lg R/C/D stk, av cal, cnd & prices. BR: Tunbridge Wells, Oos on town side, turn right, right over bridge & left.

BASKERVILLE BOOKS 0892 26776
13 Nevill Street, Tunbridge Wells, TN2 5RU.
Mon-Sat, 10-5, clsd Wed
Med size R/C stk, fast T/O & int. BR: Tunbridge Wells, Oos opp to town side & turn left & cont.

There are also two bookstls in the Pantiles.

TWICKENHAM

See LONDON

TYWYN, Wales

TOWN & GOWN BOOKSHOP **0341 250542**
9 Seafront Arcade, Tywyn, Gwynned, Wales LL36 ODG.
Every day in summer, BTR in winter
Med size R stk. Low key.

ULVERSTON

THE OLD STORYTELLERS BOOKSHOP **NOW CLOSED**

UPPINGHAM

GOLDMARK BOOKS **0572 822694**
Orange Street, Uppingham, Rutland LE15 9QH.
Mon-Sat, 9-5
Med/lg R/C stk, av cal, cnd & prices. BR: Oakham (NAST 10 miles).

NOT JUST BOOKS **0572 821306**
Market Place, Uppingham, Rutland LE15 9QH.
Mon-Sat, 9-5
Med/lg R stk, av cal, cnd, highish prices.

THE RUTLAND BOOKSHOP **0572 823450**
13 High Street West, Uppingham, Rutland.
Tues-Sat, 11-5.30, L: 1-2.15
Med size R/C stk. Spec in HSF. Av cal, cnd & prices.

UPTON UNDER SEVERN

GERSHOM WOOD **0684 583469**
31 Old Street, Upton under Severn, Hereford & Worcs.
Mon-Sat, 10-5, clsd Wed
Med size R/C stk, av cal, cnd & prices. NV. BR: Malvern, (NAST seven miles) ETF.

UXBRIDGE

See LONDON

VENTNOR (Isle of Wight)

THE VENTNOR BOOKSHOP **0983 853706**
19 Pier Street, Ventnor, Isle of Wight PO38 1ST.
Mon-Sat, 10-5, clsd Wed & Thur
Med size R/C/D stk, ab av cal, cnd & prices.

WAKEFIELD

LEO BOOKS **0924 365109**
4 Vicarage Street, Wakefield, W. Yorks WF1 1QX.
Mon-Sat, 9.30-5, clsd Wed
Med size R/C drif/Stokers Special, av cal, cnd & prices. BR: Wakefield Westgate, Oos, turn left into town, turn 1st left at Paved zone & right to bottom & left.

WALLINGFORD

TOBY ENGLISH **0491 36389**
Lamb Arcade, Wallingford, Oxon OX10 OBS.
Mon-Sat, 10-4.30
Med/lg R/C/D stk. Keen on SF and Fantasy. Ab av cal, cnd & prices. BR: Oxford (NAST 10 miles). Shop is upstairs in Antiques Arcade, etf at crossroads.

WALSINGHAM

PILGRIMS PROGRESS **032882 0399**
51 High Street, Walsingham, Norfolk NR22.
Mon-Sun, 7.30-7.30 summer, winter 2-5
Med size R/C stk. Av cal, cnd & prices. BR: Norwich (NAST 10 miles) Etf.

WAREHAM

ST JOHNS HILL BOOKS **09295 2577**
2 St Johns Hill, Wareham, Dorset.
Tues,Thur,Sat 10-5
Med size R/C stk, av cal, cnd & prices. Recently changed hands, NV. BR: Wareham, Oos turn right into town, at top of main street turn left & come back on yourself.

WARWICK

DUNCAN ALLSOP **0926 493266**
26 Smith Street, Warwick, CV34 4HS.
Mon-Sat, 9.30-5.30
Med/lg R/C/D stk, Roast Beef/Helen Hanff Special. Etf in ctr of town. Whatever you do, do NOT use the railway.

ANTICUS **0926 402004**
11 Old Square, Warwick, no postcode.
Mon-Sat, 10.30-6
Small C/Tourist's stk, newly opened. Ab av prices. Discussions. TWC. P.diff. From Allsop Oosh, turn left, first left past crossroads & opp Parish Church.

WATERFORD, Eire

BOOKWORM **NO PHONE**
Michael St (No no), Waterford.
Mon-Sat, 10-5
Med size drif special where the non-Irish bks are cast into oblivion (i.e. never more than £5). IR: Waterford, oos, cross bridge, ahead turn first left into shopping St, cont to end & turn right, SIOL at far end.

GLADSTONES **NO PHONE**
12 Gladstone Street, Waterford.
Mon-Sat 10-6, Sun 2-6, Fri - 9pm
Primarily a rmndr shop with a small stk of s/h. NESHBS only included in this part because it is open on Sunday.

WAYTOWN

HARE AND HOUNDS PUB **NOW CLOSED**

WELLINGBOROUGH

THE PARK BOOKSHOP **0933 222592**
12 Park Road, Wellingborough, Northamptonshire NN8 4PG.
Mon-Sat, 10-5, clsd Thur
Med size R/C stk, av cal, cnd & prices. TWC. P.poss. BR: Wellingborough, Oos turn right into town & right at end & straight ahead (1 1/2 miles).

WELLS

COURTYARD BOOKS **0749 07112**
Old Palace Yard, Priory Road, Wells, Somerset.
Mon-Sat, 10-5
Med/lg R/C bks. Ab av cal, av cnd & prices.

WELLS NEXT SEA

COOK **0328 710419**
65 Snaithe Street, Wells next Sea, Norfolk NR23 1AN.
Mon-Sun, 10-5, less in winter
Small R stk, ab av cal, cnd, av prices.

WELSHPOOL, Wales

CELLAR OF BOOKS **0686 650670** (Hm)
Hopkins Passage (No no), Welshpool, Powys, Wales.
Mon-Sat, 10.30-5.30
Small R/C stk, low key. NSOC. drif/silverfish special. TWC. P.poss. BR: Welshpool oos ahead & turn right into alley opp Oxfam.

WESTCLIFFE ON SEA

BARRIE ELLEN **0702 338763**
262 London Road, Westcliffe on Sea, Essex SS9 7JR.
Mon-Sat, 9.30-5.30, clsd Wed
Med size R/C stk, emphon Chess. Av cal, cnd &prices. TWC.

WESTERHAM

TAYLOR SMITH **0959 63100**
2 High Street, Westerham, Kent.
Mon-Sat, 10-5, Sun 2-6
Shop has recently moved to seperate premises from Antique shp & is near the Green. BR: Bromley (NAST 10 miles).

There are also two other antique shps with bks in Westerham.

WEST KIRBY

BOOKENDS **051 6256389**
4 Hilbre Road, West Kirby, Merseyside L48 7HD.
Mon-Sat, 10-4, L: 1-2
Med size R/C stk, av cal, cnd & prices.

WESTLETON

CHAPEL BOOKS 0728 73616
Westleton, Suffolk IP17 3AA.
usually opens 7 days a week 11-6 in summer, but always Sat & Sun at least.
Lg size R/C stk, av cal, cnd & prices. T.

WEST MALLING

FOXED AND BOUND 0732 847886
8 West Street, West Malling, Kent ME19 8QU.
Tues-Sat, 10-5
Med size R/C stk, av cal, cnd, ab av prices. Emphon Biography, folklore and Childrens.

WESTON SUPER MARE

STERLING BOOKS 0934 625056
43A Locking Road, Weston Super Mare, Avon BS23 3DG.
Mon-Sat, 9-6, L: 1-2, clsd Thurs
Lg R/C/D stk, ab av cal, cnd & prices. BR: Weston Super Mare, Oos turn right, left into main road & right at Locking Rd. SIOL.

MANNA BOOKS 0934 626228]
30 Orchard Street, Weston Super Mare BS23 1BQ
Mon-Sat, 10-5, clsd Wed
Med size R/C stk, emphon Alternative & Esoteric. Av cal, cnd & prices. From Sterling Bks, Oosh, turn right & third right. SIOR.

SEVERN BOOKS 0934 635389
48 Severn Road, Weston Super Mare BS23 1DT.
Mon-Sat, 10-5, Sun in summer.
Med size R/C stk, av cal, cnd & prices. BR: Weston Supermare, Oos, turn left, follow rd through to main road, turn left, cont & left.

WETHERBY

WORDS & MUSIC 0937 66009
Church Street (No no), Wetherby, Yorkshire.
Mon-Sat 10-5.30, clsd Wed
New bksp with small upstairs rm of s/h R/C stk, av cal, cnd & prices. TWC. P.poss. BR: Harrogate (NAST 10 miles). Etf by church.

WEYMOUTH

BOOKS AFLOAT **0305 779774**
66 Park Street, Weymouth, Dorset DT4 7DE.
Tues-Sat, 9.30-5.30
Med size R/C/D stk, Spec in Maritime. Ab av cal, cnd, av prices. BR: Weymouth, Oos directly ahead across car park. SIOL.

QUEST BOOKS **0305 789142**
13A Cove Street, Weymouth, Dorset.
Mon-Sat, 10.30-5.30, L: 1-2, Unr
Small R stk. Av cal, cnd & prices. From above, Oosh, turn left, turn left at bottom & right into High Street, cont over bridge, turn left by quay & second right. SIOR.

WHITBY

CUVVIN BOOKS **0947 880561**
1 Grape Lane, Whitby, N Yorkshire.
Mon-Sat, 10.30-5.30
Small/med size R/C stk, low key primarily pbks, av cal, cnd & prices. TWC. P.diff. BR: Whitby, oos follow seafront round to right & over bridge, turn right.

WHITCHURCH

THE PARISH BOOKSHOP **0948 4115**
47 High Street, Whitchurch, Shropshire SY13 1AZ
Tues-Sat 10-5.30.

BARN BOOKS **0948 3742**
Pear Tree Farm, Norbury, Shropshire SY13 4HZ
Fri 2-6, Sat 10-6, Sun 2-6.
Med size R/C stk, mainly rural bks.

WHITEHAVEN

MICHAEL MOON **0946 62936**
41-43 Roper Street, Whitehaven, Cumbria CA25 7BS.
Mon-Sat, 9.30-5
V lg R/C/D stk. Ab av cal, cnd & prices.

WHITSTABLE

BOOKS AND PIECES **NO PHONE**
48 Oxford Road, Whitstable, Kent.
Mon-Sat, 10-5, clsd Wed pm
Small/med size R/nrly C stk. Av cal, cnd & prices. BR: Whitstable, Oos turn right, follow road into town & right under bridge, SIOL. NV.

WIGAN

THE BOOK HOUSE **NOW CLOSED**

WILLITON

BLACKMORES BOOKSHOP **0984 32227**
6 High Street, Williton, Somerset TA4 4NW.
Mon-Sat, 9-5.30, clsd Sat 1pm
Primarily a cafe with bks. I liked the coffee.

WINCHESTER

PETER M DALY **0962 867732**
10A Jewry Street, Winchester SO23 8EZ.
Wed,Fri,Sat 10-5, L: 1-2, clsd Sat 1pm
Small/med R/C/D stk. Emphon Natural Hist, Mountaineering, Travel. Av cal, cnd & prices. BR: Winchester, Oos directly ahead, follow stream of traffic to right & shop is on right at rear of antiques arcade.

OXFAM BOOKSHOP **0992 583221(Hm)**
73 Parchment Street, Winchester, Hants.
Mon-Sat, 10-4
Med sized charity bksp, av cal, cnd & prices. No T. From Daly, oosh turn right & first left & left.

GILBERTS **0962 852832**
19 The Square, Winchester SO23 9BY.
Mon-Sat, 9-5.30
New bksp with med size R/C stk. Av cal, cnd & prices. From Oxfam, Oosh, turn left & left, right at High St & left past statue. SIOL.

Round the corner to the left is an SPCK with a small amount of s/h bks.

BOOKS AND THINGS **NOW CLOSED**

Newly opened bookfairy shop. NV.

WINGHAM

LLOYDS **0227 720774**
27 High Street, Wingham, Kent CT3 1AW.
Mon-Sat, 9.30-5, L: 1-2.15
Med size R/C stk, av cal, cnd & prices.

WITHAM

BALDWIN'S BOOKS **0376 83502**
Fossill Hall, Boars Tye Road, Silver End, Witham, Essex CM8 3QA.
BTR
Spec in Geology, Paleontogy and Archaeology.

WIVELSCOMBE

WIVEY BOOKS **0984 23506**
1 High Street, Wivelscombe, Somerset.
Some dispute about the opening hours, btr
Med size R/C stk, almost a drif special. Av cal, cnd & prices. NV & rumours that its closed.

WOLVERHAMPTON

BERRY STREET BOOKSHOP **0902 28939**
35 Berry Street, Wolverhampton.
Mon-Fri, 10-5
Med size R/C stk, low key, av cnd & prices. Oos, turn left & first right.

BOOKSTACK **0902 21055**
53 Bath Road, Wolverhampton, W Midlands WV1 4EL.
Mon-Sat, 11-5, Rel
Med/lg R/C stk, av cal, NSOC, av prices. TWC. Oos ahead to ring road, turn right & 1st left & left.

WOODBRIDGE

BLAKES **0394 380302**
88 The Thoroughfare, Woodbridge, Suffolk IP13 1AL.
Mon-Sat, 9.30-5
Med size R/C stk, av cal, cnd & prices. BR: Woodbridge, Oos towards town & look for alleyway to right, into High St turn left & SIOL.

WOODSTOCK

THE WOODSTOCK BOOKSHOP **0993 811005**
3 Market Place, Woodstock, Oxfordshire, OX7 1SY.
Mon-Sat, 10-5, L: 1-2
Med size C/D stk, Spec in OUP bks. Ab av cal, cnd & prices. BR: Oxford (NAST 10 miles).

THE AFTERNOON BOOKSHOP **0993 813445**
21 Oxford Street, Woodstock, Oxon OX7 1TN.
Mon-Sat, 12-5
Small C shp. Ab av cal, cnd, av prices. Etf.

WOOLER

THE WOOLER BOOKSHOP **NO PHONE**
High Street, Wooler, Northumberland.
Mon-Sat, 10-5
Med size R/C stk, NSOC, strange pricing. Etf.

WORCESTER

HOLBOURNE BOOKS **0905 27824**
67 Upper Tything, Worcester WR1 1JX.
Mon-Sat, 10-5
Med/lg R/C/D stk, av cal, cnd and prices. BR: Worcester/ Foregate St, Oos turn left, SIOL half a mile.

ANDREW BOYLE **0905 611700**
21 Friar Street, Worcester WR1 2NA.
Now an "unbookshop"
Med size C/D stk, emphon childrens bks. Not strictly a bksp and it is also rumoured to be closing down.

GRADUATE BOOKS AND RECORDS **0905 723959**
65 Sidbury, Worcester WH1 2HU.
Mon-Sat, 10.30-5.30.
Med size R/C stk in Record shop. Av cal, cnd & prices.

WORTHING

THE STEYNE BOOKSHOP **0903 206216**
5 High Street, Worthing, W. Sussex BN11 1NY.
Mon-Sat, 10-5.30
Lg R/C/D stk, av cal, cnd & prices. BR: Worthing, Oos through shopping precinct towards seafront, turn left at clocktower & left into the High Street.

On the way is a Help The Aged with bkrm upstairs.

KIM'S BOOKSHOP **0903 206282**
33 West Buildings, Worthing, W. Sussex BN11.
Mon-Sat, 10-5.15
Med/lg R/C stk, ab av cal, cnd, av prices. Keen on Nat Hist and Orchids. From Steyne Bks, Oosh turn right, right & cont past clocktower & third left. SIOR.

BADGERS **0903 211816**
8-10 Gratwicke Road, Worthing, W Sussex BN11 3BS.
Mon-Sat, 9.15-6
Lg R/C stk, emphon Occult. Av cal, cnd & prices. From Kim's, Oosh, turn left & left & third right.

WREXHAM, Wales

TEG'S BOOKS **0978 354224**
3 King Street, Wrexham, Clwyd
Mon-Sat, 10-5, clsd Wed
Newly opened Small/med size R/nrly C stk. Literace. Gd cnd. BR: Wrexham Central, oos into town, turn left at signs for Bus station.

GLYN'S BOOKS **0978 355797**
Bryn Mawr Arcade, Wrexham, Clwyd LL13 8LL
Mon-Sat, 10-5.
Med size R/C stk. Av cal, cnd & prices. Emphon Mod 1sts.

DOUG MILLS **NO PHONE**
New Market, Chester Street, Wrexham, Wales.
Mon-Sat, 10-5
BTA Market stall, av cnd, low prices, TWC. P.diff. From Teg's turn left oosh.

WYMONDHAM

A C & M THOMPSON **0953 602244**
1 Town Green, Wymondham, Norfolk NR18 OPN.
Mon-Sat, 10.15-5. Rel
Med size R/C stk, av cal, ab av cnd, av prices.

TURRET HOUSE BOOKS **0953 603462**
27 Middleton Street, Wymondham, Norfolk NR18 OAB.
Mon-Sat, 9-6
Med size spec in Science and Microscope bks. Some general bks. Av cal, cnd & prices.

YARMOUTH

THE OUT TO LUNCH BOOKSHOP **0983 760851**
High Street (No no), Yarmouth, Isle of Wight.
Fri, Sat 10-4, L: 12.30-1.30, Sun 1-4
Med size R/C stk, emphon Nat Hist. Av cal, cnd & prices.

YEOVIL

Rumours of new bksp with s/h bks upstairs. NFDA.

YORK

O'FLYNN'S **0904 641404**
35 Micklegate, York YO1 1JH.
Mon-Sat, 9-5.30
Print shp with med size stk of C bks & Plate bks. Looks like a Helen Hanff Special. T & D. Etgow. P.imposs. BR: York, oos turn left & follow signs for City Centre. Shop is ahead of you.

BARBICAN BOOKSHOP **0904 653643**
24 Fossgate, York, YO1 2TA.
Mon-Sat, 9-5.30, Rel
New Specialist stk with some s/h Theology upstairs. Av cal, cnd &prices. TWC. P.diff. From O'Flynns oosh, cont straight along, over bridge, through three name changes & turn right.

JACK DUNCAN **0904 641389**
56 Fossgate, York, YO1 2TF.
Mon-Sat, 10-5.30
Lg C/D stk, emphon Lit, Hist & Music. Bookfairyish at best. TWC. Directions as Barbican.

INCH'S BOOKS **0904 627082**
82 The Mound, York, YO2 2SR.
Mon-Fri, 10.30-5
Newly listed, specialist. Modern Art & Architecture stock. High Cal, high prices, high cnd. More welcoming than most Spec shops. T. P.poss. BR: York oos turn right up ramp & round to left of city walls and turn right by arch, SIOR. Looks like a private house.

MINSTER GATES BOOKSHOP **0904 621812**
4 Minstergates, York, YO1 2HL.
Mon-Sat, 10.30-5.30
Med size Literace. Not designed for R/C or D's. From Fossgate go back towards cathedral & turn right towards it. SIOR.

OBLONG BOOKS **0904 631375**
Mickelgate, York
Mon-Sat, 10.30-5.30
Newly opened R/C stk, v small emphon pbks/Students (must think of a word for this - poss pseuds) stock, low prices. TWC. P.poss. From Inch's turn left, oosh into centre of York.

PASSAGEWAY BOOK ROOM **0532 754698**
38C Fossgate, York, YO1 2TA.
Thur-Sat, 10.30-4
Newly opened. Med size R/C/D stk of int bks, lower than av York prices. T. P.imposs. SIOL at bottom of alleyway.

KEN SPELMAN **0904 624414**
70 Micklegate, York, YO1 1LF.
Mon-Sat, 9-5.30
Lg C/D stk, solid Roast Beef. Emphon Lit & Hist. Ab av cal, cnd, av prices. Res stk of D bks by request. TWC. P.diff. BR York, oos to right, follow ramp round city walls & turn left into Micklegate. SIOL.

STONE TROUGH **0904 670323**
58 Fossgate, York, YO1 2TY.
Tues-Sat, 10.30-5.30
Newly listed. C/D stk, emphon Lit & Mod 1sts. Ab av cal, cnd, av prices. T. Directions as Barbican.

TAIKOO **0904 641213**
29 High Petergate, York YO1 2HP.
Mon-Fri 10-5 but owner says btr
Spec Middle East/Africa/Oriental/Travel bks. V. high cal, v high prices. T. WAD. P.imposs.

YOXFORD

R H BOOKS **072877 439**
High St (No no), Yoxford, Suffolk P17 3EP.
Tues-Sat, 10-5, less in Winter
Small/med size R/C stk, keen on Lit. Av cnd & prices. BR: Halesworth (NAST 10 miles). Etf.

Second shop in Yoxford opened and closed at will.

* * * * * * * * * * * * * * * *

L O N D O N

ALDWYCH

THE ECONOMISTS BOOKSHOP **071 405 8643**
Clare Street (No no), London WC2A 2AB
Mon-Sat, 10-5
New bksp with small Spec stk of s/h Economics bks. Av cal, cnd & prices. Tube Aldwych, Oos ahead to right & right at Kingsway & right.

ARNOS GROVE

DENIS CAINE (ansaphone) **081 348 4888**
343 Bowes Road, London N11 1AA
Mon-Sat, 10-5
Med size R/C stk, av cal, cnd & prices. Opp Arnos Grove tube.

BALHAM

MY BACK PAGES **081 769 4851**
879 Balham Station Road, London SW12
Mon-Sat, 10.30-7.30 Rel
Med/lg R/C stk, av cal, cnd & prices. Emphon rmndrs. Tube: Balham, Oos turn right.

BATTERSEA

THE HOUSE HOSPITAL **NO PHONE**
68 Battersea High St., London SW4
Tues-Sat, 10-5
Small R/C stk, has room of bks. Newly opened. NV.

BAYSWATER

BAYSWATER BOOKS **071 402 7398**
27A Craven Terrace, London W2 3EL
Mon-Sat, 11-7
Small gen stk, av cal, cnd & prices. Tube: Lancaster Gate, Oos turn right & third right.

BELSIZE PARK

VILLAGE BOOKSHOP **071 794 3180**
41 Belsize Lane, London NW3
Mon-Sat, 11-5.30
Med size R/C stk, av cal, NSOC. Av prices. Tube: Belsize Park, Oos, turn right & left at Ornan Rd & cont.

+ second shop.

BLACKHEATH

BOOKSHOP BLACKHEATH **081 852 4786**
74 Tranquil Vale, London SE3 OBN
Mon-Sat, 9.30-5
Med/lg R/C stk, av cal, cnd & prices. BR: Blackheath, Oos turn left & keep to left.

STUDIO BOOKS **081 318 9666**
2 Montpelier Vale, London SE3 1TA
Sat only 11-6
Med/lg R/C stk, av cal, cnd & prices. Opp Blackheath Stn to left.

BLOOMSBURY

MARCHMONT BOOKSHOP **071 387 7989**
39 Burton Street, London WC1H 9AL
Mon-Fri, 11-6.30
Med size R/C stk, av cal, cnd & prices. Tube: Euston, Oos ahead to church, shop is at rear.

COLLINGE & CLARKE 071 387 7105
13 Leigh Street, London WC1H 8EW
Mon-Sat, 11-6.30, Sat 3.30
Med size C/D stk, spec in Private Press. Emphon Art & Hist. Av cal, cnd & prices. BR & Tube: Euston, Oos ahead past church & turn left.

WORLD OF BOOKS 071 436 0027
39 Woburn Place, Adjacent Royal Hotel.
Mon-Sat, 11-7
Med size R/C stk, emphon Hist. Av cal, cnd & prices. Tube: Euston, Oos straight ahead.

SKOOB BOOKS 071 404 3063
15 Sicilian Ave, London WC1A 2QH
Mon-Sat, 10.30-6.30
Lg R/C stk, av cal, cnd & prices. Emphon Acad Text & Lit. Next door is Occult Bksp.

DILLONS 071 636 1577
82 Gower Street, London WC2E 6EQ
Mon-Fri, 9.30-7.30, Sat 5.30
Lg C/D stk, Acad orientated. Ab av cal, cnd & prices.

ROBERT CONNELLY 071 430 1394
31/35 Gt. Ormond Street, London WC1N 3HZ
Mon-Fri, 12-6
Small Spec stk devoted to Medical and Scientific bks. Ab av cal, cnd & prices. A Consultancy rather than a General Practitionery. Tube: Russell Sq, oos turn right & right, past roundabout, ahead & right.

FREW MACKENZIE 071 580 2311
106 Gt. Russell Street, London WC1B 3HA
Mon-Fri, 10-6, Sat 10-2
Med size C/D stk, ab av cal, cnd & prices. Emphon Antqrn, Bindings & Sets. Tube: Tottenham Crt Rd, oos towards British Museum & turn right, SIOL.

MUSEUM BOOKSHOP 071 580 4086
36 Gt. Russell Street, London WC1E 3PP
Mon-Fri, 10-5.30, Sat 11-5.30
Med size Spec in Archaeology. Ab av cal, cnd & prices.

GREAT RUSSELL STREET BOOKS 071 637 7635
44 Gt. Russell Street, London WC1B 3PA
Mon-Fri, 10.30-5.30, Sat 12-3
Med size C/D stk. Av cal, cnd & prices. Emphon Antqrn & Prints.

FINE BOOKS ORIENTAL **071 636 6068**
46 Gt. Russell Street, London WC1B EPE
Mon-Fri, 9.30-5.30
Med/lg Spec in Middle East & Oriental. Ab av cal, cnd, av prices.

ULYSSES **071 637 5862**
31 Museum Street, London WC1A 1LH
Mon-Sat, 10.30-6, Sun 12-6
Med/lg C/D stk, ab av cal, cnd & prices. Emphon Travel, Art & Mod 1sts. TWC. (see Addendum)

BLOOMSBURY RARE BOOKS **071 636 8206**
29 Museum Street, London WC1A 1LH
Now ROE ART BOOKS.

ATLANTIS **071 405 2120**
48 Museum Street, London WC1A 1LE
Mon-Fri, 10-5.30, Sat 11-5
Med size Spec shp of Esoteric & Occult. Av cal, cnd & prices.

VANBRUGH RARE BOOKS **071 404 0733**
40A Museum Street, London WC1
Mon-Sat, 10.30-5.30
Small Spec stk of Antqrn & bks on Wine. Ab av cal, cnd, av prices.

BALLANTYNE & DATE **071 242 4249**
38 Museum Street, London WC1A 1LP
Sat,Sun 11-4
Med size C/D stk, ab av cal, cnd & prices. Emphon Industrial Hist & Art.

LOUIS BONDY **071 405 2733**
16 Little Russell Street, London WC1A 2HN
Mon-Fri, 10.30-6.30, Sat 10.30-5.30
Small C/D stk, ab av cal, av cnd & prices. Emphon Caricature, Miniatures.

SKOOB TWO **NOW CLOSED**

DAVID MAYOU **NOW CLOSED**

CENTRAL BOOKS **NOW CLOSED**

GAY'S THE WORD **071 278 7654**
66 Marchmont Street, London WC1N 1AB
Mon-Sat, 11-7, Sun 2-6
Med size new bksp spec in Homosexual bks. Mainly new. V. small s/h stk.

BOND STREET

SARAH BADDIEL **071 408 1239**
Grays Two, Davies Mews, London W1
Mon-Fri, 10-6
Small stl, Spec in Golf. Tube: Bond St, oos turn right.

S. DICKENSON **071 629 3644**
A18/A19 Grays Antique Mkt, 1-7 Davies Mews, London W1Y 1AA
Mon-Fri, 11-4.30
Med sized Spec in Chess, ab av cal, cnd & prices.

BROMLEY

THE BROMLEY BOOKSHOP **081 313 0242**
39 High Street, Bromley, Kent BR1 1LE
Mon-Sat, 10-5
Med size R/C stk, av cal, cnd & prices. BR: Bromley, Oos turn right SIOR in alleyway.

CAMBERWELL

THE CAMBERWELL BOOKSHOP **081 701 1839**
28 Camberwell Grove, London SE5 8RE
Tues-Sat, 10-6
Med size spec in Art Reference and Design. Av cal, cnd & prices. Tube Elephant & Castle & Bus (NAST 2 miles)

CAMDEN TOWN

THE ABBEY BOOKSHOP **PHONE UNKNOWN**
New Market Hall, Camden Lock, Chalk Farm Road, NW1 8AF
Mon-Fri, 11-5, Sat & Sun 10-6
Newly opened R/C stk, keen on Irish. Tube: Camden Town, oos turn right, SIOL in arcade.

Other bookstalls in this market on Saturday and Sunday.

CARSHALTON (Croydon)

THE CROYDON BOOKSHOP **081 643 6857**
304 Carshalton Road, London SM5 3QB
Tues-Sat, 10.30-5.30
Med/lg R/C stk, av cal, cnd & prices.

CHALK FARM

OFFSTAGE **071 485 4996**
37 Chalk Farm Road, London NW1 8AJ
Tues-Sat, 10-5.30, Sun 2-5.30
New bksp with v small Theatrical stk.

TOSSIE STICKLE **NOW CLOSED**

WALDEN BOOKS **071 267 8146**
38 Harmood Street, London NW1 8DP
Thurs-Sun, 10.30-6.30
Med size R/C stk, av cal, cnd & prices.

CHARING CROSS

BOOK PEDLAR **NO PHONE**
148 Charing Cross Road, London WC2
Mon-Sat, 10.30-5.30
Remndr shop with small R/C stk in bsmt.

ZENO **071 836 2522**
6 Denmark Street, London WC2H 8LP
Mon-Sat, 9.30-5.30, Sat 5
Med size Spec in Greek bks.

SHIPLEY **071 836 4872**
70 Charing Cross Rd, London WC2H OBB
Mon-Sat 10-6
Claims to be a s/h Art Dealer, but I have never been able to work out which are the s/h bks.

ANY AMOUNT OF BOOKS **071 240 8140**
62 Charing Cross Rd, London WC2H OBB
Mon-Sun, 10.30-7.30
Med size R/C/D stk, av cal, cnd & prices.

MURDER ONE **071 734 3483**
71-73 Charing Cross Rd, London WC2
Mon-Sat, 10-7
New bksp with lg Spec stk of True Crime & Detective Fiction. Ab av cal, cnd & prices.

PORDES **071 836 9031**
58-60 Charing Cross Rd, London WC2H OBB
Mon-Sat, 10-7
Med size R/C stk, av cal, cnd & prices. Emphon Rmndrs.

CHARING CROSS RD BOOKSHOP **071 836 3697**
56 Charing Cross Road, London WC2
Mon-Sat, 10.30-9
Med/lg R/C/D stk, fast turnover, ab av cal, cnd, av prices. WAD.

QUINTO **071 379 7669**
48A Charing Cross Road, London WC2
Mon-Sun, 10-7.30
Lg R/C stk, bl av cal, cnd, ab av prices, well worth avoiding. TWC.

FRANCES EDWARDS **071 379 7669**
13 Gt. Newport Street, London WC2H 7JA
Mon-Sat, 10.30-7
Med size Spec in Military Hist. Av cal. Bl av cnd. Ab av prices.

ALAN BRETT **071 836 8222**
24 Cecil Court, Charing Cross Rd, London WC2 4HE
Mon-Fri, 9.30-5, Sat & Sun 9-5
Med sized Spec in Prints & Ill bks. Libricide.

ANN CREED **071 836 7757**
22 Cecil Court, Charing Cross Rd, London WC2N 4HE
Mon-Sat, 10-7 Rel
Med/lg Spec in Art Reference & Design. Ab av cal, cnd & prices.

REG & PHILIP REMINGTON **071 836 9771**
18 Cecil Court, Charing Cross Rd, London WC2N 4HE
Mon-Fri, 10-5
Med size Spec in Travel & Topography. Ab av cal, cnd & prices.

MARCHPANE **071 836 8661**
16 Cecil Court, Charing Cross Rd, London WC2N 4HE
Mon-Sat, 11-7
Med size Spec in Childrens bks, av cal, cnd & prices.

PAUL HILTON **071 379 9825**
12 & 14 Cecil Court, Charing Cross Rd, London WC2N 4EE
Mon-Sat, 10-7
Med size R/C/D stk, av cal, cnd & prices. Emphon Lit and Antqrn.

THE CLEARING HOUSE **NO PHONE**
10 Cecil Court, Charing Cross Rd, London WC2N 4HE
Mon-Sun, 9-9
Med size R/C stk all £1.50 each.

BELL BOOK & RADMALL **071 836 5888**
4 Cecil Court, Charing Cross Rd, London WC2M 4HE
Mon-Fri, 10-5.30
Med size Spec in Mod 1sts. Ab av cal, cnd & prices.

E C NOLAN **071 497 2328**
1 Cecil Court, Charing Cross Rd, London WC2N 4EZ
BTR
Small Spec stk in bsmt of Print deaalers.

DANCE BOOKS **071 836 2314**
9 Cecil Court, Charing Cross Rd, London WC2N 4EZ
Mon-Sat, 11-7
Med size Spec in Dance, but I have never worked out which are the s/h bks.

PLEASURES OF PAST TIMES **071 836 1142**
11 Cecil Court, Charing Cross Rd, London
Mon-Fri, 11-5.45, L: 2.30-3.30
Med size Spec in Performing Arts, ab av cal, cnd & prices.

TRAVIS & EMERY **071 240 2129**
17 Cecil Court, Charing Cross Rd, London WC2N 4EZ
Mon-Fri, 10-6, Sat 1pm, Rel
Med size Spec in Classical Music. Ab av cal, cnd & prices.

WATKINS **071 836 2182**
10-21 Cecil Court, Charing Cross Rd, London WC2N 4EZ
Mon-Sat, 10-6
Med size new bksp with Spec stk of s/h Occult & Esoteric. Av cal, cnd & prices.

THE TRAVELLERS BOOKSHOP **071 836 9132**
23 Cecil Court, Charing Cross Rd, London WC2N 4EZ
Mon-Sat, 10-6.30
Med size Spec in Baedeckers. Ab av cal, cnd & prices.

H M FLETCHER **NOW CLOSED**
Replaced by Food For Thought. WAD.

CHEAM (Surrey)

THE WHITEHALL BOOKSHOP **081 643 8272**
45 The Broadway, Cheam, Surrey
Mon-Sat, 9.30-5.30, Wed 1pm
Med size R/C stk, av cal cnd & prices. Oos, under tunnel & into town. SIOL.

CHELSEA

THORNTON'S **PHONE UNKNOWN**
now moved to 455 Fulham Road, London SW3
Mon-Sat, 10-5.45
Med/lg R/C/D stk. Av cal, cnd & prices. Emphon Religious bks.
Tube: Sloane Sq, oos ahead.

CHELSEA RARE BOOKS **071 351 0950**
313 Kings Road, London SW3 5EP
Mon-Sat, 10-6
Med size C/D stk, ab av cal cnd & prices.

HARRINGTON BORTHERS **071 352 5689**
253 Kings Road, London SW3 5EL
Mon-Sat, 10-6
Lg C/D stk Plate bks. Voyages, Nat Hist, Sets.

BARBARA STONE **071 351 0963**
Antiquarius 135 Kings Road, London SW3 4PW
Mon-Sat, 10.30-5.30
Lg stall Childrens and Ill bks. Ab av cal, cnd & prices.

THE WORLD'S END BOOKSHOP **071 352 9376**
357 Kings Road, London SW3
Mon-Sun, 10.30-6.30
Med size R/C stk, av cal, strange quality, av prices. TWC.
From Chelsea Rare Books, oosh turn left.

CHISWICK

FAIRCROSS BOOKS **081 994 1912**
166 Thames Road, Strand On The Green, London W4
Mon-Sun, 10.30-5.30
Med size R/C stk in Antq shp, ab av cal cnd & prices for antq shp.

W FOSTER **081 994 2768**
183 Chiswick High Road, London W4
Mon-Sat, 10.30-5.30
Med size R/C/D stk, ab av cal, cnd, av prices. T discounts over £50.

THE CITY

WILDY & SON **071 242 5778**
Lincoln's Inn Archway, Carey St, London WC2A 3JD
Mon-Fri, 8.45-5.15
Spec shp of Law bks. Ab av cal, cnd, av prices. Tube: Chancery Lane, oos turn towards Centre Point & left into Chancery Lane & right into Carey St.

CLARKE HALL **071 353 4116**
7 Bride Court, Bride Lane, London EC4Y 8DU
Mon-Fri, 10.30-6.30
Med size R/C/D stk, av cal, cnd & prices. Emphon Mod 1sts, Ills and Samuel Johnson.

ASH RARE BOOKS **071 626 2665**
25 Royal Exchange, London EC3V 3LP
Mon-Fri, 10-5.30
Small C stk, ab av cal, cnd & prices. Emphon Prints. By Bank Station.

FARRINGDON ROAD BOOKSTALLS **NO PHONE**
London EC1
Mon-Fri, 11-3, Sat 10-12
The legend lives. Tube: Farringdon Road, oos turn right & right.

CLAPHAM

OLD TOWN BOOKS **071 498 0998**
30 Old Town, Clapham, London SW4 OLB
Mon-Sat, 10.30-6.30
Newly opened R/C stk, emphon Mod 1sts & Lit. Ab av cal, cnd &prices. T. P.poss. Tube: Clapham, Oos towards the pavement & follow round to bus stn. SIOL.

COVENT GARDEN

BERTRAM ROTA **071 836 0723**
9-11 Langley Court, Long Acre, London WC2H 9RX
Mon-Fri, 9.30-5.30
Med size Spec in Mod 1sts and Lit. Ab av cal, cnd & prices. Tube: Covent Garden, oos turn left into Long Acre & court is on left.

CRAYFORD

DARTFORD HEATH BOOKS **NO LONGER BOOKING**

CROUCH END

CROUCH END BOOKSHOP **081 348 8966**
60 Crouch End Hill, London N8 8AG
Mon-Sat, 9-6
New bksp with small R/C stk. Av cal cnd & prices. Tube: Finsbury Park & bus.

EALING

OXFAM BOOKSHOP **NO PHONE**
2 The Green, Ealing, London W5
Mon-Sat, 10.30-4
Small R stk, usual uncharitable prices. No T. Tube: Ealing Broadway, Oos turn left & cont south. SIOL.

G L GREEN **CLOSING 1 JULY**
Mail Order only.

EARLS COURT

RESPONSE **071 370 4606**
300 Brompton Road, London SW5 9JE
Mon-Sat, 12-7
Small R stk, bl av cal, cnd, ab av prices. No T. Tube: Earls Court, oos turn right (South) & right at Brompton Road.

EARLSFIELD

BOOKCELLAR **081 944 6458**
404 Garret Lane, Earlsfield, London SW18
Mon-Sat, 10-6
Med size R/C stk, slightly rmndry, av cal, cnd & prices. TWC. BR: Earlsfield, oos turn left, SIOR.

EAST MOLESEY (Surrey)

THE MOLE BOOKSHOP **0784 483467**
81 Walton Road, East Molesey, Surrey KT8 ODP
Sats only
Med size R/C stk, av cal, cnd & prices.

BROWSERS **NO PHONE**
74 Walton Road, East Molesey, Surrey
Tues-Sat, 10-5, clsd Wed
Small R stk, av cal, cnd & prices. BR: Hampton, follow sings for Molesey.

EDGWARE (Middlesex)

THE TWO JAYS **081 952 1349**
14 Whitchurch Lane, Middlesex, HA6 6JZ
Tues,Wed,Fri,Sat 10-5
Med size R/C/D stk, av cal, cnd & prices. Tube: Edgware oos turn left, cross main road, cont and SIOR.

BOOKMARK **081 952 1349**
67 High Street, Edgware, London
Tues,Thur,Fri,Sat 10-5.30
Med size R/C stk, av cal, cnd & prices. Tube: Edgware, Oos turn left & left into High St. SIOR.

ELEPHANT & CASTLE

MY BACK PAGES **081 769 4851**
Elephant & Castle Shopping Ctr, London SE1
Mon-Sat, 10.30-6.30
Med size R/C stk, Emphon pbks. Av cal, cnd & prices. Tube: E & C, cross to Shopping Ctr.

ENFIELD

THE ENFIELD BOOKSHOP **NO PHONE**
36 Gordon Road, Enfield, Middlesex EN2 OAN
Tues-Sat 10-5, clsd Thurs
Med size R/C stk, av cal, cnd & prices. BR: Enfield Town, oos turn left & right at crossroads & left at 2nd parade of shops. SIOR.

NORMAN ADAMS **081 364 4010**
72 St Marks Road, Bush Hill Park, Enfield EN1 1BB
Mon-Sat, 10-5, clsd Wed
Med size R/C stk, av cal, cnd & prices. TWC. P.poss. BR: Bush Hill Park oos ahead 500 yds & SIOR.

EPPING (Essex)

BROWSERS BOOKSHOP **0992 572260**
9 Station Road, Epping, Essex CM16 4HA
Mon,Tues,Thurs,Fri,Sat 10-5
Med size R/C stk, ab av cal, cnd & prices. Tube Epping, oos turn right & left at end.

EUSTON

FLINDERS **071 388 6080**
10 Woburn Walk, London WC1H OJL
Mon-Fri, 9.30-5.30, Sat 10-4
Med size Spec in Australiana. Av cal, cnd & prices. There is not much to say about Spec shps unless they are really bad. As I know nothing about Australia I am in no position to comment. Tube: Euston oos & left past church which abuts Euston Rd.

FINCHLEY

MANOR HOUSE BOOKS **081 349 9482**
80 East End Road, London N20 8HR
Mon-Thurs, 10-4, Sun 10-2
New bksp with small Spec stk of Judaica. Ab av cal, cnd & av prices.

MARTIN GLADMAN **081 343 3023**
235 Nether Street, Finchley, London N3 1NT
Tues-Fri, 11-8, Sat 10-6
Newly opened. Med/lg R/C stk, emphon Hist. Ab av cal, cnd, av prices. Etgow. P.poss. Tube: West Finchley, Oos turn left, SIOL.

FRIERN BARNET

THE HISTORY BOOKSHOP **NOW CLOSED**

FULHAM

THE CONSTANT READER **071 731 0218**
627 Fulham Road, London SW6 5DQ
Mon-Sat, 10.30-6.30, Sun 11.30-4
Med/lg R/C stk, av cal, cnd & not av prices. TWC. Tube: Fulham, oos turn right down Fulham Road.

GLOUCESTER ROAD

THE GLOUCESTER RD BOOKSHOP **071 370 3503**
123 Gloucester Road, London SW7 4TS
Mon-Fri, 8.30-10.30, Sat & Sun 10.30-6.30
Lg R/C stk, av cal, cnd & prices.

GREENWICH

MARITIME BOOKS **081 853 1727**
23 Nelson Road, London SE10 9JB
Mon-Sat, 10-6
Med size Spec in Maritime bks. Ab av cal, cnd & prices. BR: Greenwich, oos turn left & behind cinema to right.

ROGERS TURNER **081 853 5271**
27 Nelson Road, London SE10
Tues-Sun 10-6
Med size C/D stk, Spec in Clocks, Science & German. Ab av cal, cnd & prices.

MARCET BOOKS **081 853 5408**
4A Nelson Road, London SE10
Mon-Sun, 10.30-5.30
Med size R/C stk, Emphon Maritime. Av cal, cnd & prices.

SOUTH LONDON BOOKCENTRE **PHONE UNKNOWN**
18-19 Stockwell Street, Greenwich, London SE10
Wed,Thur 10-6, Sat & Sun 9-5, Rel
Lg R/C stk mini bookfair. Av cal, cnd & prices.

SPREAD EAGLE BOOKS **081 305 1666**
8 Nevada Street, Greenwich, London SE10
Mon-Sun, 10.30-5, L: 1-2.30
Med size R/C stk, av cal, cnd & prices.

Newly opened shop nearly opp station.

HACKNEY

ARCADY **PHONE UNKNOWN**
59 Wilton Way, Hackney, London E8
Thur-Sat, 11-6, Sun 3-6
Med size R/C stk, av cal, cnd & prices. Keen on Entertainment.

HAMPSTEAD

KEITH FAWKES **71 435 0614**
1-3 Flask Walk, Hampstead, London NW3
Mon-Sat, 10-5.30
Med size R/C stk, av cal, cnd & prices. Tube: Hampstead, oos turn left towards Belsize Park and left into Flask Walk.

HAMPTON (Middlesex)

IAN SHERIDAN **81 979 1704**
34 Thames Street, Hampton, Middlesex
Mon-Sun 10-7
Lg R/C stk, NSOC. Av cal, Ab av prices. BR: Hampton, oos turn right & left & follow path to river & left.

HAMPTON CHARITY BOOKSHOP **NO PHONE**
Hampton Station, Middlesex
Mon-Sun, 10-4
Small R stk, av cal, cnd & prices.

HIGHBURY CORNER

FANTASY CENTRE **071 607 9433**
157 Holloway Road, London N7 8LX
Mon-Sat, 10-6
Med size Spec in SF and Weird Fiction. Ab av cal, cnd & prices. Tube: Highbury & Islington, oos turn left.

HIGHGATE

FISHER & SPERR **081 340 7244**
46 Highgate High St, London N6 5JH
Mon-Sat, 10.30-5.30
Med/lg R/C/D stk, av cal, cnd & ab av prices. Tube: Archway & follow signs for Highgate.

RIPPING YARNS **081 341 6111**
355 Archway Road, Highgate, London N6
Mon-Sat, 10.30-5.30, Sat 5, Sun 11-4
Med/lg R/C stk, av cal, NSOC. Ab av prices. Tube Highgate, Oos and right.

Another newly opened shop opp tube.

BONAVENTURE **081 341 2345**
259 Archway Road, Highgate, London N6 5BS
Wed-Sat, 10.30-6
Med size R/C stk, av cal, NSOC, av prices. Tube Highgate, Oos turn right up steps and left, SIOR.

HOLLAND PARK

BERNARD SHAPERO **071 493 0876**
80 Holland Park Avenue, London W11 3RE
Mon-Fri, 10-7, Sat 5
Lg C/D stk, ab av cal, cnd & prices. Emphon Plate bks & Travel. Tube: Holland Park, Oos turn right.

ICKENHAM (Middlesex)

THE HAYES BOOKSHOP **08956 37725**
6 Glebe Avenue, Ickenham, Middlesex UB10 8FB
Mon-Sat, 9.30-5.30
Med size R/C stk, ab av cal, cnd, bl av prices. Tube: Ickenham, Oos turn left.

ILFORD (Essex(

TERRY'S **081 478 2850**
26 Chapel Road, Ilford, Essex IG1 2AH
Mon-Sat, 10-4
Small R/C stk, primarily pbks. Av cal, cnd, ab av prices. BR: Ilford, Oos turn right.

ISLEWORTH (Middlesex)

CHATER'S MOTORING BOOKSELLER **081 568 9750**
8 South Street, Isleworth, Middlesex
Mon-Sat, 9-5.30, Wed 1pm
Med size Spec in Motoring, new & s/h. Bl av cal, cnd, av prices.

ISLINGTON

BOUTLE & KING **071 278 4497**
23 Arlington Way, London EC1R 1UY
Mon-Sat, 10.30-6
Med size R/C/D stk, av cal, cnd & prices. Keen on Lefties. Tube: Angel, Oos turn right to Crossroads turn left & first left & left.

UPPER STREET BOOKSHOP **071 359 3785**
182 Upper Street, London N1 1RQ
Tues-Sat, 10-6
Med size R/C stk, emphon Architecture & Entertainment. Currently undergoing change. Tube: Highbury & Islington, Oos turn right into Upper St.

KEW GARDENS

LLOYDS **081 940 2512**
9 Mortlake Terrace, Kew, TW9 3DT
Mon-Sat, 10-4, clsd Wed
Spec Gardening bksp with med size Gen stk. Av cal, cnd & prices. BR: Kew Gardens, Oos turn right & right towards bridge & right at parade of shops.

KINGS CROSS

PORCUPINE BOOKCELLAR **071 837 4473**
5 Caledonian Road, London N1 9DX
Mon-Sat, 10.30-6.30
Newly opened. BTA. Bsmt rm in new bksp. Emphon Leftie/Trendy subjects. A branch of the indoor revolution. TWC. P.imposs. Tube: Kings Cross, Oos turn left up Pentonville Rd & first left.

KINGSTON (Surrey)

DERRICK NIGHTINGALE **081 549 5144**
32 Coombe Road, Kingston, Surrey KT2 7AQ
Mon-Sat, 9.30-5.30, L: 1-2
Med size R/C/D stk, av cal, cnd & prices, emphon Lit. BR: Norbiton, Oos turn left.

KNIGHTSBRIDGE

THE OLD NEWSPAPER & EPHEMERA SHOP **071 235 7788**
37 Kinnerton Street, London SW1X 8ED
Mon-Fri, 10-5, Thurs 8, Rel
Spec in Ephemera. Tube: Knightsbridge, Oos towards Hyde Pk Corner, turn right at Berkeley Hotel & right & left. SIOR.

MARBLE ARCH

HOSAIN'S **071 262 7900**
25 Connaught Street, London W2 2AY
Tues-Fri, 10.30-5.30
Med size Spec Indian & Middle Eastern Travel bks, av cal, cnd & prices. Tube: Marble Arch, Oos into Edgware Rd, & end left at Connaught St.

MARYLEBONE

SPCK **071 387 5282**
Holy Trinity Church, Marylebone Rd, London NW1 4DU
Mon-Thur, 9-5.30, Fri 5, Rel
V lg Spec stk of Theology. Ab av cal & cnd, av prices. Tube: Great Portland St, Oos, Shop is opposite.

STEPHEN FOSTER **071 724 0876**
95 Bell Street, London NW1 6TB
Mon-Sat, 10.30-6, Rel
Med size R/C/D stk, av cal, cnd & prices. Tube: Edgware Rd, Bakerloo Line, Oos & turn right.

BIBLIOPOLA 071 724 7231
Alfie's Antiques Market, 13-25 Church St, London NW8
Tues-Sat, 10-6
Med size Spec in Antqrn, Childrens and Ill. Ab av cal cnd & prices.

ARCHIVE BOOKSTORE 071 402 8212
83 Bell Street, London NW1 6TB
Mon-Sat, 10-6
Med size R/C stk, av cal, cnd, ab av prices. Emphon Antqrn & Sheet Music.

MAYFAIR

MAGGS BROS 071 493 7160
50 Berkeley Sq., London W1X 6EL
Mon-Fri, 9.30-5
Lg C/D stk, ab av cal, cnd & prices. Military Hist, Antqrn, English Lit, Autographs & Letters, Find Bindings, Ill bks. Not a bksp, more a collection of superlatives, heavy men in heavy overcoats spending heavy money in a heavy atmosphere.

SOTHERANS 071 439 6151
3-5 Sackville Street, London W1 2DP
Mon-Fri, 9.30-5.30, Sat am, V Rel
Lg C/D stk, ab av cal, cnd & prices. WAD. T. ABA only. Tube Piccadilly Circus, Oos into Piccadilly & 2nd right into Sackville St.

M & R GLENDALE 071 4875348
9a New Cavendish Str, London W1M 7RN
Mon-Fri, 10-6
Med size C/D stk, emphon Juvenile, Entertainment, Games. Ab av cal, cnd & prices. TWC.

HEYWOOD HILL 071 629 0647
10 Curzon Street, Mayfair, London W1Y 7FJ
Mon-Fri, 9.30-5.30, Sat 9-12.30
Med size R/C/D stk, av cal, cnd & prices. Tube: Green Park, Oos turn right & right & left into Cavendish.

THE QUEEN STREET BOOKSHOP 071 629 0532
18 Queen Street, London, W1X OJU
Mon-Fri, 10-5 Rel
Med size D stk, Lthrwr & Libricide. Av cal, cnd & prices. From Heywood Hill Oosh turn right & right, SIOL.

NOTTING HILL GATE

MUSIC & VIDEO EXCHANGE BOOKSHOP **071 229 8420**
560 Notting Hill Gate, London W11
Mon-Sun, 10-8
Med size R/C stk, av cal, cnd & prices.

NOTTING HILL BOOKS **071 727 5988**
132 Palace Gardens Terrace, London W8
Mon-Sat, 10.15-6, Thurs 1pm
New bksp with small R/C stk, av cal, cnd & prices.

MELLOR & BAXTER **071 229 2033**
121 Kensington Church Street, London W8 7LP
Mon-Fri, 10-6.30, Sat 10-4
Med size C/D stk of Lthrwr and Bindings, av cal, cnd & prices. From Notting Hill bks, oosh turn left & right & left. SIOR.

OSTERLEY

THE OSTERLEY BOOKSHOP **081 560 6206**
168A Thornbury Road, Osterley, London TW7 4QE
Mon-Sun, 10.30-5.30, Sun 4.45
Med size R/C stk, av cal, cnd & prices. No T.

PIMLICO

BOOKS OF ASIA **071 821 6544**
47 Moreton Street, London SW1V 2NY
Tues-Sat, 10-6
Med/lg Spec stk India, South East Asia, Middle East and the Pacific. Ab av cal, cnd & prices.

PORTOBELLO ROAD

The following bkstls open on Sats only. Phone numbers are home numbers. They are listed in the best order to visit them all.

FOSTER **071 724 0876**
87 Portobello Road, London W11
Tues-Fri, 11-3, Sat 8-4
BTA bkstl in Mkt. Av cnd &prices. TWC. Tube: Notting Hill Gate, Oos follow signs for Portobello Rd and first stall is on left.

S BILTCLIFFE 081 740 5326
289 Portobello Rd, London W11
KAY BOOKS 071 640 7770
291 Westbourne Grove, London W11
D ALTMAN 071 637 7635
291 Westbourne Grove, London W11
B BAILEY 071 229 1692
113 Portobello Road, London W11
FEM POEL 071 731 2736
113 Portobello Road, London W11
DEMETZY BOOKS 0993 702209
113 Portobello Road, London W11
R BARKER 071 289 3042
284 Westbourne Grove, London W11
L CHRISTIE 081 672 4024
282 Westbourne Grove, London W11
H TRUSCOTT 0403 730554
139 Portobello Road, London W11
BOOKS & THINGS 071 370 5593
157 Portobello Road, London W11
QUADRILLE 081 450 9008
146 Portobello Road, London W11

plus TRAVEL BOOKSHOP in Blenheim Crescent has some s/h bks.

RICHMOND (Surrey)

THE RICHMOND BOOKSHOP **NOW CLOSED**

HOUBEN **081 940 1055**
2 Church Court, Richmond TW9 1JR
Mon-Sat, 10-5
New bksp with small R/C stk, av cal, cnd & prices. TWC. Tube & BR: Richmond, oos turn left & look for alleyway past toilets on left.

BALDUR BOOKSHOP **081 940 1214**
44 Hill Rise, Richmond, Surrey TW10 6UB
Mon-Sat, 9.30-5.30, clsd Wed
Med size R/C stk, av cal, cnd & prices. Tube: Richmond, oos turn left & follow track up hill past bridge. SIOL.

ST JAMES'S

SIMS REED **071 493 5660**
58 Jermyn Street, London SW1 6LX
Mon-Fri, 10-5.30
Med size Spec in Art Reference. Ab av cal, cnd & prices. Office shop.

THOMAS HENEAGE 071 720 1503
42 Duke Street, London SW1Y 6DT
Mon-Fri 9-5
Now only Mail Order. Lg Spec Art Ref stk, ab av cal, cnd & prices.

PICKERING & CHATTO rumoured to be closing.

SHEEN

VANDELEUR 081 878 6837
69 Sheen Lane, London SE14
BTR
Med size C/D stk, ab av cal, cnd & prices.

SOHO

QUARITCH 071 734 2983
5-8 Lower John Street, London W1R 4AU
Mon-Fri, 9.30-5.30
Lg Spec in Antqrn, Nat Hist, Science. Ab av cal, cnd & prices.

CHARLOTTE ROBINSON 071 437 3683
55 Gt Pulteney St, London W1R 5DE
Mon-Fri, 11-6
Med/lg C/D stk. Emphon Mod 1sts & Ill. Ab av cal. Tube: Piccadilly, Oos on Shaftesbury Ave exit, turn left into Gt Windmill St & left at Brewer St & second right. SIOL.

STAMFORD HILL

PENDLEBURY'S 081 809 4922
Church House, Portland Rd, Stamford Hill, London N16 7HJ
Mon-Sat, 9.30-5, Sat 10.30-5
Med size Spec in Theology. Av cal, cnd & prices.

STOKE NEWINGTON

VORTEX 071 254 6516
139-141 Stoke Newington Church St, London N16
Mon-Fri, 11-6, Sat 10.30-6, Sun 12.30-6
Med size R/C stk, bl av cal, cnd & prices. BR: Stoke Newington, oos turn let & right into Stoke Newington Church St.

CIRCA **071 249 9775**
144 Stoke Newington Church St, London N16
Mon-Fri, 12.30-6.30, Sat 11.30-6
Small Spec in Acad pbks. Ab av cal, cnd & prices. Dir as above.

STRATFORD

K SCOTT **081 519 1593**
27 Romford Road, Stratford, London E15
Mon-Sat, 9-5.30
Med size R/C stk, av cal, cnd & prices. Emphon Rmndrs.

STREATHAM

J G BOOKS **081 764 4669**
27 Streatham Vale, London SW16
Mon-Fri, 10-6, L: 1-2, clsd Wed, Sat 10-5
Small Spec stk of bks on Lizards & snakes. Av cal, cnd & prices. Tube: Brixton & bus to Streatham, Police Station & left.

VILLAGE BOOKS **081 677 2667**
17 Shrubbery Road, London SW16 2AL
Mon-Sat, 10.30-7, Rel
New bksp with small R/C stk. Av cal, cnd & prices. TWC.

SWISS COTTAGE

FITZJOHN'S BOOKS **071 722 9864**
Northways Parade, College Cres., Swiss Cottage, London NW3
Mon-Sat, 11-6
Med size R/C stk, primarily rmndrs. Tube: Swiss Cottage, follow signs towards Hampstead, SIOL.

SYDENHAM

KIRKDALE BOOKSHOP **081 778 4701**
272 Kirkdale, London SE26 4RS
Mon-Sat, 9.30-5.30
Med size R/C stk in new bksp. Av cal, cnd & prices. BR: Sydenham, oos onto Main Road, turn left & SIOR almost opp.

HILLYERS **081 778 6361**
301 Sydenham Road, London SE26
Mon-Sat, 8.30-4, Sat 2, clsd Wed
Antq shp with small R/C stk, av cal, cnd & prices. From Kirkdale, oosh turn right & cont. SIOL 1 mile.

THAMES DITTON (Surrey)

ELIZABETH GANT **081 398 0962**
52 High Street, Thames Ditton, Surrey KT7 OBA
Mon-Sat, 10.30-5.30, clsd Wed
Med size R/C stk, emphon Childrens and Ill. Ab av cal, cnd & prices.

ROBIN BOOKS **NOW CLOSED**

TWICKENHAM

ANTHONY HALL **081 898 2638**
30 Staines Road, Twickenham TW2 5AU
Mon-Fri, 9-5.30, Wed 1pm
Med size Spec shop Russia & East European. Ab av cal, cnd & prices.

MARION PITMAN **081 898 7165**
29 Hampton Road, Twickenham TW2 5QE
closing down

UXBRIDGE

T H BARNARD **0895 258054**
11 Windsor Street, Uxbridge, UB8 1AB
Mon-Sat, 9-5, clsd Wed
Med/lg R/C stk, av cal, cnd & prices. Tube: Uxbridge, oos ahead past Mkt Hall, SIOL.

WALTHAMSTOW

RAYMOND PORT **NOW CLOSED**

THE SPORTING BOOKSHOP **081 5204032**
Antique City Market, Unit 13, 98 Wood St, London E17 3HX
Mon-Sat, 9.30-5.30, clsd Thur
Med size spec in Sports bks, av cal, cnd & prices. TWC.

NORMAN LORD **081 520 8300**
Antique City Market, Unit 3, 98 Wood St, London E17 3HX
Mon-Sat, 10-5, clsd Thur
Med size R/C stk, av cal, cnd & prices. Keen on Performing Arts.

PSYCHIC SENSE **081 520 4032**
Antique City Market, Unit 1, 98 Wood St, London E17 3HX
Mon-Sat, 9.30-5, clsd Thur
Med size Spec in Esoteric & Occult. Av cal, cnd & prices.

WATERLOO

There are a small number of bkstls mainly selling pbks outside the National Theatre in summer pm.

WATERLOO STATION BOOKSHOP* **PHONE UNKNOWN**
29 Tenison Road, London SE1
Mon-Sat, 10.30-6.30
Med size R/C stk, emphon rmndrs. By station.

SECONDHAND BOOKS **PHONE UNKNOWN**
20 The Cut, London SE1
Wed-Sat, 11-7
Med size R/C stk, av cal, cnd & prices. Emphon rmndrs. Oos Waterloo, turn right into Waterloo Rd, & right into The Cut.

WELLING (Kent)

FALCONWOOD TRANSPORT & MILITARY BKSP **081 303 8291**
5 Falconwood Parade Grn, Welling, Kent DA16 2PL
Thur-Sat, 9.30-5.30
Med size Spec Transport. Opp Falconwood BR.

WEST DULWICH

COLLECTED WORKS **PHONE UNKNOWN**
3 Melbourne Terrace, London SE22 8RE
Mon-Sat, 10-6, clsd Wed
Med size R/C stk, av cal, cnd & prices. Emphon Mod 1sts. BR: West Dulwich, Oos turn right & right.

WEST HAMPSTEAD

FORTUNE GREEN BOOKS **PHONE UNKNOWN**
74 Fortune Green Road, London NW6.
Wed-Sat, 10-5
Emphon Lit & Feminism. Tube: West Hampstead, oos turn right & keep going.

H. BARON **081 459 2035**
76 Fortune Green Road, London NW6
Fri & Sat only
Above av cal, spec in Classical Music. Dir as above.

WHETSTONE

WHETSTONE BOOKS **081 368 8338**
368 Oakleigh Rd North, London N20 OSF
Mon-Sat, 10-3.30, Sat 10-5
Med size R/C stk, av cal, cnd & prices. Tube: Arnos Grove, Oos turn right & cont past roundabout (NAST 1 1/2 miles).

WILLESDEN GREEN

GABRIELS **81 451 2047**
47 Walm Lane, London NW2 4QU
Mon-Sat, 10-7
Med size R stk, av cal, cnd & prices. By Willesden Grn Tube.

WIMBLEDON

BOOKS & LYRICS **081 543 0625**
Unit 6, Merton Abbey Mills, Sth Wimbledon, London SW19 2RD
Tues-Sun 11-6, Rel
Med/lg R/C stk, av cal, cnd & prices. Low key. Tube: Colliers Wood, oos turn left with mainstream of traffice & right at roundabout (1/2 mile) & right & SIOL.

PSEUD BOOKS **PHONE UNKNOWN**
Merton Abbey Mills, Wimbledon, London SW19 2RD
Sat & Sun only
Small shp with Spec Lit/Intellectual stk.

TLON BOOKS **081 543 4681**
Merton Abbey Mills, Wimbledon, London SW19 2RD
Sat & Sun, 10-6
Small R stk, av cal, cnd & prices.

ADDENDUM

ULYSSES

The newly opened ULYSSES at 40 Museum Street, London WC1 (071 831 1600) specialises in Modern First Editions, Literature and Illustrated Books. It has gone missing from the guide book and the directory for a very good reason which other bookshop owners would do well to consider.

In the last edition of this guide there was a shop in Museum Street called CHECK BOOKS which was one of the few in Britain that I admired, even if I could not afford the prices. This shop has not disappeared from the guide; it has not however disappeared from Museum Street, but is living under the pen name of ULYSSES. There is no indication that it was formerly CHECK BOOKS.

Across the road is another bookshop called ULYSSES. These two establishments are run by the same people, but have entirely different stocks.

Having an established shop called Check Books and changing the name to Ulysses is folly, opening a second shop and calling them both Ulysses is moronic.

What happens is that you lose all the customer base you have built up over the year for the shop whose name was Check Books and when people discuss the shop, which happens more often than the owners may realise, if only to comment on their egregious prices, nobody is certain as to which bookshop you are referring. It may well be perfectly obvious to the people that own the shops that they are two different establishments, but other people do not remember that it is now called Ulysses.

And further when madmen are compiling guide books the typists assume that the compiler who is notorious for his mistakes and inventions has just made yet another bloomer.

To add to the general mayhem one of the Ulysses is now rumoured to be closing down.

MR MICHAEL GOLDMARK
AN APOLOGY

On page 160 it is alleged that Mr. Michael Goldmark of Goldmark's Books Uppingham has secret video recording cameras in his bookshop. I have subsequently been informed that this is untrue and wish to withdraw the remarks unreservedly.There are no televison snooper cameras in the bookshop: they are in Mr Goldmark's art gallery next door.

ALPHABETICAL

SHOP INDEX

(excluding LONDON)

ABACUS BOOKS Altrincham 061 8285106
ABINGDON BOOKS Honiton 0404 47180
ABINGTON BOOKS Northampton 0604 32932
ADAM BOOKS Glasgow 041 649 1314
ADAMS, JUDITH Ludlow 0584 872 758
ADDYMAN BOOKS Hay on Wye 0497 821136
ADELPHI BOOKS Southsea 0705 833381(home)
ADELPHI BOOKS Aberdeen 0224 898 779
AFTERNOON BOOKSHOP, THE Woodstock 0993 813445
ALBATROSS BOOKSHOP Tenby 0834 2113
ALBION BOOKSHOP Broadstairs 0843 62876
ALCOMBE BOOKS Minehead 0643 703425
ALEC SMITH, ALEC Beverley 0482 869453
ALISTAIR & GARON Cambridge 0228 62086
ALL BOOKS Maldon 0621 856214
ALLERTON BOOKS Leeds 0532 695 012
ALLSOP, DUNCAN Warwick 0926 493226
ALMAR BOOKS Leeds 0532 755611
ALPHABETS Colchester 0206 572751
ALTON SECONDHAND BOOKS Alton 0420 89352
ANGEL HILL BOOKSHOP Tiverton No phone
ANGEL HILL BOOKSHOP, THE Tiverton 0884 257783
ANGLESEY BOOKS Holyhead 0407 60988
ANNIE'S BOOKSTALL Mold 03526 5683
ANTIQUARIAN BOOK CENTRE Stoke on Trent 0782 261352
ANTIQUARIAN & SECONDHAND BOOKS Swanage 0929 424088
ANTIQUE MAP AND BOOK STORE, THE Puddletown 0305 848633
ANTIQUE & BOOK COLLECTOR, THE Marlborough 0672 514040
ANTIQUES, BOOKS & CURIOS Burntwood 0543 682217
APIDISTRA Bath 0225 461 948
APPLEBY'S Keswick 07687 74054
APPLEBY'S BOOKSHOP Morpeth 0670 512 960
ARCADE BOOKS Carndomagin phone unknown
ARCADE BOOKS Belfast 0232 438474
ARCHER, R G Lavenham 0787 247229

ARGANTE Penzance no phone
ARMSTRONGS Sandown 0983 406226
ARMSTRONG'S BKS & COLLECTIBLES Coventry 0303 714344
ARROW BOOKS Kington 0544 230729
ARTICUS Warwick 0926 402004
ARUNDEL BOOKSHOP, THE Arundel 0903 882680
ASBAH Southsea no phone
ASHBURTON RARE BOOKS Ashburton 0364 53341
ASHLEY BOOKSHOP Bournemouth 0202 302499
ASPIDISTRA Bath 0225 424677
ATHENA BOOKS Doncaster 0302 322913
ATHOLL BROWSE Blair Atholl 079 681 530
ATTICUS Lancaster 0524 381413
ATTICUS BOOKS Southend on Sea 0702 353630
ATTIC, THE Henley on Thames 0491 579107
AVENUE BOOKS Newcastle upon Tyne 091 257 5836
BADGERS Worthing 09903 211816
BAGGINS BOOK BAZAAR Rochester 0634 811651
BAILEY BOOKS, JOHN Rossington 0302 864 581
BAILEYS BOOKSHOP Chipping Sodbury 0454 313399
BAIN SMITH, PETER Cartmel 044 854359
BALCONY BOOKSHOP, THE Caernarvon 0286 671 152
BALDWIN, M & M Cleobury Mortimer 0299 270 110
BALDWIN'S BOOKS Silver End 0376 83502
BALDWIN'S BOOKS Witham 0376 83502
BANGOR BOOKS Bangor, Wales 0248 352659
BANKES BOOKS Bath 0225 444580
BARBICAN BOOKSHOP York 0904 653643
BARBICAN BOOKSHOP Plymouth 0752 664597
BARLOW, BRIAN Chorlton Cum Hardy 061 881 1327
BARN BOOKS Whitchurch 0948 3742
BARN COLLECTOR'S MARKET, THE Seaford 0323 890010
BARNARD GALLERY Stockton 0642 616203
BASKERVILLE BOOKS Turnbridge Wells 0892 26776
BATES & HINDMARCH Boroughbridge 0423 324 258

BATH BOOK EXCHANGE Bath 0225 66214

BATH OLD BOOKS Bath 0225 426722

BATSTONE BOOKS Malmesbury 066 682 3072

BATTLE ANTIQUES Battle No phone

BAY BOOKS Newcastle Upon Tyne 091 251 4448

BAY BOOKSHOP Colwyn Bay 0482 531 642

BAYNTUN, GEORGE Bath 0225 466000

BEACH, D M Salisbury 0722 333801

BEACON HILL BOOKS, Hindhead 0428 606783

BEAGLE BOOKS Sway 0590 683421

BECKHEAD BOOKS Kirkby Lonsdale 05242 71314

BEECH BOOKS Birmingham 021 559 9822

BELL, MRS T Framlingham 0728 723046

BERRY STREET BOOKSHOP Wolverhampton 0902 28939

BESLEY'S BOOKS Beccles 0502 715762

BEWARE OF THE LEOPARD BOOKS Bristol 0272 257277

BEWICK BOOKS Newcastle Upon Tyne 091 281 2711

BIDDY'S BOOKSHOP Goodrington, Devon 0803 556151

BIFF BOOKS & RECORDS Sheffield No phone

BILLSON'S St Andrews 0334 75063

BIRD, TONY Presteigne 0544 260316

BIRMINGHAM BOOKSHOP Birmingham 021 472 8556

BLACK CAT BOOKSHOP Leicester 0533 512756

BLACKLOCKS Englefield Green 0704 434856

BLACKMORES BOOKSHOP Williton 0984 32227

BLACKWELLS Oxford 0865 792792

BLAKES Woodbridge 0394 380302

BLAKEWAY BOOKS Hungerford 0488 683581

BLITZGEIST Birmingham 021 4264122

BLORE'S BOOKSHOP, GEOFF Nottingham 0602 691441

BODHRAN, THE Saltaire 0274 530 102

BOOK A BRAC Sutton in Ashfield 0623 553 667

BOOK ACADEMY Southsea 0702 816632

BOOK BARGAINS Londonderry no phone

BOOK CABIN Harpenden 058 2768581

BOOK CELLAR Braunton 0271 815061

BOOK CELLAR, THE Penzance 0736 60320

BOOK ENDS Kirkcaldy 0592 205 294

BOOK END, THE Settle 072 92 3879

BOOK EXCHANGE, THE Louth no phone

BOOK HOUSE Sheffield No phone

BOOK IN HAND, THE Shaftesbury no phone

BOOK WARREN, THE Brixham 08045 58531

BOOK & ART SHOP, THE Sheffield No phone

BOOKBOX Stow on Wold 0451 31214

BOOKCASE Carlisle 0228 445560

BOOKCELLAR, THE Matlock 0629 57644

BOOKENDS West Kirby 051 625 6389

BOOKENDS Havant 0795 470094

BOOKENDS Fowey 072 683361

BOOKEND, THE Brentwood no phone

BOOKFARE Edinburgh 031 225 9237

BOOKFINDERS Belfast 0232 328 269

BOOKHOUSE, THE Ravenstonedale 058 73634

BOOKHOUSE, THE Preston 0772 201576

BOOKLEAFS Chester 0244 680 290

BOOKLORE Sherbourne 0939 814191

BOOKMART Falmouth 0326 211 252

BOOKROOM Petworth 0798 42073

BOOKROOM, THE Cambridge 0223 69694

BOOKS AFLOAT Weymouth 0305 779774

BOOKS AND BYGONES Blandford Forum 0258 456407

BOOKS AND MAPS Bournemouth 0202 421373

BOOKS AND PIECES Whitstable no phone

BOOKS AND PRINTS Bradford on Avon 0225 868300

BOOKS AND THINGS Billingshurst 0403 815131

BOOKS AND THINGS New Milton 0425 617 521

BOOKS ETCETERA Inverness 0463 712040

BOOKS FOR EVERYBODY Preston phone unknown

BOOKS & CHATTELS Ludlow 0584 876 191

BOOKS & COLLECTORS Hebden Bridge phone unknown

BOOKS & MAPS Bournemouth 0202 521373

BOOKSHELF Perth no phone

BOOKSHELF, THE Mansfield 0623 648231

BOOKSHOP BY THE ARCH, THE Totnes 0803 864088

BOOKSHOP SQUARE EDGE, THE Aylesbury 0296 89480

BOOKSHOP UNDER THE CHURCH, THE Richmond 0748 818703

BOOKSHOP, THE Cashel 062 616 05

BOOKSHOP, THE Oxford 0865 251075

BOOKSHOP, THE Emsworth 0243 372617

BOOKSHOP, THE Gloucester 0452 331 011

BOOKSHOP, THE Crewkerne 0460 76579

BOOKSHOP, THE Lytham St Annes 0253 728278

BOOKSHOP, THE Conwy 0492 592137

BOOKSIDE Leeds 0532 744021

BOOKSTACK Bridgnorth 0746 767 0891

BOOKSTACK Wolverhampton 0902 21055

BOOKSTOP BOOKSHOP Harrogate 0423 505817

BOOKSTORE, THE Belfast 0232 242 046

BOOKWORM Leatherhead 0372 377443

BOOKWORM Teknmouth 0626 775177

BOOKWORM Waterford no phone

BOOKWORMS Cromer 0263 515078

BOOKWORMS Evesham 0386 45509

BOOKWORM, THE Teignmouth 0626 775177

BOON, HENRY Liverpool 051 7094501

BOOTH, RICHARD Hay on Wye 0497 820322

BORDER BOOKSHOP Todmorden 0706 814721

BOUQUINISTE St Andrews 0334 76724

BOW WINDOWS BOOKSHOP Lewes 0273 480780

BOX OF DELIGHTS, THE Skipton 0756 790111

BRIDGE BOOKSHOP Deeping St. James 0778 343175

BRIDGE OF ALLAN BOOKS Bridge Of Allan 0786 834 483

BRIDGEND BOOK BARN Bridgend, Wales 745540

BRIDGEWATER BOOKS Macclesfield 0625 424763

BRIDGE-END BOOKSHOP, THE Burton on Trent 0283 46743
BRIMSTONE'S Brighton no phone
BRISTOL BOOKS Bristol 0272 245548
BRISTOL BOOKS Bristol 0272 634 716
BROADHURST Southport 0704 532064
BROCKWELL BOOKS Honiton 0404 43460
BROOKES, N F Brighton 0273 23105
BROUGHTON BOOKS Edinburgh 031 557 8010
BROWSE AWHILE Midhurst 0730 815425
BROWSERS Llangollen no phone
BROWSER'S BOOKSHOP Falmouth 0326 313 464
BROWZERS BOOKSHOP Prestwich 061 798 0626
BRYNBOOKS Bethesda 0248 602134
BURY BOOKSHOP Bury St Edmunds 0248 703107
BYGONES Farnham 0252 737865
BYRNES SECONDHAND BOOKSHOP Galway 091 61766
CAFE BOOKSHOP, THE East Grinstead 0342 322 669
CALEDONIA BOOKS Glasgow 041 334 9663
CALVERT, KIT Hawes 0969 667667
CAMDEN BOOKS Bath 0225 461606
CAMMILA'S BOOKSHOP Eastbourne 0323 36001
CAMPBELL'S BOOKS Menston 0943 879903
CANAL BOOKSHOP, THE Bradford on Avon 0225 723 812
CANDLE LANE BOOKS Shrewsbury 0743 65301
CAPITAL BOOKSHOP Cardiff 0222 388423
CARMARTHEN BOOKS Carmarthen 0267 2356676
CARNFORTH BOOKSHOP, THE Carnforth 0524 734588
CARRAIG BOOKS Blackrock 010 3532 882575
CASSIDY, P J Holbeach 0406 26322
CASTLE BOOK CENTRE Northwich 0606 781269
CASTLE BOOKS Edinburgh 031 556 0624
CASTLE BOOKSHOP Holt 0829 270 382
CASTLE BOOKSHOP Hertford 0992 586537
CASTLE BOOKSHOP Colchester 0206557550
CASTLE HILL BOOKS Kington 0544 231195

CATHACH BOOKS Dublin 010 3531 718 676

CATHAIR BOOKS Dublin 010 3531 6792 406

CAUSEWAY BOOKS Rushmills 02657 31033

CELLAR OF BOOKS Welshpool 0686 650 670

CHANTREY BOOKSHOP Dartmouth 0803 832796

CHAPEL BOOKS Westleton 0728 73616

CHAPTER HOUSE BOOKSHOP&GALLERY Sherborne 0935 816262

CHAPTERS Hereford phone unknown

CHAPTERS Dublin phone unknown

CHARD BOOKSHOP, THE Chard 0460 67046

CHAUCER BOOKSHOP, THE Canterbury 0227 453912

CHAUCER HEAD BOOKSHOP Stratford on Avon 0789 415691

CHESTERS, G & J Polesworth 0827 894743

CHEVET BOOKS Blackpool 0253 751 858

CHEYNE LANE BOOKSHOP Stamford 0780 51079

CHICHESTER BOOKSHOP, THE Chichester 0243 785473

CHILDREN'S BOOKSHOP, THE Hay on Wye 0497 821450

CHILTON BOOKS Skipton 0756 798939

CHIMERA BOOKS, Hurstpierpoint 0273 832255

CHRYSALIS Chesterfield 0246 69950

CINDERFORD BOOKSHOP Cinderford no phone

CLARENDON BOOKS Leicester 0533 701856

CLASSICS BOOKSHOP, THE Oxford 0865 726466

CLENT BOOKS Halesowen 021 5500309

CLEVEDON BOOKS Clevedon 0272 872304

COBWEBS Farnham 0252 734531

COBWEBS Newent 0531 821734

COLERAINE BOOKSHOP, THE Coleraine 0265 52557

COLERIDGE BOOKS Nether Stowey 0278 733338

COLES, T V Peterborough 0733 77268

COLLARDS Totnes 0548 550246 (Home)

COLLARD'S BOOKSHOP Totnes 0548 550246

COLLECTORS CORNER St Columb Major 0637 880715

COLLECTOR, THE Halifax 0422 363895

COLLECTOR'S CORNER Morecambe phone unknown

COLLECTOR'S CORNER Dublin no phone
COLLINSON, HENRY Norwich 0603 66348
COLNE BOOKS Colne 0282 870952
COLWYN BOOKS Colwyn Bay 0482 530683
COOK Wells Next Sea 0328 710419
COOPER BOOKS, FRED Newcastle Emlyn 0239 711230
COOPER HAY Glasgow 041 226 3074
COPNAL BOOKS Crewe 0270 580470
CORN EXCHANGE BOOKSHOP Stirling 0786 473112
CORNERSTONE BOOKS Plymouth 0752 661165
CORRAN BOOKS Laugharne 0994 427444
COTHAM HILL BOOKSHOP Bristol 0272 732344
COTSWOLD BOOKSHOP, THE Burford 099382 3308
COTTAGE BOOKSHOP, THE Penn 049 481 2632
COTTINGHAM BOOKSHOP, THE Cottingham 0482 845567
COUNTY BOOKSHOP Oakham 0572 722403
COURTHOUSE BOOKSHOP Brighton 0273 600365
COURTNEY, J E Harrogate 0423 500341
COURTYARD BOOKS Wells 0749 07112
COX, CLAUDE Ipswich. 0473 254776
CRAFT BARN Broxbourne phone unknown
CROFT BOOKSHOP Ashby de la Zouche 0530 417034
CROWE, PETER Norwich 0603 624800
CUMMING, A J Lewes 0273 472319
CURFEW BOOKS Lowestoft 0502 589096
CURLEWS Barnard Castle 0833 31090
CUVVIN BOOKS Robin Hood's Bay 0947 880561
CUVVIN BOOKS Whitby 0947 880561
DAISY LANE BOOKS Holmfirth 0484 688409
DALY, PETER M Winchester 0962 867732
DANDELION BOOKSHOP Dublin 0101351 784759
DARENTH BOOKSHOP, THE Otford 09592 2430
DARTMOOR BOOKSHOP, THE Ashburton 0364 53356
DAVID, C Cambridge 0223 354619
DAVID'S BOOKSHOP Letchworth 0462 673767

DAVIS BOOKS Newcastle upon Tyne 091 261 4580
DEIGHTON BELL Cambridge 0223 353939
DEJA VU Glastonbury 0273 600400
DEJA VU Brighton 0273 600400
DIAMOND BOOKSHOP, THE King's Lynn 0553 775230
DICKENS CENTENARY BOOKCASE Exeter 0392 431 587
DICKSON, JAMES A Edinburgh 031 225 6937
DORSET BOOKSHOP Blandford Forum 0258 52256
DOWANSIDE BOOKS Glasgow 041 945 2787
DRAYCOTT BOOKS Chipping Camden 0386 841 392
DRIFFIELD BOOKSHOP, THE Driffield 037744210
DUFFTOWN BOOKSHOP Dufftown 0340 20027
DUFFY & CO Dublin phone unknown
DUNCAN'S, JACK York 0904 641389
DUNDAS BOOKSHOP Edinburgh 031 556 4591
DUNKELD ANTIQUES & BOOKS Dunkeld 035 028832
DURHAM BOOK CENTRE Sunderland 091 567 4389
DYFI VALLEY BOOKSHOP, THE Machynlleth 0564 703849
DYLAN'S BOOKSTORE Swansea 0792 655255
D'ARCY BOOKS Devizes 0380 726922
EARL'S EYE BOOKS Chester 0244 319688
EASTGATE BOOKSHOP Beverley 0482 868579
EATON'S, PETER Aylesbury 0296 641393
ELHAM VALLY BOOKSHOP Elham 0303 840359
ELKIN MATTHEWS Coggeshall 0376 561730
ELKIN MATTHEWS Blakeney 0263 740475
ELLEN, BARRIE Westcliffe on Sea 0702 338763
ELLIS, J R & H E Norwich 0603 623679
ELY BOOKSHOP, THE Ely 0353 661 824
ENGLISH, TOBY Wallingford 0491 36389
ETON ANTIQUE BOOKSHOP Eton 0753 855534
EUREKA BOOKSHOP Godalming 0843 426968
EVANS, D G & A S Brecon 0874 2714
EX LIBRIS Bradford on Avon 02216 3595
EXETER RARE BOOKS Exeter 0392 431587

FARNBOROUGH BKSP & GALLERY Farnborough 0252 518033

FAVERSHAM BOOKSHOP, THE Faversham 0795 532873

FENNEL BOOKSHOP Manchester 061 835 3759

FERROW, DAVID Great Yarmouth 0493 843800

FIFTEENTH CENTURY BOOKSHOP Lewes 0273 474160

FITZJOHN'S BOOKS Ilfracombe 0271 866888

FIVE OWLS BOOKSHOP Richmond 0748 823648

FOREST BOOKS Leicester 0533 627171

FORGE BOOKSHOP, THE Chilham 0227 730267

FOURSHIRE BOOKS Stow on Wold 0451 30755

FOURSHIRE BOOKSHOP Moreton in Marsh 0608 51451

FOXED AND BOUND West Malling 0732 847886

G T BOOKS Edinburgh 031 556 8032

GARRETTS ANTIQUARIAN BOOKS Douglas, I.O.M. 0624 629660

GEORGE OF STAMFORD BOOKSHOP, THE Stamford 0780 55171

GIBBS BOOKSHOP Manchester 061 2367179

GILBERT H M Southampton 0703 226420

GILBERTS Winchester 0962 852832

GILMOREHILL BOOKS Glasgow 041 339 7504

GLADSTONES Waterford no phone

GLANCE BACK BOOKS Chepstow, Wales phone unknown

GLYN'S BOOKS Wrexham 0978 355797

GOLDEN HIND, THE Deal 0304 375086

GOLDEN PAST, THE Peel, I.O.M. 0624 842170

GOLDMARK BOOKS Uppingham 0572 822694

GOLDNEY BOOKS Bristol 0272 237408

GOSFORD BOOKS Coventry 0203 220813

GOUGH, SIMON Holt 0263 712650

GRANT BOOKS Droitwich 0905 778155

GRANT & SHAW Edinburgh 031 229 8399

GREAT AYTON BOOKSHOP, THE Great Ayton 0642 723358

GREAT GRANDFATHERS Leyland 0772 422268

GREAT OAK BOOKSHOP, THE Llanidloes 05512 2959

GREEN STREET BOOKSHOP Cambridge 0223 353939

GREENE'S BOOKSHOP Dublin 762 554

GRENVILLE STREET BOOKSHOP Stockport 061 4771909
GREYFRIARS BOOKS Colchester 0206 563138
GUILDHALL BOOKROOM, THE Eye, Suffolk 0379 871439
GUILDMASTER BOOKS Nantwich 0270 629108
HADDANS BOOKSHOP Glastonbury 0458 31753
HADFIELD, G K Shepshed 0509 503014
HALEWOOD & SONS Preston 0772 52603
HALL BANK BOOKSHOP Buxton, Derbyshire 0298 70889
HALL'S BOOKSHOP Tunbridge Wells 0892 27842
HAMBLETON BOOKSHOP Thirsk 0845 22343
HAMLEY'S Jurbey, I.O.M. 0624 897 670
HANCOX, ALAN Cheltenham 0242 513204
HANNA, FRED Dublin 010 3531 771 255
HANNA, INES Dublin 010 3531 771 255
HARLEQUIN Lincoln 0522 522589
HARLEQUIN Totnes 0803 866406
HARLEQUIN Totnes 0803 866406
HARROGATE BOOKSHOP, THE Harrogate 0423 500479
HASLEMERE BOOKSHOP, THE Haslemere 0428 6652952
HASLINGDEN BOOKSHOP Haslingden 0706 831170
HATCHARD & DAUGHTERS Hebden Bridge 0422 845 717
HAUNTED BOOKSHOP, THE Cambridge 0223 312913
HAZELDEAN BOOKSHOP Liverpool 051 708 8780
HEAD, JOHN & JUDITH Salisbury 0722 327767
HEATONS BOOKSHOP Stockport 061 431 5905
HEDGER, JEAN Cookham phone unknown
HELMSLEY BOOKS Helmsley 0439 70014
HENCOTES BOOKS AND ANTIQUES Hexham 0434 605971
HEREFORD BOOKSHOP, THE Hereford 0432 357617
HERITAGE BOOKS Ryde 0983 62933
HEYNES BOOKSHOP Cheltenham 0242 515423
HIGHLAND ANTIQUES Inverness 0463 231 316
HILL BOOKS, T S Dorking 0306 886468
HILL, ALAN Bakewell 0629 814841
HILL, ALAN Chesterfield 0246 231158

HILL, ALAN Sheffield 0742 747721
HOLBOURNE BOOKS Worchester 0905 27824
HOLCOMBE, PAUL Canterbury 0227 457913
HOLDENHURST BOOKS Bournemouth 0202 397718
HOLLETT, R F G & SON Sedbergh 05396 20298
HOLLEYMAN & TREACHER Brighton 0273 25954
HONITON OLD BOOK SHOP Honiton 0404 47180
HORSHAM BOOKSHOP, THE Horsham 0403 52187
HOWDEN BOOKSHOP Howden 0430 432 071
HOWES BOOKHOP Hastings 0424 423437
HUBBARD, MARY Emsworth 0243 377394
HUGHES & SMEETH Lymington 0590 676324
HUGHES, DAVID Llandudno 0492 77700
HULL, TRISTRAM AND JULIA Norwich 0603 624890
HUMM, ROBERT Stamford 0780 66266
HUTTON BOOKS Launleston 0566 776 503
IDLER, THE Hadleigh Suffolk 0473 827752
IMPRINT Stroud 0453 759731
INCH'S BOOKS York 0904 627082
INCREDIBLE'S Alston 091 5674389
INVERNESS BOOKSHOP, THE Inverness 0463 239 947
INVICTA BOOKSHOP, THE Newbury 0635 31176
IONA BOOKSHOP, THE Iona 06817 304 / 305
IRISH DRIF'S SPECIAL, THE Coleraine 0265 54024
J L BOOK EXCHANGE Bridlington 0262 601285
JABBERWOCKY Horncastle 0507 522112
JARVIS BOOKS Matlock 0629 55322
JERMY & WESTERMANN Nottingham 0602 474522
JUST BOOKS Truro 0872 42532
KEEL ROW BOOKS Newcastle upon Tyne 091 296 0664
KELSALL, GEORGE Littleborough 0706 370244
KEMMISH, A R Bristol phone unknown
KEMPTOWN BOOKS Brighton 0273 682110
KENDONS (BOB GILBERT) Grays 0375 372187
KENNY'S BOOKSHOP & ART GALLERY Galway 091 627 39

KEN'S Newport Pagnell 0908 610003
KERNAGHAN, BRYAN Southport 0704 546329
KIM'S BOOKSHOP Worthing 0903 206282
KINGSTON, RICHARD J Henley on Thames 0491 574 535
KIRKLAND BOOKS Kendal 0539 740 841
KNOWS HORRENDA BOOKSHOP Belfast 0232 244 137
LAFAYETTE BOOKSELLERS Cleethorpes 0472 699244
LAMBS TALES Modbury 0548 830317
LAMB'S TALES Modbury 0548 830317
LANDGATE BOOKS Rye 0797 222280
LATTO BOOKS Musselburgh 031 665 2651
LAURA'S BOOKSHOP Derby 0332 47094
LAURENCE OXLEY Arlesford 0962 732188
LAWSON, JEAN Haddington 062 082 5851
LEAVES BOOKSHOP Belfast 0232 664600
LEEK BOOKSHOP, THE Leek 0538 373 391
LEEK BOOKSHOP, THE Leek 0538 373391
LEEK OLD BOOKS Leek 0538 399033
LEE'S BOOKSTORE Cork 010 021 272 307
LEIGH GALLERY BOOKS Leigh on Sea 0702 715477
LEO BOOKS Wakefield 0924 365109
LEWIS, JOHN Coggeshall 0376 561518
LINDY'S Newton Abbot 0626 63221
LITTLE BOOKSHOP, THE Oxford 0865 591176
LITTLE BOOKSHOP, THE Ambleside 05394 32094
LITTLE HOLCOMBE BOOKS Ramsbottom 0706 825322
LLOYDS Wingham 0227 720774
LOCKYER, H K Abergavenny 0873 5825
LUCKMAN'S ANTIQUES Coventry 223 842
MACCLESFIELD OLD & RARE BKS Macclesfield 0625 610 861
MACNAUGHTON, D & K Berwick upon Tweed 0289331502
MAGPIE RARE BOOKS Shaldon 0626 872896
MAGPIE, THE Totnes 0803 325944
MAGPIE, THE Totnes 0548 830082 (Home)
MAIDSTONE BOOK & PRINT SHOP Maidstone 0622 662878

MAINLY BOOKS Leominster 0568 615722
MAIR WILKES BOOKS Newport on Tay 0382 542 352
MALVERN BOOKSHOP, THE Malvern 0684 575915
MANNA BOOKS Weston Supermare 0934 66009
MARINE BOOKSHOP Lyme Regis 0297 442 088
MARLBOROUGH BOOKSHOP, THE Marlborough 0672 515054
MARRIN, G & D J Folkestone 030353016
MARTIN, RICHARD Gosport 0705 520642
MAXINE'S CAFE Llangollen 0978 860334
MAXWELLS BOOKSHOP Acocks Green 021 7068379
MAYNARD AND BRADLEY Nottingham 0602 484824
MAYNARD & BRADLEY Leicester 0533 532712
McCARTY, M E Kirkwall no phone
McCLAREN BOOKS Helensburgh 0436 76453
McCORMACK'S Lancaster 0534 36405
McGILLS BOOKSHOP Chorlton on Medlock phone unknown
McGILLS BOOKSHOP Manchester 061 232 9620
McILREAVY, A & F St Andrews 0334 72487
McNAUGHTON'S BOOKSHOP Edinburgh 031 556 5897
MEETING ROOM, THE Dublin no phone
MERE BOOKS Ormskirk 0695 77570
MEWS ANTIQUES & BOOKS Belfast 0232 751 319
MICHAELS BOOKSHOP Ramsgate 0843 589500
MILES, ARCHIE Gosforth 094 05792
MILES, DAVID Canterbury 0227 464773
MILLER'S BOOKS AND PRINTS Southsea 0705 755796
MILLS, BRIAN Newcastle upon Tyne 091 251 5380
MILLS, DOUG Wrexham no phone
MINSTER BOOKS & ANTIQUES Leominster now closed
MINSTERGATES BOOKSHOP, THE York 0904 621812
MIRROR AND THE LAMP, THE St Ives no phone
MITCHELL'S BOOKSHOP Glenrothes 0592 758 737
MONTROSE BOOKSHOP, THE Montrose 0674 73082
MOON, MICHAEL Whitehaven 0946 62936
MOORE, ERIC T Hitchin 0462 450497

MOORLAND BOOKS Oldham 0457 871306

MORRIS, A E Bethesda 0248 352 695

MORTEN, E J Manchester 061 445 7629

MOSTLY BOOKS Barrow 0229 836808

MOTHER GOOSE BOOKSHOP St Helens 0983 873897

MOVIE SHOP, THE Norwich 0603 615239

MR MICAWBER Newport 0983 525320

MR MILES Leeds 0532 455 327

MRS LOFTHOUSE Scarborough 0947 880561

MURRAY & KENNET Horsham 0403 54847

MURRAY'S BOOKSTALL Dundee No phone

NAUGHTON BOOKSELLERS Dun Laoghaire 0101 3531 2804 392

NEEDWOOD BOOKSHOP, THE Burton on Trent 0283 41641

NEVER OPEN BOOKSHOP, THE Cowes, Isle of Wight 0983 2935

NEVILLE, ANTHONY Rye 0797 224552

NEVILLE, TONY Tentenden 0797 224 552

NEW STREET BOOKS Penzance 0736 62758

NEWGATE BOOKS Oswestry 0691 650 178

NINER & HILL Oxford 0865 726105

NORTH SHIELDS BOOKS Newcastle upon Tyne 091 296 1918

NORTHAM BOOKS Southampton phone unknown

NORTHFIELD BKSP & FURNISHINGS Northfield 021 477 7704

NOSTALGIA PUBLICATIONS York 0904 624901

NOT JUST BOOKS Uppingham 0572 821306

NOT JUST BOOKS Port Stewart 026 583 4543

NSF Godalming no phone

OBLONG BOOKS York 0904 631375

OCCULTIQUE Northampton 0604 32932

OFFA'S DYKE BOOKS Ludlow 0584 873 854

OLD APOTHECARY BOOKSHOP, THE Ripponden 0422 822 214

OLD BOOK MART, THE Swansea 0792 474919

OLD BOOKSHOP, THE Langport 0458 252644

OLD BOOKSHOP, THE Dawlish 0626 886026

OLD CATHAY FINE BOOKS Hatfield 0707 274200

OLD CLOCK REPAIR SERVICE, THE Aberdeen 0224 627 695

OLD CURIOSITY SHOP, THE Axminster 0297 33010

OLD CURIOSITY SHOP, THE Frome 0373 64482

OLD GALLERY BOOKSHOP, THE Hythe 0303 269339

OLD GRINDLE'S BOOKSHOP Edinburgh 031 229 7252

OLD HALL BOOKSHOP, THE Brackley 0280 704146

OLD HASTINGS BOOKSHOP Hastings 0424 446413

OLD RAMSGATE BOOKSHOP Ramsgate 0843 586 377

OLD SOKE BOOKS Peterborough 0733 64147

OLD STORYTELLERS BOOKSHOP, THE Ulverston 0229 56123

OLIVER'S BOOKSHOP Newcastle upon Tyne 091 2513552

OSCAR'S ANTIQUES Crewkerne 0460 72718

OTHER BOOKSHOP, THE Bangor 0247 58778

OUT OF PRINT BOOKSHOP, THE Liverpool 051 7089700

OUT TO LUNCH BOOKSHOP, THE Yarmouth, I.O.W. 0983 760851

OXFAM BOOKSHOP St Albans 0992 583221

OXFAM BOOKSHOP Hertford 0992 583221

OXFAM BOOKSHOP Winchester 0992 583221

OXFAM BOOKSHOP Cambridge no phone

OXFAM BOOKSHOP, THE Oxford 0865 310145

OXFAMS WORST BOOKSHOP Aberdeen 0224 642490

O'BRIEN BOOKS & PHOTO GALLERY Limerick 061 342 604

O'FLYNN'S York 0904 641404

PACE ONE Redcar phone unknown

PAGE, COLIN Brighton 0273 25954

PARAMOUNT BOOK EXCHANGE Manchester 061 834 9509

PARISH BOOKSHOP, THE Whitchurch 0948 4115

PARK BOOKSHOP, THE Wellingborough 0933 222592

PARKINSON, ANTHONY Southport 0704 547016

PASSAGEWAY BOOKROOM York 0532 754698

PATON BOOKS St Albans 0727 53984

PATTERSON & LIDDLE Bath 0225 426722

PATTERSON & LIDDLE Bristol 0272 257277

PEDLAR'S PACK Totnes 0803 866423

PEDLAR'S PACK BOOKS Totnes 0803 886423

PENDEES, Herne Bay 0227 374778

PENNY FARTHING, THE North Berwick 0602 4400

PENNYFARTHING ARCADE BOOKSHOP Tipperary no phone

PENZANCE RARE BOOKS Penzance 0735 6214

PERIWINKLE PRESS Faversham 0795 426242

PERTH BOOKSHOP Perth 0738 33970

PETER'S BOOKSHOP Sheringham 0263 823008

PICKEN, ROBERT A Stafford 0785 53425

PIC's BOOKSHOP Bridport 0308 25689

PIK A BOOK Cleethorpes phone unknown

PILGRIM BOOKS Boston 0205 356931

PILGRIMS PROGRESS Walsingham 03882 0399

PLEASURES Southwold 0702 723776

PLOUGH BOOKS Caistor, Lincolnshire 0472 852073

POCKET BOOKSHOP, THE Paignton 0803 529804

POETRY BOOKSHOP, THE Hay 0497 820305

POMES PENNY EACH Newcastle Under Lyme 0782 630729

POMES PENYEACH Stoke on Trent 0782 630279

PONTCANNA OLD BOOKS Cardiff 0222 641047

POOLE BOOKSHOP, THE Poole no phone

PORTER BOOKSHOP, THE Sheffield 0742 667762

PORTLAND BOOKS Leamington Spa 0926 338 793

POST HORN BOOKS Giggleswick 072 823438

POWELL, TONY Falmouth no phone

PRIMROSE HILL BOOKS London 071 586 2022

PRINGLE, ANDREW Edinburgh 031 556 9698

PRIORY BOOKS Malvern 0684 575915

PROSPECT BOOKS AND PRINTS Llanrwst 0492 640111

PROSPECT HOUSE BOOKS Belfast 0232 245 787

PUGH BOOKS, IAN K Pershore 0386 552681

QUARRY BOOKS Shrewsbury 0743 61404

QUARTO BOOKSHOP St Andrews 0334 74616

QUAYSIDE Teignmouth 0626 775436

QUAYSIDE BOOKSHOP Gloucester 0452 300422

QUAYSIDE BOOKSHOP Teknmouth 0626 775436

QUEST BOOKS Weymouth 0305 789142

QUILL BOOKS Burford 099382 3594
R H BOOKS Yoxford 072877 439
RAINBOW Bideford 023 7478592
RALPH/ROBERTS Swansea no phone
RARE & RACY Sheffield 0742 701916
RATHMINES BOOKSHOP Dublin 010 3531 961064
READERS RETURN, THE Hinckley 0455 61107
READER'S REST Lincoln 0522 543217
RECYCLED BOOKSHOP, THE Haye on Wye 0497 821450
REDCAR BOOKSHOP Redcar 0642 486122
REDMOND BOOKS, ALAN Billingborough 0529 240215
REDRUTH BOOKSHOP, THE Redruth 0209 211308
REID & REID Edinburgh 031 225 9660
REID'S OF LIVERPOOL Liverpool 051 709 312
REIGATE GALLERIES Reigate 0737 246055
REYNER, MICHAEL Cheltenham 0242 515423
RHOS POINT BOOKS Rhos Point 0492 545236
RIEVAULX Helmsley 0439 70912
RIPPON BOOKSHOP Harrogate 0423 501835
ROATH BOOKS Cardiff 0222 490523
ROBERTS, JOHN Bristol 0272 268368
ROBLINS Huddersfield 0484 516793
ROCHDALE BOOKSHOP, THE Rochdale 0706 31136
ROLPH, JOHN/THE OLD COACH HOUSE Lowestoft 0502 572039
ROMA RYAN Belfast 0232 242 777
ROMILLEY LITTLE BOOKSHOP Romilley 061 427 4853
ROOM AT THE TOP Kingsbridge 0548 856364
ROSEMOUNT BOOKSHOP Aberdeen 0224 639 355
ROSS OLD BOOKS Ross on Wye 0989 67458
ROTHWELL AND DUNWORTH Taunton 0823 282476
ROTHWELL AND DUNWORTH Dulverton 0398 23169
ROUNDABOUT SHOP, THE Bradford on Avon 02216 3421
ROWAN, H & S Bournemouth 0202 398820
ROWLANDS RECORD EXCHANGE Swansea no phone
RUSKINS Romsey 0794 523881

RUTLAND BOOKSHOP, THE Uppingham 0572 823450
RYDE BOOKSHOP, THE Ryde, IOW 0983 65227
SALTBURN BOOKSHOP Saltburn 0287 623335
SANDERS Oxford 0865 242590
SCARBOROUGH BOOKS Scarborough 0723 368813
SCARTHIN BOOKS Cromford 0629 823272
SCENT WITH LOVE Mold 0352 700374
SCIENTIFIC ANGLICAN Norwich 0603 624079
SCORPIO BOOKS Bungay 0986 5743
SCUDDERS Bideford 023 727567
SECOND CHAPTER Market Drayton 0630 57410
SECOND EDITION Edinburgh 031 556 9403
SECOND READING Cardiff 022 461404
SECONDHAND BOOKSHOP, THE Broxbourne phone unknown
SEVERN BOOKS Weston Supermare 0934 635389
SHAMBLES DRIF SPECIAL, THE Malton phone unknown
SHERIDAN'S Hull 0482 28759
SHOP FOR DERANGED LADDER CARRIER Halifax phone unknown
SIDMOUTH ANTIQUE BOOKS Sidmouth 0395 516 028
SIDMOUTH OLD BOOKS Sidmouth 0395 514461
SILVERFISH SPECIAL BOOKSHOP, THE Bradford no phone
SIMMONS BOOKSHOP Wednesbury 021 502 4622
SIMMONS BOOKSHOP Birmingham 027 5024622
SIMON'S BOOKS Somerton 0458 72313
SIOP LUFRAU'R HEN BOST Blaenau Frestinog 0766 831 802
SKLARROF Totland, I.O.W. 0983 754960
SMALLEST BOOKSHOP, THE Buxton No phone
SMITH BOOKS, KEITH Ledbury 0531 5336
SMITH, RAYMOND Eastbourne 0323 34128
SMITH'S BOOKS, TIM Horncastle 0507 527139
SPCK Chester 0244 323753
SPEAKS VOLUMES Birkenhead 051 647 6076
SPELMAN, KEN York 0904 614414
SPEY BOOKS Elgin 034 387 1284
SPREAD EAGLE BOOKS Ruthin 08242 3840

ST ANDREWS BOOKSHOP Penrith 0768 64455
ST JOHNS HILL BOOKS Wareham 0925 2577
ST MARGARET'S BOOKSHOP Ripon 0765 2877
ST MARY'S BOOKS Stamford 0780 63033
ST MICHAEL'S BOOKSHOP Leeds 0532 746067
ST PETERS BOOKSHOP Chichester 0243 778477
STACPOOLE, GEORGE Adare 061 86409
STAFFORDS Tealby 0673 83557
STAFFS BOOKSHOP, THE Lichfield 0543 264093
STANILAND Stamford 0780 55800
STAPLEGROVE BOOKSHOP Taunton 0823 336450
STAR BOOKSHOP Southsea 0705 737 077
STEADMAN, A & E Kirkwall phone unknown
STEEDMAN'S Newcastle upon Tyne 091 232 6561
STERLING BOOKS Weston Supermare 0934 625056
STEVENS, BRIAN Monmouth 0600 713701
STEYNE BOOKSHOP, THE Worthing 0903 206216
STIRLING BOOKSHOP, THE Stirling 0876 81771
STOKES BOOKS Dublin 010 3531 713 584
STOKESLEY BOOKSHOP, THE Stokesley 0642 712514
STONE TROUGH York 0904 670323
STORNOWAY BOOKSHOP, THE Stornoway phone unknown
STOUR BOOKS Sturminster Newton 0258 73561
STRAND BOOKS Sandwich 0304 611948
STRAND BOOKS Padstow no phone
STRAND BOOKSHOP, THE Talgarth 0874 711195
STRATFORD TREVERS Broadway 0386 853668
STRATHERN ANTIQUES Crieff 0764 4344
STRATHTAY BOOKSHOP, THE Aberfeldy 0887 29519
STROTHERT'S Chester 0244 340 756
SUFFOLK RARE BOOKS Sudbury 0787 72075
SUSSEX BOOKS Pulborough 079 823030
SWAN GALLERY Sherbourne 0935 814465
TAIKOO BOOKS York 0904 641 213
TALISMAN BOOKS Manchester 061 4499271

TALL STOREY'S Brighton 0273 697381

TAMARISK Hastings 0424 420591

TAPLINS BOOKSHOP Birmingham 021 7796505

TARKA BOOKS Lostwithiel 0208 873 407

TARKA BOOKS Barnstaple, Devon 0271 74997

TAYLOR SMITH Westerham 0959 63100

TAYLOR SMITH BOOKS, ALAN Westerham 0959 63100

TAYLOR, BERNARD Stoke on Trent 0752 824682

TEG'S BOOKS Wrexham 0978 354 224

TEG'S BOOKS Chester 0244 311017

TEMPLE GALLERY Derby 0332 293 752

THESAURUS Jersey, Channel Islands 0534 37045

THIN, JAMES Edinburgh 031 556 6743

THOMAS RARE BOOKS Lanchester 0207 529066

THOMPSONS BOOKSHOP Cirencester 0285 655239

THOMPSON, A C & M Wymondham 0953 602244

THORNTONS Oxford 0865 242939

THORNTON'S Cranbrook 0580 712965

THORPE, THOMAS St Albans 0727 865576

THORP, THOMAS Guildford 0483 62770

THRIFT BOOK CENTRE Edinburgh No phone

TILLEY'S Chesterfield 0246 454270

TILLEY'S VINTAGE MAGAZINE SHOP Sheffield 0742 752442

TILL'S BOOKSHOP Edinburgh 031 667 0895

TIN DRUM BOOKS Leicester 0533 548236

TIN DRUM BOOKSHOP, THE Fakenham 0533 548 236

TITLES Oxford 0865 727928

TOLL HOUSE BOOKSHOP, THE Holmfirth 0484 686 541

TOMBLAND BOOKSHOP, THE Norwich 0603 760610

TOR BOOKS Torrington 0805 23791

TORC BOOKS Snettisham 0485 54188

TOWER BOOKSHOP King's Lynn no phone

TOWN & GOWN BOOKSHOP Twyn 0341 250542

TRAFALGAR BOOKSHOP, THE Brighton 0273 684300

TRAYLEN, THOMAS Guildford 0483 572424

TREASURE CHEST, THE Felixstowe 0394 270717
TREWINS BOOKS Aldebergh 098 684649
TRIANGLE BOOKS Lymington 0590 670 934
TRINDERS BOOKSELLERS Clare 0787 277130
TUCKER, ALAN AND JOAN Stroud 0453 764738
TURN OF THE CENTURY ANTIQUES Hexham 0434 603988
TURRET HOUSE BOOKS Wymondham 0953 603462
TWENTIETH CENTURY BOOKS Ludlow 0584 874 441
UNIVERSITY BOOKSHOP Durham 091 3842095
UNMAUDLIN BOOKSHOP, THE Cambridge 0223 62457
UPPER DECK BOOKSHOP, THE Londonderry no phone
VALENTINE'S BOOKS Nailsworth 045383 832483
VAUGHAN, ROBERT Stratford on Avon 0789 205312
VENTNOR BOOKSHOP, THE Ventnor I.O.W. 0983 853706
VICTORIA BOOKS Brightlingsea 0206 302374
VICTORIA BOOKSHOP Swindon 0793 527364
VICTORIA GALLERY Cambourne, Cornwall 0209 719268
VILLAGE BOOKSHOP, THE Leek 0538 372092
VILLAGE BOOKSTORE, THE Stoke on Trent 0782 543005
VINTAGE MOTORSHOP Batley 0924 470 773
VIRGINIBUS Honiton 0404 43460
VOKES & SON Darlington moved to Bookroom
VOLTAIRE & ROUSSEAU Glasgow 041 339 1811
VOLUME ONE Belfast no phone
WALLIS, DEREK AND GLENDA Bath 0225 424677
WAR ON WANT Belfast 0232 232 064
WATERFIELDS Oxford 0865 721809
WAX FACTOR Brighton 0273 673744
WAYFARER BOOKS Tewkesbury 0684 293337
WAY, RICHARD Henley on Thames 0491 576663
WEBBS Dublin phone unknown
WELL READ Belfast no phone
WELLINGTON BOOKS Bristol 0272 739848
WENLOCK BOOKS Much Wenlock 0952 727 877
WEST HOUSE BOOKS Hay on Wye 0497 821225

WEST RIDING BOOKS Halifax no phone
WEST WALES BOOKS Lampeter 0570 423778
WESTGATE BOOKSHOP Sleaford 0529 304276
WESTWORDS Greenock 0475 892 467
WHITE BOAR ANTIQUES Leyburn 0969 23901
WHITEHILL BOOKSHOP Bradford on Avon 02216 2402
WICKS, E S Farnborough 0252 544876
WILBRAHAM, JOHN Hastings 0424 446413
WILDMAN, RICHARD Bedford 0234 43905
WINDING STAIR BKSP & CAFE, THE Dublin 0103531 733 292
WINDMILL BARGAIN BOOKS Ramsgate 0843 591334
WINKWORTH Cockermouth 0900 824984
WINRAM, G R Aberdeen 0224 630 673
WIRRAL BOOKSHOP, THE Birkenhead 051 638 0160
WISE OWL BOOKSHOP, THE Bristol 0272 262783
WITCH BOOKS AND ANTIQUES Galway 091 68388
WIVEY BOOKS Wivelscombe 0984 23506
WOODHEAD, G M Honiton 0404 42969
WOODHEAD, GEOFFREY M Honiton 0404 42969
WOODSTOCK BOOKSHOP, THE Woodstock 0993 811005
WOOLER BOOKSHOP, THE Wooler no phone
WOOTTON-BILLINGHAM Northampton 0604 34531
WORDS & MUSIC Wetherby 0937 66009
WORDS & MUSIC Chester 0244 311910
WORDSWORTH BOOKS & CARDS Paisley 041 887 7303
WORLD OF BOOKS Belfast 0232 454 272
WRIGHT, SIDNEY Bournemouth 0202 397153
WYCHWOOD BOOKS Stow on Wold 0451 31880
YARBOROUGH HOUSE BOOKS Bishop's Castle 0588 638318
YESTERDAY'S BOOKS Bournemouth 0202 302023
YORK, GRAHAM Honiton 0404 42074
YOUNG, R M South Molton 0271 890273
YSTWYTH BOOKS Aberstwyth 0970 617511
Y.S.F Sheffield 0742 6806787

ALPHABETICAL

SHOP INDEX

LONDON

ADAMS, NORMAN Enfield 081 364 4010

ALTMAN, D Portobello Road 071 637 7635

ANY AMOUNT OF BOOKS Charing Cross 071 240 8140

ARCADY Hackney phone unknown

ARCHIVE BOOKSTORE Marylebone 071 402 8212

ASH RARE BOOKS The City 071 626 2665

ATLANTIS Bloomsbury 071 405 2120

BADDIEL, SARAH Bond Street 071 408 1239

BAILEY, B Portobello Road 071 229 1692

BALDUR BOOKSHOP Richmond 081 940 1214

BALLANTYNE AND DATE Bloomsbury 071 242 4249

BARKER, R Portobello Road 071 289 3042

BARNARD, T H Uxbridge 0895 258054

BAYSWATER BOOKS Bayswater 071 402 7398

BELL BOOK & RADMELL Charing Cross 071 836 5888

BIBLIOPOLA Marylebone 071 724 7231

BILTCLIFFE, S Portobello Road 081 740 5326

BONAVENTURE Highgate 081 341 2345

BONDY, LOUIS Bloomsbury 071 405 2733

BOOK MARK Edgware 081 952 1349

BOOK PEDLAR Charing Cross No phone

BOOKCELLAR Earlsfield 081 944 6458

BOOKING HALL, THE Marylebone 071 255 2123

BOOKS AND LYRICS Wimbledon 081 543 0625

BOOKS AND THINGS Portobello Road 071 3705593

BOOKS OF ASIA Pimlico 071 821 6544

BOOKSHOP BLACKHEATH Blackheath 081 852 4786

BOUTLE & KING Islington 071 278 4497

BRETT, ALAN Charing Cross 071 836 8222

BROMLEY BOOKSHOP, THE Bromley & London phone unknown

BROWSERS East Molesey phone unknown

BROWSERS BOOKSHOP Epping 0992 572 260

BUTCHER, PABLO Portobello Road phone unknown

CAINE, DENIS Arnos Grove 081 348 4888

CAMBERWELL BOOKSHOP Camberwell 081 701 1839

CHATER'S MOTORING Isleworth 081 568 9750
CHELSEA RARE BOOKS King's Road 071 351 0950
CHRISTIE, L Portobello Road 081 672 4024
CIRCA Stoke Newington 071 249 9775
CLARKE HALL The City 071 353 4116
CLEARING HOUSE, THE Charing Cross no phone
COLLECTED WORKS West Dulwich phone unknown
COLLINGE AND CLARKE Bloomsbury 071 387 7105
CONSTANT READER, THE Fulham 071 731 0218
CREED, ANN Charing Cross 071 836 7757
CROUCH END BOOKSHOP Crouch End 081 348 8966
CROYDEN BOOKSHOP, THE Carshalton 081 643 6857
DANCE BOOKS Charing Cross 071 836 2314
DEMETZY BOOKS Portobello Road 0993 702209
DERRICK NIGHTINGALE Kingston 081 549 5144
DICKENSON, S Bond Street 071 629 3644
DILLONS Bloomsbury 071 636 1577
ECONOMISTS BOOKSHOP, THE Aldwych 071 405 8643
EDWARDS, FRANCES Charing Cross 071 379 7669
ENFIELD BOOKSHOP, THE Enfield phone unknown
FAIRCROSS BOOKS Chiswick 081 994 1912
FALCONWOOD TRANSPORT&MILITARY BKSP Welling 081 303 8291
FANTASY CENTRE Highbury Corner 071 607 9433
FAWKES, KEITH Hampstead 071 435 0614
FISHER & SPERR Highgate 081 340 7244
FITZJOHN'S BOOKS Swiss Cottage 071 722 9864
FLINDERS Euston 071 388 6080
FOSTER Notting Hill Gate 071 724 0876
FOSTER, STEPHEN Marylebone 071 724 0876
FOSTER, W Chiswick 081 995 2768
GABRIELS Willesden Green 081 451 2047
GANT, ELIZABETH Thames Ditton 081 398 0962
GAY'S THE WORD Bloomsbury 071 278 7654
GLADMAN, MARTIN Finchley 081 343 3023
GLENDALE, M & R Mayfair 071 487 5348

GLOUCESTER ROAD BOOKSHOP, THE Gloucester Road 071 370 3

GREAT RUSSEL STREET BOOKS Bloomsbury 071 637 7635

GREEN, G L Ealing - mail order only 081 997 6454

HALL, ANTHONY Twickenham 081 898 2638

HAMPTON CHARITY BOOKSHOP Hampton no phone

HARRINGTON BROTHERS King's Road 071 352 5689

HAYES BOOKSHOP, THE Ickenham 08956 37725

HENEAGE, THOMAS - now mail order St James 071 720 1503

HEYWOOD HILL Mayfair 071 629 0647

HILLYERS Sydenham 081 778 6381

HILTON, PAUL Charing Cross phone unknown

HISTORY BOOKSHOP, THE Friern Barnet now closed

HOSAIN'S Marble Arch 071 262 7900

HOUBEN Richmond 081 940 1055

HOUSE HOSPITAL, THE Battersea No phone

J G BOOKS Streatham 081 764 4669

KAY BOOKS Portobello Road phone unknown

KIRKDALE BOOKSHOP Sydenham 081 778 4701

LLOYDS Kew Gardens 081 940 2512

LORD, NORMAN Walthamstow 081 520 8300

MAGGS BROS Mayfair 071 493 7160

MANOR HOUSE BOOKS Finchley 081 349 9484

MARCET BOOKS Greenwich 081 853 5408

MARCHMOUNT BOOKSHOP, THE Bloomsbury 071 387 7989

MARCHPANE Charing Cross 071 836 8661

MARITIME BOOKS Greenwich 081 853 1727

MELLOR & BAXTER Notting Hill Gate 071 229 2033

MOLE BOOKSHOP, THE East Molesey 0784 483 467

MURDER ONE Charing Cross 071 734 3483

MUSEUM BOOKSHOP Bloomsbury 071 580 4086

MUSIC & VIDEO EXCHANGE BKSP Notting Hill Gate 071 22984

MY BACK PAGES Elephant and Castle 081 769 4851

NIGHTINGALE, DERRICK Kingston 081 549 5144

NOLAN, E C Charing Cross 071 497 2328

NOTTING HILL BOOKS Notting Hill Gate 071 727 5988

OFFSTAGE Bond Street 071 485 4996

OLD NEWSPAPER & EPHEMERA SHOP, THE Knightsbridge 071 23

OLD TOWN BOOKS Clapham 071 498 0998

OSTERLEY BOOKSHOP, THE Osterley 081 560 6206

OXFAM BOOKSHOP Ealing No phone

PARK BOOKSHOP Wellingborough 0933 222 592

PENDLEBURY'S Stamford Hill 081 809 4922

PITMAN, MARION Twickenham 081 898 7165

PLEASURES OF PAST TIMES Charing Cross 071 836 1142

POEL, FEM Portobello Road 071 731 2736

PORCUPINE BOOKCELLAR Kings Cross 071 837 4473

PORDES Charing Cross 071 836 4872

PREDOMINANTLY PRINTED Purley 081 667 1671

PSEUD BOOKS Wimbledon phone unknown

PSYCHIC SENSE Walthamstow 081 520 4032

QUADRILLE Portobello Road 081 450 9008

QUARITCH Soho 071 734 2983

QUEEN STREET BOOKSHOP, THE Mayfair phone unknown

QUEEN STREET BOOKSHOP, THE Mayfair 071 629 0532

REMINGTON, REG & PHILIP Charing Cross 071 836 9771

RESPONSE Earls Court 071 370 4606

RICHMOND BOOKSHOP, THE Richmond 081 940 5512 closed

RIPPING YARNS Highgate 081 341 6111

ROBBIE'S BOOKSHOP Muswell Hill 081 444 6957

ROBIN BOOKS Thames Ditton

ROBINSON, CHARLOTTE Soho 071 437 3683

ROGERS TURNER Greenwich 081 853 5271

ROTA, BERTRAM Covent Garden 071 836 0723

SCOTT, K Stratford 081 519 1593

SECONDHAND BOOKS Waterloo phone unknown

SHAPERO, BERNARD Holland Park 071 493 0876

SHERIDAN, IAN Hampton 081 979 1704

SHIPLEY Charing Cross 071 836 4872

SIMS REED St James 071 493 5660

SOTHERANS Mayfair 071 439 6151

SOUTH LONDON BOOKCENTRE Greenwich phone unknown
SPCK Marylebone 071 387 5282
SPORTING BOOKSHOP, THE Walthamstow 081 520 4032
SPREAD EAGLE BOOKS Greenwich 081 305 1666
STONE, BARBARA King's Road 071 351 0963
STUDIO BOOKS Blackheath 081 318 9666
TERRY'S Ilford 081 478 2850
THORNTONS King's Road 071 736 6181
TLON BOOKS Wimbledon 081 543 4684
TRAVELLERS BOOKSHOP, THE Charing Cross 071 836 9132
TRAVIS & EMERY Charing Cross 071 240 2129
TRUSCOTT, H Portobello Road 0403 730554
TWO JAYS, THE Edgeware 081 952 1349
ULYSSES Bloomsbury 071 637 5862
UPPER STREET BOOKSHOP Islington 071 359 3785
VANBRUGH RARE BOOKS Bloomsbury 071 404 0733
VILLAGE BOOKS Streatham 081 677 2667
VILLAGE BOOKSHOP Belsize Park 071 794 3180
VORTEX Stoke Newington 071 254 6516
WALDEN BOOKS Chalk Farm 071 267 8146
WALFORD, G W Highbury 071 2265682 not bksp
WATERLOO STATION BOOKSHOP Waterloo phone unknown
WATKINS Charing Cross 071 836 2182
WHETSTONE BOOKS Whetstone 081 368 8338
WHITEHALL BOOKSHOP, THE Cheam 081 643 8272
WILDY & SON The City 071 242 5778
WORLD OF BOOKS Bloomsbury phone unknown
WORLD'S END BOOKSHOP Chelsea 071 352 9376
ZENO Charing Cross 071 836 2522